Cerebus the
Barbarian Messiah

Cerebus the Barbarian Messiah

Essays on the Epic Graphic Satire of Dave Sim and Gerhard

Edited by ERIC HOFFMAN

McFarland & Company, Inc., Publishers
Jefferson, North Carolina, and London

LIBRARY OF CONGRESS CATALOGUING-IN-PUBLICATION DATA

Cerebus the barbarian messiah : essays on the epic graphic satire of Dave Sim and Gerhard / edited by Eric Hoffman.
    p.   cm.
Includes bibliographical references and index.

ISBN 978-0-7864-6889-8
softcover : acid free paper ∞

1. Sim, Dave, 1956– Cerebus 2. Gerhard, 1959– Cerebus
3. Comic books, strips, etc.— Canada — History and criticism.
    I. Hoffman, Eric, 1976–
PN6734.C47C47 2012   741.5'971— dc23   2012007782

BRITISH LIBRARY CATALOGUING DATA ARE AVAILABLE

© 2012 Eric Hoffman. All rights reserved

No part of this book may be reproduced or transmitted in any form or by any means, electronic or mechanical, including photocopying or recording, or by any information storage and retrieval system, without permission in writing from the publisher.

Reprint with corrections

Cover art by Dave Sim, colored dyes and black ink on illustration board, 11½" × 17", 2005 (from the collection of Darren O'Shaughnessy)

Manufactured in the United States of America

*McFarland & Company, Inc., Publishers
Box 611, Jefferson, North Carolina 28640
www.mcfarlandpub.com*

Acknowledgments

I would like to thank each of the contributors for their time and talent in helping make this volume a reality.

Utmost appreciation goes to Dave Sim and to Gerhard, for their immense contribution to the art of the comics medium. Together, they have expanded the medium's visual and verbal lexicon. I sincerely hope that this volume is worthy of its subjects.

Table of Contents

Acknowledgments   v

Preface   1

Introduction: Alone, Unmourned and Unloved
   Eric Hoffman   5

Part One: A Map of Estarcion

Growing Complexity; or, the *Cerebus* Effect
   Sebastian Domsch   65

Audacious Tenacity, Tenacious Audacity: *Cerebus*' Grand (and Changing) Narrative Strategies
   Eric Hoffman   77

Part Two: Ignore It, It's Just Another Reality

"Does This Seem Right to You?" Stories Within *Cerebus*
   David Groenewegen   97

Aardvarkian Intertexts and True Stories
   Dominick Grace   103

"Why Certainly Dear Boy…" Incorporating Oscar Wilde into the Aardvark's World
   Gregory John Fink   118

Part Three: Becoming Synonymous with Something Indescribable

Seeing Sound
   C.W. Marshall   127

Negative Space and Guttural Noise: Gerhard's Psychological *Reads*
   Sabin Calvert   148

Part Four: Mind Games

Testing the Limits of Genre/Gender
   Dominick Grace   163

Anti-Feminist Aardvark? Gender, Subjectivity and Authorship
    Isaac J. Mayeux   175

The Aardvark and the Beautiful Women: Male Sexuality and
Gender Politics
    Mario N. Castro   190

Part Five: Ye Booke of Sim

YHWH's Story, or, How to Laugh While Reading "Chasing YHWH"
and Still Have Enough Stamina for *The Last Day*
    Edward M. Komara   199

Appendix: An Introduction to the Cerebus *"Phonebooks"*
    Lenny Cooper   217

Bibliography   221
About the Contributors   225
Index   227

Preface

In 1977, a struggling Canadian comics artist named Dave Sim self-published the first issue of *Cerebus the Aardvark*. A *Conan the Barbarian* satire utilizing the *Howard the Duck* setting of a funny animal trapped in a human world trope, at first *Cerebus* was largely a story of a foul-tempered, sword-wielding aardvark, traveling the "northern territories" of the imaginary world of Estarcion, seeking fortune and strong drink. Sim's bi-monthly black and white comic was one of the few success stories of the comic industry's direct market, then a relatively new comics distribution phenomenon. Within a decade, Sim single-handedly helped revolutionize the comics medium by showing other comics artists they too could forgo the usual route of publication by way of a major publisher. In so doing, Sim inspired such successes as *Teenage Mutant Ninja Turtles* and *Bone*, along with dozens of other self-published black and white comics that began appearing in subsequent years and decades.

The reasons for Sim's success with *Cerebus the Aardvark* (later just *Cerebus*) are manifold: its humor, its artful design, Sim's knowledgeable, tongue-in-cheek satire of the comics medium, and perhaps most importantly, its predictable bi-monthly (later monthly) publishing schedule. As critic R. Fiore observes, "Sim's success was the result of a fan boy's understanding of what made a comic successful: a regular publishing schedule and the same ingredients as what the majors had to offer: superheroes, buxom women, and, at the time, a funny animal and swords and sorcery" (Fiore October/November 2004, 105). Over the course of 26 years, from December 1977 to March 2004, Sim, and later collaborator Gerhard, produced over 6,000 pages of narrative, totaling 300 separate issues subsequently collected into sixteen trade paperbacks.

When he set out to write *Cerebus*, Sim intended to break every rule of the medium. The title of this book suggests this unique aspect of *Cerebus*; namely, the ability to transform, transgress and violate. As the essays collected here demonstrate, with *Cerebus*, Sim meant to upset multiple boundaries, be they aesthetic, sexual, political or religious.

Comics in the late 1970s were staid, predictable stuff. The Marvel revolution of the late 1960s had long since devolved into cookie-cutter homogeneity, and unchallenging, formulaic work cluttered comics racks. *Cerebus* became the outlet for Sim's dissatisfaction with the medium he loved. As the series progressed so too did its satirical reach. Sim began incorporating other comics characters, notably through the agency of The Roach, a schizophrenic whose sundry personalities are comprised of parodies of various popular-at-the-time superheroes, including Moon Knight, Wolverine, Captain America and The Sandman, among others. Yet Sim also satirized non-superhero characters, including Michael Moorcock's Elric, Hal Foster's *Prince Valiant*, and even Groucho (and later Chico) Marx. His satires were spot on, and his wicked humor won him a modest number of dedicated fans. Gradually, the print run of the comic climbed to over 30,000 copies, a perhaps insubstantial number when compared with *Batman* or *Spider-Man*, yet practically unheard of for a small self-publisher of black and white comics.

Sim's outspoken advocacy of self-publishing and critique of work-for-hire contracts resulted in some controversy. *The Comics Journal*, a respected (if highly opinionated) magazine of comics journalism, criticism and comment, frequently attacked Sim for his allegedly myopic view of the publisher's role in the comic industry. What even the *Journal* had to admit, however, was that, at least during the 1980s, Sim was producing some of the finest work in comics.

Cerebus' venture into politics, *High Society*, the first major story arc of the *Cerebus* narrative, is a smart critique of United States realpolitik, a kind of comic book *Duck Soup*, following *Cerebus* out from the barbarian setting into the city-state of Iest (pronounced Yest) into a world of high politics, political campaigning, and war. The subsequent volume, *Church & State*, itself an 1,100-page work, remains a masterful meditation on power, corruption, greed and the inevitable tarnishing of religious and social ideals. In it, Cerebus becomes pope, commits rape, infanticide and demands gold on the threat of death. He eventually ascends to the Moon where he encounters George, a mysterious judge, who warns him of his imminent death, "alone, unmourned and unloved." The story up to this point is, according to Sim, largely a study of the futility of power (see Brownstein Winter 1997a, 14). Cerebus, despite having achieved what he believed he wanted, wealth and total control, finds he is unfulfilled. The remainder of *Cerebus* explores the aftermath of this realization.

With *Jaka's Story*, Sim, at the height of *Cerebus*' popularity, produced a 500-page meditation on the politics of domesticity. With this story arc, Sim relegates Cerebus—no longer pope and in hiding from the Cirinists, a totalitarian matriarchal army that assumed control of Iest at the end of *Church & State*—to the background while Sim focuses his attention on a then-minor character, Jaka Tavers, Cerebus' love interest. In part because of the Judge's pronouncement of Cerebus' eventual fate, Cerebus takes up residence with Jaka and her new husband Rick. Here, Sim explores the more intimate power struggle of a marriage, as Jaka strives to balance a relationship with her husband, household and career, all the while coming to terms with events from her past and the uncertainty of her future.

Key to Sim's widening narrative scope was the addition, in the midst of *Church & State*, of background artist Gerhard, whose elaborate set pieces considerably enriched the world of *Cerebus*, giving Sim's often Mort Drucker–ish caricatures a baroque counterpoint, adding to the comic an undeniably original visual style. The addition of Gerhard had the effect of not only freeing Sim somewhat from the constraints of single-handedly writing, drawing and publishing *Cerebus*, but also allowed him to concentrate more fully on the development of both his own art and the structure of the series, and to further develop his skills as a comics letterer. Gerhard's elaborately crosshatched backgrounds lent *Cerebus* a unique classicism, allowing Sim to incorporate increasingly complex themes while adding to Sim's vision of the comic as the visual equivalent of a Russian novel. The religious iconography, late medieval architecture, and fully realized set pieces provided Sim the storyteller with a richly imagined world wherein he could place his characters and fashion their storylines. Because of Gerhard's contribution to *Cerebus*, the development of Sim's narrative was less restricted and the comic's mise-en-scène unquestionably enlarged.

Sim also began to devote more and more of the comic narrative and supporting materials (the Note from the President, letters page and essays included in its back pages) to his decidedly non-mainstream views of feminism, labeling his writings as "anti-feminist." Many of Sim's critics disagreed, decrying these essays as misogynistic. Not one to be swayed by public opinion, Sim gradually began to incorporate these views on feminism into *Cerebus*, mostly notably in *Mothers & Daughters*, a study of the opposing forces of Cirinism, and Kevillism, a political movement similar to the political feminism of the 1970s. Also key to his criticism of feminism is Cerebus' decision to abandon his trajectory as a world-changing force (a "magnifier") in pursuit of a doomed relationship with Jaka, a kind of allegorical figuration of Sim's own destiny as an ascetic, devoted comic book creator whose 300-issue project is persistently threatened by outside temptations or forces, women foremost among them.

The final 100 issues of the series act as an extended epilogue, wherein Cerebus finds vocation as a bartender, again meets Jaka, travels north with her to his childhood home, only to reject her. He wanders for decades finding work as a sheepherder, sportsman, and leader of a bizarre new religion, an interpreter of the Bible, and finally a doddering and nearly senile leader, trapped in a prison of his own making. Cerebus' journey into seclusion has its counterpart in Sim's personal life during these years. His position as an anti-feminist, Sim felt, had resulted in a self-described "pariah" status in the comics industry.

Whatever Sim's reasons for believing the comics community has rejected him, *Cerebus* is routinely included in most critics' selections as one of the most important comics of the medium. Critics cite *High Society*, *Church & State* and *Jaka's Story* in particular as examples of a high-water mark among independent comics. His work has received notable mention from a variety of media outlets, including *Entertainment Weekly*, *The Village Voice* and *The Believer*. Young comics artists still point to Sim as a major influence, an accomplished letterer, and an inspiration for self-publishers and independent comics artists worldwide.

This present volume comprises five sections plus a general introduction that provides an historical and cultural context for Sim and Gerhard's work, briefly addressing their various thematic, textual and visual concerns, while also providing a biography of Sim. The sections that follow feature essays that link thematically with the others. If, as Mario N. Castro states in his essay in the present volume, *Cerebus* "works as an evolving narrative that moves from the most specific ideas to the most general abstraction," then this book works in the opposite direction, beginning with a broad canvas, a kind of "high altitude mapping" (to borrow a phrase from Sim), that gradually increases its magnification as subsequent sections focus on more specific aspects of the work.

The first section, "A Map of Estarcion," explores the various techniques (beyond those techniques inherent to the form — panels, word balloons, etc.) Sim utilized in fashioning his unique accomplishment of 300 monthly discrete issues of an ongoing story, in particular the high degree of flexibility Sim employed to allow the significant changes in theme, tone and structure, and how Sim developed this elaborate plot over the period of the 26 years he composed the comic book.

The essays of the second section, "Ignore It, It's Just Another Reality," concern Sim's use of storytellers *within* the larger story, and how each storyteller represents a shifting perspective that opposes any verifiable claims of truth. Use of this technique allowed Sim to transcend his own limitations, providing him with the freedom to shift the focus as he saw fit, so that, as in an extreme example, *Cerebus* simultaneously satirizes religion (largely characterized in the comic as outright delusion and a means of coercion and control) and elucidates Sim's evolving religious beliefs. Similarly, *Cerebus* itself is a claim to truth that opposes the "story" of feminist politics and political correctness, particularly in the text interpolations dispersed throughout the comic, both internal and external to the storyline proper.

"Becoming Synonymous with Something Indescribable," the third section of this book, consists of a meticulous study of *Cerebus'* visual virtuosity and technical sophistication, addressing in particular Sim's imaginative and descriptive use of lettering.

The fourth section, "Mind Games," is an exploration of perhaps the most problematic, yet important, of *Cerebus'* themes, namely the use of gender, both as a narrative device within *Cerebus* proper and in Sim's supplementary essays, which together comprise an extended critique of institutionalized feminism. The interplay between genders represents some of the best and worst aspects of *Cerebus*. The introduction of feminist critique, both within the *Cerebus* storyline and the tangential material accompanying the primary text, compromises the narrative by a blurring of authorial intention. From the nuanced representation of gender roles and female-male relationships in *Jaka's Story*, to the anti-feminist polemics of *Reads*, these essays address Sim's views of gender both within the context of *Cerebus'* storyline and its larger social implications.

The fifth and final section, "Ye Booke of Sim," consists of one reader's attempt to salvage what most readers and critics generally consider *Cerebus'* most unreadable segment, the "Chasing YHWH" section of *Latter Days*, by offering a new way of reading the text and viewing it within the larger context of Sim and Gerhard's work.

Cerebus is a substantial work requiring a substantial critical response. Its many facets— as satire/parody, as comic book, as political statement — receive comprehensive treatment in these essays. Addressing the aesthetics of the comics form, cohesion in comics narrative, sexual identity, and power politics, these essays will also appeal to a more general audience, for both established fans of *Cerebus*, casual readers, newcomers or for anyone interested in comics or comics history, and in particular the transformations of the medium over the last forty years.

Introduction:
Alone, Unmourned and Unloved

> I did have an idea that comics would survive and go on to become great literature, as a graphic combination of pictures and words, and eventually would become ... books in which novels and stories are presented in that form rather than just flipping pages.... Of course, I still have that kind of a dream in the back of my head.—Carl Barks

As a medium, comic books are largely resistant to change. After decades of innovation by the likes of Carl Barks, Winsor McKay, E.C. Segar, and Will Eisner, among others, the advent of the super-hero in the late 1930s introduced what remains the medium's dominant visual, stylistic and generic vocabulary. To be sure, there are notable exceptions, yet they are exceptional enough to prove the rule; for example, the EC horror, humor and war comics of the post-war era, truncated or watered down by 1950s government censorship, the underground comix movement of the late 1960s and early 1970s, or the indie comics movements of the 1980s to the current era. Yet in the post–Watergate, post–Vietnam era of disillusionment and economic recession, for many purveyors of comic books it was business as usual, a studio system of considerable editorial control and little creative freedom. Reliable and predictable, the superhero genre reclaimed the mentality of the comic book as comfort food, the increasing sophistication of its audience temporarily appeased by the ironic self-consciousness of Marvel Comics in the early 1960s.

During that decade, head shops, a unique subculture environment where hippies and leftist political activists congregated, developed from existing candle and poster stores. There, self-published and Xeroxed magazines were sold, along with comic books. A new style of comic, "comix," began to appear, appealing to this hip, urbane audience. These comix existed outside the establishment of Marvel and DC, and thereby avoided the self-censorship of the Comics Code Authority, established a decade before. As Charles Hatfield observes in his book *Alternative Comics*, "comix opened the door" to creator-owned comic books, "pav[ing] the way for a radical reassessment of the relationships among publishers, creators, and intellectual properties" as well as "introduc[ing] an 'alternative' ethos that valued the productions of the lone cartoonist over collaborative or assembly line work" (Hatfield 2005, 16).

The head shops gradually transformed into comic book shops, which fed a growing demand by an increasingly older (and therefore wealthier) clientele of collectors and hobbyists, adults who grew up reading comics and possessed a shared nostalgia for the medium, a subculture that gradually evolved into what is now known as comic fandom. According to Hatfield, the rise in comics fandom correlates directly to the appearance of comics fanzines, price guides, and subsequent fan conventions, beginning in 1964. A gradual decrease of newsstand sales resulted in a marketing adjustment that saw comics fandom as its primary market and the superhero genre as its dominant genre (Hatfield 2005, 21). Moreover, the proliferation of comic book shops and fan conventions led to new methods of distribution. These stores and conventions made possible new marketing possibilities for distribution outside of the established newspaper/magazine distributor method that made it nearly impossible for small publishers to achieve any real exposure to potential audiences.

In 1968, Phil Seuling, an enterprising businessperson and comic book fan from Brooklyn, New York, established the New York Comic Book Convention, which he ran until the end of the 1970s. Seuling's conventions were very popular among comic book enthusiasts and proved to those who still viewed comic books as disposable kids' stuff that they were a serious art form worthy of critical attention and, perhaps more importantly, of value and collectability. In 1972, Seuling founded East Coast Seagate Distribution, creating a new distribution system wherein stores could purchase comics directly from publishers on a non-returnable, non-refundable basis, in return for heavy discounts. This made it safer for a publisher to enter the market, as publishers were required to publish only the amount solicited from vendors in advance of publication. As a result, direct market distribution made it possible for many smaller comic book publishers to enter the field and challenge the Marvel and DC hegemony, which, aside from Archie and Warren, made up nearly 100 percent of the comic book market.

Less cost for the publisher meant more opportunity for experimentation. One form publishers experimented with were longer-form narratives within a single book, a format that later came to be known as a "graphic novel." Moreover, monthly comic books benefited from this transformation in the way comics collectors and readers now viewed comics, i.e., as a viable art form as opposed to disposable "kid's stuff."

Subsequently, comics matured in both form and subject matter. This transformation was made possible in part by the consistent publishing schedule offered by direct market distribution and the removal of the self-imposed censorship of the Comics Code Authority, as well as the entry of new writers and artists, those who had grown up with comics and long dreamed of expanding the potential of the narrative form they loved.

As Hatfield observes, another factor in this increased experimentation was the "relative prosperity of the market in the 1980s" (Hatfield 2005, 23). The comics that began appearing thanks to direct market were named "ground level" (because, Hatfield says, "they attempted to reconcile underground and mainstream attitudes" [ibid., 26])—later termed "alternative" comics—the most popular among them being Wendy and Richard Pini's *Elfquest*, Jack Katz's *First Kingdom* and Mike Friedrich's *Star*Reach* and *Quack!* Aside from their reliance on clichéd fantasy trappings, writes Hatfield, these comics acknowledged the "influence of the undergrounds and represented a first, tentative turning toward more personal and innovative approaches" (ibid.). Typically, these "ground level" comics featured low production values, low print runs and inconsistent print schedules and, as a result, comic book fans accustomed to regular, weekly releases of new comics titles for the most part lost interest. Not surprisingly, then, independent comics came and went with surprising rapidity. Yet an observant comics fan in the late 1970s would find amongst the latest issues of *Rom: Spaceknight*, *Champions of Xandar* and *Commander Steel* another regularly appearing title, first every two months, then monthly, in a slightly larger format, with four-color covers but a black and white interior. This comic appeared to be a mutant offspring of *Conan the Barbarian* and *Howard the Duck*, a parody of the former in the spirit of the latter. Its main character was a diminutive, ill-tempered barbarian aardvark named Cerebus.

When *Cerebus* first appeared in the late 1970s, it was without peer. The comix movement died, and comic book shops were only beginning to consider untested markets. As R. Fiore notes, Sim was among a handful of "cartoonists with mainstream sensibilities [that] saw a possibility of breaking out of the serfdoms of the newsstand companies and the stranglehold of the Comics Code by applying the methods of underground comics to the content of mainstream comics in the new market" (Fiore October/November 2004, 105). During its 300-issue, 26-year, self-published run, *Cerebus the Aardvark* challenged every cliché and broke nearly every rule of comics. Like Will Eisner's *The Spirit* before it, *Cerebus* helped to redefine the possibilities of the medium. Its unique achievement, a self-contained work with a beginning, middle and an end, written by a single author and artist (later joined by a background artist and inker), will never again be repeated. Its creator, an enterprising twenty-two-year-old Canadian artist named Dave Sim, with only a handful of previous publication credits — including sporadic work in fanzines, horror magazines, a failed comic strip and a handful of comics that never reached issue two — decided after a dozen issues to dedicate the majority of his adult life to telling a single tale: the life of a barbarian aardvark.

Because it is largely the work of one artist without any editorial interference, *Cerebus* underwent significant changes in tone and style and, in keeping with its "ground-level" roots, grew increasingly personal and innovative. In many ways, Sim's decision to commit himself to a single comic story was foolhardy, particularly in an environment where survival beyond several issues is difficult to accomplish. Yet even a cursory examination of Sim's life before *Cerebus* makes it unlikely that Dave Sim would consider doing anything else.

Sim was born 17 May 1956 at St. Joseph's Hospital in Hamilton, a port city in Southern Ontario, its third largest city and part of its manufacturing base. His mother, Mary Sim, was an elementary school secretary and his father, Ken Sim, worked for Budd Automotive as a factory supervisor. Denise Loubert, who later married Sim and helped publish *Cerebus* during its early years, tells author Blake Bell that she found Sim's parents "sophisticated.... They were college educated. Dave's mother was a very strong person. His father was creative and wasn't into the traditional macho role" (Bell 2002, 127). Sim's father also worked as a labor negotiator, and, as a result, adds Loubert, Sim had grown up "with much more liberal concepts in many ways of male and female roles" (ibid., 128). Sim claims that he learned from his father, "a naturally funny person ... that if you're going to make somebody laugh," you do so "legitimately" (Thompson August 1983, 79). His father was also a source of knowledge, wielding a "scalpel of rhetorical precision" with which he would make "mincemeat" of his son's opinions, a skill Sim would acquire and use successfully against those who later challenged him (Sim and Gerhard June 1998).

At the age of two, Sim's parents moved him and his older sister Sheila to neighboring Kitchener, approximately 60 miles to the northwest. A smaller city that includes nearby Waterloo and Cambridge, Kitchener is home to a nine-day annual Oktoberfest, the largest outside of Germany. Pulp fiction writer Ross Macdonald grew up in Kitchener. It is the birthplace of his wife, Margaret Millar, also a crime writer, and of David Morrell, author of *First Blood*, and creator of Rambo. Not that Sim cared. His interests were elsewhere, namely the comic books he began collecting from an early age. "Comic books have always, except for very brief time periods in my early teens, been at or near the number one position in my life since I was eight years old," Sim later told interviewer Tom Palmer, Jr. (Palmer, Jr. 1996, 60). "When I was ten or eleven there were about [a] half-dozen kids in the neighborhood who were collecting comic books," Sim observes. "By the time I was thirteen I was the only one ... comics were all that I was genuinely interested in, all that I thought about. All that I did" (Sim and Gerhard June 1998).

When Sim first started reading comics, he initially gravitated toward DC, and did not read Marvel until after 1970 (Thompson August 1983, 66). Typical of initiates into comics, Sim was more interested in the artists, preferring a more realistic drawing style and in his own work striving toward realism (particularly in his later, post–*Cerebus* work *glamourpuss*, a comic wholly comprised of a kind of neo-realism that involves tracing from other artists' work or from women's magazines). Among his favorites were *Superman* artist Curt Swan, Jim Mooney and Kurt Schaffenberger. "I think to this day, I try to put a lot of the Curt Swan quality in my work," explains Sim. "So I guess my influences come down to a war between the writer who wants everything to look like Curt Swan, and the artist who always wants to be out there, using complicated page layouts" (Darnall 1993, 65). Sim told interviewer Steve Bissette that he owes "an enormous debt to [Swan] in terms of drawing people and making you really believe that they are interacting on the page. It's still difficult for me to believe the Curt Swan stories were actually drawn by somebody — because the posture and the attitude and facial expressions were so perfect" (Bissette 1992, 23).

In his adolescent years, Sim began gravitating toward the work of "the flashier guys," particularly Neal Adams, Berni Wrightson and Barry Windsor-Smith (Darnall 1993, 65). The first comic book Sim purchased because of the artist was Wrightson's *Badtime Stories* (1971), a 48-page black and white anthology of Wrightson's work. Sim was 14 or 15 years old at the time and, after reading it, began drawing in earnest (Spurgeon February 1996, 70).

The Freelance Years (1971–1976)

Sim had no formal art training. He dropped out of high school after having to repeat the eleventh grade (Thompson August 1983, 67), telling his parents that "school had nothing left to teach him as a cartoonist" (Bell 2002, 127). During adolescence, Sim wrote and drew his own comics but it was not until he read about a DC comics fanzine, *The National Adviser*, in the first issue of *Rocket's Blast Comics Collector Fanzine* (also known as *RBCC*), that he would mark his first attempt at publication.

RBCC brought fans together in a large forum. Originally a science fiction fanzine, *The Rocket's Blast*, it later merged with another fanzine, *The Comics Collector*. When it began publication in the early 1960s, the print run was small (at first around 1,000; gradually increasing to about 2,250 per issue), yet its influence helped to shape the industry. The fanzine helped collectors to locate hard-to-find comics, sell their own, and gauge their values. Prior to *Overstreet*, it was the most trusted price guide for comic collecting, featuring interviews with notable comics talent, including Adams, Wrightson, or Wally Wood, Frank Frazetta, and Vaughn Bodé, among others.

RBCC also included a variety of advertisements, including those for other amateur fanzines. The ad Sim answered with his first submission, he tells Kim Thompson, was "one of those ads that you don't see quite as often now as used to: 'Artists and writers wanted for a comic fanzine of this. Submit samples'" (Thompson July 1983a, 68).

Sim sent samples, including articles and artwork. The fanzine decided to publish the articles, but passed on the artwork. Sim recalls receiving the finished copy in the mail "about a year and half later," disappointed by its lack of professionalism (ibid.). Something good came out of the experience, however, as he began a correspondence with its editor, Gabe Quintanilla, who encouraged him to continue submitting materials to a growing market of fanzines, some of which paid money. Idealistically, Sim dedicated himself to making a living by being a comics writer and artist (ibid.). He began submitting to fanzines in earnest and would in fact accomplish a great deal of fanzine work during these heady days of the early part of the decade. Nevertheless, it was not enough on which to live.

In fall 1971, Sim convinced Harry Kremer, owner of a Kitchener book, record and comic shop Now and Then Books, to publish a fanzine, *Now and Then Times.* According to Loubert, "Harry's was the place to go if you were into science fiction," adding that Kremer was a "big, funny, warm-hearted bear of a guy who would do anything for the people who were part of his universe. He was generous to a fault, quiet and yet when he said something, you paid attention" (Bell 2002, 127). Observes Blake Bell, Now and Then was at that time "a gathering place with an owner more than willing to assist prospective writers and artists in producing a couple of issues of whatever pie-in-the-sky project walks in the door" (Bell 2002, 127).

The appearance of *Now and Then Times* and another fanzine, John Balge's *Comic Art News and Reviews* (*CANAR*), created, writes Canadian comics historian John Bell, "a degree of continuity" between Canadian comic art in the 1940s and that of the 1970s (Bell 1986, 38). In 1974, Bell continues, Canadian-produced comics shifted from those themes associated with the comics underground of the late 1960s into "more traditional [science fiction and fantasy] themes," yet, Bell notes, these new comics, while sharing similar subject matter with mainstream comics, involved a "more adult approach" in part thanks to the "large amount of artistic freedom which they afforded creators" (ibid.).

The first issue of Sim's fanzine appeared in summer 1972. "A thousand copies were printed," writes Sim, "and over the next thirty years as many as twelve to twenty copies were sold (slight exaggeration)" (Sim April 2009, 1). A second issue of *Now and Then Times* appeared in 1973, but by then, *CANAR* and other freelance jobs kept Sim busy. He set up a studio in the basement of his parents' house and did the occasional interview for *CANAR* whenever a comic convention rolled through town. One of his subjects in 1973 was Barry Windsor-Smith, the artist of *Conan* and a significant influence on Sim's early style.

During his interviews, Sim gradually came to the realization that many of his subjects considered those artists he most admired, like Curt Swan or Jim Mooney, dated. Sim did not mind holding "minority opinions," yet after he decided to make a career for himself in comics, he "weeded out" his collection of comic books from about 4,000 to 200, keeping only those select few comics "drawn by guys that really get me fired up just by looking at the work [they are] doing" (Spurgeon February 1996, 70). As with many other young comics artists, Sim began imitating the work of those artists that most impressed him, which, he tells interviewer Tom Spurgeon, is "really how you learn—copying something and moving to the point where you understand what you're copying" (ibid.). While he admits he was "always a better writer than ... artist," the art is more enjoyable and more gratifying because when it is complete "you have something to look at" (ibid., 71).

Another early influence on Sim was *MAD Magazine*, which he first read around the age of 12 or 13. *MAD*'s satirical edge was unlike anything else in comics at that time, except for comix, which, in Kitchener at least, Sim could not purchase at the local drugstore. Sim considered underground artist Jack Jackson's *Conan* parody, together with Wood and Harvey Kurtzman's "Superduperman" particularly influential, if only for the "*sheer* exaggeration" (Spurgeon February 1996, 74) (Sim used a similar amount of exaggeration to great effect in the character of The Roach in *Cerebus*).

Throughout 1975 and 1976, Sim was busy developing *The Beavers*, a proposed weekly comic strip, the inspiration for which came from a small cartoon book entitled *Outhouses of the North*, published by Highway Bookshop in Northern Ontario, and the *Peanuts* strips Sim was then collecting. Highway Bookshop was looking for a similar project to follow up this successful book, and commissioned Sim to produce it. Sim set up a template of his beaver characters and completed the book (entitled *How's Your Beaver?*—see figure 1) in about three days. For his efforts, he was paid $125. "The good news?" remarks Sim. "I made $40 a day. The bad news? The monstrosity now existed and had my name on it" (Sim April 2009, 5).

If Sim seemed to be having difficulty getting *The Beavers* off the ground, other projects kept him busy enough to keep from being discouraged. In the fall of 1975, Charlton and Warren published some of his work. Importantly, he became friends with Gene Day, with whom he began corresponding in 1973. Augustine Funnell, a writer whom Sim interviewed for *CANAR*, introduced Sim to Day via letter. During the interview, Funnell suggested that Day, who rented the second floor of Funnell's house, might be interested in contributing some artwork to *CANAR*. Still living at home and not making much money from his artwork, the older artist impressed Sim with his ability to eke a living doing his artwork. Sim met Day physically in 1974 and they remained friends until Day's death less than a decade later.

Figure 1. Cover to Dave Sim's *How's Your Beaver?* (© 1974 Dave Sim).

During this period, Day was producing a significant

amount of work based on Howard's *Conan* characters. From Day Sim learned "the value of doing a Conan picture and then running it around the circle of prozines [professional fanzines] until someone would agree to pay anywhere from twenty to forty dollars" for the work (Sim and Gerhard September 2001) (see figure 2 for an example of Sim's early barbarian-themed work). The quantity of Day's work Sim saw on that initial visit helped Sim to realize that "sheer productivity was an inherently good thing and ... an essential element in making the jump from amateur to professional" (ibid.). As a result, Sim developed a similar work ethic and, in this sense, Day's example contributed to Sim's later achievements.

Around this time, Day and Sim were also developing a character named "The Partisan" (actually a rip-off of Jim Steranko's *Nick Fury, Agent of S.H.I.E.L.D.*) for a proposed series to run in the pages of *Orb Magazine*, a magazine published and edited by Jim Waley. Importantly, Sim assumed editorship for the magazine's last two issues. Sim assumed he was offered the job of senior editor at *Orb* due to a recommendation from Day, as Waley "didn't know me from a hole in the ground and Gene was their second most popular creator" (Sim December 2009, 13). Also during this period, Day published his story "Samurai" which drew the attention of Marvel and directly resulted in his being hired as the inker on *Master of Kung-Fu*. Day, perhaps feeling sorry for Sim, may have suggested him to Waley (Sim February 2010, 1).

Working with Waley, remarks Sim, was far different from working with Day. It was, Sim describes, "non-stop creativity versus total inertia" (Sim February 2010, 1). The experience would prove crucial in Sim's development as a publisher and contributed immensely to his later success with *Cerebus*. "I learned most of what I know about publishing by avoiding what [Waley and Mike Friedrich] did wrong," writes Sim (Sim October 2009, 21–22).

Until *Cerebus*, success had eluded Sim. The reason for this, Sim believed, was the interference and prejudices of publishers and editors who either did not know worthwhile material or interfered to such an extent that any value the work originally had became obliterated by editorial interference or a lack of vision. "In the larger context of the history of comics," writes Sim,

there is every indication that what comic book fans desire most is a creator who ... maintains a

Figure 2. Early barbarian work (© 1976 Dave Sim).

reliable level of productivity.... In many cases, with many of our best talents, those productive times were interrupted by the capricious intrusion of editors and publishers, unforeseen changes in company policy, the imposition of guidelines unacceptable to the creator's sense of right and wrong. Implicit in self-publishing, which puts all controls and all decision making in the hands of the creator, is the opportunity—for the first time in the history of the medium—to circumvent these inevitable and destructive intrusions [Sim and Gerhard June 1996].

"Every time I worked for someone," Sim explains, "it seemed like they spent so much time talking about what was going to happen in the next issue as opposed to sitting down and doing it" (Darnall 1993, 64). For example, when Waley demanded Sim cut a nine-page story to eight pages in order for him to fit his next issue and needed it done in "roughly 24 hours," "What I was starting to think was, 'there must be a way to do comics *without* people like this," writes Sim. "There was: self-publishing" (Sim October 2009, 23–24).

Eventually, *Orb* folded. Looking back at his experiences working on *Orb*, Sim mentions several crucial errors he made with the magazine (errors that he intended not to repeat): first, that super-heroes don't do well in a black and white format (the reason Cerebus has a gray tone); second, that changing format (for example, going from magazine size to digest size) can ruin a comic; third, that reliability is key to success; and fourth, that on-going storylines do not work unless the deadline is being met (Sim February 2010, 4–10).

Orb's collapse gave Sim the opportunity to focus again on his own career. Comic book companies "came and went," Sim explains, and page rates were abysmally low, making "a syndicated comic strip ... more sensible and appealing" (Sim April 2010, 1). Sim's attention turned to *The Beavers*. Syndication of the strip would allow Sim to retain creative control and rights, along with any merchandizing. By comparison, doing work for comic book companies meant handing over all creative control "so all you could ever hope for was a page rate" (ibid.). Another hazard of the comic book business, Sim soon found out, was the tendency for publishers to disappear with the artwork and to not pay on time, or not pay at all (ibid., 2–3).

A sequel to *How's Your Beaver?* was proposed, entitled *Son of How's Your Beaver?* Before Sim could finish it, however, the publishers shut down production. In the wake of this disappointment, Sim turned his attention toward the possibility of undertaking a weekly comic strip, believing *The Beavers* might be his best chance at success in comics (Sim April 2009, 8). At Day's suggestion, Sim attempted to sell *The Beavers* idea to the *Kitchener-Waterloo Record*. "I used to bug Sandy Baird, the editor-in-chief, about running better comics (although they did carry *Rip Kirby* almost from the beginning) but this was the first time I pitched one of my own," Sim writes. "His answer was, basically, 'I've tried this before and the cartoonist always loses interest and I get the blame for cancelling the strip.' This was as close as I had come to getting a 'yes' out of anyone ... I just had to find a way around his argument" (Sim June 2009, 4).

Baird's rejection of *The Beavers* gave Sim the idea to complete an entire year's worth of strips ahead of schedule; to save time, Sim would write and pencil and Day ink the strips (Sim June 2009, 22) (figure 3). Sim and Day completed the year's weekly strips, 52 in all, in three days (Sim August 2009, 2). "I met with Sandy Baird and dropped off the roughs," explains Sim. "His answer in retrospect was predictable: 'These are just rough sketches. How do I know you would actually be able to produce finished strips?' If his intention was to discourage me it didn't work since his was still the only answer I was getting

Figure 3. *The Beavers* weekly strip (© 1975 Dave Sim).

that wasn't a definite no" (ibid., 4). The completed strips display Sim's developing political humor, territory he would revisit several years later with *High Society* (Sim June 2009, 23).

Another project important to the development of *Cerebus* was Sim's solo, 32-page comic book *Oktobertfest* (produced with the assistance of Gene Day), which served a dual purpose. First, it would capitalize on the local Oktoberfest mania and second, it would add a "solo vehicle" to his growing portfolio with which he hoped to land a job with Marvel or DC (Sim June 2010, 17). As he writes in *Cerebus Archive*, "what could make more sense than to link this enormous beer festival to a children's comic, modeled on the work of Carl Barks ... particularly his legendary 'The Golden Helmet' storyline from *Dell Color Comics* #408, of which I had, then, recently obtained a copy? ... It was basically an act born of desperation for paying work" (ibid., 11). Sim again approached Harry Kremer, who had subsidized Sim's *Now and Then Times*, to foot the bill.

Oktoberfest attracted scant media attention. An article in the *Kitchener-Waterloo Record* written by Max Southall (later technical director of Sim's *Cerebus TV* some thirty-odd years later) featured a photo of Sim in his parent's basement at 282 Westmount Road East, where Sim worked on a "shallow drafting board" placed atop his parents' kitchen table while seated at a barstool. Sim tells Southall, speaking of *Oktoberfest*, "I'd been practicing strips in the old Walt Disney style" (Sim August 2010, 12). According to the article, Sim "decided to try a comic book featuring a hero-type spoof and whimsical animals. Mr. Kremer bought the idea, reckoning it would appeal to adults and children as an Oktoberfest souvenir" (ibid.). Sim and Day completed the Uncle Hans section of the book, Southall reports, in just fifteen days while Sim visited Day in Gananoque. "We lived on cheese and peanut butter sandwiches," explains Sim, "drawing like mad" (ibid.).

Oktoberfest does not have much to recommend it, but, as Sim explains, it did give him "hands-on experience of seeing exactly how much work it was to fill 32 pages even with simple cartoon drawings" (Sim August 2010, 19). Sim sees the comic as his self-conscious attempt to work within a larger tradition of Canadian comic books, in particular those comic books mentioned in *The Great Canadian Comic Books* (1971) by Michael Hirsh and Patrick Loubert. "Thinking in terms of Canadian comic art 'traditions,'" comments Sim,

> I was in for a rude awakening over the course of the next year or so. Even at the time, people who did comics in Canada weren't really on anyone's radar screen but their own — isolated individuals who had found some strange patron or other who would pay them a wage to produce comic strips or comic books or cartoons. Usually the best hope was for such accidental patronage, followed by benign neglect mingled with inertia and apathy, which allowed a comics feature to continue to exist because no one really noticed it [ibid., 18].

Success continued to elude Sim. He begrudgingly took up work in the basement of Now and Then; Kremer had recently expanded his operations, selling comics upstairs, and records and collectibles downstairs. Originally, Kremer planned to have his mother work the register downstairs but Sim offered to do it for $75 a month, working ten A.M. to eight P.M. Thursday and Friday and ten A.M. to six P.M. Saturday. To help supplement his income, Sim sold his comic book collection to Kremer, keeping only the Adams, Wrightson, Mike Kaluta and Windsor-Smith material for himself. This garnered Sim an additional $1,000 with which he moved into a one-bedroom apartment in a converted pantry at 379 Queen Street South. "My rent was $120 a month, I was making $75 a month, and I had $1,000 in the bank from the sale of my comic book collection. It was 'sink or swim' time," writes Sim (Sim August 2010, 22).

Enter the Aardvark (1976–1980)

On 1 December 1976, Sim moved out of his parents' home into an apartment. He named his new apartment studio ComicGraphics and placed an ad in *The Comics Journal*. The ad did bring him some work, including drawing a script by the talented, if eccentric, T. Casey Brennan. Sim met Brennan previously, at the June 1972 Southern Ontario Panel Art Festival (SOPAF), held at Now and Then Books. Brennan agreed to conduct an interview in Kitchener, and to do it at Sim's parents' house. "It was a weird, weird break-point for a sixteen-year-old comic book writer just hanging out in the half of the basement where I kept my comic books" (Sim June 2009, 22).

Reviewing Brennan's work prior to the interview, Sim came to realize just how unique it was. They were allegorical, "dark fables," writes Sim. "The stories and Casey's approach to them were a revelation to me. There was the surface of the story and then there was your own interpretation — or various interpretations — to be had in the aftermath" (Sim June 2009, 22). Brennan's comics "fundamentally changed my view of what constituted a good comic book story," Sim explains (ibid.). Encouraged, Sim, ever the ironist, sent Brennan a short parody of one of Brennan's own stories. Brennan liked it and when proposing his own title, sent Sim several scripts, one of which was entitled, notably, "A Boy and His Aardvark." The Brennan comic never materialized, but the story was eventually published in the first issues of *Power Comics* in March 1977, just ten months prior to the publication of the first issue of *Cerebus* (ibid.).[1]

Brennan was also an invited guest at a 1976 comic convention held at Sim's high school, along with Gene Day and, at "one of those humiliatingly sparsely attended events," Sim, Brennan and Day sat together on a panel. "One of [the] four people [in the audience]," writes Sim, "was an attractive brunette with long straight hair ... I talked with her for a little while and then Casey and I had a back-and-forth exchange or two" (Sim and Gerhard November 1995). Sim noticed that when Brennan or Day spoke, she wrote down what they said in a notebook, but wrote down nothing when it was Sim's turn to speak. Following the panel, Sim mentioned to Kremer that he was available to work the downstairs at Now and Then Books if Kremer needed him. Soon after, Sim passed the brown-haired person in the hall and she again caught his eye. "It would be another two months before I found out her name, Denise Loubert" (ibid.).

On 16 December, just two weeks after Sim moved out of his parents' house, 22-year-old Denise Loubert walked into Now and Then Books. Born in 1951 in Timmins, Ontario, Loubert lived in a number of places as a child, due to her father's work as a miner and a railroad worker. She lived in the United States for a time, in Arizona and in California, attending high school in San Francisco in the heady mid-to-late 1960s. She and her friends smoked marijuana and read *The Fabulous Furry Freak Brothers*, but for the most part she was not interested in comics, preferring science fiction. Eventually, Loubert's father moved the family to Kitchener, where she found work in a plastics factory. Attending a science fiction and comics convention, she was "blown away by this whole other world I had no idea existed" (Bell 2002, 127). "At the time," Loubert tells interviewer David McDonnell, "I had not very serious ... aspirations to be a writer" (McDonnell 1983, 21). Seeing firsthand the fanzines distributed among comic shops and collectors, Loubert was eager to contribute her own science fiction fanzine. She and her brother Michael and sister Karen "decided to try and publish our own magazine, modeled after Gene Day's *Dark Fantasy*. I got elected to get it done and went to the local comic shop, Now and Then Books, to talk about buying copies" (ibid.). When she walked into Now and Then, she was looking for Kremer to talk about promoting and selling a proposed fanzine in his store. Kremer was not in at the time, so she instead struck up a conversation with Sim, explaining to the then-18-year-old Sim that she wanted to publish something in digest format similar to Day's *Dark Fantasy* (erroneously referring to it as *Dark Shadows*). When Sim mentioned to her that he had work published in Day's magazine, she became immediately interested in him.

"When I met Dave," Loubert tells Blake Bell,

> I was surprised there were guys who penciled and guys who inked. I started talking about my project and he had all these questions. Before you know it, we're talking about Gene's publication, fanzines, comics, science fiction, and we talked for two hours. We totally clicked the first time we met. He was bright, cute and into all this weird kind of stuff I was. Dave's very charming. Even back then, he was very charming. I was a little bit more pop; he was a little bit more on the edge [Bell 2002, 127].

Loubert returned the following day and invited Sim over for dinner. After the meal, Loubert showed Sim a file containing various stories and poems, written by Loubert, Michael and Karen. An artist, Eric Hope, had contributed some drawings and Sim was pleased to see Hope lacked talent as it meant they needed his. Sim, if not for his attraction to Loubert, would have waved this project away as too amateurish for his increasingly professional pen. Instead, he "took control of the magazine as a means of ingratiating myself to [Loubert]" (Sim and Gerhard December 1995). Working on Loubert's comic, however, served the additional purpose of feeding his ego: "It was an unexpected switch for me to go from being a marginal presence at *Dark Fantasy*, a largely unpublished 'wannabe,' and to find myself a kind of final authority on creative, production and business matters on Denise Loubert's proposed magazine" (ibid.). The name of Loubert's fanzine was to be *Cerebus*, a misspelling of *Cerberus*, the three-headed hound that guards the gates of hell (Loubert admits to being a lousy speller).

Sim had considerable ambition, remarks Loubert, and she was attracted to his confidence. "I remember Dave telling me I'm going to be a millionaire before I'm thirty." She recalls that he told her this on their third date together (Bell 2002, 128). What's more, his connections to industry creators that he had established conducting interviews for *Now and Then Times* and *CANAR* served them well in their pursuit of self-publishing. As Loubert remarks, "it meant we had footing with these people" (ibid.). Sim's attraction to Loubert, quite simply, was because she was an older, more experienced woman, and attracted to him. She was the first woman he had ever dated (ibid.).

When Sim set to work designing a logo for the magazine, the same logo that appears on the first 50 issues of *Cerebus the Aardvark* (Sim and Gerhard December 1995), he felt something was missing. He suggested to Loubert that she come up with a name for the publishing imprint. Loubert decided to task her brother and sister with the job. Michael suggested "Vanaheim Press," which Sim later interpreted as being "synonymous with Valhalla"— unbelievable given that Vanaheim in fact is a region from the mythology of *Conan the Barbarian*, of which *Cerebus the Aardvark* was largely a parody — and Karen suggested "Aardvark Press" (ibid.). Karen's suggestion allegedly stemmed from an activity popular among her high school friends involving placing one's fingers flat on the table and raising the middle finger, to make the hand look like an aardvark (ibid.). Sim, with designs on someday becoming Mr. Denise Loubert (he and Loubert had recently moved in together), decided to be democratic about the situation and named the press Aardvark-Vanaheim. He then drew a mascot, an aardvark, he says, because he did not know how to draw a Vanaheim (Sim and Gerhard December 1988). "We looked [aardvark] up in the dictionary and there was a really bad, teeny thumbnail drawing," recalls Loubert. "Dave made it up from there ... Barry Smith's *Conan* was all the rage. He had all the medallions and the helmet with the horns, so we put these accoutrements on a really crude drawing of an aardvark" (Bell 2002, 129). Sim doesn't recall doing the drawing of the small gray barbarian aardvark, but he was doing so much freelance work at the time that any work he did on Loubert's fanzine seemed to him more of a hobby than anything (ibid.). As the date of publication neared, Loubert realized that the title *Cerebus* was mis-spelled. Sim, not looking forward to having to redesign the logo, suggested that instead they simply say that Cerebus was the name of the mascot (ibid.).

One week after drawing the aardvark mascot, Sim drew a single comic book panel featuring the aardvark, "just to see what he looked like from a different angle," writes Sim (Sim December 1995). Several months after the originals for the fanzine were lost, he drew a splash page, again featuring the aardvark (figure 4). Clearly, Sim felt he had something here; he just was not sure what. The splash page, he notes, "sat on a shelf in my studio in Deni's and my first apartment ... through the spring and summer of 1977, as I completed

Opposite: Figure 4. Splash page from *Cerebus* issue 1, December 1977/January 1978 (© 1977, 1978 Dave Sim).

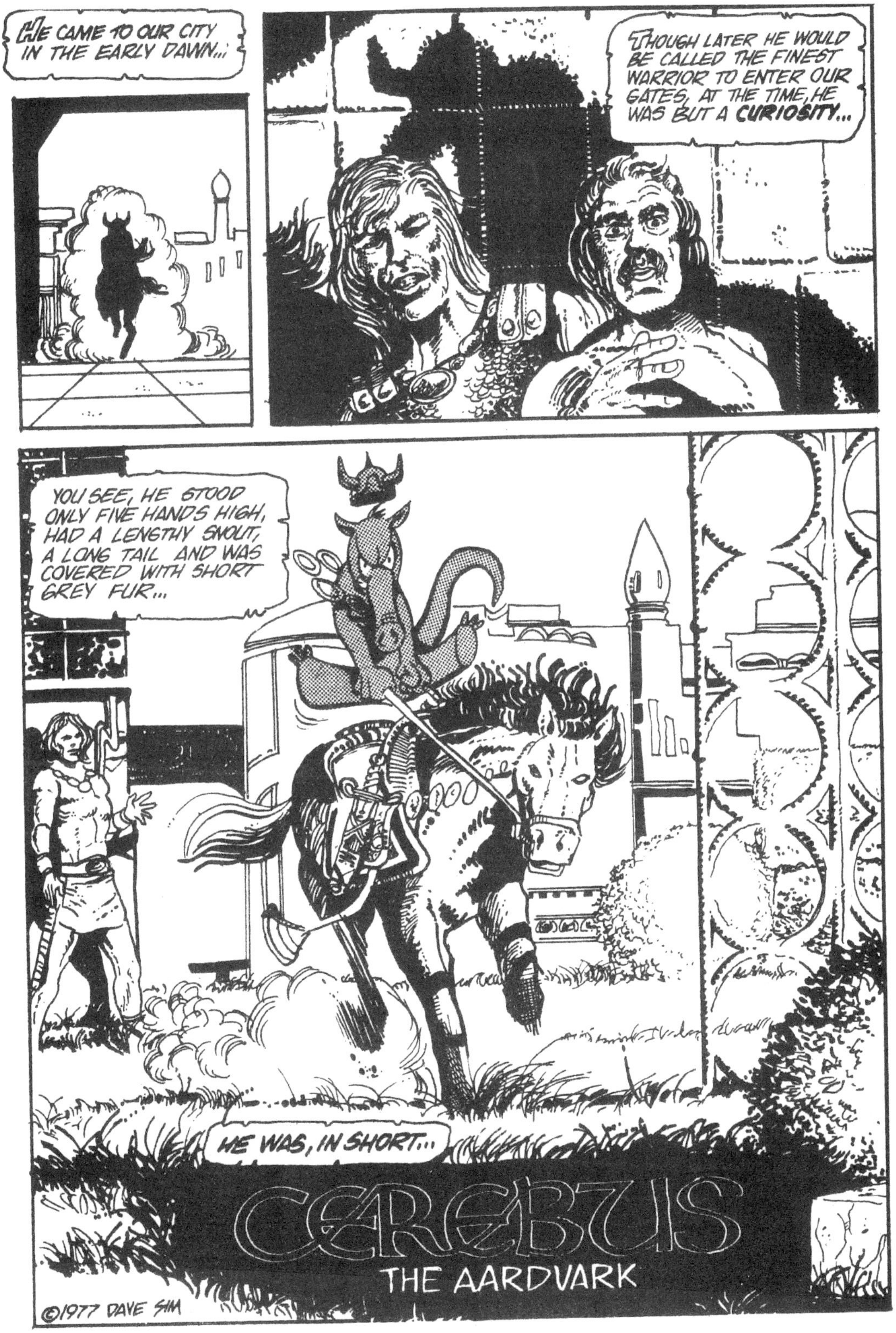

Phantacea No. 1" (ibid.). As Sim explains, "the [*Cerebus* splash] page was just lying there and it sure beat making up a new character. I drew the first issue the same way I have drawn each successive issue ... at page one, pencil, ink and letter it, and then go on to page two" as opposed to penciling a book in its entirely, then lettering it, and then inking it. "If I were to try and do *Cerebus* that way, I'd fall apart after four issues" (Sim January 1981a).

In the twenty-fifth episode of the second season of *Cerebus TV*, Sim remarks that the clearest memory he has of writing and drawing the first issue of *Cerebus* is trying to complete it in a hurry because he would not receive payment for it. At the same time, he recalls trying to do his best work because the comic was his property and no one else's (Sim 2011a). This dichotomy of the pressures of regular publication combined with the production of a quality comic became the comic's primary driving force for its remaining 299 issues. Sim, and later Sim and Gerhard, became masters at producing a quality comic on a (mostly) consistently monthly publication schedule, largely getting the comic right the first time around, without the need for revision when reprinted in its collected format.

Another reason why Sim chose *Cerebus* as his next project was due to the "demand for sword and sorcery and funny animal books," noting the popularity of Steve Gerber and Val Mayerick's *Howard the Duck*, Frank Thorne's *Red Sonja* and Roy Thomas and Barry Windsor-Smith's *Conan the Barbarian* (Sim and Gerhard December 1988). In fact, there *was* a considerable amount of boilerplate swords and sorcery produced in the mid-to-late 1970s. During the early part of that decade, the work of Howard experienced a resurgence of popularity. Originally published in *Weird Tales* in the 1930s, in 1966 science fiction writer L. Sprague de Camp made arrangements with popular science fiction and fantasy publisher Lancer Books to republish Howard's *Conan the Cimmerian* and to expand the character into other media, including comic books. It proved a winning formula. *Conan* fanzines proliferated. Windsor-Smith's notable comic book adaptations of Howard's Barbarian were particularly successful. Other related swords and sorcery novels also flourished, including Michael Moorcock's *Elric*. Sim found he could draw *Conan*-style swords and sorcery drawings for the fanzines and manage to bring in some income. As he told Thompson, an artist could sit in his basement doing drawings based on Howard's short Conan story "Red Nails" or "Rogues in the House," or an Elric drawing and "find a market somewhere" (Thompson August 1983, 68). Sim's contributions to the Howard fanzines in 1976 came about in large part because "it was still the widest market open to the aspiring illustrator at the time" (Sim April 2010, 10). This was work about which Sim was "dispassionate" (ibid.), a perception that gradually devolved into what Sim describes as "jaded irony." "Did I really want to be making a living reiterating these same tired rhetorical tropes, postures and sophomoric 'tudes?" Sim asks rhetorically (ibid., 11).

Like so many of Sim's other projects at this time, *Cerebus* the fanzine never materialized. Loubert and Sim hired a printer Day suggested because they were inexpensive, mailing a check for $175 and the original artwork to the printing firm in California. They saw neither the check nor the artwork ever again. "I recall optimism of the arrival of the printed first issue gradually giving way to anxiety, then anger, and finally resignation," writes Sim. "The awareness that a magazine like *Dark Fantasy* operated in the red, financed by Gene's freelance paychecks, and that *Cerebus* would be lucky to break even in some distant future ... dashed the original dream on the rocks of hard truth" (Sim December 1995).

Day had recently acquired additional freelance work at Marvel, including inking *Star Wars*. As a result, *Dark Fantasy* went on hiatus as Day concentrated on increasingly lucrative projects. Sim began to feel he and Day were moving in opposite directions. Particularly after the first few issues of *Cerebus the Aardvark* were published, Sim saw the small press as a much better opportunity than slaving away for Marvel for ridiculously low page rates. "In visiting Gene," remembers Sim, "the first rush of seeing actual Marvel Comics penciled pages in my friend and mentor's studio gave way to the disheartening awareness of the crippling workload [and] Gene's new status as a small cog in the Big Machine" (Sim December 1995).

Other jobs that came Sim's way because of his ComicGraphics ad was *Phantacea* for Jim McPherson's McPherson Publishing Company, standard black and white science fiction fare, with a masthead proclaiming "This Is Where Phantacea Really Begins." Sim, who wrote and drew the September 1977 first issue and provided an additional ten pages artwork for the second issue, not published until June 1978, did not like doing work-for-hire. The script simply made no sense and having to draw a story that he could not understand was immensely frustrating. He also came to find out that McPherson was paying a "middleman" fifty dollars a page for the pages Sim was drawing for twenty. "A few situations like that," Sim explains to Thompson, "convince you that if you can just eliminate all the middleman and all the excess baggage you're carrying around there would be more money in it for you personally" (Thompson August 1983, 68).

Another comic Sim worked on at this time, *Revolt: 3000*, "a quartet of Super-hero stories I had written and drawn as a commissioned work from the long-departed and never-lamented Irjax Enterprises" (Sim December 1995), never even saw publication. Both titles, Loubert tells Thompson, were intended "to be continuing series" (Thompson August 1983, 68). These frustrations later contributed to his decision to begin self-publishing with *Cerebus*, though he still had feelings of self-doubt about his success relative to Day. "As much as I thought Gene had taken a wrong turn with his Marvel freelance, I was left contemplating my own situation — doing second-rate imitations of the (even then) formulaic Marvel style at a fraction of the Big Two's pay rates and for publishers who could only muster a fraction of Marvel or DC's circulation" (Sim December 1995). Sim recalls cautioning Day about creator's rights, particularly in dealing with the Big Two, "important points ... that Gene should have paid closer attention to as he embarked on his collision course with Marvel seven years down the road" (Sim April 2009).

Marvel's treatment of Day was influential in Sim's decision to self-publish. The workload they gave him and the tight schedule for its completion, was highly stressful for the chain-smoking young artist. Day also faced pressure from having to pay the mortgage and support his wife (Sim and Gerhard September 2001). Yet the quality of Day's work resulted in improved sales on *Master of Kung-Fu*. Regardless of the increased sales, Editor-in-chief Jim Shooter removed Day and collaborator Doug Moench from the book. "Because sales were increasing," writes Sim "suddenly everyone [at Marvel] wanted to fiddle" with it (ibid.).

According to Sim, Day's dedication to his craft, and Marvel's opportunistic exploitation of that dedication resulted in Day's death at thirty-one years of age. Marvel required an emergency inker to meet a weekend deadline. Marvel called Day, who took a train from Montreal to New York during a snowstorm "and began inking as soon as he arrived" (Sim and Gerhard September 2001). Marvel put him up in a rat-infested hotel for the night. Day balked; they offered him a couch in the reception area. "He developed an infection in his kidneys as a result," writes Sim (ibid.). Shortly before his death, Shooter allegedly fired Day, who found work at DC soon thereafter. Day, however, was hurt, as he preferred Marvel to DC, and, according to Sim, this indirectly resulted in the heart attack that killed him while out walking on the night of 23 September 1982.[2]

Self-publishing increasingly seemed like the only viable option for the struggling artist. "Dave was really working hard on these books for other publishers," explains Loubert, "taking a lot of crap, and *not* getting much money" (McDonnell 1983, 21). Sim adds, "I had grown very tired of arbitrary judgments and editorial directions" (ibid.). Sim told Thompson that self-publishing was a "natural outgrowth from.... 'Well, I want to do it myself, I want to do a book that will be my book' because I was getting tired of drawing scripts that people were sending me. People who were looking for an artist to draw their stories just for ego's satisfaction" (Thompson August 1983, 68). As Sim says in a 1989 *The Comics Journal* interview with Gary Groth, the advantage of self-publishing is that the artist is able to "make decisions that are artistically important ... on the basis of art, and flying the face of business if it's necessary" (Groth July 1989, 101).

According to Sim, direct sales changed the market for comics in a fundamental way. "With the direct-sales market, the publisher's role changed to that of a service industry to the artist," remarks Sim (Groth July 1989, 101). "The publisher is there to take an unduly large percentage ... for what is basically taking [an artist's work] to a printer, phoning distributors, finding out how many copies they want, telling the printer, getting the printing bill, getting the checks from the distributors, and then taking an unconscionably large percentage.... As the publishers conceive it, they squeeze you in somewhere between the paper and the ink" (ibid.). In direct sales, there is much less risk for the publisher.

At first, Sim self-published for practical reasons; only later would he translate his success into advocacy of self-publishing for other comics artists and refigure the practice as a locus for his larger analysis of the business of comics, in particular the work-for-hire model as practiced by Marvel and DC. As comfortable as Sim became with self-publishing, acting as publisher of another's work left him cold; he felt pressured to adopt tactics he as self-publisher routinely criticized. The hypocrisy was too much to bear. "I became aware that most creators use publishing companies and whoever's in control of these publishing companies as a crutch," Sim told interviewer Stephen Darnall. "It's up to the creator to just sit there and create it, and then [the publisher] is supposed to make it a success" (Darnall 1993, 65). Creative freedom, argues Sim, is not something an artist simply acquires; it is something earned, just as Sim struggled to win his "territory" in the comics industry in his publication of *Cerebus* on a (mostly) reliable monthly basis. "As soon as you become a publisher for someone else," Sim continues, "you're talking about taking most of the business knocks for them, and essentially you're talking about trying to run two careers simultaneously.... At some point, you just start feeling like Dad" (ibid.).

Sim later came under fire by some publishers in the industry, notably Groth, who found Sim's advocacy of self-publishing reckless and unethical. Sim, Groth believed, was the exception that proved the self-publishing rule. Not all comics artists are as talented as Sim, Groth maintained, therefore, to encourage young artists to self-publish is to risk condemning them to financial ruin. Sim would later retract some of his bolder statements about self-publishing and refashion his advocacy as mere encouragement, telling Tom Palmer, Jr., for instance, that self-publishing is "worth a try.... Having said that, I will acknowledge that self-publishing is not for everybody. But I think the only way to find that out is to actually do it" (Palmer, Jr. 1996, 60).

It was while working on *Revolt 3000*, that Sim, drawing "five different characters in 12-page first chapters of longer stories, set on Earth," realized he could not only produce work on schedule, it was something he wanted "to do for the rest of my life" (McDonnell 1983, 21). Sim decided that publishing a comic himself and adding it to his samples package, consisting of *Revolt: 3000* and *Phantacea* would help bring in work. The only problem now was coming up with an idea.

Quite by chance, Sim landed on the idea of expanding the one-page splash page of *Cerebus the Aardvark* he'd designed and sent to Mike Friedrich of Star*Reach Productions for publication in his funny animal comic *Quack!* Friedrich famously passed on the idea, the same month he passed on Wendy and Richard Pini's *Elfquest*. "I felt Mike had pretty much missed the boat on what made *Howard the Duck* successful," says Sim. "With *Howard*, it was the idea of a funny animal in today's world of humans. So, the obvious thing for me would be either a science fiction or a barbarian funny animal ... I had a bizarre idea [for] a Barry Smith–style funny animal" (McDonnell 1983, 21). Friedrich, Sim explains, did not think the property had any commercial potential. "Mike had rejected the aardvark, and I wanted to take my own shot at publishing. Why not *Cerebus*? I had already put a reasonable amount of thought into the premise" (ibid.). According to Loubert, Friedrich first suggested Sim self-publish the comic book (Bell 2002, 129).

Loubert recalls that at the time Friedrich passed on *Cerebus the Aardvark*, she was working full time for a local printer to help support Sim's fledgling career as a comics artist. "Basically, what I remember is sitting in the kitchen talking about it, Dave sitting down with a pen and a piece of paper and saying, 'Well, we'd have to sell this many issues to break even'" (Thompson August 1983, 70). Sim came up with the idea of doing three issues initially; then, if by the third issue they were not making a profit, they would discontinue the book. "I will now have *Phantacea*, *Revolt: 3000* and three issues of *Cerebus* to advertise the fact that this guy does, indeed, do full comic books, chock full of thrills," reasoned Sim (ibid., 71). "I thought, 'Okay, regular publication is a key, having a continuing character is a key, and if I can't keep going, then I will have put out three issues of a comic book in the space of six months, and use these to get more work" (Palmer Jr., 64–65).

Loubert, through her printing connections, knew someone who could print the inside pages cheaply, and they kept the print run down to a modest 2,000 copies, of which 500 would be sold to Harry Kremer at a discounted distributor's rate, with an option to buy an additional 500 if the first 500 sold well (Thompson August 1983, 71). Sim and Loubert sold an additional 500 copies to Jim Friel (who incidentally inked Sim and Brennan's story, "A Boy and His Aardvark") (ibid.). After printing the first issue, Sim and Loubert received a call from Phil Seuling asking to increase his order from 500 copies to 1,000. Thus, all 2,000 of the comics sold the moment Sim and Loubert received the published comics. It was an auspicious beginning.

Loubert assumed the management end of Aardvark-Vanaheim, with Sim there to teach her what he knew about the comics business. It would prove to be a learning experience for both of them, but moreso for Loubert. Sim kept controlling interest of the company as a "moral point," believing that giving the artist controlling interest assures that the artist will produce his or her best work, as it is their integrity on the line (Thompson 1983, 75). Sim argued that there are limits to what an artist can earn when working for Marvel or DC, whereas, in the case of self-publishing it is a rather more "straightforward" matter, which is to say, "if the book sells more we make more money" (ibid., 76). Comparatively, if Marvel sells more of an artist's comics the artist does not always see an increase in salary.

Sim's single-minded drive to translate his passion for comic books into a living spilled over into his personal life. Loubert, he writes, "was pressed into service as an agent for my commercial art skills" (Sim and Gerhard March 1996). Loubert enlisted her brother Michael to write a number of stories to help enlarge and evolve the mythos of *Cerebus*; Michael would contribute the "Aardvarkian Age" map closely based on the Hyborean Age map found in the Marvel *Conan* series (figure 5). Sim's first apartment prior to meeting Loubert, he writes, "was all drawing board and art supplies, promotional brochures for my studio ... tear sheets and news clippings filling the corkboard wall which separated the single living room/bedroom from the kitchenette, the limited drawer and cupboard space occupied by comic books and reference books" (ibid.). After moving in with Loubert, Sim transformed their apartment into the Aardvark-Vanaheim studio and "fanzine publishing office" (ibid.).

Sim learned from the example of Day, whose responsibilities in paying the mortgage and supporting his wife, that one's "comic-book life" and "real life ... might exist in diametric opposition to each other" (Sim and Gerhard March 1996). Sim remarks that a "discerning reader will recognize a large measure of Viktor Davis' genesis in the above"—Viktor Davis being one of the protagonists of the *Cerebus* volume *Reads*—"in this case the marital residence itself serving as a creative void to devour [the artists'] energies and idealism" (ibid.). Sim resolved to "avoid" as best he could a situation similar to that of Day's. Sim slips into the third person (reminiscent of the third person used in *Reads*) to describe his situation further, "As he eyed his lifemate ... he could congratulate himself that he ... had chosen wisely. He intended to conquer the world, to become indescribably wealthy and equally famous" (ibid.).

While Sim could later lament the female urge to devour artistic energy and idealism,

Figure 5. "The Aardvarkian Age" map by Dave Sim and Michael Loubert, from *Cerebus* issue 3, April 1978 (© 1978 Dave Sim).

in the late 1970s, Loubert was supporting him as he struggled to make it as an artist (Bell 2002, 130). As Loubert comments, self-publishing was an extremely risky undertaking and there was no one they could turn to for support, no example with which to base their decisions, artistic, financial, or otherwise. They were charting entirely new territory. "There were no independent comics at the time," Loubert tells Bell. "There was Mike Friedrich doing *Star*Reach* and Dean Mullaney just starting Eclipse" but that was all (ibid.). Loubert worked full-time until the fourteenth issue; she worked on the *Cerebus* business on "nights and weekends" (McDonnell 1983, 21). She was happy to support Sim, telling McDonnell that "I've always had a very big conviction that if you're an artist, you *shouldn't* have to worry about rent. I grew up wanting to be somebody who made it possible for somebody else to be artistic, though not necessarily in comics because I wasn't 'into' comics until I met Dave" (ibid.). Loubert readily admits that her knowledge of both comics and publishing came from her husband: "Every attitude that I have about publishing is from Dave," she confesses. "The big decisions have basically been made by Dave. He knows how, more than I" (ibid., 22).

Based on the nearly imperceptible reaction to the comic, it seemed at times as if they were working in a vacuum. "I can remember when one letter a day was a pretty heavy response," Sim tells McDonnell (McDonnell 1983, 22). In addition to the depressing and somewhat alarming lack of response to the work, the task of self-publishing provided many opportunities for financial ruin: "checks bounced, books were damaged" or buyers demanded refunds (ibid.). Distributors were late with payments while printers demanded their money on time. "Cash flow was a problem," Sim explains (ibid.).

Gradually, however, the situation changed. Attending the 1978 Toronto Comic Convention, the couple discovered that *Cerebus* had acquired a substantial following. According to Loubert, Sim was overjoyed (Sim October-November 1978). After another comics artist approached Loubert to inquire if Aardvark-Vanaheim was interested in publishing his book, Loubert took it upon herself to re-fashion Aardvark-Vanaheim from Sim's original concept of the company as a means of self-publishing into something more like a regular publishing company. Sim would later state that Loubert simply did not have enough to do beyond secretarial work, and allowing her to pursue the publication of others' work was a means of placating her and allowing him to concentrate more fully to *Cerebus* (Sim and Gerhard March 1996).

With the reassuring realization that *Cerebus* had a following, Sim began expanding the world of Estarcion, pursuing a larger story, epic in scope, not limited to simply *Conan* satires and all but abandoning his (rather poor) Barry Windsor-Smith style for an increasing sophistication and experimentation. Early issues of *Cerebus* show Sim trying to find his voice as an artist, borrowing here and there from artists as diverse as Day, Adams and *Batman* artist Marshall Rogers, whom Sim met at a convention in Ottawa (Bell 2002, 131).

Cerebus issue 11 is an important issue, as it is the first appearance of a non-barbarian setting, that of a roughly fourteenth- to fifteenth-century landscape. When Sim and Marshall Rogers next met at the 1979 Toronto Comic Convention, Rogers was drawing DC's *Batman*. Rogers told Sim he felt Batman was a "sicko" for his being compelled to dress up in tights (Sim 1982b). Stimulated by the idea, Sim created the character of The Roach, the longest running of *Cerebus*' supporting characters, and Sim's first interjection of overt comics parody beyond the Conan/Red Sonja variety (figure 6). Because of copyright laws, Sim obviously could not use a character dressed as a bat, so he "opted for the most disgusting critter I could think of" (ibid.). The Roach was also the catalyst for the introduction of two

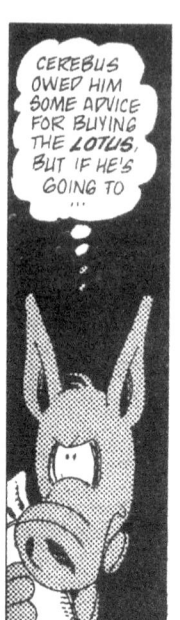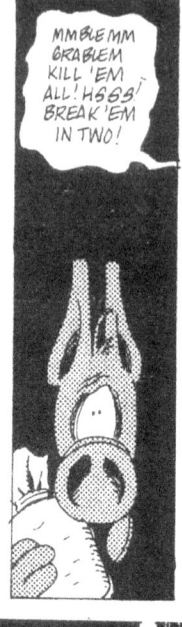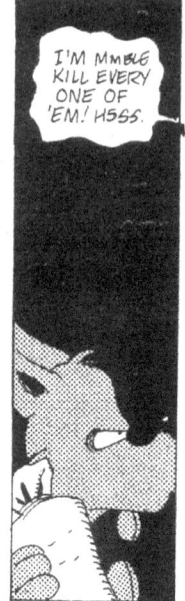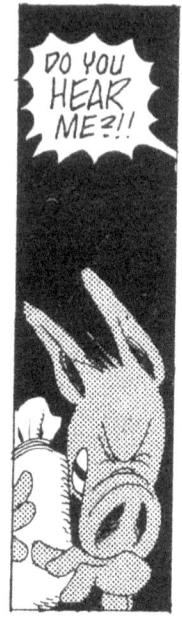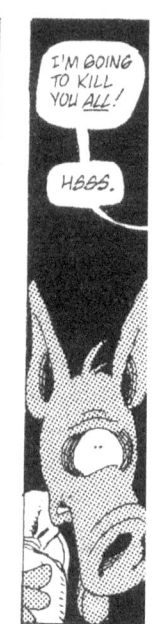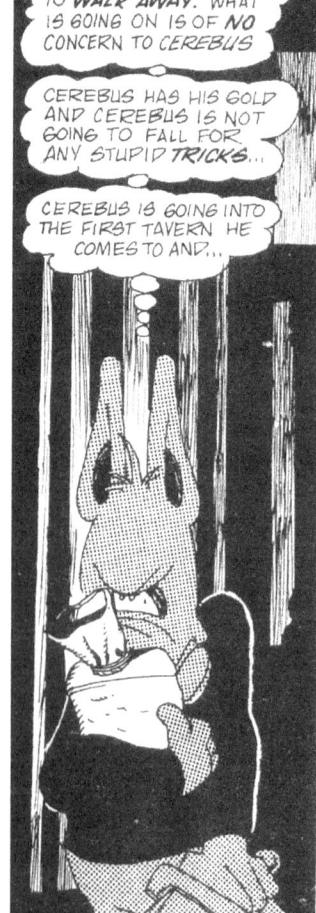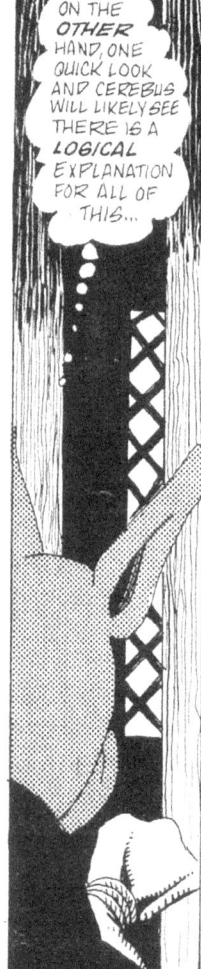

additional key characters, Weisshaupt and Astoria, both of whom helped shift the tone of the series.

With the Roach, *Cerebus* made a crucial step forward in its self-awareness as a comic book at the same time substantially increasing the title's popularity. The Roach's second incarnation, The Moon Roach, is a satire of Bill Sienkiewicz's *Moon Knight*. Similarly, the Petuniacon Cerebus must attend as part of his campaign for Prime Minister is nothing more than a thinly veiled comics convention. Sim did not consider it anachronistic to include them in what was otherwise a serious political satire. He also was not overly concerned that a reader's lack of familiarity would detract from their enjoyment of the satire. "I'm doing a comic book for the comic book environment because that seems and has seemed sensible to me," Sim explained to Spurgeon.

> You put all your efforts into comic books, and you deal with the language the people in that environment know.... To me it was necessary to have this one really ridiculous superhero character in the story who just recurred.... The context that I'm in, and certainly the context that *Cerebus* evolved in, you had to bring in a guy with long underwear or it just wouldn't have the proper resonance.... That was about superhero fans and superhero stores and superhero comic book companies and the weight it exerts in my life [Spurgeon February 1996, 86–87].

In effect, *Cerebus* bridges a "schism" between the comic book medium and comic books as a conduit for the superhero genre (Spurgeon February 1996, 87). *Cerebus'* satirical edge self-reflexively examines media representations of super-hero genre clichés, while simultaneously functioning as a self-conscious commentary on the comics medium.

Comprehension of a considerable amount of *Cerebus* depends on abundant familiarity with the history of the comics medium from the mid–1970s to the early 2000s, a requirement that detractors believe will severely affect *Cerebus'* longevity. Its allusions, at times obscure, render the comic almost nonsensical to an uninitiated reader. For some, *Cerebus* became so much a comic *about* comics that they found it too distracting, too much an interruption of the elaborate world Sim and Gerhard worked so exhaustively to create. Yet, the obscurity of Sim's references at times deepens the meaning of the comic substantially and hardly seems extraneous to the narrative action or meaning. The introduction of a satire of a comic book convention in the context of a political convention, for example, suggests the political content of any activity. In *Jaka's Story*, Sim finds a more subtle expression of the comic book culture in the character of Pud Withers, a shy and withdrawn tavern owner who fantasizes about the beautiful tavern dancer Jaka, who is symbolic of the "fanboy" mentality.

High Society (1982–1983)

By the late 1970s, things were looking good for Sim. *Cerebus* was beginning to sell more steadily and, though there continued to be financial emergencies and other ongoing problems inherent with publishing, he began to feel more secure about the comic's long-term viability. Moreover, Sim was to attend Seuling's 1979 New York Convention to receive the Ed Aprill Award. Shortly before the convention, however, Sim suffered a nervous breakdown, allegedly from an overdose of LSD.[3]

Opposite: Figure 6. The Roach, the earliest example of Sim's comics satire, in *Cerebus* issue 11, August 1979 (© 1979 Dave Sim).

Because of this overdose, Sim radically revised the scope of *Cerebus*. First, he announced the book would run to 156 bi-monthly issues, a quarter-century commitment. In addition, Sim apparently developed much of the broad outline that would carry the plotline to its end (Thompson August 1983, 60). He then changed the publishing schedule of *Cerebus* from bi-monthly to monthly, upping the final issue count to 300, due to the "psychological strain" of stopping work on the comic for a month at a time to do work on advertising or other commercial work (Bissette 1992, 21). *Cerebus* had become easier to produce without the additional commitments getting in the way (Thompson July 1983, 73). Limiting the series to 300 issues assured there would be an end in sight. As he tells Palmer, Jr., he would not "be 75 years old and racked with arthritis trying to do the next page"; at the same time, the number of issues also required Sim to commit to some longevity and not simply "do the character for another year or two until I got bored. Doing 300 issues seemed like a good compromise" (Palmer, Jr. 1996, 60). Going monthly and writing and drawing all of the issues himself also allowed him to tell a large story with a "consistent viewpoint [and] story" as opposed to the "immense, complicated, self-contradictory mythos" of other long-running comics, one usually written and drawn by regularly changing staff of artists who possessed "no real interest in manufacturing or adding to it" (Thompson August 1983, 60).

Sim had in his month off decided to sell *Cerebus* as a "regular feature," eventually selling a number of single page strips to *The Buyer's Guide*, a comics ad newspaper with a large circulation, essentially receiving payment for a free one-page advertisement for *Cerebus* (Sim drew the comic as a wonderfully knowing send-up to Hal Foster's *Prince Valiant*) (Sim 1982a). "The time between Cerebus #13 and #14 was very interesting," explains Sim. "I was right royally sick of doing commercial art ... and working for people who wouldn't know a marketable idea or [an] effective drawing if they tripped over it" (ibid.). In January 1980, Sim decided to stop doing the strips. When Loubert warned him he could not simply end the strip abruptly, Sim replied that he would rework the strip so that it functioned as a bridge between the two issues. Sim already had in mind that the Lord Silverspoon character, around which Sim wrote and drew the strip, had a wealthy and powerful father, the ruler of a complex government bureaucracy centered in Palnu, a wealthy Estarcion city.

It was while attending the 1979 Christmas Con that Sim read the first review of *Cerebus* in *The Comics Journal* 52, dated December 1979, exactly two years after the comic's inaugural issue. The review, by editor Kim Thompson, praises Sim for "surmount[ing]" his comic's origins as a "line-for-line pastiche of Roy Thomas and Barry Smith's *Conan* ... to stand on its own two ... feet as a delightful and admirable work of art" (Thompson 1979, 25). He notes Sim's increasing popularity, in addition to his "ever-increasing craftsmanship," and it is on this artistry that Thompson concentrates for the bulk of the review (ibid.). Thompson calls *Cerebus* a "true heir to Carl Barks' duck stories," in part because, like Barks, Sim shows "the sensitivity to develop an almost organic feel for their characters that are far removed from ... intellectual manipulation" (ibid., 25–26).[4] Because of this, Sim is able to achieve something Steve Gerber in *Howard the Duck* could not, because Gerber was too "insistent on using [Howard] to make points in his stories" (ibid., 26). Thompson notes how even the supporting cast has acquired depth, "doubly remarkable" in that these characters initially began as one dimensional parodies, yet, writes Thompson, "once Sim had turned the originals inside out, he found that the resultant contortion had its own charm and took off from there" (ibid., 27). Thompson, amusingly given the later context, did not think that the theological background for the series should be "taken ... seriously" (ibid.). What *should* be taken seriously, however, is Sim's talent as a comics artist; Thompson writes at length of Sim's developing skill, in particular his "command of the comics language ... a clean, uncluttered, pleasant storytelling style ... Sim knows exactly when to use split panels, tilted and odd-shaped panels, silhouettes, triptychs, zooms, and does so expertly that these techniques blend into the fabric of the narrative to create a seamless tapestry of images" (ibid., 26).

Thompson's review was "immensely reassuring to me," writes Sim. "One of the points Kim made was that (except for Red Sophia) most of the parodies I had done became, to him, solid characters in their own right.... After reading Kim's review ... I decided to see if I could apply an outside figure to the role of Grandlord and make him stick" (Sim 1982b). That character was Lord Julius, a masterful parody of Groucho Marx. "Groucho came to mind almost immediately," explains Sim. "Groucho's flair for improvising [and] quality of verbal manipulation became the essence of Lord Julius" (ibid.).

In his 1983 interview with Sim, Thompson points out that he has "never seen anything quite like [Sim's] rhythm, the silent panels, the use of dialogue," and asks Sim if any particular comics artist had influenced his comics style (Thompson August 1983, 76). Sim replies with a short list: Adams, Day, Jim Steranko, Harvey Kurtzman and Berni Krigstein. The extension of their philosophy is, for Sim, to make "every page interesting [or] distinctive in its own way, have its own character" (ibid., 78). Because Sim does not need to "get by an editor," he has the freedom to experiment: "the whole world opens up, because so few interesting approaches have been done" (ibid.). This statement helps to illustrate one of Sim's intents with *Cerebus*; not only to break the rules of how a comic is made (self-published on a regular, monthly basis) but to break the rules of what the comic is composed, its structural and thematic content, as well.

Once the 300 issues were decided, Sim realized he could not do single issues exclusively, but would need to allow the reader the experience of duration, of a story unfolding *over time* as opposed to the entirely static and unreal time of most comics, whose characters never age even though the fashion, technology and cultural references surrounding them do. These other comics, Sim points out, are largely super-hero comics, with an entire stratum of narratives not adequately dealt with. "If I were writing a novel it would be difficult ... to think of a theme that hasn't been done before," Sim tells Thompson, "but in comics there's nothing but open space" (Thompson August 1983, 78). Pointedly, Sim is not bothered by the fact that most comics enjoy brief periods of avid readership but then generally fall by the wayside when the next big thing arrives; titles with the significant longevity of, say, *Batman*, are exceptions which prove the rule. Any creative artist, argues Sim, is always faced with a "highwire act; at any moment they might be surpassed by the Next Big Thing and forgotten about" (ibid., 64). Asked if he is worried that the subjects he is satirizing will fade away and *Cerebus* will lose its impact as a result, Sim replies that many things in *Alice in Wonderland*, for example, are parodies and the audience's lack of knowledge of their sources does not affect their enjoyment in any significant way. Moon Roach, for example "has his own personality," Sim tells Thompson, and his psychoses can be "overlay[ed onto] any super-hero [with] a standard psychotic personality "and they will fit each other like glue" (ibid.).

The change in format of the comic book from a medieval swords and sorcery setting to that of a roughly fourteenth- or fifteenth-century cosmopolitan, European setting was first introduced in "The Palnu Trilogy" in issues 14 through 16. The three-issue storyline was both a first attempt at a longer storyline and an enlargement of the *Cerebus* mythos, the introduction of new, long-running characters, coupled with an expansion of those characters already introduced, and increasingly perceptive commentaries on politics and religion.

High Society was the first of these long-running "novels," as they came to be called, having increased in issue length from three to roughly 25, amassing some 500 comic pages in length. Sim's development of these cohesive, serialized "novels-within-a-series," and subsequent collecting them in a trade paperback format, anticipated the standard industry practice of twenty years hence. (His ability to complete these longer "novels-within-a-novel" was another benefit of self-publishing, afforded by his having complete editorial control of *Cerebus*.) Sim flirted with returning to single issue stories only once after *High Society*, in the first dozen or so issues of what came to be the single longest-running "novel-within-series" *Church & State*, running some 1,100 pages in length in collected form. After *Church & State*, every issue of *Cerebus* was designed as the beginning, middle and end of a self-contained and relatively coherent (some more than others) "novel."

Sim's decision to adopt a more sophisticated air to his comic than a straightforward satire of swords and sorcery, may have resulted from his first reading the work of Norman Mailer (in particular the serialization of his Muhammad Ali biography *The Fight* in *Playboy*) (figure 7). Writing in a 2004 letter shortly after the conclusion of *Cerebus*, Sim wrote Mailer attesting to Mailer's "*unimaginably large* ... contribution to my own life and work (Sim 2005, 280). "It was your writing which weaned me off the exclusive diet of fantasy and science fiction that I had consumed to that point, your writing which first made the real world interesting to me" (ibid.).[5]

Another influence in Sim's decision to transition the comic from a swords and sorcery format was Richard and Wendy Pini's *Elfquest*. Sim was impressed with the direction Wendy Pini had taken the comic; he could "just feel that radiating quality of somebody doing exactly what they wanted.... At the same time, I was basically still trying to be Barry Windsor-Smith, and trying to do *Conan* material, and finally, I had to acknowledge to myself that I had no great love of swords and sorcery" (Darnall 1993, 65).

Sim was not the first comics artist to devote himself to a lengthy project, as he readily admits, yet he may have been the first to announce his intention from the outset. To do so evinces a remarkable faith in the project's longevity and an assumption that an audience will continue to read a comic book for well over twenty years when so many comic books have trouble lasting more than a year or two. Sim recognized that the primary reason for the cancellation of comics is not simply any lack of quality (although that is often a contributing factor). Rather, they face cancellation because they do not stay on schedule and are constantly changing artistic personnel, in particular the pencillers and inkers, who have difficulty maintaining the intense schedule of a monthly comic.

One typically finds the longest and most successful comics on the Sunday pages among strip cartoonists such as Charles Schulz, who wrote and illustrated *Peanuts* for 50 years, while Milton Caniff's *Steve Canyon* and Frank King's *Gasoline Alley* lasted 41. Sim's work stands in marked contrast to these other works in that Schulz, King and Caniff had only to produce a few dozen panels per month while Sim had to create twenty pages of comic art plus a cover. King and Caniff's work anticipates Sim's extended narrative in that each series had a narrative continuity in a general sense. Discussing the length of the series, Sim tells McDonnell that he decided to do 300 issues because Will Eisner's *The Spirit* lasted thirteen years (1940–1952) "and it wasn't enough ... I'm saying, yes, *Cerebus* is implausible, ludicrous and ridiculous, but the 6,000 pages of story will hold together" (McDonnell 1983, 23–24).

Opposite: Figure 7. Sim's narrative begins to increase in complexity. From *Cerebus* issue 14, March 1980 (© 1980 Dave Sim).

CEREBUS HAD NEVER BEEN TO PALNU, BUT, IN THE COURSE OF HIS TRAVELS, HAD HEARD MUCH ABOUT IT! MOST OUTLANDERS DWELT AT SOME LENGTH ON ITS SIZE AND WEALTH! SINCE HE HAD DECIDED TO REMAIN HERE, HE WOULD NEED TO KNOW MORE! THERE WAS AN EXPRESSION IN SERREA, "WHEN THE DRUNKARD SPEAKS THE SOBER MAN LEARNS MUCH." WITHIN THE HOUR, CEREBUS HAD LOCATED A SUITABLE BUREAUCRAT AT THE "FROG AND DUCK" AND, FOR THE PRICE OF A FEW TANKARDS, IS SOON UP TO HIS MEDALLIONS IN INFORMATION.

THE ARISTOCRACY HAD ALL BUT VANISHED IN PALNU! BOUND AS THEY WERE TO THEIR ENORMOUS ESTATES, THEY WERE NO COMPETITION FOR THE THRIVING MERCHANT CLASS WHOSE ASSETS NOW GENERATED UNDREAMT OF INCOME. THERE WERE FIVE DOMINANT MERCHANT "HOUSES" WITHIN THE CITY WALLS. THESE HOUSES EMPLOYED "CLIENTS," EACH CITIZEN OF VOTING AGE BEING A CLIENT, THEIR LIVING EXPENSES PAID BY THE HOUSE "LORD" IN EXCHANGE FOR THEIR VOTE. THE LORD, BY PAYING FOR THESE VOTES, ASSURED HIMSELF OF A PLACE ON THE "GRAND COUNCIL OF PALNU." THE LORD WHO OWNED THE MOST CLIENTS, AND, HENCE, VOTES WAS MADE "GRANDLORD" OF THE CITY AND ITS SURROUNDING TERRITORY! AT THE MOMENT, THIS WAS LORD JULIUS! THE WRINKLE THAT JULIUS HAD ADDED TO THIS IDEA WAS THE SELLING OF TITLES FOR ADDITIONAL REVENUE! THE LORDS OF THE NOUVEAU-RICHE MERCHANT HOUSES, HAVING, SOME TIME BEFORE, RUN OUT OF THINGS TO BUY, NOW FILLED JULIUS' COFFERS IN EXCHANGE FOR THE TITLE OF THEIR CHOICE! THESE THEY HANDED OUT LIKE PARTY FAVOURS TO CONCUBINES, FAMILY BODYGUARDS, ACCOUNTANTS, NIECES, NEPHEWS AND, OF COURSE, THEMSELVES. JULIUS HIMSELF WAS GRANDLORD SUPREME, BARON OF THE HOUSE OF TAVERS, RIGHT HONOURABLE PRIME MINISTER OF PALNU, PRESIDENT OF PARMOC, COUNT OF CIHNU...

THERE WERE A NUMBER OF OTHER TITLES HE HAD PAID FOR, BUT CEREBUS HAD FORGOTTEN ANOTHER SERREAN EXPRESSION;

"WHEN THE BUREAUCRAT SPEAKS, THE SOUND OF SNORING SOON FILLS THE ROOM."

Sim points to how *Cerebus* retains its appeal because it has remained relatively constant whereas the rest of the comics industry has changed. "Since I've begun, the top comics titles have changed," he tells McDonnell. "We went through the *Red Sonja* administration, then *Howard the Duck*, *The X-Men*, *Daredevil* and now *Teen Titans*. Those changes happened because the guy who made it to the top book took up his pen and left. That's the difference. I'm not going to leave" (ibid., 24).

Even though *Cerebus* was only selling around 30,000 copies, Sim earned more based on that small circulation than those comics artists whose work sold 250,000 to 300,000 copies. Thus, Sim's financial and artistic autonomy were at the time highly unconventional in the comics industry. Because of this, Sim could maintain his artistic integrity and resist temptations to "cash in" on the *Cerebus* phenomenon, no matter how small it may have been by comparison. Sim resisted an offer from Marvel to write *Howard the Duck* and from DC Comics to purchase the rights to his character, and, for the most part, the temptation to merchandise or to otherwise capitalize financially on his creation (aside from producing a quality monthly title).[6] Sim's decision not to sell the rights to his characters, thereby retaining his creative independence, was influenced by two high-profile creator disputes in the early 1980s: Steve Gerber's battle to recover his rights to *Howard the Duck* and Jack Kirby's highly publicized effort to recover his artwork and acknowledgment and credit for his part in creating *The Fantastic Four, Captain America*, and many other Marvel characters.

Sim's ongoing satires of the "flavor-of-the-month" comic book, primarily filtered through his perpetually transforming character The Roach, were at times so on-the-mark that they caused a small amount of furor. The first, and most notorious, instance of this controversy came with Sim's parody of the *X-Men* character Wolverine (figure 8). Marvel Comics' lawyers sent Sim a cease and desist letter after Sim featured the Wolveroach character prominently on three consecutive covers of *Cerebus*, numbers 54 through 56. The letter stated that Sim's use of the parody character represented an "unauthorized use" and that it "constitutes an infringement of Marvel's copyright, trademark, and other proprietary rights" (*The Comics Journal* July 1984 news feature, 11; Sim reprinted the letter in *Cerebus*). Sim and Loubert were quick to acknowledge to *The Comics Journal* that the Wolveroach character was their most "extensive" parody yet. Sim told the *Journal* that "Marvel felt it was unfair usage to put the character on the cover for three consecutive issues ... I guess Marvel felt that Wolverine was a more valuable commodity than Moon Knight.... But I didn't give [Marvel] any flak for having S'ym [a *Cerebus*-derived villain created by Chris Claremont in response to a Sim parody that merged the Professor X character with Claremont] in *The X-Men*" (ibid.). Sim decided not to push the issue any further, though he remained critical of Marvel's handling of the matter, which he felt would have been better served by sending an inquiry letter prior to a cease and desist from their lawyer. Sim "faulted the lawyers ... for acting in such a matter" (ibid., 12).[7]

As *Cerebus* increased in popularity, and as Aardvark-Vanaheim's list of titles grew, Sim and Loubert's marriage began to fall apart, with Loubert eventually asking for a trial separation (Sim October 1983). In discussion with Bell, Loubert states that she was beginning to feel as if she did not have an identity outside of her husband. The fan club and limited merchandising that took up most of her time had less to do with finances than with feeding Sim's ego (Bell 2002, 136). Moreover, she was disappointed that Sim was not interested in pursuing projects that might have resulted in financial gain. "Every time I tried to push him that way, he didn't want to do it," she tells Bell. "We had people very early on approaching us about [a] film. He wouldn't do it unless he had total control, which we knew how likely that was" (ibid., 135). Loubert admits that publishing other comics and the comics in the "Unique Stories" back up was a means of asserting her independence. Sim had to sell ad space in the back of *Cerebus* in order to cover the printing costs of the additional titles.

In the fall of 1983, the couple underwent a trial separation; Loubert moved out (Sim November 1983). In spite of their rapidly deteriorating relationship, she and Sim continued to publish *Cerebus* together, and she continued to expand Aardvark-Vanaheim's monthly roster of titles, including Arn Saba's *Neal the Horse*, Jim Valentino's *normalman*, Bob Burden's *Flaming Carrot* and William Messner-Loebs' *Journey*. They continued to attend conventions, and Loubert maintained her title as publisher and contributed her Note from the President for each issue of *Cerebus*. Her last issue was issue 70 dated January 1985. Loubert moved to Los Angeles, moving all the Aardvark-Vanaheim titles other than *Cerebus* to her new imprint, Renegade, which went bankrupt a few years later.

Figure 8. Sim's parody of a Marvel character, Wolveroach, on the cover of *Cerebus* issue 54, September 1982 (© 1982 Dave Sim).

Sim's first act in the absence of Loubert was to cut the book back to a more manageable 24 pages (from 32) and to jettison Loubert's "Unique Stories" back up which displayed other Aardvark-Vanaheim talent. In issue 72, Sim announced that the current storyline on which he was working was *Church & State* and was ongoing since issue 52, an attempt to complete what he started in *High Society*.

Loubert's departure occurred only a few months after the arrival of Gerhard, who began working on *Cerebus* with issue 65 (figure 9). Gerhard met Sim while working as a deliveryman for an art supply store where Sim purchased his supplies. At the time, Gerhard was doing freelance work, and Sim saw some samples of his work. Intrigued, Sim asked him to do some paste-up and design work in-house advertisements and promotionals that appeared both in *Cerebus* and in the *Comic Buyer's Guide*. Gerhard's freelance work was mostly comprised of colored landscape settings, in both urban and natural environments

(Brownstein Winter 1997b, 31–32). Archie Goodwin, editor of *Epic Illustrated*, asked Sim if he might contribute some color *Cerebus* stories for the magazine. Sim, inexperienced with color, asked Gerhard to add color backgrounds to inked pages Sim produced. The *Epic* stories went over well with readers, and eventually Sim asked Gerhard to work on the monthly comic (ibid., 32).

Sim and Gerhard maintained a unique partnership in the comics industry. Not only did their creative partnership last longer than any other comics artist team (including Jack Kirby and Stan Lee on *The Fantastic Four*), but Sim also granted Gerhard part ownership of the company. Sim told Gerhard that he could produce his own *Cerebus* comic or reprint their comic if he so desired, plus gave him the ability to withdraw money from the company, and so on. In fact, Sim's agreement with Gerhard is a real world example of the type of gentleman's agreement Sim favored over the typical work-for-hire contract utilized by DC or Marvel, or espoused by Groth as necessary to protect the publisher and artist.

Rape, Infanticide, Self-Publishing and Other Sins: Little Controversies (1983–1988)

During his monthly serialization of *Cerebus*, one of the virtues Sim himself hoped to extol was maintaining the integrity of *Cerebus* as a pure comics experience. As long as he was in control, a summer blockbuster would not make *Cerebus* into a comics advertisement. This meant Sim naturally rejected any form of merchandising, aside from the few mom and pop-type businesses that licensed characters from him, only producing a few hundred plush dolls, T-shirts, and so on. Most of these merchandisers were fans, which is to say, primarily inexperienced and entirely inadequate concerning advertising or any other marketing strategies. "I was never tempted by merchandising and whatnot," Sim tells Bissette, "because you are then dealing with those guys in the three-piece suits" (Bissette 1992, 25).

Sim remarks that no matter how great the sum of money, he could not be obliged to sit in the same room with these businesspersons and lawyers (Bissette 1992, 25). "I passionately disagree" with businesspeople, says Sim, "and dealing with them would diminish what it is I enjoy about *Cerebus*, [namely] the autonomy of *not* having to talk to people like that" (ibid.). "If you start doing licensing, merchandising, translations and all of those sorts of things," Sim continues, "they all have to be accommodated into your day. Then you have to be accommodated into your day. Then you have to start allocating specific amounts of time" (ibid.). Sim witnessed the transformation of comics artists into account managers in Peter Laird and Kevin Eastman, following the success of their *Teenage Mutant Ninja Turtles*.

Despite Sim's recognition of the need for a consistent publishing schedule, *Cerebus* did not always ship on schedule. The comic fell behind schedule more than once during its run. Heidi MacDonald writes in her February 1987 "Generally Speaking" column in *The Comics Journal*, that one of the comic's primary annoyances is its "erratic" scheduling, in part because the reader "has become fatally *accustomed* to his/her *monthly Cerebus* fix"

Opposite: Figure 9. Gerhard's first issue, from *Cerebus* issue 65, August 1984 (© 1984 Dave Sim and Gerhard).

(MacDonald 1987, 95). MacDonald claims this frustrates enjoyment of the comic because of its serial cohesion, and because one's memory of the last installment has "*faded* somewhat" (ibid.); this claim begs credulity in a medium based on discrete installments, at the same time it is an affront to the intelligence of the average comics reader. However, MacDonald's argument does at least point to the inherent difficulty in seeing *Cerebus* as an ongoing serial, and thus necessarily incomplete, as opposed to seeing it as a whole, which is to say, reading *Cerebus* as a comic versus reading it as a graphic novel. According to MacDonald, "ideally we *should not read* Cerebus *until all 300 issues have been completed*," yet she admits that this would ruin what she calls the "gestaltic factor: the pleasure of reading each issue as it arrives, the pleasant anticipation between issues, the slow rumination over previous events and what is yet to unfold, the speculation and occasional displeasure" (ibid.). To frame the argument more simply: *Cerebus* was, for a time, a twofold method of storytelling: a sequential comic book and a graphic novel composed of gradually accumulating volumes.[8]

Charles Hatfield notes how the earlier issues of *Cerebus* were comprised of "tightly structured chapters [that] eventually gave way to roughly twenty-page allotments divided without regard to the monthly series as such. These allotments would sometimes end, for instance, in mid-scene" (Hatfield 2002, 160). When *Cerebus* began, it had no apparent pretense to being a "graphic novel," either in Sim's later description of the 300 issues as a cohesive storyline, or in the collected story arcs.

Sim later collected a handful of issues into the six volumes of *Swords of Cerebus*, initially as an attempt to provide newcomers an affordable means to own the complete series. Early issues, with their 2,000 copy print run, had become increasingly scarce. It was not until the conclusion of *High Society* that the impracticality of this republication format became apparent. Therefore, Sim began publishing the story arcs in large format (11 × 12 inch) trade paperbacks, roughly the size of a phonebook with similar newsprint paper. These "phonebooks" proved immensely successful, and served the dual purpose of providing a reader with much-needed background for the ongoing series (in essence an advertisement for the comic book, which gradually reversed as the number of phonebooks increased and remaining issues decreased), but also reinforced *Cerebus* as a respectable literary work with "graphic novel" pretensions.

Sim's phonebooks capitalized on the growing numbers of affluent comics fans, in addition to the self-perception among comics artists (influenced by their underground comix progenitors) that comic books be considered "art." Will Eisner coined the term "graphic novel" in 1978 to describe his 64-page single volume *A Contract with God* (a work Sim, whose phonebooks regularly run to as many as 500 pages, considers a short story). Eisner used the term not just to lend credibility and legitimacy to his work but also as a means of getting his work into bookstores. Eisner was not successful and it was not until nearly a decade later that Warner Books published Alan Moore and Dave Gibbons' *Watchmen* and Frank Miller's *The Dark Knight Returns* under standard paperback distribution to bookstores. These works were, like *Cerebus*, serialized prior to paperback publication, yet unlike *Cerebus*, their coherent structure did not depend as much on serialized form. As a result, *Cerebus* problematizes any simple description as either "comic book" or "graphic novel," at least from a certain point in Sim's narrative. On the other hand, *Cerebus* also helpfully demonstrates the difference between the "comic book" and "graphic novel" when its earlier issues are presented as cohesive individual units with beginning, middle and ending, while later issues begin and end *in media res*, retaining no dramatic cohesiveness, at least until their later appearance in collected form. Sim's decision not to include certain issues of the series in the paperback reprints (nor any of the covers or supplementary material) suggests a re-envisioning of the series from "comic book" to "graphic novel." Now that the storyline is complete, the latter description is dominant: *Cerebus* as a graphic novel composed of sixteen discrete volumes. The 300 back issues are in some way a relic, something for collectors to amass, or those who read it upon publication to sell.

For all the acclaim Sim was receiving by 1987, sales of *Cerebus* had not substantially increased. When Sim arranged for the publication of *High Society*, comprised of issues 26 through 50, he decided to sell the books direct only, and cut out distributors completely. This decision was reached based on financial factors (the monthly comic was not making money, sales were not increasing) for which he blamed the distributors and comic shops[9]; in other words, they were not doing enough to increase sales of Sim's comic. Sim was punishing them by not making the collected edition available to them at discount. Conversely, the distributors and comic shops argued that whatever success Sim currently had was thanks, in part, to their efforts, and Sim's cutting them out was an unforgivable slight. As a result, Diamond Distributors, one of North America's largest direct market distributors, retaliated by refusing to carry the Aardvark One International title *Puma Blues*, an environmental allegory written by Stephen Murphy and lushly illustrated by Michael Zulli. Diamond's share of the series' distribution amounted to roughly one-third of its print run. Sim held firm. "[Diamond] realized there was very little business pressure they could put on me," says Sim. "They couldn't complain to my publisher or my advertisers" (Darnall 1993, 66). The incident forced Sim to consider the extent to which creator's rights also applied to distribution and sales (ibid.).

At a Capital City conference held in Madison, Wisconsin, on May 8–10, 1988, Sim announced that he and eleven other creators were considering a boycott of Diamond, a matter that the creators would vote on in July at the Capital City Distributors Sales Conference. The twelve creators involved were Sim, Gerhard, Kevin Eastman, Peter Laird, Michael Zulli, Stephen Murphy, Steve Bissette, John Totleben, Alan Moore, Dave Gibbons, Bill Sienkiewicz, and Frank Miller, at that time the hottest names in comics (Darnall 1993, 66). That July, Sim gave a speech at the Capital City conference, and the *Journal* noted that as of late June it appeared that the twelve had abandoned the idea of a boycott (*The Comics Journal* July 1988, 6). Sim funded a dinner for Capital City employees, wherein he told the audience that Geppi was "hypocritical, adopt[ing] one attitude when he spoke at the Diamond conference and another when he spoke with Sim" (ibid.). Sim also discussed the dissolution of the "Gang of Twelve" (what he wanted to call the "Government of Associated Self-Publishers" or GASP). This coalition began when Frank Miller, weary of his battles with Marvel and DC over the content of his comics, requested a meeting with Sim, whom he considered one of the oldest and most successful self-publishers in the market. They held the first meeting in Northampton, Massachusetts, the second in Northampton, England (attended by Moore and Gibbons) and the third in Los Angeles (attended by Miller). The "Gang of Twelve" was then to meet in Toronto over the Fourth of July weekend. The intent of the initial Northampton, Massachusetts, meeting, according to Sim, was to "debate a motion to withdraw our work from Diamond Comics Distribution network" (ibid.). The meeting was to include "the drafting and approval of a joint statement of intent, a self-publishers' manifesto" (ibid.). The reason for this meeting was to establish the rights of retailers, distributors and creators, respectively. Sim told the audience that the manifesto would "affirm that (1) the creator is the source of the work and is entitled to determine its direction, (2) there are a variety of means for the creator to get his work to the public, and

(3) self-publishers are not empire-builders, their sole concern is to get their work to the public" (ibid.).

That November, Eastman and Laird, hosted a two-day summit in Northampton, Massachusetts. Among those who attended were Ken Mitchroney, Mark Martin, Michael Dooney, Steve Lavigne, Laird, Eastman, Ryan Brown, Zulli, Richard Pini, Larry Marder, Rick Veitch, Bissette, Eric Talbot, Sim and Gerhard. The meeting resulted in the drafting of a "Creator's Bill of Rights." According to Sim, "the creative community got a pretty good guideline as to the rights you inherently have once you create something" (66).

The ramifications of this meeting were widespread, eventually leading to the exodus of several popular Marvel artists — including Todd McFarlane, Jim Lee and Rob Liefeld — to form their own comics company, the wildly successful Image Comics. McFarlane later invited Sim, along with Neil Gaiman and Alan Moore, to write and draw an issue of McFarlane's *Spawn*, for which he was paid $100,000. Sim donated his salary to the Comic Book Legal Defense Fund (CBLDF).

The CBLDF and the Creator's Bill of Rights were indicative of a growing awareness in the comic book community of the generally poor treatment artists received from Marvel, DC, and other comics publishers, particularly after these business entities fused with larger entertainment conglomerates and produced substantially profitable film franchises. This, together with more creator-friendly contracts offered by new direct market comic book companies like Eclipse, First and Pacific, and Sim's exceptional and comparatively moderate success, would for a time mean the death-knell for the traditionally abysmal work-for-hire contracts once endemic to the medium. Sim would play a crucial role in this battle, speaking against Marvel and DC's abhorrent treatment of their artists at every opportunity, raising awareness and funds for various creators' rights issues, and becoming an outspoken advocate of self-publishing. So tenacious was Sim's advocacy that it caused no small amount of ire from that bastion of comic book commentary, *The Comics Journal*, which now took every opportunity and advantage to critically savage Sim.

For example, in early 1987 the *Journal* focused its attention on another Sim controversy when, in issue 94 of *Cerebus* (January 1987), Cerebus, newly ensconced as pope, uses his power to rape a bound and gagged (with her own underwear) Astoria. Critic R. Fiore predictably condemned this rape as "sick ... something that shouldn't be passed over lightly" and yet Fiore admits that it is entirely "within character" for Cerebus to rape her, noting that, after all, he did toss a baby off of a roof a few issues before (Fiore 1987, 37) (figure 10). If *Cerebus* were not a comic book, but "legitimate fiction," observes Fiore candidly, "Sim would merely have to face up to the fact that his main character is an evil little motherfucker" (ibid.). The difficulty is that the reader identifies with Cerebus, as he is the comic's protagonist and while the baby tossing is forgivable, as the action possesses a satirical, over-the-top character, the raping of Astoria is certainly an imaginable offense. "A reader cannot identify with a rapist and live with himself," Fiore argues (ibid.). Fiore predicts Sim will face "serious consequences" for this transgression, his autonomy threatened as he increasingly alienates his audience from which he makes a living (ibid.).

As it turns out, audiences are willing to accept most anything, including rape, as long as the tone of the comic remains relatively consistent. Thus, the Astoria rape would not

Opposite: Figure 10. Cerebus throwing a baby. From *Cerebus* issue 66, September 1984 (© 1984 Dave Sim and Gerhard).

alienate nearly as many readers as did the continuing transformation of the *Cerebus* storyline in *Jaka's Story* and *Melmoth*, a transformation that led numerous critics (in particular R. Fiore in *The Comics Journal* 154) to claim Sim had, like Charles Dickens with Oliver Twist, simply grown tired of his character. In these books, the character of Cerebus becomes a supporting character, more scenery than the driving force of the series as he had been in the first 113 issues of the series. Sim, the critics claimed, had trapped himself in a single storyline for 300 issues and since his interests had naturally developed and shifted away from swords and sorcery to more literary subjects, such as a comics biography of Oscar Wilde, Sim had merely used the comic as a means for exploring these new interests. Sim spoke of this mis-perception in his 1992 Bissette interview, saying that the "widely spread, widely believed impression" that Sim was "sick of Cerebus, that the reason Cerebus wasn't the central character ... is that ... I wanted to do other things. This was in one review [R. Fiore's] and then gradually just became conventional wisdom about Dave Sim" (Bissette 1992, 12).

"Comics: Not Just for Kids Anymore": Dave Sim the Legitimate Artist (1988–1991)

Another development of the *Church & State* period was Sim's conception of *Cerebus* as a sophisticated alternative to the standard adolescent superhero-type comic fare, wherein muscle-bound heroes and buxom women are constantly battling with one another. In his 1986 interview for filmmaker Ken Viola's documentary *The Masters of Comic Book Art*, Sim describes *Cerebus* as a comic book about

> two people in a room.... If you're going to do a film or a comic book that isn't just two people talking you're missing the whole essence of what's human. We are human because we sit and talk. How many fistfights does the average person get into in their lifetime? How many people go flying off their balcony? How many people get into a car chase? These become clichés in entertainment and [are] virtually non-existent in real life.... Art is something that is supposed to speak to the human condition and you see very little of the human condition in most popular culture [Viola 1987].

Jaka's Story was the result, in part, of Sim reading Jaime and Gabriel Hernandez's celebrated comic book *Love and Rockets* (published by Groth's imprint Fantagraphics) and wanting to try something similar, what Sim describes as a "human drama story" utilizing a more limited set of characters than the three previous story arcs. This was determined by Sim's desire to delve deeper into their lives, to capture the minutiae of their existence, the mundane, day-to-day aspects of life in Iest.

When asked by Spurgeon if Sim's anti-feminism had already been established at the time he wrote *Jaka's Story*, an arc that includes a somewhat sympathetic portrayal of a female character, Sim responds that his anti-feminism "evolved over an extended period, starting with my lack of satisfaction with the conclusion of *Church & State*" (Spurgeon February 1996, 93). Sim meant to address feminism in *Church & State* but, as with *High Society*, he simply ran out space. Thus, the marriage between Jaka and Rick is a microcosm of the larger male-female dichotomy that he would address on a larger scale in subsequent volumes. Rick thinks he is in control of his domestic situation, yet it is clear that Rick does nothing without Jaka's approval. Jaka is the more experienced of the two; not only that, she is employed while Rick is unemployed, she also maintains their home while Rick loafs around and spends time cavorting with their homosexual neighbor Oscar, who clearly finds Rick attractive. Rick is oblivious to this attraction while Jaka is fully aware of Oscar's inclinations.

Jaka's Story seems to suggest that women are the more sophisticated and more practical sex. Yet as the title *Jaka's Story* suggests, this view of women is artificial, a "story" society chooses to believe as opposed to what actually is. That Oscar's "read" *Jaka's Story* is comprised of what Rick knows about Jaka's life reinforces this unreliability. Sim's entitling a later volume *Rick's Story* underlines the fact that what constitutes "reality" is largely the result of individual or social perception and usually faulty at best. Jaka's decision to marry Rick as opposed to waiting for Cerebus to return, Sim explains, was a result of her willingness "to put the idea of swept-off-your-feet romance on the shelf in favor of somebody she can control" (ibid.). Rick, for example, would never think of interfering with her career. Another reason for Jaka marrying Rick, according to Sim, is his lack of jealousy: "Any guy who has gone out with an exotic dancer for more than four or five days is going to have to have that type of personality" (ibid, 94). Yet Sim cautions against a simple feminist reading of Jaka in *Jaka's Story*, telling Spurgeon that Jaka exhibits a degree of "duplicity" in her behavior, chastising her husband for his loafing at the same time she is financially dependent on a man, Pud Withers, for her income, a relationship she exploits for her own gain as she is obviously aware of Pud's feelings for her (ibid, 94). Moreover, Rick's lack of employment, Sim explains, does not necessarily connote his inability to provide for his wife. Sim speculates that had Jaka opted not to abort their unborn child, a decision she made in part due to Rick's unemployment, a baby would have likely forced Rick to assume more responsibility and become the very provider Jaka decided he was not (ibid., 95).

In addition to being a study of domesticity, *Jaka's Story* also operates as an allegory for artistic freedom and integrity. To Sim, freedom and integrity were of utmost importance. Jaka's uncompromising attitude, her devotion, perfectionism and seriousness toward her "art" is symbolic of Sim's relationship with his. The character of Oscar, composing Jaka's biography in secret, is on the other hand, a metaphor for the work-made-for-hire artists who cede artistic credibility in exchange for money. Oscar is obviously wealthier than Jaka and Rick. His painfully purple prose suggests a work paid for by the word and thus overly padded. Moreover, the fact that he is composing a biography of Jaka, a princess, indicates this is a book intended for the popular press and destined to end up on a bestseller list, much like the bestsellers of today that concern themselves with celebrity status above literary substance. The dark side of Jaka's artistic integrity, however, is her willingness to sacrifice her family in order to pursue it, indicated by her decision to abort her child in favor of her career, a decision that results in the eventual destruction of her marriage at the hands of the Cirinists.[10] Arrested for pursuing her art, the Cirinists execute Pud Withers and she, Rick and Oscar are imprisoned. The Cirinists reveal to Rick that Jaka had their child aborted so she could continue dancing. Thanks to her station in life, the Cirinists spare Jaka. Rick, devastated by the revelation, leaves her. Oscar remains in prison. Cerebus, running an errand when the arrest occurs, believes Jaka to be dead.

In *Jaka's Story*, Sim's anti-feminism is already in place. To Sim, a woman's independence and desire for a career is a destructive societal force, resulting in a contamination or outright rejection of what Sim perceives to be correct gender roles (Rick plays a part in this, too, by not fulfilling his masculine obligations). In the end, *Jaka's Story* is largely a parable about the ways feminism and female careerism pervert the natural order of things, ultimately resulting in the breakdown of family and, by extension, society. Mrs. Thatcher (a caricature of conservative 1980s British Prime Minister Margaret Thatcher) represents the invasiveness of feminist controls on this social order. According to Sim, the feminist agenda, out of interest of increasing safety and eliminating discrimination, is by design a totalitarian force and a means of wresting power and control from their patriarchal counterparts.

Melmoth (figure 11) grew out of *Jaka's Story* just as *Church & State* grew out of *High Society*, which in turn grew out of "The Palnu Trilogy." Sim, in fact, considers *Jaka's Story* and its sequel closely enough related as to comprise a single story arc. "In the sense that *High Society* and *Church & State* could be put into one book and called *State and Church / Church & State*, *Jaka's Story* and *Melmoth* could be put under one cover and be called *Love and Death*" (Spurgeon February 1996, 96). The primary link between the two arcs is the character of Oscar Wilde. Oscar in *Jaka's Story* ends up imprisoned and a few weeks or months later, a much older Sebastian Melmoth walks out of prison, incarcerated for the crime of homosexuality. Confusingly, "Melmoth" was the real Oscar Wilde's pseudonym, and Sim's Melmoth is a caricature of Wilde, as is Oscar from *Jaka's Story*. Yet the two characters, while based on the same historical persona, are different. Melmoth dies at the end of *Melmoth* but Oscar is later shown to be alive and in prison in *Mothers & Daughters*, the next story arc. Melmoth even mentions Oscar's work (disparagingly, of course).

Figure 11. Sebastian Melmoth, also known as Oscar Wilde. One of Sim's numerous caricatures of well-known authors. The cover to *Cerebus* 140, November 1990 (© 1990 Dave Sim and Gerhard).

Melmoth's death is, according to Sim, meant to be symbolic of Cerebus' "death of ... spirit" (Spurgeon February 1996, 97). Comprised of twelve issues, the story arc is the shortest in *Cerebus*, yet it is exceptional in other ways. If Sim's modus operandi with *Cerebus* was to push boundaries, *Melmoth* perhaps pushed more boundaries than the four previous story arcs combined. Sim told Spurgeon that in fact he pushed it "*past* the breaking point, to the point where the overall story is *broken* for a fair number of readers. Having done that, I could retreat back to more comfortable territory" (ibid., 98). *Melmoth*'s storyline is perhaps the most easily summarized of all the story arcs: Cerebus, despondent at having lost Jaka, sits outside a café, while Sebastian Melmoth, a writer, dies a slow death with a friend by his side. Yet Sim and Gerhard's achievement, in pacing, tone and overall structure, is notable; the book is perhaps the series' most concise and emotionally resonant. Key to the story's success is the contribution of Gerhard's meticulously rendered backgrounds. Without his richly imagined setting, *Melmoth* would not have been as convincing.

Because Cerebus remains a largely superfluous supporting character during these storylines, R. Fiore in his 1990 review of *Jaka's Story* in *The Comics Journal* 158 (October 1990) remarks that perhaps it is time for Sim to "lose the aardvark" (Fiore October 1990, 37). Fiore then adds that he has always been under the impression that Sim believes *Cerebus* "can encompass everything he wants to say without alienating the reader who doesn't normally read comics," a position that Fiore finds "mistaken" (ibid.). For example, quips Fiore, who would have ever suspected that one of the central themes of the comic would be feminism, "and pretty radical feminism at that" (ibid.). Sim's miscalculation, adds Fiore, is that he expects his work taken seriously *despite* the aardvark. Fiore believes based on the evidence of *Jaka's Story*, that Sim may have come to a similar conclusion, as Cerebus "is hardly there.... He is peripheral to the story at best, and neither motivates nor performs any vital story action, and it could be he just didn't fit" (ibid., 38). Sim countered Fiore's argument by stating that Cerebus' diminished importance to be intentional, a reflection of how during certain periods in everyone's life you seem to melt into the background, your importance, your ability to have any effect on others, or even yourself.

The Cirinists' arrest of Oscar on the grounds that he has no license to write and thus "no artistic license" (a poor pun, it must be said), further illustrates the extent to which Cirinist controls have reached totalitarian proportions. On a much smaller scale, suggests Sim, the "confrontation between Rick and Jaka ... is what happens when [relationships between men and women] go wrong. Rick's declaration to Oscar that he would never do anything to keep [Jaka] from dancing is ironic because what he most wants, a son, would do just that" (Spurgeon February 1996, 95).[11]

Oscar provides, for critic Keith R.A. DeCandido, the first instance of self-reflexivity: In *Jaka's Story*, "Oscar has one bit where he says that he met the author of *Church & State*. 'Funny looking chap ... I heard someone say that the ending was less of a grand finale than a grand finally" (DeCandido 1990, 40). Similar things, remarks Candido, might be said about Sim's 1,100-page *Church & State*. It is also, Candido observes, the first unabashed example of a "misogynist" in *Cerebus*, as Oscar defines a wife as a "perfect acquisition for any gentleman feeling himself to have excessive control over his personal affairs" (ibid.). The real Wilde, of course, shared a similar view of women.

The Story He Wants to Tell: Cerebus as Political Tract, or the Big Controversy (1991–2001)

Sim could not understand why some readers took exception to his portrayal of the Cirinists. To him, he did not feel he was "doing anything wrong"; in fact, he felt justified in their portrayal in that they were portrayed as *"really good soldiers,"* Sim tells Bissette. "If you are going to argue that a woman can do anything a man can do, then women can be soldiers" (Bissette 1992, 37) (figure 12). Sim's point, as he explains to Bissette, is that if a group has absolute power, they will exercise that power regardless of whether or not they are male or female. "I can understand somebody saying I don't understand women, but I can definitely counter in my own mind by saying you don't understand power and the people that are drawn to it" (ibid., 38).

The Cirinists, first introduced in issue 20, act as Sim's straw man for his critique of feminism. "A phrase popped into my head years and years ago," Sim told Charles Brownstein in a 1997 interview,

> "No one rules without opposition." That is, the mere fact of governance, the imposition of authority[,] implies opposition and the opposition is usually going to be in a suitable size ratio to the authority. Mothers? Daughters ... I had some time to develop the history, the back-story, the fundamental arguments.... Since Cirinism prevailing was the whole point of the first two hundred issues, it occupied quite a bit of my attention from 1980 to 1991.... Outside the story? Well, the Ontario teachers are on strike and the primary thrust of the news coverage is how costly and inconvenient it is for working mothers who have to find a place to put their kids while they're at work. The loss of education ... is a minor note compared with the loss of free daycare. Someone's even putting together a class action suit to recover daycare costs from the Ministry of Education. Cirin and Astoria could've had a right old donnybrook over something like that.... Actually, it started with a Feminist society—women on top [Brownstein 1997, 11–12].

Sim began writing more earnestly about the Cirinist/Kevillist division near the end of *Jaka's Story* and *Melmoth*. He knew at that time that the next story arc was to be entitled *Mothers & Daughters*. Described by Sim as a sequel to *Church & State*, in *Mothers & Daughters*, Sim transfers his distrust of certainty to that of feminist politics. Sim finds feminism more damaging to the fabric of society than religious faith, as feminism makes every act, both public and private, a political act and therefore subject to political control. Religion, on the other hand, is largely a matter of personal conviction and, in any truly democratic society, safely separated from political machinations.

Sim began researching for the book by not only reading, "a debilitating amount of feminist writing" (Spurgeon December 1996, 81), but also

> having conversations with women to, basically, interrogating women.... It was extremely hard to keep the sequential, logical male thinking out of the equation. Because [the interviews] didn't follow a logical progression ... I finally got a glimmering of what they were all about: emotion-based collectivism.... Then it all started to make sense [ibid., 71].

Watching *The Oprah Winfrey Show*, it dawned on Sim that women were "mad" (ibid.). He found he simply could not fathom how they viewed the world. He finally concluded, based on his so-called "research," that a woman's worldview was not based on logic but emotion, and emotion alone. A woman's objective was to achieve happiness. "What was said, the words themselves," continues Sim, "went from secondary importance to complete unimportance to a state verging on complete meaninglessness" (ibid.). Feminists had "usurped the civil rights [movement] and its whole purpose was not so much to advance women as it was to undermine and destroy fatherhood" (Sim and Gerhard July 2001). Sim believed feminists to be part of a "Marxist-feminist-homosexualist" axis (Sim and Gerhard August 2001).[12] This, he insists, does not suggest a "monolithic conspiracy" so much as a "number

Opposite: Figure 12. First mention of the Cirinists in *Cerebus* issue 20, September 1980 (© 1980 Dave Sim).

of shared misapprehensions that are proliferating unchecked in our society because of [this] hegemony, commonly referred to as 'political correctness'" (ibid.). Sim elaborated on his anti-feminist theories in a series of essays published in the pages of *Cerebus*, both as part of the story and external to the story ("Tangent").

Sim had long considered *Church & State* to be an "incomplete" work; *Mothers & Daughters* formed its second half and together they comprised a single narrative. Both story arcs, Sim notes, are "centered on the Big Bang" (Spurgeon December 1996, 73). The primary dilemma of both storylines is the conflicting views mothers and daughters hold of one another: mothers view the daughters as "raw material for what she, the daughter, will become and the daughter [views herself] as a finished product" (ibid.). In the end, Astoria, the Kevillist who helped Cerebus' rise to power in *High Society* in order to achieve political victory for herself by manipulating Cerebus, comes to realize after having listened to Suenteus Po's [a mystic aardvark and leader of the Illusionists, an ideology in competition with Kevillism and Cirinism] monologue that "collectivist thinking about the individual [is] a complete waste of time" (ibid., 74).

With *Reads*, Sim's comic becomes decidedly meta-fictional. Sim explained to Spurgeon the necessity of this literary device: "In examining the totality of [*Cerebus*] there are ... three parts to the equation: There's *Cerebus*, there's me, and there's the other person reading it.... So what I was doing was bringing those three individuals as close together as I possibly could" (Spurgeon December 1996, 75) (figure 13). In *Flight* and *Women*, Suenteus Po, Sim tells Spurgeon, is essentially a "stand-in" for Sim (ibid.). But in *Reads* and its many text pieces, Sim forgoes the stand-in, and includes a more autobiographical character, Victor Reid (Victor is Sim's middle name and Reid his mother's maiden name), based in part on Gene Day, and who "mirrors a series of incidents and attitudes and failings that I see in myself, looking back over 30 years of ... existence" (ibid.). In fact, Reid is Sim's tongue-in-cheek attempt to describe biography, no matter how accurate, as essentially consisting of "a handful of bits of information ... extrapolated into an 'accurate' word-portrait of a human being" (ibid.). Reid is a fictional "reads" (a comic book in Cerebus' universe that, like *Reads* itself, alternates between a page of illustration and a page of text) author who, unlike Oscar, holds fervently to an ideal artistic integrity which he finds compromised at every turn.

Comics are, in Harvey Pekar's oft-quoted definition, comprised of words and pictures. In a sense, the definition is sacrosanct. True, words are not entirely necessary — a comic book can be comprised of images only and still be a comic book — yet the series of panels, the choices of page design, of character expression, of angles and scale, comprise a language in and of itself. In *Reads*, Sim, in keeping with his intent to push the boundaries of comic books as far as possible, took these two components to their logical extremes: if either there are words without pictures, or pictures without words, is it possible to refer to what results as a comic book?

"*Reads* was a rhetorical writer question," Sim explained to Spurgeon:

> Does this violate parameters? Is it a fact that you can have a really good comic book story *without* words but as soon as you have pages without *pictures*, then you don't have a comic book anymore? Is there a limit to the number of text pages that you have before you have violated the basic structure of what a comic book is? I don't know if there is a good answer to that ... I knew going in I wasn't going to come up with a suitable answer to that question [Spurgeon February 1996, 101].

Yet this violation of what constitutes a comic book is only one of numerous violations in *Reads*, which is comprised of three storylines: the storyline that dominates the "picture" half of the book is that of the confrontation between Cerebus, Cirin, Astoria and Suenteus Po, particularly Cerebus' sword duel with Cirin. As it is the most physical aspect of the storyline, relegating this almost entirely to the visual end of the spectrum makes perfect sense. The other two storylines predominantly consist of words, supplemented with single-panel pictures. The third storyline, that of Viktor Davis (an even more thinly veiled Dave Sim than Victor Reid—Dave Sim's middle name is Victor), another "reads" author, consists of only words. Davis provides an essay which puts forth a view of gender based on the idea of a "male light" and "female void," thus reversing the Judge's proclamation at the end of *Church & State*.

Sim made his critique of feminism explicit when Sim decided to publish the anti-feminist essay in issue 186 of Cerebus.[13] The finale of the *Reads* storyline, which had featured an ongoing prose section written by Davis, the essay eschews any pretense to being a fictional work by a fictional author, no matter how thinly disguised. It appears to be Sim himself doing the talking. In it, Sim declares that feminism consists of a belief in the interchangeability of men and women, and the concomitant shift of women from the home to the workforce (and the child from home to daycare). Moreover, Sim points out the seeming contradiction that arises when one takes into consideration that the majority of alimony and child support are paid from men to women and that, despite a woman being "genetically predisposed" to childbirth, men bear the "fault and responsibility" for any unwanted pregnancy (Sim and Gerhard August 1996). "When you engineer a society whose primary purpose is to make sure that no one is made to 'feel bad' ever, the vast majority end up 'feeling bad,'" observes Sim (Sim and Gerhard July 1998). To Sim, one result of a feminist agenda that obsesses over security and the lack of discipline in childcare and school is that men have become "feminized" (ibid.). Robbed of the experience of emotional pain and conflict, they are left with

> profound societal terror, the magnification of apprehension into anxiety, anxiety into fear, and fear into terror. With no sorting-out process, no incremental challenges met, no inclination or ability to push individual limits of endurance and capability, whole generations of males haven't the first clue as to who or what they are, since they have grown up in a structure where their only measure of themselves is in female terms: how sensitive, how caring, how compassionate, how environmentally aware, how safe they are. Every other measure of maleness—forget masculinity—is deemed irrelevant and stupid [ibid.].

Gary Groth devoted an entire section of *The Comics Journal* issue 174 (February 1993) to Sim's anti-feminism, accompanied by a cartoon by Jeff Wong portraying Sim as a Nazi guard with naked, emaciated women held captive in a concentration camp; where the words "Arbeit Macht Frei" should appear on the iron gates is written "Aardvark-Vanaheim." Entitled "Misogynist Guru of Self-Publishers," the section begins with an essay by previous Sim champion Kim Thompson and J. Hagey, entitled "The Story That Wasn't: 'Reads' [sic] and the Comics Industry." "What should be done," asks Hagey and Thompson, rhetorically, "when an artist expresses ... ideas or convictions that are utterly repugnant to the majority of his contemporaries?" (Thompson and Hagey February 1993, 112). To be fair, Sim is utilizing descriptions meant to evoke an earlier conclusion made by the Judge, that a "Male Void" had violated a "Female Light." Nevertheless, *Reads* does argue, from Sim's perspective, no less, that, in Hagey and Thompson's words, "Almost all women are greedy leeches who prey upon male energy" (ibid.) (figure 14). Man's only recourse is to avoid women at all costs. Hagey and Thompson interpret this as a "justification of—even a call for—misogyny" (ibid.). "As a philosophical stance," the authors continue, *Reads* "comes on like a combination of bitter post-break up barroom rant, biologic conspiracy, and bizarre male Objectivism" (ibid.). While Hagey and Thompson do allow for the possibility that

Figure 13, opposite: "Reads," Estarcion's version of a comic book. Here is their first mention in the series, from *Cerebus* issue 59, February 1983 (© 1983 Dave Sim). Above: *Cerebus* issue 175, October 1993 (© 1993 Dave Sim and Gerhard).

Figure 14. Sim on male-female relationships: "the parts of yourself that have been consumed to that point," *Cerebus* issue 224, November 1997 (© 1997 Dave Sim and Gerhard).

the essay was a Swiftian "provocation inserted into what is, after all, a clearly fictional framework" (ibid., 113), Sim's admission that "It wouldn't be that big a stretch to categorize [*Reads*] as Hate Literature Against Women," is to Hagey and Thompson a "fair description" (ibid., 112). Had this essay been published in any medium other than a comic, the authors allege, "there would have been immediate public uproar ... at the very least within the confines of the industry or medium affected" (ibid., 113).

The *Journal*'s "token feminist" Anne Rubinstein's article "The Saddest Fate" rightly perceives the influence of Norman Mailer in the Victor Reid story, which is that of a writer unable to complete a major work, whose progress is interrupted by contractual obligations and relationships with women, suffering the final indignity when a baby girl smears strained spinach on his manuscript. Victor Reid "becomes" Viktor Davis, whose troubles are, to Rubinstein, far less specific than Victor's, resulting from a "vast conspiracy" of the "Devouring Rapacious Female Void" (Rubinstein February 1993, 120). Rubinstein disagrees with Sim on three points: (1) that the differences between men and women "transcend all our similarities and explain all our behavior"; (2) that in relationships women exert greater control than men, and; (3) "that there is some amorphous, evil 'Life Force' behind all this, leading women in the great male-controlling conspiracy" (ibid.).

The *Comics Journal*'s letters column "Blood & Thunder" from April 1995 (issue 176) features several responses to the *Journal*'s coverage on Sim's misogyny. One reader found it interesting that Cerebus raping a woman or killing a baby (events that took place in *Church & State*) were for readers less disturbing than Sim's anti-feminist essay appearing in the final issue of *Reads*. Was it because the essay was written instead of being drawn, the reader wonders? Tom Spurgeon responds that he felt more weight given to the essay because the former is a work of fiction while the latter is "widely believed to be a personal statement by the author" (Spurgeon April 1995, 5). Spurgeon goes on to describe the essay as a "crock of shit, poorly presented, with a circular logic that discourages rational counter-argument" (ibid.). Another reader, a female, points out that the character Rick was in fact a "male void" leeching off his more successful wife, Jaka (ibid., 9). Yet another female reader states that, overall, Sim's female characters "are often stronger and more competent than the men around them, and they do *not* drain the males dry" (ibid., 10).

Colby Cosh, a conservative columnist for *The National Post*, a Canadian newspaper to which the now right-wing Sim subscribes, contributed an essay to the 2004 *The Comics Journal* critical roundtable that followed the conclusion of *Cerebus*, defending Sim's views of feminism. Cosh admits, after having familiarized himself with Sim's work, that while his politics are out of step with the majority of Canadians, and contain rhetoric that "veers at times into the pathological," his "rather nightmarish images of matriarchy in *Cerebus* do remind me of Canada at its worst" (Cosh October/November 2004, 125). Canadian feminists, writes Cosh, "rallied behind the creation of a universal federal registry for legal firearms" (ibid.). Cosh also points to Canada's strict obscenity laws, which he believes violate Canada's constitutional amendment protecting freedom of speech. The Women's Legal Education and Action Fund (LEAF) established in cooperation with feminist scholar Catherine MacKinnon, is designed to protect women from pornography that includes explicit sex that is dehumanizing and violent, or features children (ibid., 127–28). The laws are broadly written and therefore interpreted to justify the ban of any number of materials from entering Canada, explicit or otherwise, including, for instance, comic books by Robert Crumb. Cosh also points out the audaciousness of family law, including its "draconian provisions against 'deadbeat dads' while being lazy to the point of malfeasance about enforcing access orders for divorced fathers already deprived of equal custody of their children" (ibid., 128). Moreover, LEAF successfully won numerous lawsuits to change laws concerning "the definition of sexual assault, the admissibility of evidence in sex-assault trials, workplace discrimination, sexual harassment, abortion, and child-care benefits.... When Dave Sim speaks of a 'dictatorship' he is merely using another word to describe [an] historical project of which its executors are exceedingly proud" (ibid.).

In response to his critics, Sim carefully noted that his concept of "merged permanence," which sees a woman as something akin to a parasite is similar to the feminist view that men act to dominate their wives. He also insisted that telling a man to be "wary" of women (the title of four consecutive volumes act as a warning: *Women — Reads — Minds — Guys*) was not the same as advocating active hatred of them. Realistically, he did not expect warm acceptance of his views, but also did not expect the vitriolic response he received. "If you adhere to masculine principles, ethics and scruples," Sim concluded, "you will, likely as not, end up having few if any friends, scrupulously silent and anonymous supporters, universally despised and maligned, called a Nazi" (Sim and Gerhard July 2001). Sim fully expected he would eventually be arrested "under Canadian laws of recent feminist vintage ... for promulgating hate literature against feminists" (ibid.). In the end, Sim felt satisfied he had contributed a small voice of opposition among the dominant "pro-androgyny propaganda" that insists, "men and women are interchangeable apart from minor biological details" (Spurgeon December 1996, 75–76). In his interview, Spurgeon suggests that Sim intentionally tried to achieve an emotional reaction from his readers by using intense rhetoric. Sim responds, yes, he agrees, but only for "any being who is degraded in their nature to a point where their emotional reaction to something supersedes any intellectual assessment. That's the centerpiece of my argument: 'Look at what you have become'" (ibid., 76).

Sim's essay "Tangent," indistinguishable from Davis' essay but unlike its predecessor external to *Cerebus* and credited to Sim, is his "last word on gender" (Sim and Gerhard April 2001). In it, Sim declares that feminism, like Marxism before it, is utopian and like all utopias before it, destined for failure (ibid.). As a self-described "masculinist," Sim grew tired of having to alter reality willingly in order to believe what he calls the "Five Impossible Things Before Breakfast." These include:

- the lack of difference between a working mother who places her children in daycare and a mother who rears her own children
- government-funded daycare wherein a working woman can, in theory, produce enough tax revenue to cover daycare costs
- a doctor's input on a woman's decision to have an abortion is more important than a father's
- a woman's decision to have an abortion is ethical given she has her doctor's approval
- two people cannot simultaneously control a marriage — one person must lead, the other should follow.

Sim adds additional "impossible things," including:

- women should have access to "men's only" gathering places, but not vice-versa
- the concept of affirmative action
- the lowering of physical standards for fire and police in allowing women to be hired in place of men
- the disproportionate number of women in colleges and child support and alimony paid from men to women

- the disproportionate amount of alimony paid from successful men to less successful women
- the disproportionate responsibility between child-rearing and financial support expected of men
- moreover, that to disagree with any of the above necessarily makes one a misogynist or anti-woman (ibid.).

Nevertheless, in looking at *Cerebus,* it appears Sim's view of men is no less damning than his view of women. His subsequent story arc, *Guys,* explores the world Cirin creates when, after establishing an agrarian matriarchal society, she consigns all men uninterested in work or family to spend the rest of their days drinking in pubs. Often cited as one of the funniest of the *Cerebus* books, it is also among the most sneering, painting a portrait of men without women that is far from positive.

The Final Ascension (2001–2011)

The final volume of *Mothers & Daughters, Minds,* largely consists of a discussion between Cerebus and his creator, "Dave." For Sim, "Dave" is another level of truth obtained by Cerebus; the Judge has become Suenteus Po has become Viktor Reid has become Viktor Davis has become "Dave." Each is a distinct character in Cerebus, yet each represents the story's author, and each has a specific role to perform. "Dave" is Cerebus' maker. "I knew if I could get past *Reads,*" Sim tells Spurgeon, "that Cerebus and I were going to have a little chat" (Spurgeon December 1996, 80) (figure 15). Sim improvised the dialogue in his notebooks, and was surprised when Cerebus mentioned Jaka. Cerebus' potential as a world changing force (a "magnifier") is squandered. As a result, Cerebus is consigned to a life without consquence, reversed only when Cerebus finds himself the inadvertent inspiration for a new religion. In a sense, "Dave" could not forgive Cerebus of his interest in Jaka above all else, primarily above a more lasting and substantial relationship with God. When Sim himself underwent a religious awakening while researching the Bible for the *Rick's Story* arc, it, and the subsequent storylines, *Going Home* and *Latter Days,* are a unique example of a character undergoing continuous punishment by his angry author/God.

Sim's religious awakening resulted from his view that true happiness results from devotion to God. As a practicing atheist of many years, Sim sought solace in the usual places and with, he declares, predictable results. In his 1983 Thompson interview, Sim's description of Cerebus reads like a self-description, 20 years hence: "He's never going to be completely happy. Even with absolute power, riches, there is always something lacking. It's an attempt to outwardly make up for some inward lack" (Thompson August 1983, 72). Cerebus' dissatisfaction is symbolic of the curious emptiness Sim felt after having achieved critical and commercial success. With each new accomplishment, Sim tells Thompson, there is the recognition that the feeling of success falls short of what he would imagine it to be. Asked if Cerebus will ever be happy, Sim replies, "Probably not. He doesn't learn from being unhappy" (ibid.).

In a sense, Cerebus was one of a number of relationships Sim sacrificed in his new relationship to a higher power. The conversation Cerebus has with Sim in *Minds* is pre-awakening yet anticipates Sim's ongoing conversation with his maker. It also signals a shift in authorial perspective where Sim's treatment of his main character becomes less a passive

befuddlement than a more active critique. Sim has grown exhausted by and intolerant of his creation. Having awakened to a new profound reality of God, Sim punishes Cerebus for not having had the same realization, for returning to Jaka in *Rick's Story* and *Going Home*. As a result, Cerebus is not there when his parents die; he wanders for years in shame and self-disgust, only to become captive of a bizarre new religion. When he finally succeeds in vanquishing the Cirinist dictatorship, he only supplants it with one of his own, and it is equally dictatorial, violent and despotic as Cirin's. The final issues of *Cerebus* find him a prisoner of his own making, a tired, geriatric king whose time has passed, while the world outside his tower walls falls sway to the very evils his creator (Sim, in this case) denounces.

I will not address Sim's religious beliefs here. They are, like any religious belief, highly personal and arguably do not have much bearing on the history of *Cerebus* beyond providing its title character with an ideology that alienates him from a larger heathenistic society out of step with God. Much like his creator, this ideology forces Cerebus to retreat to a life of solitude.

Latter Days (comprised of two volumes, *Latter Days* and *The Last Day*) is the most overtly religious, dogmatic and downright weird of the series' nine story arcs. In it, Cerebus becomes the object of cult devotion by the Three Wise Fellows (a parody of The Three Stooges), who imprison Cerebus for an excruciatingly long period in a church undergoing construction both figuratively and literally: the church undergoes physical construction at the same time as the religion it is to represent. This religion is the result of the insane ravings of Jaka's husband Rick, who, in *Rick's Story*, suffers a blow to his head and, as a result, sees Cerebus as a holy entity. Here, Rick is akin to John the Baptist heralding the advent of Christ (in fact, Cerebus witnesses Rick baptizing his religious devotees in "Fall and the River"). Eventually, the Three Wise Fellows release Cerebus who, in the guise of a parody of Todd McFarlane's *Spawn*, leads an army of emasculated men (equipped with their own "spawn" of little children) in a revolt against the Cirinists (figure 16). Following their defeat (which takes place, for the most part, off the page), Cerebus institutes new laws to punish women as vipers, keeping only those who are physically attractive. Moreover, he creates a new calendar, and becomes a fan of Garth Inniscent's read *Rabbi* (a parody of Garth Ennis' *The Preacher*) (figure 17).

Sim's portrayal of religion as a kind of mental illness fits his earlier atheistic mentality, yet, strangely, Sim himself underwent a religious awakening while researching the Bible ostensibly to lampoon it for the purposes of *Rick's Story*. Something similar happens in *Latter Days* when Konigsberg, the Not-So-Good Samaritan (a parody of Woody Allen), brings Cerebus the Torah, a book that, in the warped timeline of *Cerebus*, has been suppressed for hundreds of years. Cerebus begins a long examination of the text, and this examination (Chasing YHWH, referred to by fans as the "Cerebexegesis") is simultaneously serious and satirical. Exasperatingly small type fills page after page (figure 18) as Cerebus pores through the text, attempting to make sense of it, leaving the reader with the sense that this is not Cerebus' thoughts we are reading, but Sim's. Frustrated, Cerebus eventually tires of the exercise.

The Last Day begins years later, with Cerebus in geriatric decrepitude, ensconced in a tower, irrelevant to the society he keeps at bay behind barbed wire encasements (figure 19). The book opens with a dream Cerebus is having of the origin of the universe, the third variation on the male-female identification of the universe. "I think God gave me two tries

Opposite: Figure 15. The introduction of "Dave," Cerebus' creator, from *Cerebus* issue 181, March 1994 (© 1994 Dave Sim and Gerhard).

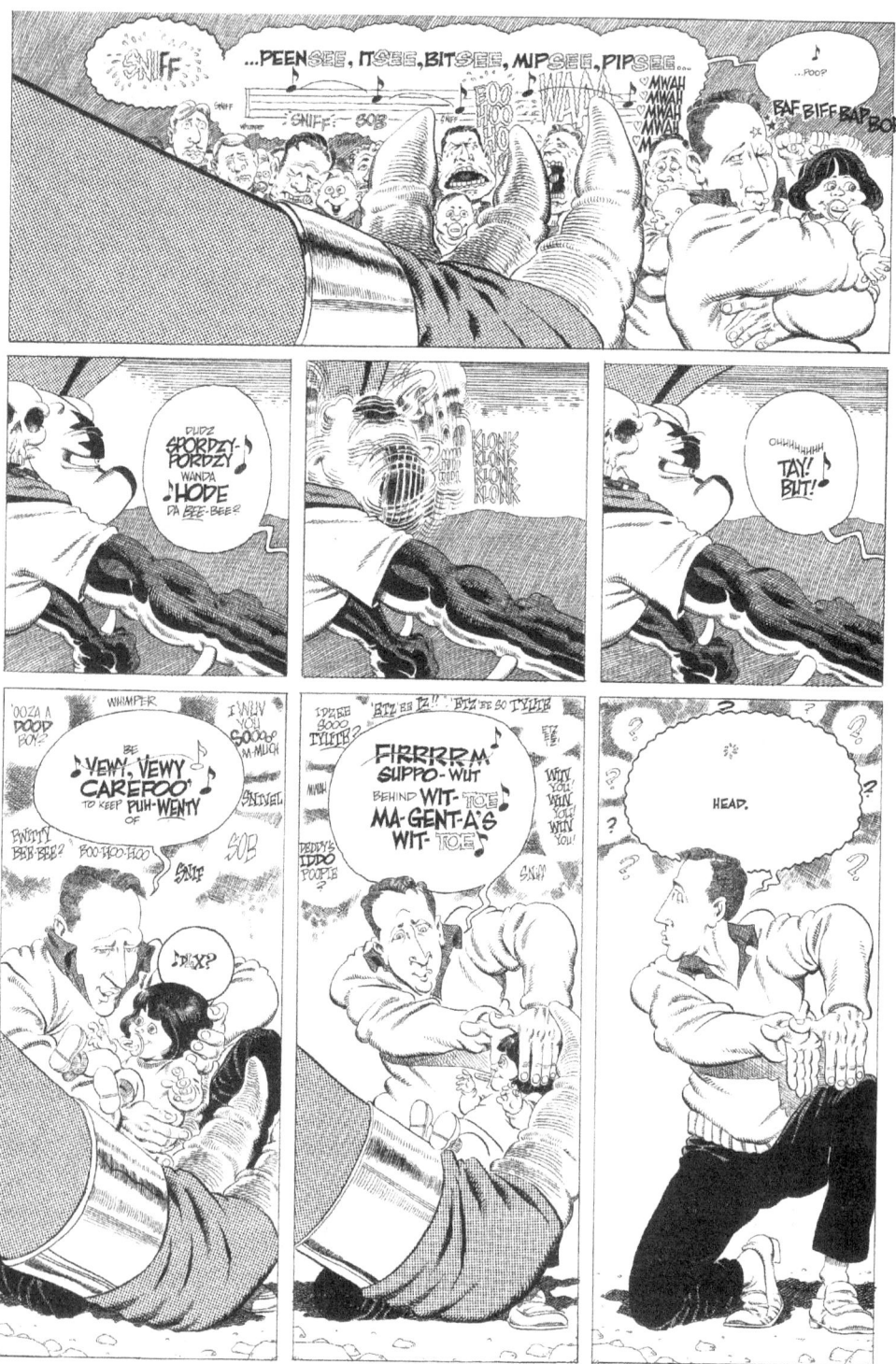

Above: Figure 16. Another baby is tossed, this time from *Cerebus* issue 276, March 2002 (© 2002 Dave Sim and Gerhard).

Opposite: Figure 17. Sim's satire of Gary Groth's *The Comics Journal*, with which Sim has had a long and contentious relationship. From *Cerebus* issue 279, June 2002 (© 2002 Dave Sim and Gerhard).

GROWTH: [laughs] *Our fearless leader.*
INNISCENT: [laughs] Yes, exactly. Our fearless leader. So, I said to him, "You mean, it's the only thing he reads for *entertainment.*" And he shakes his head. "No, *Rabbi* is the only thing he reads, *period.*"
GROWTH: [loud, raucous laughter]
INNISCENT: [laughs] Careful, Gary. [laughs] With this one, it is possible to start laughing, go completely "'round the bend" and not be able to stop even when they show up to haul you off to, you know, wherever. I've seen it.
GROWTH: [laughing] Oh, God. Oh, God.
[After a few minutes they manage to compose themselves, the stenographer as well, who misses the first few sentences of the discussion as it resumes]
INNISCENT: ...dwarfs the absolute authority of any Emperor or Pontiff, Western or Eastern, Lord Julius, Lord Julius' Council of Heirs before that was dissolved. And the only thing he reads is a juvenile religious pulp fiction satire tailored to the sensibilities and tastes...of a thirteen-year-old boy. Actually, I think Kyle had *outgrown Rabbi* by the time he was thirteen. [laughs] And that isn't the worst of it.
GROWTH: [laughs] *It isn't?*
INNISCENT: No, it isn't. You know the thing I dreaded most of all? The one thought that haunted my every waking moment? [pauses] What if he wants to *meet* me? [laughs]
GROWTH: [new gales of laughter] [again, the stenographer, as well, who misses the next couple of sentences]
INNISCENT: What if he wants to, you know, have dinner? And sends some...goons...over to get me?
GROWTH: [laughing] [high-pitched strangulated voice] My ribs are starting to ache.
INNISCENT: [laughs] It gets worse. After a year or so, when he *hadn't* contacted me, I realized how...strange...that was. He had been reading *Rabbi* for...oh, God...what would it have been, at that point? Eight years? Ten [high-pitched strangulated voice]
...nd yet!...He ...v about *Rabbi's* ow do you

INNISCENT: Name a favourite author of yours..
GROWTH: You mean, like Jaime De...
INNISCENT: No no. Someone you *don't* publish yourself.
GROWTH: Oh, uh. William S. Joyce, Fran Kafka......
INNISCENT: Joyce. Joyce is a good one. Let's say for some reason you've gone on an absolute William S. Joyce [laughs] *binge.* That experience that we've all had. You know, picking up something at random out of your library and re-reading a few pages and finding it just mesmerizing. And suddenly you're re-reading everything Joyce ever wrote and appreciating it at a completely new level.
GROWTH: Actually, that just happened to me a while ago with F. Stop Kennedy.
INNISCENT: Kennedy. Another good example. Someone you appreciate at one level when you're twenty and a completely different level when you're forty. So, you're in the midst of this binge and you have the level of power and absolute authority that Cerebus has. What are you going to do?
GROWTH: [laughs] *Send some goons out to find F. Stop Kennedy and drag him over to my place for dinner.*
INNISCENT: [laughs] Exactly! Now. Let's leave aside the fact that people with political power are usually textbook cases of arrested emotional development insofar as what little need they have for emotional support they prefer to receive in the form of mass adoration from strangers. In Fraudian terms, a political leader is an infantile personality, driven purely by his core of ego that is virtually unchanged from when he was a baby. A mentally unhealthy state of affairs that was, I saw, dramatically worse in Cerebus. My fear, that he would take a sudden interest in me, was really my fear of the pathological levels of displacement he was exhibiting. Do you know Fraud, at all?
GROWTH: *Probably.*
INNISCENT: [laughs] Oh, I forgot! You're a publisher. Well, for the sake of your readers who *aren't* publishers let me oversimplify by saying that displacement is the transfer of a subject's emotional attachment from the original object of whatever has caused his serious mental problems to another object in a way unrecognized by the subject in order to avoid addressing the primary conflict. As distinct from transference, whereby the subject's emotional attachment is transferred, ...ally to the therapist, but in a way recognized ..._ subject which is non-evasive of reality. ...ing again, the latter resembles

imprinting.
GROWTH: [laughs] *You mean, Cerebus thought you were his mother?*
INNISCENT: [laughs] No, that was certainly what I was *afraid* of. The whole anaclitic symbiosis which would be the inevitable result of the displacement Cerebus was enacting, that is, the neurotic reduction into narrower and narrower parameters of those elements of reality he was willing to accept. But, the whole point was that *I* didn't enter into it in any way. In fact, Garth Inniscent was just another reality he had turned his back on in his gradual descent into psychosis. The anaclitic symbiosis was there, but it wasn't directed at *me*, it was directed at *Rabbi.*
GROWTH: [laughs] *You mean, Cerebus thought the one hundred and fifty issues of Rabbi were his mother?*
INNISCENT: [laughs] No, as I told you it's worse than that. Cerebus thought that Rabbi, the fictional character, was his mother. [They both laugh uproariously, the stenographer as well, causing another gap in the transcription]
...mother, father, primary narcissistic event, sole object of his ego libido, narcissistic libido *and* his object libido. That's why I kept giving Rabbi more and more and more powers. On the one hand, all indications were that Cerebus' entire psychic apparatus was breaking down, his schizophrenia was acute or soon would be. On the other hand, by feeding his psychoses, reinforcing his infantile wish tendencies, I really thought that if anyone could get rid of the Cirinists, he could.
GROWTH: *And he did.*
INNISCENT: And he did. Which left me with only one problem: I could get Cerebus to get rid of the *Cirinists*, but how was I going to get rid of *Cerebus* when the time came?
GROWTH: *And?*
INNISCENT: I decided to do this interview and leave strict instructions that a copy of it is to be given to him after my death.
GROWTH: *You think it will work?*
INNISCENT: I'm sure it will. The moment he reads all this, every one of the myriad interrelated complexes I've implanted within him will sponteously implode and leave him drooling human vegetable.

Left: A drooling human vegetable. But why not now, when we can *all* enjoy it?

GROWTH: *Wow.*
INNISCENT: [laughs] I knew that the sheer ...oulless sadism of it would appeal to you .
GROWTH: I'll say! But why *after* you're dead? Why not now when we could all enjoy it?
INNISCENT: No, there's apt to be a neurasthenic abreaction during the latency period when he would want to hunt me down and kill me in a horrible fashion.
GROWTH: *Spoilsport.*
INNISCENT: So. Can I get a discount c the copy of the *Reads Journal* I'm leaving
GROWTH: *No.* ▫

pillar, shall be Gods house, and of all that thou shalt giue me, I will surely giue the tenth vnto thee." So, nine-tenths of whatever Jacob gets, Jacob keeps and one-tenth of whatever Jacob gets [laughs] Jacob will give to his rock. [looks around the Sanctuary] Hard to believe that the idea for all this [laughs] came from a rock. Jacob is a very, very funny guy. He just doesn't *know* that he's a very, very funny guy. Okay. Chapter twenty-nine. *"Then Iacob lift up his feet, and came into the land of the children of the East. And he looked, and behold, a well in the field, and loe, there three flocks of sheepe lying by it: for out of that wel they watered the flocks: and a great stone was vpon the welles mouth."* [laughs and laughs and laughs a *lot* through this part of the story] God is going along with it! Why not? If he can pretend for *Hagar* that His house is inside of a *well*, what kind of a big problem would it be for God to put His *new* house on top of His *old* house? No problem at all. *"And thither were all the flockes gathered, and they rolled the stone from the wels mouth, & watered the sheepe, and put the stone againe vpon the wels mouth in his place."* [laughs] God knows his place! Inside the stone on top of the well's mouth. *"And Iacob said vnto them, My brethren whence be ye? and they saide, Of Haran are we. And he said vnto them, Know ye Laban the sonne of Nahor?"* [laughs]. Laban isn't the son of Nahor. Laban is the son of *Bethuel*. Bethuel is the son of Nahor. [laughs] Jacob can't remember who is whose father and who is whose grandfather any better than Yoohwhoo can! *"And they sayde, We knowe. And he said vnto them, Is there peace to him? and they said, He is well: and behold, Rachel his daughter commeth with the sheepe."* [laughs] See, this is the part where Jacob, like Abraham's servant did, is supposed to say something in his heart like "Let it come to pass that the damsel to whom I shall say, let down thy pitcher and give the cattle drink, etc. etc." And he was probably thinking that he'd have to kill a few hours until the cattlemen showed up. Instead, here she comes with *the sheep* and he gets so nervous when he finds out that *this is her!* that it comes out: *"And hee said, Loe, yet the day is great, neither is it time that the cattell should be gathered together: water yee the sheepe, and goe and feed."* [laughs] All the guys by the well must've thought he had lost his mind! *"And they said, We cannot, vntill all the flockes bee gathered together, and till they rolle the stone from the welles mouth: then wee water the sheepe. And while hee yet spake with them, Rachel came with her fathers sheepe: for she kept them. And it came to passe, when Iacob saw Rachel the daughter of Laban his mothers brother; that Iacob went neere, and rolled the stone from the wels mouth, and watered the flocke of Laban his mothers brother."* [laughs] What a comedian! He's got it *backwards*. He's supposed to think in his heart of something Laban's daughter can do to identify herself to *him* and *instead* [laughs] he takes *one* look at her and *he* rolls the stone off of the well's mouth and *he* waters all the sheep for *her*. [laughs] *"And Iacob kissed Rachel, and lifted vp his voice, and wept."* [laughs] This boy really knows how to play "hard-to-get". *"And Iacob told Rachel, that hee was her fathers brother, and that hee was Rebekahs sonne: and she ranne and told her father."* [laughs]. Well, he was *half* right. [laughs]. He's Rebekah's son, but he sure isn't Rachel's father's brother. He's Rachel's father's *nephew*. Can you imagine when Rachel came running in? [laughs] Your brother is here! The son of Rebekah! "Oh, crap," he must've thought with this excited young girl bouncing all around him. [laughs] "Not *this* again." *"And it came to passe, when Laban heard the hearing of Iacob his sisters sonne, that he ranne to meet him, and imbraced him, and kissed him, & brought him to his house: and hee tolde Laban all these things. And Laban said to him, Surely thou art my bone and my flesh: and he abode with him a moneth of daies."* [laughs] "My bone and my flesh," that's what Adam called *Hawwa*: "bone of my bone and flesh of my flesh" [laughs] So Laban [dangling his hand from a limp wrist] has figured Jacob out in the first five seconds. [laughs] Oh, Laban is going to take this one re-e-al slow after what happened with Rebekah. Oh, this is going to be fun. Stick around, kid. Which Jacob does. Which gives Laban a month to figure out what he's going to do with him. So, a month later, Laban just...pops...him with: *"And Laban said vnto Iacob, Because thou art my brother, shouldest thou therefore serue me for nought? Tell me, what shall thy wages be?"* Well, the answer to *that* is: who said *I* was going to serve *you*? The *elder* is supposed to serve the *younger*. If *anybody* serves *anybody*, *you* should be serving *me*, Uncle Laban. But that's "man stuff" and Yoohwhoo and Jacob don't [laughs] don't know from "man stuff". Jacob's only reaction is, Wages? Hmm. [laughs] What do I want for my wages to serve my brother Laban? Oh, this kid is "easy pickings" all right. *"And Laban had two daughters: the name of the elder was Leah, and the name of the yonger Rachel. Leah was tender eyed: but Rachel was beautiful and well fauoured. And Iacob loued Rachel, and said, I will serue thee seuen years for Rachel thy yonger daughter. And Laban said, It is better that I giue her to thee, then that I should giue her to another man: abide with me."* Jacob completely misses the insult: It's better that I give her to you than to someone like me. You know, to another *man*. Whatever Jacob is [laughs] a man wouldn't serve another man for *seven years* just for a *wife*. What? No cattle? No property? No gold? [laughs] For Laban this is about as

Above and opposite: Figure 18. The text overtakes the page. Konigsberg overwhelmed by the "Cerebexegesis." From *Cerebus* issue 284, November 2002 (© 2002 Dave Sim and Gerhard).

and made a feast." [laughs and laughs] He gathers together all the *men* of the place? [laughs and laughs] Oh, this is going to be good. Heh. Well, aye, Cerebus feels a little bad for Jacob. But [laughs] This is going to be good. *"And it came to passe in the euening, that he tooke Leah his daughter, and brought her to him, and he went in vnto her. And Laban gaue vnto his daughter Leah, Zilpah his mayde, for a handmaid."* [laughs] That's too funny. [laughs] He gives his daughter a *dowry* to marry Jacob! [laughs] He has to "sweeten the deal" for his daughter! *And it came to passe, that in the morning, behold it was Leah: and he said to Laban, What is this thou hast done vnto mee? Did not I serue with thee for Rachel? Wherefore then hast thou beguiled me?"* Oh, the boys were probably just killing themselves laughing in the bunkhouse. [laughs and laughs] "Saaay. *You're* not Rachel." *"And Laban said, It must not be so done in our place, to giue the yonger, before the first borne. Fulfill her weeke, and wee will giue thee this also, for the seruice which thou shalt serue with mee, yet seuen other yeeres. And Iacob did so, and fulfilled her weeke: and he gaue him Rachel his daughter to wife also.* [laughs] Oh, Cerebus wishes he could've been there when he told the boys. "Guess what, fellas? He's going to serve me *seven more years for Rachel!"* [laughs] What a putz! [laughs and laughs and laughs] *Fourteen years...*for two *women*! *"And Laban gaue to Rachel his daughter, Bilhah his handmaid, to be her mayd."* [laughs] Laban figures that Rachel should have a dowry for marrying Jacob, too. Something to sweeten the deal. [it takes him a while to stop laughing] [thinks] You know, in a way, Cerebus feels bad laughing at this. But, at the same time, Cerebus has been around guys all his life. You just can't be that, *that*...[dangles his hand from a limp wrist]...and not expect that some guy is going to—you know—give you "the business". *"And he went in also vnto Rachel, and he loued Rachel more then Leah, and serued with him yet seuen other yeeres. And when the Yoohwhoo saw that Leah was hated, hee opened her wombe: but Rachel was barren."*

That's as far as Cerebus got. Actually, Cerebus got *further* than that, but the next part is complicated with Jacob's twelve sons and all of their names, so it's probably better to just stop before the last four verses of chapter twenty-nine where Jacob's first four sons are born. [thinks] [laughs] Well, at least he wasn't a *total* [dangles his hand from a limp wrist] [we both laugh] Cerebus feels like having an ale. [smacks his lips] Aye, Cerebus definitely feels like having an ale. How about you?

        Me:
        Me? Sure.

        Cerebus:
Great. Let's go. There's a place about four doors down on Two Mile Road. [Sees me looking over at Konigsberg] Oh. Uhhh. [thinks] Uhhh. You...uh...[thinks some more] You have a good night, there, Konigsberg!

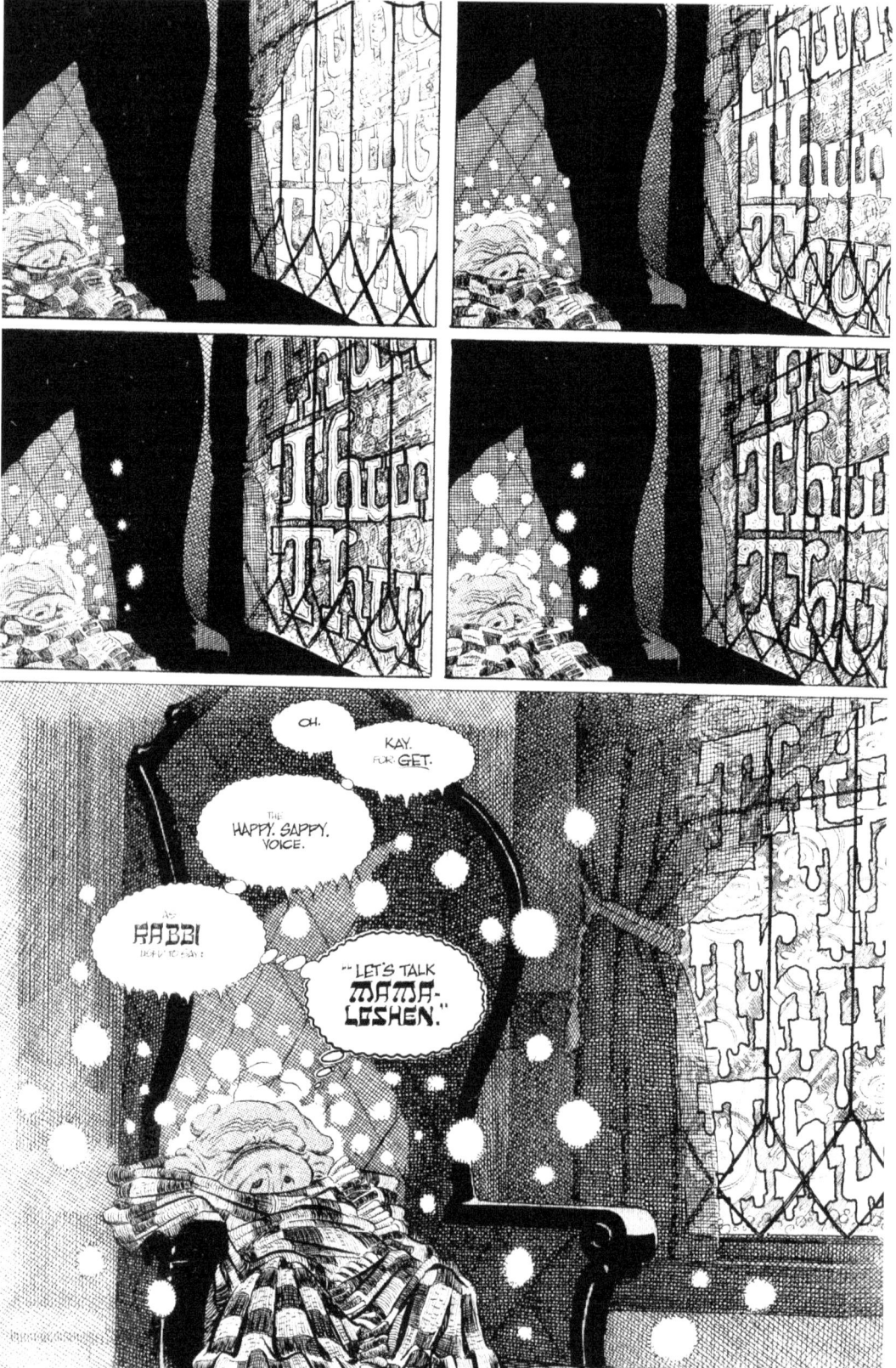

at the Origin of Everything on my own (as a secular humanist," writes Sim in his notes to the work, "knowing I would get the 'straight goods' only after reading The Bible and the Koran and submitting myself to his will" (Sim and Gerhard 2004, vii).[14] Sim seems to have fully predicted that no one would pay any serious attention to his theories of the origin of the universe. After a beautifully illustrated forty pages, Sim never mentions it again, perhaps implying that any such grand revelation will have no effect on a world conditioned by secular humanism, feminism and Marxism. That nobody paid attention to Sim's reconciliation of *Genesis* with Einsteinian physics is because, he claims, he is not a feminist: "how long are the feminists going to be able to keep a lid on the fact that an anti-feminist has come up with an interpretation of Genesis that functions as an actual historical narrative and ... possibly discovered the Unified Theory that eluded Einstein all his life?" (ibid., viii).

Following the conclusion of *Cerebus*, Gary Groth published a series of essays in the October/November 2004 issue of *The Comics Journal*. The first essay, by Rich Kreiner, asks "Can Cerebus Survive Dave Sim?" (Kreiner October/November 2004, 101). How will *Cerebus*' longevity be affected by the fact it is no longer appearing monthly on the comics stand? Kreiner's question raises interesting questions about how it is we are to read and experience *Cerebus*. As Charles Hatfield observes in *Alternative Comics*, *Cerebus* essentially operated as two separate media constructs: (1) the ongoing story appearing in discrete, monthly installments of twenty pages each and; (2) a series of "graphic novels" containing (except for the first volume) self-contained story arcs. Each served the other: the availability of the "phone books" helped the monthly comic. A new reader could pick up a handful of paperback books and catch up on the necessary back-story, while the monthly comic acted in part as a monthly advertisement for the phone book collections, essentially keeping the comic on the fickle reader's radar screen. (Hatfield 2002, 160)

Kreiner's question also raises the question of exactly what of *Cerebus* will receive "ongoing public recognition" and "sustained vitality and relevance"; would it be, for example, "the formidable virtues, and superlative execution of the series or Sim's outspoken nature and controversial notions?" (Kreiner October/November 2004, 101). If the latter, then it will prove problematic, for Sim's beliefs have, to Kreiner, become "progressively disassociated" (ibid.). Kreiner likens the development of the series to a volcanic eruption: the initial blast being issue 186. Since then, Sim "has become more thematically broad [and] rhetorically unstinting" (ibid.). Kreiner rightly observes that as Sim's beliefs begin to take over more and more of the comic's action, the greater the comic suffers both artistically and commercially (ibid.). Which brings Kreiner to his central question: is it possible for *Cerebus* as a creative work to overcome its creator's polemics? Kreiner says yes, pointing to the work of Leni Riefenstahl, Ezra Pound and Richard Wagner (ibid.).

Kreiner was among those readers Thompson and Hagey mention who initially believed the Viktor Davis sections to be an elaborate trick or joke of some kind. Then, Kreiner has intentionally avoided Sim's "Chasing YHWH" sections for the same reason he overlooked the Viktor Davis material — it bored him. As the ending of *Cerebus* neared, Kreiner consciously avoided revisiting much of this material, focusing his reading almost entirely on those sections he found of greatest interest to him on an initial reading, namely *Jaka's Story*, *Melmoth* and *Going Home*. In fact, *Going Home* is for Kreiner representative of what is most problematic about *Cerebus* as a whole, namely, the "nature, depth and accomplishment" of

Opposite: Figure 19. Cerebus contemplates his life during ***The Last Day***. From *Cerebus* issue 292, July 2003 (© 2003 Dave Sim and Gerhard).

Sim's caricature of F. Scott Fitzgerald, F. Stop Kennedy (figure 20), would be largely lost on Sim's audience were it not for the lengthy notes ("Chasing Scott") that accompany the main text in the *Going Home* phonebook. At the same time, these notes present the reader with the worst of Sim's proselytizing and, in Kreiner's view, "threaten admiration and pleasure of the comic narrative" (Kreiner October/November 2004, 102).

Longtime critic of Sim, R. Fiore in his essay "Quixote Triumphant" accuses Sim of tilting at windmills, namely feminists, Marxists and homosexuals, whom Sim blames "for every depravity committed" in the name of pluralism (Fiore October/November 2004, 103). Since his religious awakening, continues Fiore, to disagree with Sim is "not only wrong but immoral" (ibid.). In fact, Sim's outspokenness raises the question of the effect of an artist's views on his or her artwork. Fiore (in his typically rhetorically overheated style, like Sim's, written to provoke) compares Sim's *Cerebus* to Hitler writing a great oratorio about killing Jews. What *Cerebus* might have been, had it not been for Sim's willingness to utilize the comic as a mouthpiece for his political and religious convictions, would be something akin to Hitler writing "pure music the content of which could not be anything other than sublime" (ibid.). In the end, observes Fiore, it is best to place the aesthetic and moral qualities of the work into separate categories. Fiore argues that, in the case of Sim, beliefs do not necessarily invalidate his art on the basis that they are so clearly out of the mainstream and therefore of no real threat to anyone. Thankfully, writes Fiore, enjoyment of *Cerebus* does not require the reader to confront Sim's beliefs head-on, you can take them or leave them. "The bitterness and self-pity that are often on display in the explanatory material," Fiore notes, "is almost entirely quarantined from the comics. Whatever his peregrinations as a philosopher, [Sim] remains a storyteller with a storyteller's instincts" (ibid., 104).

For Fiore, *Cerebus* "jumped the shark with the anti-climax of *Church & State* [and] Cerebus' conversation with the Judge"; at that time, "Sim made his decision for self-indulgence.... His motto from that point on seemed to be 'Whatever I do is right'" (Fiore October/November 2004, 105). After *Church & State*, Sim seemed less and less interested in Cerebus and more interested in pursuing other subjects, most notably his eleven-issue meditation on Oscar Wilde's death in *Melmoth*, or his extended prose sections in *Reads*. Had art been Sim's primary concern, argues Fiore, he would have then wrapped up the series around the mid-way point and gone on to other things. According to Fiore, however, Sim was afraid of losing his guaranteed audience at the same time he was determined to finish the 300 issues he had promised; therefore he made the decision to have *Cerebus* fit his interest. "Sim convinced himself that *Cerebus* could accommodate any content he wanted it to," yet in doing so Sim stretched credulity (ibid.). With *Melmoth*, Sim alienated the mainstream audience he'd won with his Wolveroach and Secret Sacred Wars [a parody of Jim Shooter and Mike Zeck's bestselling crossover *Marvel Super Heroes Secret Wars* (1984–1985)] issues while those interested in comics as an art were alienated by "the fantasy trappings and the commercial comics idiom" (ibid.). Sim's most "disastrous" decision argues Fiore, was to "start interpolating lengthy prose passages into his comics" (ibid.).

To Fiore, *Latter Days* represents Sim at his "best and worst," the best being the early chapters that chronicle Cerebus' years as a sheep-herder and Five-Bar Gate player (an imaginary game devised by Sim), the worst being, for example, a scene wherein the men, recently thrown off the yoke of years of oppression by the Cirinists, cast votes to decide which women will live and which will die. Fiore admits that the context of the Cirinist oppression

Opposite: Figure 20. Sim and Gerhard's masterful composition. F. Stop Kennedy surrenders to his demons. From *Cerebus* issue 241, April 1999 (© 1999 Dave Sim and Gerhard).

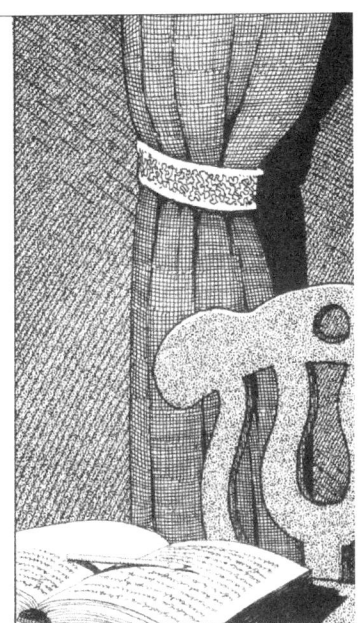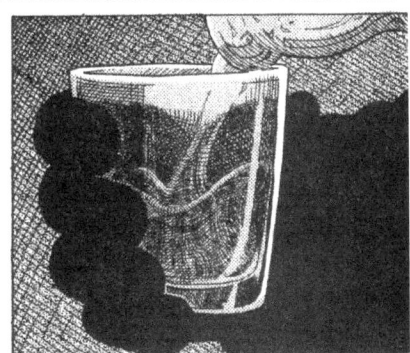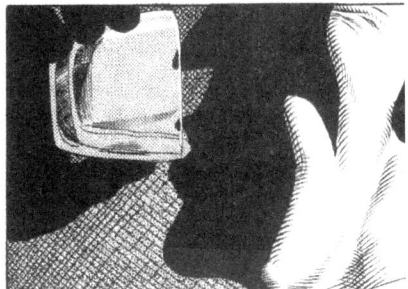

(and a simultaneous parody of Todd McFarlane's mean-spirited and wildly violent *Spawn*) is important, and may help to explain the men's behavior; that the men routinely allow beautiful women to live while voting the ugly ones to death is equally damning of men's self-serving prerogatives, for example. What Fiore cannot tolerate, however, is that among the women executed is the cartoonist Julie Doucet. "Suggesting violence against an actual living person, even in effigy, and even when that person is a character in a work of art subject to satire, is really a violation of any kind of civilized norm," Fiore steams (Fiore October/November 2004, 106). Equally untenable is Sim's decision to include a sixty-page sequence including a caricature of The Three Stooges, or, worse, an almost unreadable exegesis of the *Book of Genesis* incomprehensibly accompanied by meticulously rendered pages of fictional movie stills involving Konigsberg. To Fiore, this material is the "direct result of [Sim's] totally arbitrary decision to fill 300 issues, even if he doesn't have the story to fill them" (ibid., 109).

In a 1993 "Aardvark Comment" column, Sim wrote of his plans after *Cerebus*, remarking that he would keep the reprint volumes in print, and would publish any of Sim's additional comics stories or graphic novels. Sim doubted that he would do anything with the Cerebus character again or that he would ever do a monthly comic. As for further collaborations, Sim was hopeful that Gerhard would continue to work with him. Both he and Gerhard planned long vacations, whatever might happen. In actuality, when 2004 finally came around, Sim first responded to a backlog of mail, resulting in his alternately fascinating and aggravating letters collections *Collected Letters 2004* (2005) and *Collected Letters 2* (2008). He took part in Craig Miller's *Following Cerebus* (2004–), a comic-sized magazine that includes essays on Sim's work and the occasional essay or original art by Sim. In addition, Sim began work on his next series, *glamourpuss* (2008–), a largely disappointing comic containing an uneasy mix of vicious satires of women's fashion magazine, combined with a rambling history of photorealism in comics (*glamourpuss* is rendered in the neorealistic style Sim first introduced in *Latter Days*, and later explored in his meticulously rendered and researched *Judenhass* [2009], which recounts the troubling history of the abandonment of the Jews during World War Two). Two other projects, *Cerebus Archive* and *Cerebus TV* (both 2009–) are extensions of the *Cerebus* franchise. The former largely concerns making available previously published and unpublished works and providing an historical context for the development of *Cerebus*—as of this writing eighteen issues have appeared and Sim is only now beginning to discuss the early stages of *Cerebus'* publication—while the latter is a good-natured anthology series that includes everything from interviews with other comics artists, monologues and skits by Sim, commentaries on the history of the medium, or the promotion of Sim's own works or the works of others.

Eight years after the final issue of *Cerebus*, it is clear that this work remains, and will remain, Sim's magnum opus. It is extremely unlikely that anyone will ever again publish anything similar to *Cerebus*, particularly in the rapidly changing comics industry. The previous methods of publication and distribution had, since the late 1970s, transformed. The speculation boom of the early 1990s severely diminished the number of outlets available to self-publishers. Moreover, increased access to publish-on-demand (something Sim makes use of for *Cerebus Archive* and *glamourpuss*) and desktop publishing has opened up the field to countless talents that, previous to these technological developments, might have languished publishing poorly published and distributed material, if anything at all. The flipside of this is that, with more talent comes increased competition for each artist's share of the market. With a limited market to begin with, and one largely dominated by the ever-present super-hero genre (which, thanks to Hollywood shows no sign of diminishing), many comics artists find they are unable to make a living wage from their art, let alone rent penthouses and limousines, and thus their longevity is diminished by the disappointment of ever-diminishing returns.

Sim addressed some of these concerns in his 1993 and 2010 editions of the *Cerebus Guide to Self-Publishing*. In a sense, that work functions as a useful method of coming to terms with Sim's body of work. It provides an historical, economic and artistic explanation of Sim's accomplishments. There is no question that *Cerebus* had a profound effect on the comics medium, yet it is difficult to gauge *Cerebus*' reputation among comics, or to predict how future generations of readers and comics creators will view this brilliant and maddening work. Recent appraisals of the work from Douglas Wolk (2007) and Tim Kreider (2011) are positive, with reservations. Both recognize Sim and Gerhard's accomplishment, note its many praiseworthy aspects, and, predictably, criticize Sim for severely hampering the work with cumbersome expositional tracts on feminism and religion. Blogs and internet reviews, as to be expected, lean toward the extreme: accusing Sim of outright misogyny or uncritical accolades, with little in between.

The essays that follow represent an alternative to the criticisms of *Cerebus* that have so far appeared. Aside from a handful of critical responses, there has been, for the most part, a lack of serious scholarship addressing Sim and Gerhard's important work, a complete realization of the dream of Carl Barks. Here, the authors provide new ways of looking at *Cerebus*. In so doing, they are helping to establish a context for new or established readers hoping to better comprehend *Cerebus* and the reasons why it deserves our attention. It is my hope that this collection represents a beginning of continuing scholarship devoted to Sim and Gerhard's work, as opposed to a scholarly curiosity about a comics curiosity.

Notes

1. It was not the first time an aardvark entered into Sim's life; previously, Sim won a copy of the rock band Kensington Market's *Aardvark* after correctly answering a radio call-in question (the answer presumably had something to do with comics) (Sim November 2009).

2. Jim Shooter posted his version of the events on his blog. According to Shooter, Day came to New York at Marvel's expense to meet editor Denny O'Neill and others. O'Neill chose the Chelsea Hotel for Day to stay, because, according to Shooter, it had "literary history and would be an interesting place to stay" (Shooter 2011). A few days later, Shooter took Day out for lunch and did not voice any complaints about roaches, but did say he felt the hotel was "sort of shabby" (ibid.). Shooter asked his secretary to move him to a better hotel; no one at Marvel asked him to sleep in the Marvel offices, which, Shooter adds, had heat during the night. Shooter admits to finding a few of Day's layouts "confusing," but he did not fire Day over it. Shooter insists that he tried to find more work for Day, either on *Indiana Jones* or *Star Wars*. "Gene died right around then," writes Shooter. "I was told he had a heart attack.... Gene had a sedentary lifestyle—too many hours at the board—his diet wasn't the healthiest and I believe he smoked. It was a tragic loss" (ibid.). David Day, Gene's younger brother, adds to Shooter's blog that Day was not overweight and did not die of a heart attack, but of a heart aneurysm. He was, according to David Day, undergoing significant stress in his life, including marriage and financial problems and any disappointments over Marvel's treatment of him would only have added to the stress, but could not have been the sole cause of his death (ibid.).

3. Loubert attended the convention alone. "We didn't want people to know what was going on with Dave," she tells Blake Bell, "we just said he had work to do" (Bell 2002, 131).

4. One could argue that this is *exactly* where Sim goes wrong in the latter half of *Cerebus*, with its sacrifice of narrative in the service of anti-feminist and religious polemic.

5. In fact, in his 1983 Thompson interview, Sim compares *High Society* with a "fictional biography" of Richard Nixon. "I think we miss the point if we make Richard Nixon into a villain, or an anti-hero, or a figure of tragedy, or a grand comic figure.... He was just an individual who got in out of his depth, whose ambition exceeded his abilities, and we tend to find out that presidents on the whole are that

way. Their ambition in the office is very often what gets them there, but the abilities to win a campaign are not the skills you need in office" (Thompson August 1983, 70). Mailer's account of the 1972 United States presidential race between Nixon and George McGovern, *Saint George and the Dragon*, paints a very similar picture of Nixon as the one Sim presents here, and reaches the same conclusions concerning Nixon's campaign ability surpassing his talent as president. Sim writes in an e-mail that Mailer's work was not an influence on *High Society*, yet "Mailer's *Miami and the Siege of Chicago*, I suspect, would have had a HUGE influence had I found a copy and read it at that time." However, Sim suspects he did not locate a copy of that book "until the mid- to late-90s" (Sim, e-mail to author 4 August 2011).

6. DC approached Sim about doing a "colorized" version of *Cerebus* while allowing Sim to continue self-publishing the black and white version.

7. Jim Shooter writes on his blog that the legal issue arose because the Wolveroach issues "sold well, and therefore, Dave kept doing it" (*Jim Shooter Blog*, accessed 1 September 2011). Single use of a trademarked character as parody is copyright protected, writes Shooter, "but multiple uses constitute infringement, which if left unchallenged, can weaken a trademark" (ibid.). Lawyers sent a cease and desist letter. "Dave went ballistic (though he was wrong) and ranted against Marvel in his book" (ibid.). To solve matters, Shooter alleges that he spoke with Marvel's in-house lawyer and "convinced them that Dave was actually a friend and that we should solve the trademark problem by retroactively licensing the use of the Wolverine trademark for Dave's parodies for a dollar," which they did (ibid.). Shooter was befuddled when, in a subsequent issue of *Cerebus*, Sim "continued ranting" (ibid.). Later, Shooter spoke with Sim at a convention and inquired as to his reasons. "He said he'd gotten such an enthusiastic response to his ranting that he didn't want to stop," writes Shooter. "And he seemed stunned that I would be offended" (ibid.).

8. Comments in his interview with Charles Brownstein support this interpretation: "telling the story in serial form but being aware that it would be issued as a collection meant that I was really telling two different stories simultaneously. In any instance where I had a choice to make between something that would serve the story better in serial form or collected, the collected choice was always the one I chose" (Brownstein Winter 1997a, 21).

9. There was also the matter of DC offering Sim "six figures" for the rights to *Cerebus*. "Lying in bed at night picturing five zeroes can drive you bug fuck," Sim explains. "The only way I could get any sleep was to find a way to get five zeroes without giving anything away. 6000 twenty dollar books. Simple as that" (Sim and Gerhard September 1987).

10. The autobiographical elements in *Jaka's Story* (Loubert worked to support Sim while he wrote and drew his early comics) suggest that the breakdown of Sim's own marriage was the result of his devotion to the comic book, but that is probably incorrect; the end of Sim's marriage seemingly had nothing to do with his devotion to *Cerebus*. What's more, Sim, for all practical purposes a workaholic, bears little commonality with the slacker Rick.

11. Depressingly, Sim suggests that had Jaka decided to have the baby, she and Rick "would have been a pretty happy family" (Spurgeon February 1996, 95).

12. Sim's equation of feminism and Marxism is not as far-fetched as it might first appear. Keep in mind, modern feminism (as distinguished from its 19th century forebears) developed in the late 1960s, a period when, as Neil Lydon notes in his controversial critique of feminism, *No More Sex War*, "many of the concerns, protests, and disenchantments of the young [took] focus ... in the political philosophies and terms of expression of the old (Marxist-Leninist) Left" (Lydon 1992, 60). At times Lydon's rhetoric matches Sim's: "If you look my way into the bottom of the feminist approach," he writes, "what you will find ... is not a set of humane and loving principles discerned with noble intelligence and applied with all the finest distinctions of literacy and judgment, to the advancement of civilization. What you will discover is a mess of pseudo–Marxist crudities, swirling in a pot of terror, cooking up in an oven of unprecedented social change. You find blind panic disguised as clear-eyed militancy; you find rank selfishness disguised as philanthropy; and you find sophistries of base prejudice disguised as political sophistication" (ibid., 59).

13. In a note in "Aardvark Comment" from June 1986 (issue 87), Sim writes of his readiness to "take custody" of *Cerebus*' back pages "to have a bit of a go at any topic that I feel like blathering on about" (Sim and Gerhard June 1986).

14. Sim in a 2004 letter to Stephen Notley: "there's the pre–Bible *Cerebus* and the post–Bible *Cerebus*. The former seems to me now like so many secular humanist shots in the dark" (Sim 2005, 200).

PART ONE
A MAP OF ESTARCION

Growing Complexity; or, the Cerebus Effect
Sebastian Domsch

The specific attributes of the medium, such as the techniques of creation, the production, distribution, and consumer expectations, enabled Dave Sim to develop *Cerebus* in a way that revolutionized the genre of the graphic novel. Regarding the evolution of the genre graphic novel and the medium comic book, *Cerebus*' main achievement is continually increasing complexity, what has been termed the "Cerebus Effect."[1] With issue after issue, the story and the characters developed into something infinitely larger than the initial starting point, as is especially apparent throughout the first 25 issues leading up to the first larger story-arc of *High Society*. Sim's own (often self-reflexive) artistic approach to comics, graphic design, and storytelling was productively reinforced by the medium he was working in at that specific moment in time; its history, its conditions of production and distribution, and its perception among readers, many of whom were also creators themselves. This will not only help to better contextualize *Cerebus* within the history of the graphic novel, but also to show that this work is even more important for what it *became* than for what it *is*.

The Medial Conditions for Cerebus' Development

Very few artworks produced, distributed, and perceived in a given time grow completely independent of the outward factors that determine the media they are using. Those works not determined by the prevailing conditions of production often tend to influence them in turn. The rise of the modern novel, for example, resulted as much from the increase in general literacy, the spread of lending libraries and improved printing technologies as it does from the works of its groundbreaking creators.

The development of genres is closely tied to conditions of productions, and there is probably no other modern art form that exemplifies this better than comics do. As a medium that demands a technically laborious method of creation — disregarding all considerations of the intellectual effort involved in creating, the pure process of putting words on a page is less laborious than that of drawing, coloring, *and* writing — and whose distribution is dependent on relatively advanced technologies of distribution, comics were for the longest time strongly determined by factors not directly connected to the medium's potential for artistic expression. The purely arbitrary restrictions imposed by the Comics Code Authority in 1954 are only the most glaring example.

From the beginning, the opportunities, restrictions and demands of the different media in which they appeared influenced comics. As daily or weekly strips published within newspapers, they were able to reach a mass audience very quickly, while the use of color made them the most eye-catching and visually sensational part of these newspapers. On the other hand, the serialization in discrete, brief chapters—continuous storytelling over a long period of time was rare but not impossible, as the example of *Gasoline Alley* shows—almost excluded the development of longer storylines or interconnected events and rather invited a form of narration that used constant variations on a limited set of themes, adapting techniques of jazz improvisation.

All throughout the period that marked the height of comics' popularity, the format of the comic book dominated. This had major consequences for their artistic potential. The standard comic book was of a relatively short length, it told stories about one or several recurring fictional characters in a serialized form with an indefinite end. Depending on their success, titles could potentially run forever, as evinced by those titles from the 1930s, like *Detective Comics* or *Action Comics*, still published as of this writing. Furthermore, the distribution through newsstands, which included the ability to return unsold comics, meant that at any given time, readers could only purchase one issue of a title, strongly discouraged the development of longer storylines, since they would make issues interdependent, alienating casual readers who did not read every issue. Thus, editors insisted on self-contained issues as well as characters and story worlds that remained reliably fixed and therefore easily approachable.

This worked very well with superhero stories, invented for the comic book format, while maintaining a storytelling structure similar to mythical narratives. Both tell stories of superhuman heroes that, after a characteristic origin story, remain unchanged and unchangeable throughout all their adventures. Their time does not work in a linear way, implying change and consequences, but in a cyclical way, emphasizing constancy. Readers who picked up a copy of *Superman* or *The Amazing Spiderman* had the reassurance of familiarity, they knew that they could expect spectacle within an unchanging framework: Superman would never be anything but the perfect hero, and Spiderman would never stop being a teenager.

Superhero stories and newsstand comic books were indeed a perfect match—in fact, they worked so well together that for decades they seemed to eclipse even the idea of telling different stories in the comics medium, and telling them in a different way. In addition, the longer their reign continued, the harder it became for the monthly visual spectacle to hide the fact that it had no consequence at all. After all, no matter what unimaginable feat Superman achieved, in the big picture it made no difference.

The late 1960s and early 1970s had seen a rebellious countermovement with the rise of underground comix, breaking with the Comic Code's ideas about what comics can portray and with the predominant aesthetics of perfect bodies, stereotyped indistinguishably. Comix were radical in their break with tradition and as a general movement—they are certainly a major force of liberation in the development of western comics—yet their importance lies very much in preparing the ground for future artists and their works. In 1977, it appeared the creative and subversive surge of underground comix lost most of its momentum. Much of it became formulaic and the more complex and mature artworks it inspired, such as Will Eisner's *A Contract with God* and Harvey Pekar's *American Splendor*, had not yet surfaced. Furthermore, they had not managed to break the economic stranglehold the two main publishing houses held over the comics market. Independent publishing, though existent, was still very marginal. Marvel and DC held an unbreakable monopoly, defending their market share with the ever increasing number of titles they launched, endlessly recycling the same types of stories, "locked into their own narrow and confining view of what comics should be," as Sim writes on the letter page for issue 7 (Sim February 1979).

One of the problems causing this "narrow and confining view" was mainstream comics' continued dependence on infinite serialized publishing, as this led to repetitive stories, stereotypical characters and stagnant, interchangeable story worlds. However, there simply seemed to be no other way to publish comics at the time. The financially potent publishers did not want to support an artist through the creation of a large-scale work (as they would start to do in the 1980s) and the independent publishers *could* not do it. Choosing self-publication, Sim had no alternative to using the format that had for the longest time created the artistic stalemate he was so disappointed with in the first place. Nevertheless, this compromise turned out to be the condition for his artistic success. The very serialization of comics that, when used by a profit-oriented company employing multiple authors, neither of whom owned their own copyrights, had for decades limited the artistic growth of comics, became, in the hands of an individual self-publishing artist, the mode of publishing that made the *Cerebus* effect possible.

As a serialized comic book, *Cerebus* from the beginning fit into consumer expectations and distribution channels. When people looked for new comics, they expected to buy monthly or bi-monthly issues. Underground comix had already established an acceptance for a higher cover price for independent titles, but it would have been difficult to sell one of the *Cerebus* phone books in 1977. Thus, with the serialized form, Sim could get his comics project started, surviving financially from month to month, and securing the series' continuation. However, the fact that he was the sole copyright owner also meant that he could change all of the paradigms for the project whenever he wanted. Choosing the serialized format gave Sim the structural framework to grow into his own project in the way that he did. Moreover, choosing to use fantasy as his genre gave him a narrative mode that, when combined with the structural framework, made the *Cerebus* effect possible. Just as the superhero stories had adapted ideally to the cyclical and static form of infinite series, fantasy enabled the telling of stories that continuously grew in complexity.

The fantastic in fiction has its story roots in myths and legends and granted access to literature through Romanticism's interest in folk tales and the imagination, leading to the highly successful and influential Gothic style. Nevertheless, at the beginning of the 20th century, fantasy as a genre in its own rights (and distinct from the fantastic, Gothic, or science fiction) came into being. From the outset, fantasy evolved into two distinct and individually successful sub-genres, namely swords and sorcery on the one hand, and epic fantasy on the other. However, as a term a coinage of 1961, swords and sorcery derived from the 1930s stories of Robert E. Howard, particularly those dealing with the character Conan the Cimmerian. These stories are set in medieval fictional worlds containing supernatural elements, but their focus is on the personal struggle of a main protagonist rather than on the general fate of that world. This is where they differ most from works of epic fantasy, the latter being concerned with large-scale world-threatening events, in which individual protagonists are often just pieces of a larger game (the defining work of this latter genre is, of course, J.R.R. Tolkien's *The Lord of the Rings* trilogy).

It is obvious that the two approaches to telling fantasy stories also entail different narrative modes. Swords and sorcery stories are a direct ancestor of picaresque storytelling and legendary tales, suspending time and linear change in a series of potentially endless Homeric adventures. It is less the final homecoming than the endless digressions that he encounters on the way. Epic fantasy, on the other hand, modeled much closer on the *Iliad*, is tied to the larger mythological narratives of creation and destruction; it is a story about the world's construction.

It is surely no coincidence that, of these two modes of telling fantasy stories, swords and sorcery style that was first successfully adapted into the comics medium. Having grown out of a similar environment of production and distribution, the pulp magazines, these stories worked well within a form that relied on serialization and a wide distribution to an audience only loosely committed to single publications. As long as customers were able to casually pick up any given issue of a comic book and enjoy the story, it was impossible to introduce the long story arcs and complicated plots involving a wealth of detailed information that high or epic fantasy required, or so publishers thought. After all, it had taken two Oxford dons with a lot of arcane knowledge, a lot of free time, and no economical considerations to influence their mode of production to create the genre-defining models for epic fantasy; *The Lord of the Rings* and C.S. Lewis' *The Chronicles of Narnia* virtually created their own sub-genre as well as a market for it, leading to decades of innumerable imitations through all media.

Market demand and modes of publication enhanced the differentiation of the fantasy sub-genres, but they were by no means completely distinct from each other. There is a strong tendency in all fantasy storytelling to shift the emphasis of interest from individual events and even characters (the sword and sorcery style) towards the story world as a fictional setting (high or epic fantasy). After all, this strangeness is the *differentia specifica* and the main selling point of fantasy. This strangeness breeds reader curiosity. With curiosity comes a stronger commitment to an ongoing story — readers will be more eager not to miss parts of the story in order to get the full picture — and this (economically desirable) commitment of readers necessitates consistency in its structure.

This tendency of fantasy storytelling to gravitate from episode to epic enabled *Cerebus* to evolve seamlessly in scope and ambition without having to change narrative gears in a disruptive way. The narrative mode of *Cerebus* did not change suddenly and categorically, rather it moved within the full range that the different sub-genres of fantasy enabled. In its swords and sorcery form, fantasy was ideally suited for a serialized comic that could start with no narrative obligations, taking the economically risky business of starting an independent comic book one step at a time while delving right into the significant part from the first issue. In addition, the fluid boundaries between this sub-genre and that of epic fantasy made the transition towards more involved storylines, a widening and interconnecting of characters' back-stories, and an increasingly elaborate structuring of the story world.

Creating and enlarging *Cerebus*' back-story was short-lived. The map of Cerebus' world appeared from issues 3 to 10 (the first three issues of the *Conan the Barbarian* comic book had a very similar map). In issue 7, Sim announced plans for a book called *The Aardvarkian Age* that he would publish in collaboration with Michael Loubert. This book, a clear parody/imitation of "The Hyborean Age," a prose text by Robert E. Howard describing the fictional setting of his Conan stories, appeared only in piecemeal form for a few issues and then was quickly dropped. Instead, Sim created his stories in a way that they gradually revealed more and more about their fictional world, keeping his own responses to the many urgent appeals for clarification in the letters pages ambivalent and noncommittal, though he later admitted to the urge to tell all of it in one long prose essay (see below).

The Artistic Development of Cerebus and the "Allmähliche Verfertigung der Gedanken beim Sprechen"

In the following, I will show both how *Cerebus* developed and grew artistically, and how Sim continuously reflected this process in authorial comments and interaction with his readers' comments on the letter page of the series. This is what is meant by this growing complexity, a growth that is not pre-planned or somehow engrained into the DNA of the original starting point, but evolves in the dynamics between producing parts of an artwork. Sim published these parts before the whole was finished, reflecting on the published parts while planning the continuation, a type of process that Heinrich von Kleist had speculated about in his famous 1805 essay "Über die allmähliche Verfertigung der Gedanken beim Reden" (On the Gradual Production of Thoughts Whilst Speaking).

Serialization was a necessary precondition for this type of development. Moreover, not only did it enable this development, it also allowed readers (and, in retrospect, scholars) to listen in on the artist all the while. It is part of the peculiar nature of the "Cerebus Effect" that artistic growth becomes, to an extent, a public event. With the serialized form, parts of the artwork exist in public in a finished form at a stage when the plan for the structure or scope of the artwork as a whole is unknown.

It is always fascinating to watch an artist at work, or have him talk about creating his work, and with *Cerebus*, readers could do both, and not only in retrospect, but right in the middle of the creative process. All throughout the creation and publication of *Cerebus*, Sim has been very outspoken about his own work (though in later stages, and until recently with *Cerebus Archive*, his more political commentaries came to dominate his public comments). As was common practice, Sim reserved one or more pages in each of his issues for letters from readers and his occasional answers. Though he obviously had to fake the letters for the early issues—there was one issue (number 9) for which not enough letters had arrived—for many years to come there was no dearth of comments from readers. Many of the earliest letters are merely encouraging or congratulatory in a general way, giving support to a fresh and humorous take on other successful comics genres. Soon enough readers started to become more involved in the specifics of the series, starting to debate the story world and the direction it was taking. Sim never tired of answering these letters, though not all of his answers are as straightforward as readers might have wished. A further source of highly interesting information in this regard are the introductions that Sim wrote for the first six volumes of *Swords of Cerebus*, which reprinted the first 25 issues and were published between 1981 and 1984, while the project was still in its early stages.

Artistic Development

The artistic development that marks the achievement of Sim as a comics innovator can be traced through a number of aspects, from technical ones like his drawing style and the panel layouts through the narrative mode that is employed (from self-contained parody to deep and intricate storylines) to the structuring of the fictional world in general. All of these aspects radically changed throughout the first couple of years of *Cerebus*' publication.

Probably the least surprising artistic development is the gradual improvement of Sim's drawing style, though the speed at which this development took place is still impressive. Part of this might have been mere practice — especially when it comes to drawing the main character, Sim did get a lot of practice over the years, yet part of it derives out of the shift from stylistic imitation to original creation. This happened early on in the series, as Sim mentioned himself: "As for the art, this issue [number 7] was my first radical departure from my intention to be a major Barry Smith sequel [sic] — the cross-hatching on the splash page. I was trying to find a Barry Smith–style texture that would allow me to render the webbing in two different shades. I broke down and did tight weave cross-hatching even though Smith had never used it. Suddenly I was free. Why — I bet I could do anything I wanted!" (Sim 1982a). Talking about the next issue, Sim also stresses the close relation between the desire for stylistic imitation and a limited view on comic narrative in general:

> The splash page and the top panel of page six were expressions of my own personality without filtering through someone else's style. This was around the time that I started developing a lighter touch to the pace of my stories. The plot seems to bounce along inside the panels. No longer restricted to seeing the world through Barry Smith–colored glasses, I started seeing each panel as a link in a chain. My priority was no longer to copy Smith's pen lines, but to use each drawing as a connecting fragment. It was like a dormant time-sense had leaped into my head from nowhere. It had been there all along of course, but it had been overruled most times by the part of me that was determined to be Barry Smith. The emphasis shifted from the finished art to the layout of the story. From cosmetic technique to narrative flow [Sim 1982a].

As with most other artists, Sim's drawing style evolved through a series of appropriations, rejections, and innovations. He quickly transcended the original style he was aiming to imitate, but continued to let others influence him on top of that. The introduction of the Batman parody in issue 11 brought with it the much more elaborate and atmospheric rendering of the urban scenery as background that is common to the superhero genre, but the improvement in the visual atmosphere and depth is very pronounced, and it stayed with *Cerebus* from there on. As Cerebus' story world became fleshed out and gained in complexity, Sim spent more and more energy in visually contextualizing him in this world, even long before he took on Gerhard.

More clearly recognizable as a conscious decision but also a testimony to Sim's fast developing capabilities as a comics creator is the development of the layouts. Already in issue 8, Sim started to introduce more experimental panel layouts throughout Cerebus' imaginary struggles, testing out a concept that would lead to the celebrated first "Mind Games" issue. In his 1981 introduction to the issue, he explains that his original plans had been even more daring at the time, continuing the experimental layout for several issues and increasing the swirl to a state of pure abstraction. However, this would have effectively been a categorical change of genre, turning the narrative comic book into a piece of experimental "art." Instead, by introducing experimentation in doses small enough not to explode the original format and genre, he managed to expand the artistic range of that format. Only by remaining true to its comic book form did *Cerebus* change what a comic book could be (Sim August 1982b).

Issue 20 was one of the more noticeable steps in the artistic development of *Cerebus*. Sim knew that with issue 20 he was entering new terrain, taking a step against reader expectations (always commercially dangerous) but one that could be artistically liberating, if successful. In a note on the letters page of issue 19, Sim acknowledges his debt to Wendy Pini whose recently published issue 7 of *Elfquest* had given him courage for his own experimentation to come ("Attagirl, Wendy. Next issue is my turn" [Sim August 1980]). By stressing this connection, Sim once more situates himself in the context of a broader movement for a greater range of what was possible between the covers of a comic book. Issue 20 is crucial in two respects: first as an artistic experiment, especially when considering the layout and storytelling. Second, because it strongly introduces the element of social and theological intrigue into Cerebus' fictional world, setting the ground for much that would preoccupy the series in the time to come.

This was a decisive though gradual shift in narrative mode, further de-emphasizing the series' starting point as a parody, but then, *Cerebus* could hardly have started as full-fledged novel of political machinations between numerous fictional factions. This would have been a hard sell for an almost unknown comics author. The parodist origin was a necessary decision to create reader interest, one natural to the comics medium.

One of the hallmarks of mainstream comics' storytelling is fictional crossovers. No other narrative medium has ever employed the combination and connection of different fictional worlds to the extent that comics have. The main reason for this was that the same institution, the publishers, who were not identical with their creators held the ownership rights of several ongoing fictional worlds. Thus, crossovers were not artistic appropriations but sanctioned combinations of intellectual properties that had not yet had narrative closure. However, this also meant that participation in this form of fictional crossover was only possible from within the mainstream industry, and according to their rules. No independent creator could have his or her own creation pop up in the "official" Superman world and say "Hi" to its chief hero, let alone defeat him.

But then again, the disenfranchised had other and much older narrative modes at their disposal to crash into the fictional party uninvited, the most important of them being parody. Parody is a fictional crossover from outside of copyright, a subversive form that appropriates in an ironical fashion fictional property and uses the combination to create satirical effects of incongruence. As such, parody was the ideal mode for an unconnected comics artist without direct access to any of the popular but licensed fictional worlds to situate himself at the fringes of the collected comics imagination but close enough to provide associative leads into his own story world for his readers.

Parody was a necessary first step to get readers' attention, and almost all of the elements of the first issues have their foundation in a parodist intention. At the core of *Cerebus*' creation lies the parody of swords and sorcery stories, especially the *Conan* comics and Michael Moorcock's fictional character Elric. The full initial parodist intention is already contained, in total, in the three panels that form the first page of the first issue. In the first panel, we see a figure in silhouette ride into the city, with the caption "He came to our city in the early dawn." In the second panel, the figure's shadow casts upon a wall with two war-like characters standing before it, obviously amazed at what they see. The shadow is bigger than they are, and the caption reads: "Though later he would be called the finest warrior to enter our gates, at the time, he was but a curiosity." So far, this could be the beginning of any Conan-imitating swords and sorcery comic, until the reader looks to the third panel, where he sees the actual figure of Cerebus for the first time, with the (unnecessary) caption explaining, "he stood only five hands high." This new barbarian warrior is obviously the direct opposite of the Conan stereotype: he is exceedingly short, grey, and furry: he is in fact an aardvark. This basic incongruity is the major source of the initial parodist comedy. Sim would milk it for what it was worth during the very first issues but it must have always been apparent that it would not last long as a vehicle for transporting the series. Thus, in issues 3 and 4, Sim introduced parodies of two other characters that had become synonymous with sword and sorcery, Elric and Red Sonja, or, as they are named in *Cerebus*, Elrod and Red Sophia. With them, he could draw out the parodist stance of the series, and in addition, he considerably broadened the scope of his parody when he introduced the Cockroach in issue 11, first as a jab at the Batman, but soon enough as a stand-in for multiple superhero parodies. Especially with this character, he could have gone on to work his way through all of the major Marvel and DC superheroes until nobody was left at which to poke fun.

Nevertheless, parody has a way of growing on its creators. One of the reasons for this is parody's ambivalent relation towards its source text. Though its intention is critical, making it a statement on the source text, it is also an imitation of this source, and thus partakes in what it sets out to criticize. Parodies are always heavily "tainted" by their satirical target, and a large part of their enjoyment stems from this very ambiguity. Parodist criticism is therefore never an absolute criticism, or a negation. Both the creators and the readers of parody are usually not of the opinion that the parodied art form is completely unworthy of attention, because that would invalidate the parody as well.

Often enough, those parodies that have grown beyond their original intent have been those that were dissatisfied with the way that other artists had so far explored the potential of an emerging genre, almost unwillingly providing an example of what that genre is actually capable of. In 1605, Miguel de Cervantes, dissatisfied with the ridiculousness of so many romances about knight errantry, published the first part of his novel *Don Quixote*. What started out as a rather lighthearted and formulaic parody quickly led to the creation of a memorable literary character. This character proved so successful that it provoked a spurious continuation, which in turn lead Cervantes to publish his own second part, a masterpiece of meta-fictional irony and ingenious storytelling that turned the complete book into a world classic defining the genre of the modern novel up to this day. Something similar happened in the Eighteenth Century, when Henry Fielding was at the same time driven off the stage, where he had been hugely successful as a writer, by a new censorship law, and to despair by the success of Samuel Richardson's epistolary novel *Pamela* (1740), which Fielding regarded as highly hypocritical and structurally weak. Thus, in 1741, he published a short and vicious parody entitled *An Apology for the Life of Mrs. Shamela Andrews*, poking fun at Richardson's ethics and style of writing by imitating the epistolary form. However, Fielding did not leave it at that, and one year later published *The History of the Adventures of Joseph Andrews and of his Friend Mr. Abraham Adams*. Like *Shamela*, this text took as its starting point a parody of Richardson's novel, but now Fielding merely poked fun at the characters, devising his own way of storytelling, which he styled in the preface a "comic epic poem in prose." Reading *Joseph Andrews*, it is fascinating to see how Fielding gradually loses his parodist goal out of sight while the characters take on a life of their own, rather than as satirical shadows of another writer, and the novel develops an independent artistic merit. In the end, Fielding had developed his own and highly influential form of novel writing.

Though only time will tell about the influence and longevity of *Cerebus* within comics history, one can easily detect parallels to these examples. Like the novel at the beginning of the Seventeenth Century, and the more narrowly defined realist novel at the middle of the Eighteenth Century, comics in the late 1970s were still very much a developing art form, with the concept of the "graphic novel" not yet official. There were many artists working in the medium, but, for reasons left unstated, most were content to work within the rather narrow artistic limits established by earlier practice, economic considerations, and exterior regulations. It was easy for Sim to point at the shortcomings of contemporary comic storytelling through his parodies, and he fully met the expectations of the readers of an independent comic. One of his most important artistic achievements is that he did not give in to the easy success of parody. Reviewing the readers' comments in the first few issues, it is obvious that the parodist characters, especially Elrod, were the most popular elements of the series. Even Michael Moorcock himself congratulated Sim on Elrod in a letter in issue 6.

Parody and humor were surely good for sales, but Sim wanted more than that. Humor downplays the consequence of a fictional world, and though Sim never stopped adding humor to his narrative mix, he very soon decided not to let it neutralize the serious and even tragic potential of his stories. In a comment from 1993, he looked back at the move of the first fifty issues away from pure humor, calling it the "Woody Allen syndrome." Sim writes that when he "first brought up the idea of a 'closet issue' [issue 51] it was in an attempt to explain why there wasn't as much humor in *Cerebus* as there used to be (a subject of many letters as the years went by). I found humor easy to do and I wanted to try to address weightier topics because I found it more of a challenge as a writer. The Woody Allen syndrome" (Sim 1993).

Storytelling

The most massive and, in the final analysis, most controversial development of *Cerebus* is to be found in the story-world that Sim created for his protagonist. There are two phases in the development of the story-world. The first involves an ever-increasing expansion of scope, depth, and coherence. The second phase entails a shift in emphasis of what this world regards as important. In the first phase, Sim created his fictional universe, continually making it bigger than readers expected it to be. In the second phase he explained it, effectively narrowing down the different readings of it that were possible.

The most obvious change in regards to storytelling is the growing size of the story arcs. It is clear how fast Sim moved beyond self-contained issues. *Cerebus* started rather conventionally within the narrative confines of a parody of the sword and sorcery genre, with self-contained humorous episodes, containing all the expected elements, from sword-wielding barbarians to ugly monsters, from scantily clad women to pointy-headed sorcerers. Jokes seemed repetitive and stereotyped swords and sorcery stories would run dry even faster than the material parodied. Indeed, it took Sim only very little time until he started expanding storylines beyond single issues, though he was aware of the risk of that move.

It is one of the finer instances of meta-fictional humor (even though a letter writer later complained bitterly about it) when Sim has Lord Julius exclaim at the end of issue 17, "Start praying this is more than a two-part story!" (Sim June 1980). While in the context of the specific story, Julius merely hints at the danger he is in, it can also be read as a plea of the fictional characters to their author not to treat them as disposable elements in a merely parodist game, but to give them the room to develop into fully fledged fictional characters. Interestingly, in the next issue, Julius receives a clay pipe instead of a cigar. The pipe fits better into the fictional setting of Cerebus' world, and it is a small sign that the character started to move away from being merely an imitation of Groucho Marx and his customary trademark cigar.

One story archetype that is characteristic of serialized humorous narratives is the inevitable cycle of gain and loss. In this type of story, the protagonist will each time come up with different ways or meet with opportunities to achieve his or her goal — usually to acquire a lot of money — but before the end of the single story or issue, this goal / the money will have been lost again. Such a story archetype is especially suited for swords and sorcery stories of a humorous nature, as they are mostly concerned with travelling adventurers out to find fortune and fame. *Cerebus* was no different in this regard. However, in issue 1 he manages to get away with his pouch of gold unhindered, already the next issue has him obtaining an incredibly valuable object only to see it turn into worthless iron before he has a chance of selling it. In issue 4, he throws away the Chaos Gem; in issue 5, he abstains from becoming a religious figure that would give him great power. The two-part story in issue 6 and seven finds him hunting for a treasure in a temple, only to obliviously walk past it in the last panel. Next, he does accept to become the leader of an army, but this army becomes poisoned only an issue later, and all his dreams of conquest come to naught again. Some issues later, we can see Cerebus literally bathing in gold, only to have it snatched from him in a series of misadventures.

These stories closely conform to the archetype, playing on the tension between the tantalizing hope of a momentous narrative change — making one's fortune — and the inevitable stasis of the "back to square one" endings. Thus, the archetype usually emphasizes the unchanging nature of the protagonist, who never falters in his or her hope that someday, everything will turn to the better, though it never does. What happens in *Cerebus*, interestingly, is not that Sim discards the archetype with which the series started. On the contrary, he employs it all the way to the very end in issue 300. However, when integrated into the larger and larger story arcs, not only are the stakes continuously raised (from leader of an army to prime minister and pope) but also Sim emphasizes the toll that this takes on the characters, especially Cerebus. Instead of reinforcing the unchanging nature of the protagonist, Sim begins to highlight the character's development towards disillusionment. One only need to look at the beginning of issue 112, appropriately entitled "Square One," to see that losing everything has become serious business. Cerebus is Sisyphus as a sad man, struggling stubbornly — and increasingly humorlessly — on after he has been prophesized, in the issue previous, a death "alone, unmourned and unloved" (Sim and Gerhard June 1988). Cerebus is unable to commit suicide in issue 113, but certainly not from joy of life, becoming rather tragic in his inability to end things before the 300 promised issues are up.

This fixed goal of 300 issues was an important condition both for the series' artistic successes and for failures. The number gave enough room for *Cerebus* to evolve to the full height of its potential, but also resulted in its marring by the narrowing vision of its creator. In the beginning, though, publicly projecting the length of *Cerebus* helped set the conditions for its advancement. Indeed, the statement that *Cerebus* would have a definitive end — thereby implying the promise of narrative closure and consequence — and the number of issues that he announced, were two strokes of Sim's genius. Only the longest-running titles of the big publishing houses like *Action Comics* and *Detective Comics* had, by that time, managed to best such a number. In a time when most independent titles were successful if they made it beyond issue three, 300 issues by a single self-published artist was pure hubris. Yet it not only sent out the signal that events would happen and things change with consequence in the world of Cerebus, but that these changes and events would be monumental and epic in scope.

This announcement came in two stages. First, in issue 12, Sim wrote, "I hope to make *Cerebus* and Dave Sim synonymous and produce 156. The last of which should be dated December 2004. Stick around and see if I can do it, okay?" (Sim October 1979). This was a playful challenge, both to himself—to create 156 issues, an unprecedented number in independent publishing—and to his readers to commit to the project and thereby keep it financially possible. In issue 19, sometime after the book had switched to a monthly schedule, Sim expanded his plan, writing that two years of bi-monthly and 24 years of monthly publication would finally lead to 300 issues. The goal was set.

The increasing length of storylines and the promise of a finite, yet far-off conclusion inevitably begs the question of the coherence of *Cerebus'* story world as well as its complexity. The larger stories tended to have a bigger impact both on the characters involved and on the story world in general, which demanded a stronger regard for continuity. During the first 25 issues, Sim through his comments on the letter pages started to convey the impression that he had bigger things in mind for *Cerebus*. He notes that events readers could experience at the present would have a larger significance in the story's future development, and that all the different elements, events and characters would cohere into a structure that was much larger than could be expected presently.

It is debatable how far Sim was truthful in his pronouncements regarding the extent to which he had *Cerebus'* narrative future planned out at different stages in the writing process, but this is an ultimately futile debate. What is obvious is that Sim did not have the fictional world or the complete storyline when he set out to write *Cerebus*, and that his conception of what type of story *Cerebus* would be changed radically but gradually along the way. Hinting at bigger things to come and at his knowledge of how to explain some apparent mysteries was initially a clever way to keep readers interested beyond the pleasures of a single issue. His own comments are therefore ambivalent at best.

The earlier comments evince insecurity about the changes that *Cerebus* was going through, or even his indecision about future events. In issue 7, we can find the first of the numerous questions about Jaka's potential return. Here, Sim answers, "The jury is still out on whether Cerebus and Jaka will get back together," but also hints that Cerebus did not forget her completely (Sim February 1979). When a letter writer in issue 13 starts to wonder whether Cerebus is "some sort of Aardvarkian Age God," Sim invites all of his readers to speculate about the theological significance of his protagonist, without commenting on the claim at all (Sim December 1979). In issue 31, he would do something similar, though it seems that such major aspects of the story world are not open to debate anymore, and the "public vote" that Sim agrees to is merely about the question whether Cerebus should be rendered with visibly muscular arms, curbing his readers' hopes for enfranchisement by stating that he doesn't consider the character as in the "'public domain' category ... yet" (Sim October 1981).

However, a year earlier, Sim is not quite so self-assured, half-jokingly suggesting in the notes to the letters page of issue 19 that all those readers who do not care for longer storylines with interdependent issues need only ignore pages one, two and twenty: "Voilá, self-contained unit." In one of his later introductions, he commented on the fact that at that time, he did not yet "see the book in terms of being one very long continuity.... Many was the time I would be tempted to go ahead with a bit of funny business that contradicted the major continuity I was forming in my head. I appreciate the effort more in retrospect than I did at the time and I'm often surprised at some slightly twisted turn of phrase that hints at concepts I've begun to develop more fully in the last year or so" (Sim 1982c).

With issue 20 and the surrounding issues it became more and more obvious that *Cerebus* was straying from the received serialized mode of comic book storytelling, and Sim's self-confidence as an artist grew considerably. In an answer to a letter in issue 23, Sim singles out as his most important accomplishment so far "introducing the idea of coherent plots to comic book humor" (Sim December 1980). From then on, comments that hinted at Sim's long-scale plans such as this one from issue 30 became common: "There are uses for an aardvark that Cerebus doesn't have any idea about. Fortunately, I know most of them" (Sim September 1981). Even then, he had not yet fully determined how to convey his bigger plans to his readers. In issue 31, he answers a very long letter speculating about the significance of some events: "To be quite frank, I am torn on the one hand between telling everything in a kind of monumental sixty-page-three-issue-crash-semester-of-Estarcion-501, that would keep the Continuity Wolves at bay and probably plummet sales, and my author's instinct which says that as long as you're all drooling out there, I must be doing something right" (Sim October 1981).

By issue 51, Sim has long lost his insecurity about the direction that *Cerebus* is taking, stating categorically in the letters section that he would not adjust the story arc to "pacify critics" who would like a return to the earlier character of Cerebus (Sim June 1984). There was no turning back anymore; *Cerebus* had changed for good, even though that meant alienating some of the original fans. This willingness to risk a disappointment of readers' expectations made Sim an innovator of comics, though it is arguable that in the second half of the project's creation, stubbornness outweighed originality. By then, Sim had long since made comics history.

NOTES

1. The term "Cerebus effect" was first coined by Bart Beaty in his article "*Pickle, Poot*, and the Cerebus Effect." Beaty was referring mainly to the phenomenon that sales of the series dropped while at the same time those of the collected volumes rose. There was at least one use of the term in the sense of this essay on the internet, but its source is not available anymore. The website *TVTropes* mentions what they call the "Cerebus Syndrome" as the gradual shift of a serialized narrative from comedy to more serious drama (see http://tinyurl.com/7lb122).

Audacious Tenacity, Tenacious Audacity: *Cerebus*' Grand (and Changing) Narrative Strategies
Eric Hoffman

> It was not the Truth. It was not truth. It most especially was not reality.—Viktor Davis

As a result of the length of its composition, and its being composed by a single artist who maintained complete artistic control over its content (by virtue of its being self-published) in serialized, mostly monthly installments over a 26-year period (an entirely unique storytelling apparatus for any medium), *Cerebus* remains a compelling experiment in narrative stability and sustainability. The significant changes in tone and subject matter it underwent during its run challenge its cohesiveness. Yet what is perhaps most fascinating about Sim and Gerhard's achievement is that, apart from these changes, *Cerebus* retains coherence *because* of Sim's readiness to revise earlier developments resulting from his radically shifting authorial interests and perspective.

Sim's story sometimes faltered when he tried to fit it with his shifting belief systems and interests (most controversially with his critique of feminism beginning in 1990 and his finding religion in 1996), or succumbed to the temptation to interpret later events in light of these developments. Still, Sim's narrative structure in *Cerebus*, despite its radical modifications, most notoriously when incorporating his controversial views on gender and religion in the latter half of the series, remains surprisingly resistant to the usual inconsistencies of other serialized stories.

Douglas Wolk, in his penetrating essay on Sim and *Cerebus* in *Reading Comics*, notices this remarkable quality of narrative symmetry. He notes how

> the formal symmetries and echoes within *Cerebus* are spectacular, especially given that every chapter has gone unrevised since its initial publication. It is possible to divide the series into three units, each roughly two thousand pages long and culminating in a failed ascension into Heaven. Alternately, it can be split into a "male half" and a "female half" (everything we believe is true in the first half is inverted in the second) or on a sort of angle into a "Cerebus half" and an "Astoria half" ... almost from the beginning, it's loaded with resonances and symbol systems and setups—the final few scenes abruptly detonate thematic explosions whose groundwork had been laid decades in advance [Wolk 2007, 295].[1]

Formal symmetries abound indeed. Among the more obvious are the many "talking heads" episodes (wherein characters engage in lengthy conversation with one another). In addition, there are the love triangles/quadrangles (often accompanied by a literary figure, of which society is largely apathetic or antagonistic, for instance Oscar, Viktor Reid, Viktor Davis, F. Stop Kennedy and Ham Earnestway). There are also the numerous Ascensions, each one leading to a higher level of "reality" (in quotes because in *Cerebus* reality is never entirely certain). Finally, there is the use of text as a counterpoint/challenge to the authority of the comic book image (and vice-versa) in *Jaka's Story*, *Women*, *Reads*, *Rick's Story*, *Going Home* and *Latter Days*; the Terim/Tarim and YHWH/God dichotomies. And so on.[2]

In a comment in the June 1997 "Aardvark Comment" letters column, Sim writes that the "300 issues [of *Cerebus*] exist and have always existed in specific form. The story has always ended the same way" (Sim and Gerhard June 1997). See also his comment in a 2004 letter to Dan Morris: "*Cerebus* progressed pretty much along the path that I intended for it. The emphasis changed on *Latter Days* when I realized I was discussing more serious issues at greater depth.... But yes, everything came out about the way that I hoped it would" (Sim 2005, 306). Despite Sim's intentional (and often strikingly subtle) echoes, this remains a startling claim, particularly for any long-time reader of the series. It is, rather, largely self-mythology and, indeed, Sim's desire to re-envision his work as a single, coherent story ironically diminishes his accomplishment. In fact, given the inorganic structural demands (a monthly twenty-page comic book, and all the formal symmetries *that* demands, based on panels with word balloons, and so forth) and organic interests of its author, *Cerebus'* coherence, often in spite of Sim's intentions, is nothing short of astonishing.

In his 1983 *Comics Journal* interview with Kim Thompson, Sim provides an earlier and more accurate description of the process of writing and drawing *Cerebus*. There, Sim explains that, having established a 300-issue structure to his monthly comic *Cerebus*, "a framework [began] to emerge, but the actual framework that you can see is only what you've got done so far" (Thompson August 1983, 60). Sim relates to Thompson how in the spring of 1979, the idea to do an extended storyline first came to him following a nervous breakdown, the result of "doing too much acid" (ibid.). In a July 2005 interview for the website *Coville's Clubhouse*, Sim explains that he decided to do 300 issues initially because of the flood of "thoughts and experiences that I had had over the period of the false transcendent state [of an LSD trip] ... [I] began to work towards putting them all down on paper in the *Cerebus* storyline. When I realized, a month or two later, how large and difficult a task that was going to be, I decided to make *Cerebus* into a 300 issue project in order to encompass it all.... The documentation of this state itself went from about issue 20 [the first "Mind Games" issue] to about issue 186 [the issue that includes the now-infamous essay]" (Coville July 2005).[3] Importantly, Sim also decided to dedicate himself wholly to *Cerebus* and to stop pretending that "next month I'm going to ... do something else."[4]

Sim tells Grant that he only reached the point of wondering how it is that one writes 300 issues "around the time that *High Society* first started evolving" (Grant 1993, 81). Because of this 26-year long canvas stretched out before him, Sim decided that he wanted "to do a very long story," which he considered a "radical idea, so contrary to how the market worked." As Domsch notes above, issue 20 of *Cerebus*, "Mind Games," was a watershed in the series, not just stylistically (it was the first of many visual experiments; each page when combined with the others forms a large portrait of Cerebus—an idea Sim borrowed from an issue of Neal Adams' *Deadman*), but also with regards to narrative (figure 21). It is the first of many

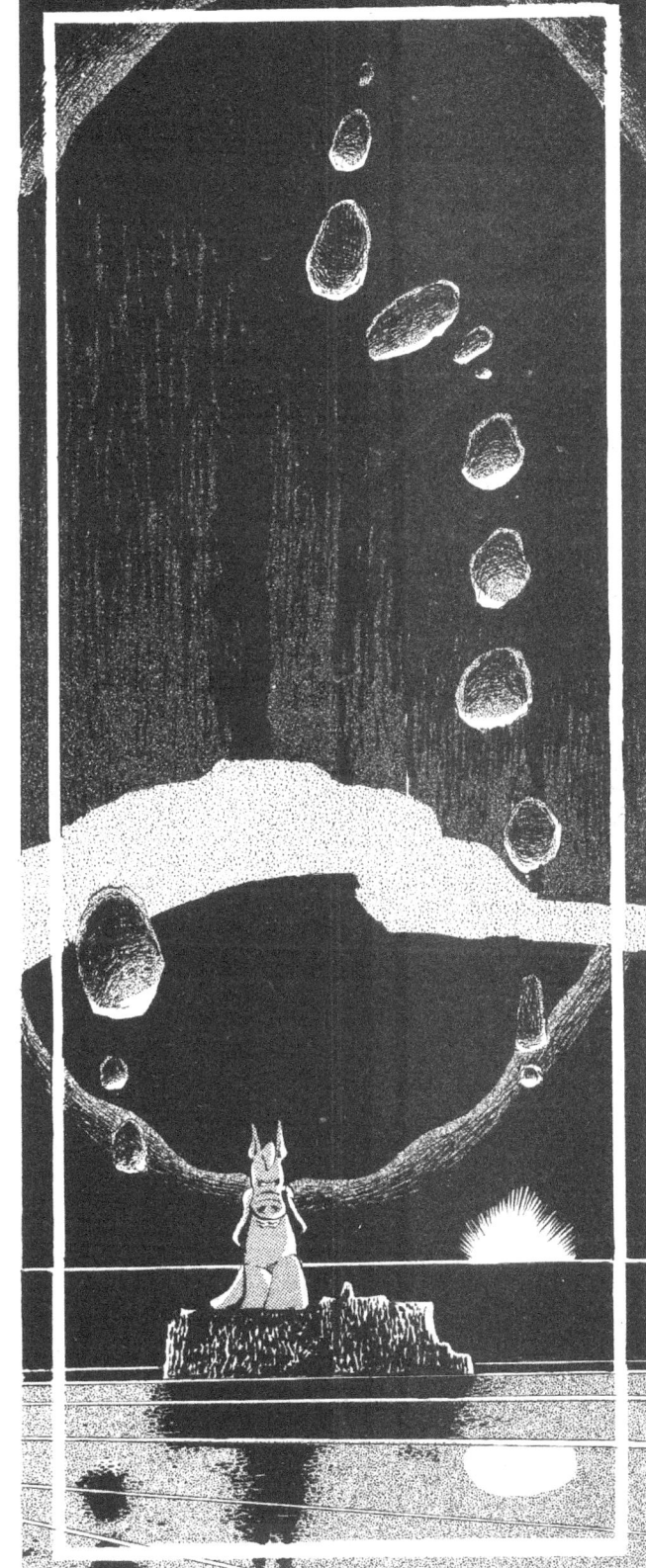

Figure 21. The mythology of *Cerebus* deepens as Cerebus explores the "Seventh Sphere." From *Cerebus* issue 28, July 1981 (© 1981 Dave Sim).

issues whose primary dramatic action is that of conversation, and it first introduces the matriarchal fascists the Cirinists and the Illusionists, of whom Suenteus Po is representative.

At the time of his decision to commit to *Cerebus* for 300 issues, Sim's foremost concern, he tells Thompson, was his ability to tell, in Sim's words, "a coherent story" with a "consistent viewpoint" (Thompson August 1983, 60). Indeed, the decision to begin telling longer stories within *Cerebus*, Sim confesses, did not occur to him until he was faced with this "enormous structure," as well as a monthly publishing schedule, as Sim worried that readers would not have the patience to wait sixty days for the story's continuation (ibid.). Shortly after establishing a monthly schedule, Sim composed *Cerebus*' first extended sequence, the three-issue "Palnu Trilogy," appearing in issues 14, 15 and 16. A seventy-one-page story, the trilogy introduces several major characters (notably Lord Julius and President Weisshaupt) and a number of themes further explored in *High Society, Church & State* and *Jaka's Story*. Sim later remarked that when he wrote the three Palnu issues he "tended not to see [*Cerebus*] in terms of very long continuity, [though he was often] tempted to go ahead with a bit of funny business that contradicted the major continuity I was forming in my head" (Sim June 16, 1989). Sim told interviewer A. Pearson in 1993 that even when fashioning the longer story arcs, such as the one thousand page *Mothers & Daughters*, he still allowed for a degree of spontaneity, if only to keep the comic interesting to himself and, by extension, to others. Sim maintained "flexibility" structurally (for example, by expanding a two-page sequence to four pages) and certain aspects of the comic, such as the character of The Roach, were improvisatory from start to finish (Pearson November 1993, 20).

Following the trilogy's completion, continues Sim,

> and having moved towards the development of a major war in issues 17, 18, 19 and 20, I was feeling the urge to do something — well — structural with the story. I had been developing the idea, albeit gradually, since issue 5 that Cerebus existed as an unwitting, but key, figure in a number of wide-ranging conspiracies and as a nexus point for a number of disparate belief systems [Sim August 25, 1989].[5]

Eager to leave behind the swords and sorcery format, and interested in pursuing storylines dealing with the political machinations of the imaginary world of Estarcion, Sim remarks in response to a letter in his "Aardvark Comment" letter column that "Cerebus is getting a little old for going into battle" (Sim January 1981). One subject of great interest to Sim was politics, and his decision to incorporate political satire into the comic was crucial in maintaining his interest in the comic once he grew tired of swords and sorcery. Writing in issue 26's "Aardvark Comment," Sim notes that it was the popularity of the character of Lord Julius, together with a "revised interest on my part in charting more of what transpires in the bizarre city of Palnu" that contributed to his decision to leave behind the swords and sorcery setting and to focus more on the "great social upheaval" taking place in Estarcion, in particular the "rise of [a] merchant class [that] is making all these chaps with big armies something of the past" (Sim March 1981). What Sim's essay-length response makes clear is that his vision for *Cerebus* in general is remarkably clear, even if the finer details are yet unknown:

> Above all, I would ask [readers] to remember that Cerebus himself is trying to adapt to a world not only *he* never made [a reference to the tag line from *Howard the Duck*—"trapped in a world he never made"]—but one that very few individuals have managed to adapt to gracefully. His simple pursuit of money, physical comfort and frivolous pastimes is becoming something of an albatross in the thriving new capitalism — it becomes too easy for him to achieve his goals.... Whether Cerebus molds the environment to suit his needs or whether society manages to change Cerebus is what I'll be exploring for the 274 issues [ibid.].

The decision to do even longer stories, Sim explains, was also the result of not wanting to "end up in the year 2004 with 100 60-page stories" as well as the "political situation of the time," namely other self-published titles like Richard and Wendy Pini's *Elfquest* and Jack Katz's *First Kingdom*, attempting fifteen and twenty issue story arcs. These factors, coupled with Sim's strict definition of what constitutes a graphic novel, also contributed to his decision to do much longer self-contained storylines. "I focused on the term and what novel means to me when someone says 'novel'" (Spurgeon February 1996, 81).

In his later contribution to the Massachusetts Institute of Technology Press anthology *Third Person: Authoring Vast Narratives*, Sim explains that applying this standard to other comic books then being marketed as "graphic novels" (as, for example, Will Eisner's *A Contract with God*, which, Sim claims, he can read in about "twenty to thirty minutes"), makes a "two-hundred page graphic novel ... the equivalent of a twenty-page short story" (Sim 2009, 42).[6] In an interview with Spurgeon, Sim comments that "reading something called a 'novel' in a short amount of time somehow makes the form seem a bit illegitimate" (Spurgeon February 1996, 77). Claiming graphic novels to be more than they actually are overstates their cultural legitimacy, falsely claiming that they have met the criteria of another art form when in fact they have not. Sim expands on this definition in a 1996 interview with Tom Palmer, Jr. Looking back over the five major story arcs completed since the Thompson interview, Sim admits that the idea to do a graphic novel of true novelistic proportions came to him only gradually. "The more I labored to get the kind of structure and characterization that you get in a really good novel into *Cerebus*, the more I started to see what else I wanted to cover in the series," he tells Palmer, Jr. (Palmer, Jr. 1996, 60).

Sim at first believed that this broad, 500-page canvas would allow him to "tell the story of the world," only to find that, having completed *High Society*, he managed to finish roughly half the story he had hoped to tell. This, Sim explains, "established for me the limit of what could be conveyed in five hundred comic book pages" (Sim 2009, 42). It also helped to establish for Sim the importance of *duration* in comics; if he was to tell a story that realistically conveys the passage of time[7] as opposed to the standard comic book fare of isolated stories with a non-linear passage of time (which is to say, it maintains its relevance by remaining current; fashion and technology changes while the character doesn't age or, what is more likely, grows *younger*), then he would have to allocate more pages to a story than he had previously done.[8] As a result, the sequel to *High Society*, *Church & State*, was over twice as long. Sim had originally "allocated a thousand pages to the other half of the story I tried to tell in [*High Society*], and I managed to get it all in about twelve hundred pages, so that gave me a clearer idea of how much story I could communicate." In writing *Church & State*, Sim "had to get over the disappointment of how little you could get into a 500-page comic-book story" (ibid.). Initially, Sim had pictured doing the equivalent of Tolstoy's *War and Peace*, an extended exploration of both the political *and* religious aspects of the city-state Iest. "By the time I had figured out how many pages I needed to do an election campaign, election night, the deciding vote and then six issues of Cerebus as Prime Minister," Sim writes,

> the book was over and I never got to the religious side. That's why I doubled the length for *Church & State* ... I'd be able to visit different parts of the city, introduce "reads" and anecdotes of various figures that I had introduced. It still ate up pages like nobody's business. So I learned to mentally scale back the book that I planned up ahead, learned to realistically assess

what I could get across in two hundred pages without having to rush everything. My best assessment now is that I hope I was able to produce over the 6000 pages the comic-book equivalent of one Russian novel, as opposed to the twelve Russian novels I originally intended [Sim 2009, 152].

Following the conclusion of *Church & State*, Sim continues,

> I switched from my ambition of wanting to tell a series of Russian-style novels in comic book form to trying to write one Russian-style novel over the course of 6,000 pages. What I decided was that you have to do ten comic book pages to communicate what you can communicate in one page of a Russian novel [ibid.].

The organization of a 6,000-page graphic novel, according to Sim, is roughly approximate to the organization of a 600-page prose novel. First, Sim tells Palmer, Jr., "you sketch out the overall parameters, touchstone moments, plot the outline, characters, themes and narrative tones, and then having macro-managed the overall project; you begin to micro-manage the parts" (Palmer, Jr. 1996, 43). In his interview with Charles Brownstein, Sim notes that a novel's length largely determines the number of "major points" that novel will address (Brownstein Winter 1997a, 13). The place within the larger structure of the series largely determines the shape of each individual issue; it must move forward what came before it and set up the following issue. Similarly, each issue itself has specific points Sim must address. In a 1985 interview with Heidi McDonald, Sim provides additional description of *Cerebus*' narrative structure:

> It's very odd, because I know where it fits and I know that just by having somebody say this to somebody else, that that implies this has to come up again later on. Largely, that's the way I have done it. I know the touchstone points, or the key points to this storyline that are coming up, and then it's matter of fleshing out what's there and hooking it up as it becomes part of it [McDonald July 1985, 145].

Using the example of issues 37 to 43 of *Cerebus*, Sim notes how these issues concentrate on Cerebus' campaign trail, while issue 43 is devoted entirely to election night. When writing the campaign trail issues, Sim explains that when he had a good idea for election night, he made notes on that idea to return to later. Individual scenes might take one or two pages, depending on the momentum of the scene, and so on. After Cerebus' election as prime minister (largely influenced by Theodore White's *The Making of a President*, a chronicle of the 1960 presidential campaign of John F. Kennedy), Sim decided to do a satire of Richard Nixon's *My Six Crises*, and by the time he reached the issues that make up the beginning of *Church & State*, "things [had gotten] easier" for him. By the middle of *Church & State*, he explains, "I had a pretty good idea the next one would be a love story: *Jaka's Story*.... So that means I had two and a half years to get the rough shape of *Jaka's Story* straight in my mind," which, for Sim, was like "living in the lap of literary luxury" (ibid., 43).

It appears Sim came up with an ending to *Cerebus* roughly around the conclusion of *Church & State* (which, ending properly at issue 111, roughly marks the conclusion of the first third of the series' run). Cerebus, ensconced on the moon following the first of several failed Ascensions (arguably three in total, marking roughly the 100th, 200th and 300th issues, the importance of which is discussed below), is told by the Judge (known to fans as "George," one of his many names, an omniscient, God-like character loosely based on Lou Jacobi's Judge from Jules Feiffer's play, *Little Murders*) that he will die "alone, unmourned and unloved" (figure 22).

Figure 22. The Judge proclaims Cerebus' destiny. From *Cerebus* issue 111, June 1988 (© 1988 Dave Sim and Gerhard).

Around the same time Sim asserted Cerebus' mortality, he came to view *Cerebus* as a story of a life. Sim in his "Note from the President," from *Cerebus Zero* notes from the vantage point of having completed roughly half of the series that

> put as simply as possible, *Cerebus* is my attempt to document a life for 26 years and 300 issues. *Cerebus* began in December 1977 and concludes in March 2004 at issue 300, with the death of the title character. It is my attempt to by-pass one of the major faults of comic books (and strips, for that matter); the fact that the characters never age or change and that most attempts at change can be summed up as gimmicks and temporary modifications introduced for the purpose of boosting sales. Sometimes the *Cerebus* story line is funny. Sometimes it is sad. Sometimes it crawls along month to month with very little happening and sometimes it flies by at breathtaking speed with everything happening at once. I create the book consciously this way because that this is the way I see life; my life and the lives of those people that I know. In some story lines, Cerebus is a central figure and a driving force behind the events taking place. At other times, he is a secondary figure, observing rather than participating. Again, this is very much like my own life and the lives I see around me [Sim 1993].

As a result, Sim sought to achieve as much verisimilitude with what he perceived real life to be, that characters age naturally, that people and events slip in and out of their lives sometimes without logic or reason, and that people are alternately active or passive participants in their own destiny.[9] The comic medium, he felt, in both its ongoing, discrete monthly format and its visual composition is well suited to realistically portraying lived experience, as, for example, when Cerebus becomes a supporting role in *Jaka's Story* and *Melmoth*. This is because, as Sim explains to Spurgeon,

> there are times in anyone's life where you suddenly have an overall sense that you're starring in your own life.... And there are other times when it seems through a series of decisions ... you're bounced like a ball out of whatever context it was and you're watching rather than participating ... since what I am doing in *Cerebus* is trying to do a life, I try to emphasize that. To do that actively through the advantages of the medium of comics, where a character can be in the background and perfectly visible while the primary action is going on somewhere else, the major decisions are being made somewhere else [Spurgeon February 1996, 78].

Moreover, the length of the story allowed Sim to probe deeper into his characters' lives than most other comics. With Cerebus, he could accurately portray changes in characters "at a glacial pace" (ibid., 79). His decision to place Cerebus in a near-catatonic state in *Melmoth* was in part autobiographical yet also results from a desire to have the story arc that occupies the middle of the entire *Cerebus* story act as a kind of allegory for "the ending up ahead" (ibid., 97). Sim tells Spurgeon that because he "was coming up to the halfway point, and really trying to get across 'This is a life,' I'm trying to do a life, and all the things that go into it. And here's a death [both the actual death of Sebastian Melmoth and the symbolic 'death' of Cerebus] to prove my point" (ibid.). Sim readily admits in "Aardvark Comment" in *Cerebus* 125 that he decided to do *Melmoth* only after researching Oscar Wilde for the character of Oscar in *Jaka's Story* (Sim and Gerhard, August 1989) deciding that Oscar's fate, essentially rendered as a punch line in *Jaka's Story*, was too abrupt, particularly after all the research Sim had done in order to fashion the character (Spurgeon February 1996, 96).

Neither Sim's announcement of Cerebus' impending mortality, nor his distinctly literary meditation on death, should be construed as a marketing gimmick, as with DC's puerile 1988–1989 *Batman: A Death in the Family* (in which the decision to kill off the Jason Todd incarnation of Batman's sidekick Robin was accomplished via a 900 number), or the 1992 *Death of Superman* storyline. As early as the 1983 *Comics Journal* interview, Sim voiced his disinterest in pursuing storylines or gimmicks that capitalize on fan interest to the detriment of a realistic "document of a life," something Sim seems genuinely surprised to have been the first in the comic book medium to attempt. "I started thinking," he tells Thompson, "what a horribly futile thing that *Superman* was up around issue #250 ... and it wasn't 250 issues of one story. It's an immense, complicated, self-contradictory mythos, blended by five or six individuals primarily, with a lot of other individuals who had no real interest in manufacturing it or adding to it" (Thompson August 1983, 60). In his 1993 interview with Paul M. Grant, Sim claimed to have kept secret the idea to do the very long story "until I was a substantial way through it," in part because he was fearful of how such a radical concept might be accepted by an audience still clamoring for more "Cerebus the Barbarian" stories (Grant 81).

At the time Sim began to consider *Cerebus* a "story of a life," he became increasingly concerned with truth. The most obvious example of this search is his characters' periodic Ascensions. The Ascensions, Sim explains to Spurgeon, are symbolic of Sim's own attempt "through the act of creativity to try and understand and ... develop some level of understanding of what is that big thing up there: the cosmic muffin, God, the Life Force, whatever you want to call it ... that's what I was dealing with in the climax of *Church & State* and *Mothers & Daughters*" (Spurgeon February 1996, 71). Cerebus, on the other hand, distracted at varying times by power, greed, and sex, is uninterested in his creator's search for truth and has little use for it, until too late. If by extrapolation we conjecture that Cerebus the character is to some extent Sim's alter ego, then Cerebus' inability to grasp this truth can be interpreted as a lengthy exercise in self-flagellation, or an example of a creator punishing his creation for his own stupidity.[10]

Sim's own late acknowledgment of his concern for finding the truth (of which his various tracts on anti-feminism, politics and religion are a record) becomes a post-facto explanation for the radical transformation in tone and substance from early to late *Cerebus*, from the relatively self-contained, mock–*Conan* issues which gradually morphed into the political and religious satires of *High Society* and *Church & State* storylines, which in turn transitioned to the domestic dramas of *Jaka's Story* and *Melmoth*, leading the comic headlong into the admittedly overly-expository cul-de-sac of anti-feminism and religious exegesis.

In a 2004 letter to reader David Bird, written in the months following Sim and Gerhard's completion of the series, Sim acknowledges these sometimes abrupt and jarring shifts because of his implementation of an elastically organic structure that allowed him to replace one truth with another (Sim 2005, 526). Sim tells Bird that his compositional method was to "supersede the previous reality with a new reality when a new reality presented itself to me," a technique he claims to have used "all along" (ibid.).[11] In an interview with Craig Miller, Sim claims that he in fact "anticipated" the inevitable changes he would undergo while writing a comic book over such a long time and therefore

> would jettison anything that wasn't working as soon as I found something preferable to it, always trying to find more accurate metaphors for what I saw as reality on the assumption that I would end up closer to the truth at the end then I had been at the beginning. That is, I actively set out to undercut — or rather, supersede — the early portions as I went along. Suenteus Po playing chess seemed a more accurate reality than the Judge just observing everything on the moon [Miller and Thorne July 2004a, 6].

Probably the most notorious of Sim's "new realities" came during the epic *Mothers & Daughters* story arc, the densest and mythologically richest of *Cerebus'* storylines. Its four books are concerned with the rise of the Cirinists, led by Cirin, a brutal collectivist and agrarian totalitarian group of "mothers" and their political challengers, the Kevillists, led by Astoria, comprised of "daughters," anarcho-feminists who believe in the woman's right to abortion, a rough approximation Sim's view of modern feminists. Here, Sim's critique of feminism takes center stage, and becomes the most pervasive example of truth searching in *Cerebus*. Sim specifically ties this theme of reality versus illusion to his attack on feminism in a 2004 letter to Dan Morris:

> If you're looking for Truth, which I was, your central theme is going to be reality versus illusion. The destruction of the latter in the interests of arriving at the former. I don't think it takes precedence over feminism and the "battle of the sexes," but is rather implicit there as elsewhere. Is feminism reality or illusion? [Sim 2005, 403].

In the introduction to *Flight*, the first book, Sim claims to have developed the "original germ" for *Mothers & Daughters* in 1979, "when I first conceived of *Cerebus* as a 300 issue series" (Sim and Gerhard 1993). Sim knew this storyline needed to touch upon specific plot points, specifically: the reversal of the light-void gender identifications from *Church & State*, and placing this reversal at a certain point (three-fourths of the way through the story arc) in *Mothers & Daughters* in order to echo the place this revelation holds in the earlier work (Brownstein Winter 1997a, 17). Sim divided the book into four chapters so as to reflect the four story arcs that preceded it (*High Society, Church & State, Jaka's Story* and *Melmoth*). *Mothers & Daughters* also acted as a means of tying together disparate gaps within the previous narrative, reconciling them to Sim's better-understood sense of its trajectory, particularly from *High Society* forward. This involved several instances of reversals of previous held beliefs, especially regarding Sim's earlier, less critical views of feminism. Writing in the introduction to the *Women* phonebook, the second book in the series, Sim notes that he is "edging closer and closer to the core of the storyline" and that book three (*Reads*) and four (*Minds*) "will come as close as anything I have written to explaining reality as I see it" (Sim and Gerhard 1994). This "reality" specifically had to do with his growing isolation because of his anti-feminism, as this isolation, he writes, is "central to who I am and ... so critical to whatever progress I have made as an artist, writer, and publisher" (ibid.).

Reads, Sim tells Brownstein, is "mathematical" in its structure, as only 25 issues of the formal storyline remained (Brownstein Winter 1997a, 20). Because Sim had planned the structure of the arc in advance, allotting a certain number of pages to text and a certain amount to imagery, he put "more energy ... into the content" (ibid.), particularly the Viktor Davis section of the text. In issue 186, the conclusion of *Reads*, Sim mirrors "the war between reality and illusion" with Cirin and Cerebus' "bloody hand-to-hand combat" (Sim 2005, 404). The issue is comprised almost entirely of a Norman Mailer-inspired third person, self-referential essay written by the "character" Viktor Davis (the essay appears to take place in our world, the real world, wholly *apart from* the world in which *Cerebus* takes place — Sim's middle name is Victor). In it, Davis describes his vision of a "Marxist-feminist" totalitarianism that had seized control of Western democracies, and there is, in effect, a war going on between genders, wherein the "Female Void" is draining its counterpart, the "Male Light" of its innate power and creative energy. This worldview effectively undermines the legitimacy of the worldview in which *Cerebus* takes place, especially the Judge's earlier claims to Cerebus concerning a Male Void threatening to consume the Female Light, which, one assumes, was the worldview the pre-anti-feminist Sim held. Sim tells Spurgeon that *Mothers & Daughters* is the "mirror image" of *Church & State* in that regard, his re-working of the gender identities of the light and void being the most radical example of Sim's talent for allowing the story enough malleability to incorporate the radically shifting beliefs of its author (Spurgeon December 1996, 70).[12]

The reversal of the male/female paradigm in the Judge's creation myth happens in the body of Viktor Davis' essay, which quotes Alan Moore's dictum "All stories are true" several times. Because the stories told by Sim's characters, whether it be The Judge or Viktor Davis, Jaka or Oscar, Cirin or Serna, are in competition with one another, Sim, in quoting Moore (who in saying all stories are true suggests that stories possess their own reality and help shape our world), suggests that each interpretation is equally valid and it is up to the reader to decide. According to David Groenewegen below, this technique is present in Sim's competing and contradictory stories of individual characters within the work, each one a claim to truth. For example, writes Groenewegen, the Judge's "biography of Suenteus Po is later denied by Po himself, at the same time when the Judge's very existence is being questioned" (Groenewegen October/November 2004, 118).

Such ambiguity allows Sim the opportunity to radically contradict (or willfully subvert) stories while in no way compromising the integrity of *Cerebus* as a whole. Characters act as mouthpieces for Sim's best estimation of Truth, and because *Cerebus* is largely about the inherent unreliability of these truths, when Sim changes his mind it doesn't impact the cohesiveness of the narrative structure as it would in a work where only one story is true. "I tend to see that as the nature of reality as well," Sim told Tom Spurgeon in his 1996 interview. "Okay, here this guy comes along. And yeah, we all believe in him. He's got the answer. All it takes is ten years and hanging back and waiting for the tell-all books to come out from the people who were in proximity or what not, and you find out that person wasn't at all who you thought they were" (Spurgeon February 1996, 91). Writing Dan Morris, Sim states, "Suenteus Po reflected much of my own best thinking on various subjects at the time.... He was my mouthpiece ... as the Judge had been before him and as Rick-as-prophet would be after him. The reader is free to see each viewpoint as superseding the previous viewpoint—as I intended—or adhere to whichever viewpoint seems wisest" (Sim 2005, 403).

Textual evidence of this method is found nearly everywhere in *Cerebus*: from Oscar's biography of Jaka which she claims entirely misunderstands her, to Rick's composition of the *Booke of Ricke,* itself a comment on how supposedly sacred texts are largely compromised by the agendas and fallibilities of their all-too-human authors. Sim, Groenewegen observes, "often stated that he never re-read his own work during its production precisely because he wanted to use an imperfect memory to demonstrate the way that real life works" (Groenewegen October/November 2004, 119). Characters' claims for truth are therefore compromised by their author's intentional misrepresentation of them, as in his portrayal of his comic alter ego "Dave," introduced near the conclusion of *Mothers & Daughters* in a sadly ironic attempt to bridge the gap between the real world and the world of *Cerebus* (sadly ironic because it destroys the elaborate textual verisimilitude Sim worked so tirelessly to create).[13] "Dave" explains to Cerebus that the Judge was rather a fake Judge (as were Death and the Regency Elf, two other mystical beings) and that he had it the wrong way around. "Dave's appearance," writes Groenewegen, shows Cerebus that "memory is fallible," an entirely appropriate lesson to be learned by the alter ego of an author who admitted to not re-reading his own work in order to more accurately capture the inherent inaccuracy of memory, that "everyone has an agenda" (ibid., 119–120), even Sim. This intentional ambiguity plays the double role of supporting the ongoing theme of Truth in Cerebus at the same time neatly covering up any plot inconsistencies that may have developed over its 26-year run. (This ambiguity led some hopefuls to believe that Sim's essay wasn't representative of Sim's thoughts about feminism but was rather Swiftian satire — later essays and the acidic tone of Sim's portrayal of women in coming issues would gradually disabuse readers of this possibility.) Sim came under fire for his use of anecdotal evidence, yet he insists its use was purposeful: "It was unbalanced just as feminist 'philosophy' is unbalanced, it was anecdotal just as feminist 'evidence' is anecdotal, it was biased just as feminist 'theories' are biased" (Brownstein Winter 1997a, 20).

Sim suggests in the introduction to the *Reads* phonebook that readers bothered by his conclusions "find [their] own summit. Weave the elements presented into something that has meaning for you. Tell your own story.... Paint yourself your own Big Picture of What It All Means" (Sim and Gerhard 1995). In a 1996 interview, Sim remarks to Sandy Atwal, "Is 186 true? Don't know if it's true or not but it makes a good story ... I think there's a case to be made that Storytellers were probably the genesis point for a lot of religions" (Atwal 84).

One year later, the then atheist Sim was exploring this very idea of storytellers as the genesis of religion in *Rick's Story*, which concerns a delusional religion Jaka's ex-husband Rick develops around Cerebus. While researching the 1611 King James Bible for this story arc, Sim became a believer, and, as a result, the subsequent exploration of religion in *Latter Days* straddles an uneasy mix of religious reverence and irreverence as Sim alternately lightheartedly lampoons and sincerely investigates religious practices and beliefs.

Importantly, in *Latter Days* Sim would again reverse gender designations for the Light/Void paradigm in the creation myth of the double-issue 289 and 290. Here, the Light is female and the Void male, yet this time the Light is a threat to the Void. Thus, Sim restores the gender designations of his *Church & State* creation myth without compromising the relationship wherein the female is an all-consuming, vampiric and destructive force, in keeping with Sim's view of women as secondary beings. They are inadequate, deceptive and largely dependent on their primary masculine counterparts.

Moreover, the periodic Ascensions (one roughly every 100 issues) undertaken by certain characters (Cerebus in the first instance, Cerebus and Cirin in the second) are also indicative of narrative malleability. Cirin seeks the Supreme Being Terim's (like herself, a matriarch) approval/acceptance as justification of her own fascistic aims; she believes all previous attempts at Ascensions have failed because in every case the ascendant was a male. Cerebus' Ascension, on the other hand, fails (not solely based on his gender, as it is later revealed that he is a hermaphrodite[14]) because his aims are rather worldlier than Cirin's. What Cerebus seeks above all is power (be it political, religious or sexual power, as in his problematic relationship with Jaka). Occasionally, this quest for power sublimates his various desires (in the early, barbarian stories, by ale or jewelry).

In issue 5 (August 1978), Cerebus is able to resist the temptation to rule the Pigts, an underground cult that has built up its belief system around the belief that an "Earth Pig" will eventually lead them to victory over what they consider their rightful turf. (Sim would later refashion the Pigts as a prophetic bunch who foresaw Cerebus' rise to power as pope, one of Sim's many re-incorporations of originally disconnected themes and ideas from the original barbarian stories in *Mothers & Daughters*.) Soon, however, ale and money are not enough for Cerebus. Once installed as Prime Minister, Cerebus becomes drunk with power, even moreso when made pope.

Cerebus' failure is a failure of self-awareness; Cerebus is too power-mad to complete his Ascension. He reaches the Moon, where he has a long discussion with the Judge. Pointedly, Sim considers this one of the series' key moments, as it reveals Cerebus' eventual fate.

What Sim does *not* reveal is whether Cerebus' subsequent Ascension represents a failure for either Cirin or Cerebus, or both. Midway through the Ascension, Cirin and Cerebus part ways, and as Cirin disappears slowly into the distance, she proclaims her victorious union with Terim. As a result, Sim gives Cirin her long awaited (though unseen and self-proclaimed) encounter with Terim. From her perspective she has clearly succeeded at her Ascension; subsequently the justification for her totalitarian regime on Earth is advocated writ large. This leaves Cerebus to his lengthy dialogue with "Dave," who describes himself as Cerebus' "creator."[15] At first, "Dave" appears to Cerebus only as a disembodied voice; he is, in fact, a thought balloon, making it ambiguous whether "Dave" is real or just hallucination.[16] From Cerebus' perspective, armed with the knowledge that he is a created being (though not specifically occupying the space of a comic book — that realization is saved for the readers of *Cerebus* — as such it's a largely unnecessary realization), Cirin's Ascension becomes nothing more than an illusion, as presciently predicted by the largely indifferent Illusionist Suenteus Po in his meeting with Cerebus and Cirin just prior to their leaving Earth. Cerebus has met his maker, literally, and it makes little difference to him. Sim the author must find this unforgivable, judging by the remaining 100 issues, quite possibly literature's longest and most uncomfortable thrashings. According to Sim, prior to his conversation the only plot points he had hoped to address were Cerebus returning to his favorite tavern at the Wall of Tsi, the return of Rick, and the establishment of the Cerebite religion (Miller and Thorne July 2004a, 5).

Sim, in improvising their dialogue, admits to being surprised that Cerebus would speak of Jaka; "despite my best efforts," comments Sim, Cerebus "couldn't get past the 'Jaka thing' ... his inaccurate perception of an inability to escape his Jaka misapprehension having doomed himself to the fate he would suffer" (ibid., 15). As a result, "Dave" and Sim return Jaka to the storyline, only after leaving Cerebus (and the reader) with the realization that what he loved was not Jaka, but his *idea* of Jaka. Sim drives this point home by presenting Cerebus with another side of Jaka. Once Cerebus has finally tired of the real Jaka, seen her for what she truly is, he violently rejects her, retreating into a self-imposed exile as a sheep herder and again, religious leader, this time of a cult based around the writings of Jaka's estranged husband, Rick.

The plasticity of the character Jaka most painfully illustrates Sim's changed view on gender and the extent to which he was prepared to alter the tone to convey this altered perspective.[17] Careful *Cerebus* readers noticed this following Jaka's re-entry into the storyline at the conclusion of *Rick's Story*. To be fair, numerous characters undergo similar transformations: Rick, for example, went from being a hopelessly unemployed and "pussy-whipped" husband to a mad prophet. Bear, Cerebus' assistant from his days as pope, and his companion at the bar in *Guys*, changes considerably when his wife once again enters the picture. The power-hungry Astoria, disillusioned with power politics, decides to go into hiding and tend to a garden. Suenteus Po, portrayed in issue 20 as a somewhat buffoonish leader of the Illusionists, then by the Judge in issue 108 as a great military leader who, referring to one of his earlier "incarnations," later describes a group of quasi-religious drug users. The Po who finally physically appears in issue 155 is a humble ascetic and a conveyer of Zen-like wisdom (from the next issue: "The more worthwhile the Road, the more seductive will be those paths divergent from it" [Sim and Gerhard 1992]), is quite the contrast from his first appearance. Several minor characters also undergo significant transformation, some out of the requirements of an increasingly complex narrative.[18] Wanting to present the final days of the incarcerated Oscar of *Jaka's Story*, yet unable to alter his timeline for the passage of several decades, Sim simply introduces another Oscar, this one named Sebastien Melmoth (a pseudonym of the real Oscar Wilde's while in exile). Sim references the other Oscar, and in interviews, Sim frustrated any clear explanation for the introduction of this other character, which, it seems, was primarily the result of the above dilemma.

In contrast to these other transformations, however, Jaka's is more upsetting in that it suggests the worst aspect of the final third of the storyline, namely Sim's tendency to foreground his anti-feminist views by moving them from the comic's supplementary essays, letter columns and opinion pieces and making them a driving force of the story. The reader can ignore Davis' essay because, though it appears as the main text of issue 186 and at the conclusion of the collected *Reads* paperback, it does not significantly intrude into the plot of *Cerebus* in any significant way. Indeed, Davis' essay stands outside the storyline proper much like the comic's accompanying texts, the "Aardvark Comment" letter column, the "Note from the President" and the essays. Prior to this, Sim conveyed his anti-feminism through his characterization of the militant matriarchy of the Cirinists and the quest by Cirin to be the first female to make the Ascension, which had failed in every earlier, masculine-directed, attempt.

Reads, arguably the most technically sophisticated, challenging and controversial book of the series, provides the reader with a key that might help contextualize this new Jaka and regard her transformation as a result of something other than simply a victim of character assassination as a result of Sim's anti-feminism.[19] Apart from the Viktor Davis texts, Sim in earlier issues of this story arc made a less overt commentary on the life of a comic book creator in his character Victor Reid. Reid is a "reads" author (in *Cerebus*, reads are, like *Reads* issues themselves, a literary form that features alternating text and illustrations and, of course, Reid visually and audibly echoes "read") hired to ghost-write Jaka's autobiography. Reid here views Jaka as something she is not, just as another of Sim's many unreliable narrators/perspectives. What Sim appears to be conveying with Reid (as with Oscar before him and later with F. Stop Kennedy in *Going Home*) is an artist who finds his muse in Jaka, what amounts to a male objectification of the female. When "Dave" appears to Cerebus at the conclusion of *Minds*, he tells Cerebus, so concerned was he with having Jaka to fulfill his fantasy of what he wanted her to be, that he never really knew who Jaka was. Thus, Sim quite subtly sets up Jaka's transformation between *Jaka's Story*, her last appearance before *Reads*, where she is portrayed as headstrong, passionate and practical, and *Going Home*, where she is presented as self-absorbed, whiny, impractical, petty, and argumentative.

Admittedly, when viewed within the context of the development of Jaka's character, it may be that fame as a Cirinist celebrity has gone to her head, or that her newfound wealth has brought out the worst of her qualities, and certainly, Jaka pre–*Rick's Story* is not without significant failures of moral character and intelligence. After all, she did decide to put Pud Withers' life at risk by dancing in his tavern, and perhaps her husband's life as well. She knew the repercussions of her act, yet she did it anyway. Either this Jaka is foolhardy or she is of mediocre intelligence. "It's horrifying to me the number of *Cerebus* readers who find Jaka this paragon of virtue even after reading *Jaka's Story*," remarks Sim (Brownstein Winter 1997a, 15). Perhaps the new Jaka is a result of Cerebus finally seeing Jaka, in Sim's description from "Aardvark Comment" in issue 268: "as she was, and as she is, and as she always would be: a spoiled, myopic, insensitive, self-absorbed and self-important harlot princess" (Sim and Gerhard, July 2001). Sim's incisive and fascinating portrayal of Jaka in *Going Home* is quite jarring when contrasted with her earlier incarnation: independent, successful, a master of her own fate, bogged down by an emotionally and financially dependent man who does not do any washing up.

As Sim would have it, that any woman can be as vain, materialistic and "bitchy" as Jaka is in *Going Home* is an anathema to a romanticized, idealized perception of female behavior. Indeed, it may be that this "new" Jaka troubled many readers because this incarnation initially appeared (however much earlier issues foreshadow her or the character circumstances in *Going Home* contextualize her) following Sim's public critique of feminism. (That fewer readers are troubled by Rick's more extreme transformation undoubtedly reassured Sim of the accuracy of his views on feminism and the extent to which his mostly male audience, many of them born after the mainstream acceptance of radical feminism, had become indoctrinated). Had Sim not made public these criticisms, would the response to this new Jaka have been as negative? Had Sim not made these revelations at all, would readers of *Cerebus* have noticed a change? If they did, would their reaction have been quite so vehement? Were Sim's plans for *Cerebus* so general that the introduction of such major thematic concerns did not result in significant changes in the comic's overall design?

Sim's transition into commentary on politics and religion had much to do with his increasing fascination with these latter subjects, coupled with his stated lack of interest in the former. Nevertheless, where in the earlier *Cerebus* Sim's interests support the plot, in the later issues, the emphasis has shifted and the narrative seems to have become increasingly subservient to Sim's extra-textual agenda. Though Sim flatly refuses to view Cerebus as in any way an autobiographical character, Cerebus of *The Last Day*— ensconced in his lonely tower, locked away from the morally depraved feminists who stand just outside his gate — can just as easily be viewed as a self-portrait of Sim the self-described "comics pariah," who later cut off many of his personal relationships following his demonization as an "evil" misogynist.[20]

Sim appears to have planned the plot of *Going Home*, Cerebus undertaking a long journey back to Sand Hills Creek, the village of his birth, early on.[21] It may be that Sim's outline for the story allowed him opportunity to continue his perceptive analysis of gender differences, whereas *Latter Days*, the final storyline, as with *Church & State* and *Minds* (which mark, respectively, the one-third and two-thirds mark of the series), is concerned with Sim's final attempt at finding the "Truth." Since both Sim and Cerebus have now found God, large chunks of the storyline consist of an unusual and at time extremely tedious commentary on the Torah.[22] Here, it seems, the plot is increasingly in service of Sim's message, much to the detriment of any remaining narrative tension.

The Last Day, aside from its Mort Drucker-inspired splash page of futuristic feminists — complete with cigarette smoking infants and posters promoting child molestation (figure 23) — is, it seems, close to what Sim had in mind for an ending, if we are to believe his claim that he knew the ending of *Cerebus* far in advance.[23] His decision to continue with the storyline started in *High Society* rather than returning to the swords and sorcery theme of the earlier issues was a conscious decision to remain true to his vision for the comic, and not allow financial enticements to compromise it.

Sim's zealous pursuit of creative autonomy and (partial) disregard for the demands of the market may help explain his later decision to incorporate his anti-feminist and religious beliefs into *Cerebus*. After issue 186, some readers wondered if Sim was joking, while others suggested that perhaps it might be a marketing ploy to draw attention to *Cerebus*, a misguided attempt on Sim's part to make the comic, with its steadily declining sales, relevant. Yet profit was obviously not Sim's motivation. Therefore, while it is disputable whether the incorporation of these subjects into *Cerebus* is at all an artistic success, whether or not Sim "pulls it off," it is indisputable that their introduction is in keeping with Sim's artistic

Figure 23. Brave New World. A Mort Drucker–esque splash page contemplates the nightmare dystopia of the "Feminist-Homosexualist Axis." From *Cerebus* issue 296, November 2003 (© 2003 Dave Sim and Gerhard).

integrity and his conviction that an artist's success is not measured by its sales but by the degree to which the artist remains true to his or her vision.

At the same time, Sim was not above toying with or even at times radically subverting the public perception of his artistic integrity. In the Viktor Davis section of *Reads*, Davis outsmarts the reader and suggests that instead of ending at issue 300, *Cerebus* would end at issue 200, only fourteen issues away (indicating, it would seem, that Davis is another of Sim's unreliable narrators).[24] Davis' announcement that the comic would end at this issue is misleading. In one sense, the comic did not end at issue 200, but continued to issue 300 as Sim originally intended. However, in another sense, the proper storyline *did* end at 200. There was a very specific reason for this: as Dave Sim told Charles Brownstein, his "dialogue with Cerebus," which he had planned early on, "couldn't happen late in the storyline or there would be no room to show, properly, the dawning of genuine self-awareness" (Brownstein Winter 1997a, 13). Sim, having wiped the slate clean, so to speak, now has the opportunity to explore anti-feminism and religious faith in the story itself. His plan for the final 100 issues, then, was, aside from a few major plot points, like his conversation with Cerebus, largely an improvisation.

When asked by Bissette in 1992 what was to follow *Mothers & Daughters*, Sim replies that it is "one long story, probably broken up into two or three smaller stories, but very tightly interconnected" (Bissette 1992, 18). Indeed, it was four stories (*Guys*, *Rick's Story*, *Going Home* and *Latter Days*, of which the latter two were lengthy enough to warrant two separate phonebooks). Further evidence for this overall lack of a specific plan for the final third is in Sim's introduction to *Minds*, quoted here at length:

> What a relief and a terror it was—putting down on the page the sequence of events and repercussions from way, way, *way* back in 1977, '78 and '79, answering the *who*, *what*, *where*, *when*, and *whys* I've been keeping secret for nearly twenty years.... And then ... I came at last to the point I thought I would *never* get to: "Your turn." And after that simple two-word dialogue balloon, it was time for complete improvisation. As difficult as it is to keep a secret for twenty years, it is at least ... as difficult to keep a secret from yourself for that long. I had no idea what Cerebus' dialogue would be from that point on. For close to ten years, I wouldn't let myself even *speculate* on it.... Disconcerting, indeed, when the capstone to a 1,000 page sequence and (in many ways) the capstone of the entire previous 4,000 pages, hinges on such a nebulous article of faith [Sim and Gerhard 1996].

Sim's decision to use the word "faith" in this instance is telling. Sim wrote the introduction in 1996, apparently the same year that he underwent an altogether unexpected religious awakening. The remaining 100 issues are on Sim's part an extended act of faith that he can successfully pull together *Cerebus* and his newfound social, political and religious agendas while continuing to maintain a coherent story. It is arguable that the entire *Cerebus* work rests on another, more substantial act of faith, namely Sim's faith in his artistry, unencumbered by editorial or fiscal concerns, together with his ability to construct a narrative structure that can withstand the verities of 26 years of experience and the considerable contradictions and transformations of his personality and beliefs.

Sim wanted to accomplish something unique in comics, and to leave his mark on its history. He saw potential in the medium of comics that others did not (or did not want to) see: an extended format made up of discrete installments that could establish its own pacing, unfolding over time, reflecting life in all its boredom and excitement, where years can pass by in the blink of an eye or an hour occupy an eternity. Regrettably, one of *Cerebus*' key strengths, its being written and illustrated (save for the backgrounds) by one artist, and its malleable structure, which allowed for almost complete revision or reappraisal of its subject, also became something of a liability. Over time, Sim gradually became less interested in telling Cerebus' life in a way that was true to the spirit of the comic, and more interested in telling his own, more personal story, not hesitating to subvert or manipulate Cerebus' story in order to do so.

In some sense, *Cerebus* was *always* about Sim: his interests and fascinations have driven *Cerebus* from sword and sorcery parody, to grand political and religious satire to quietly intimate character studies. Yet these fascinations always worked in favor of the story while Sim's later anti-feminist and religious views do not. Most know and agree, for instance, that politics are corrupt, that religious leaders are hypocritical, vainglorious and fallible, that marriage is difficult and death is tragic, and Sim provided considerable insight into these aspects of modern life. What most do not agree on, and what Sim felt was his obligation to espouse to a built-in audience that neither expected nor deserved such a betrayal of narrative cohesion, is that the collapse of modern society is the result of the insidious infiltration of a "Marxist-feminist-homosexualist" axis. As a result, *Cerebus* will always remain a difficult and problematic work. Yet, helpfully, these difficulties and problems are deeply fascinating and, to its last issue, *Cerebus* remains one of the comics medium's towering triumphs, a revolutionary and innovative work of a master of the form. Indeed, in Sim's inspired use of organic yet (mostly) coherent narrative structure and his revolutionary use of the comic book medium to tell the story of a life, *Cerebus* remains a resounding success and a singular narrative achievement, regardless of the medium.

Notes

1. Compare this with Sim's comments in a *Cerebus* Yahoo Group March 2004 Q&A session, framing the series' structural design with a strictly sexual context, seeing the first 150 issues as a "male cycle" due to its being "outward bound" or "ejaculatory ... a 3,000 page cum shot which ends with Cerebus virtually expired" and the second half as the "female cycle" in that "as in our society," the Feminist "takeover is complete." The first half, Sim continues, "is largely concerned with how uncontainable a force of nature Cerebus is," a force that "ultimately gets contained by [his love interest] Jaka," after which he becomes "immobilized to the point of catatonia" (Sim March 2004).

2. Note also the formal symmetries in the books' titles: *Women* followed by *Reads* and *Minds*, echoing Serna's explanation to Cerebus in *Women* that "all women read minds" (Sim and Gerhard 1996, 164). Sim in a letter to Margaret Liss writes, "'Women Reads Minds, Guys' was indeed the Flat Assertion Pregnant with Poisonous implication that you suspected. A kind of billboard in the middle of the mammoth project hiding in plain sight" (Sim, 11 February 2006, http://tinyurl.com/3g5hhop).

3. In a 1993 interview in *Wizard*, Sim told interviewer Paul M. Grant that the decision to do 300 issues came in "three stages." The initial stage was the attempt at doing a bi-monthly comic. The second stage

> was around issue 11 or 12, and there was enough money coming in ... it was now possible to do *Cerebus* monthly.... The third stage was, 'Okay, I know I can keep going and this is now all I have to do. Now the question is, how far do I go/where do you stop?' It's always been the same problem. I'm doing something that nobody else is doing, there's really no pattern, there's no guide, no map as how to do this [Grant 1993, 80].

4. "I decided I wanted to do *Cerebus* until issue #300 because I didn't want to be 75 years old and racked with arthritis trying to do the next page, and I also didn't want to just do the character for another year or two until I got bored. Doing 300 issues seemed like a good compromise" (Palmer, Jr. 1996, 60). More practically, Sim wanted to get his name in the history books as the longest single author-artist comic books by beating the current record holders: Stan Lee and Jack Kirby's 102-issue run of *Fantastic Four* and Marv Wolfman and Gene Colan's 63 issues of *Tomb of Dracula*. Sim admitted this aspiration to Spurgeon: "Having beaten Stan Lee and Jack Kirby's record on [*The Fantastic Four*]" (Spurgeon 1996, 60).

5. Sim and Michael Loubert's "The Aarvarkian Age" was an early attempt (in issue 13, December 1979–January 1980) at providing narrative coherence quickly jettisoned by Sim.

6. Sim adds, at the conclusion of this essay, "within my own frames of reference, I had to work for 26 years to produce one 6000-page equivalent of a prose novel. Not the happiest conclusion to come to, but I think it's an accurate one" (Sim, "On Writing Cerebus" 46).

7. Sim's experiments with duration did not only result in a radical decompression, he could also equally compress the narrative so that where one issue may only cover a few minutes, another may cover weeks or months or, as in issue 266, several years.

8. The composition of *High Society* and *Church & State* was nowhere near as planned out as that of *Jaka's Story*. In an "Aardvark Comment" comment from issue 53, Sim admits that he found the ending to *High Society* "unsatisfying." "As you can see from the past few issues," he writes, "the story goes on ... would ask you look on *High Society* as the novel within the novel. I apologize for all the loose ends that were not tied up, but I also ask that you bear with me on that as I forge ahead" (Sim *Cerebus* 53). Sim did not announce the title of the new storyline, started in issue 52, until issue 72, March 1985. Indeed, *Church & State* did not have its sub-chapters demarcated until issue 86 and even then, Sim altered the length of those chapters as the story unfolded. By comparison, at the end of *Church & State*, Sim, in his "Note from the President" in the double-issue 112/113 is announcing his "next novel," the first storyline Sim (and collaborator Gerhard) planned entirety from the outset, *Jaka's Story* (Sim and Gerhard July 1988).

9. Sim told Spurgeon that because his decision to make *Cerebus* a story of a life was arrived at so late, issues 100 to 200 possessed a "more life-like structure" (Spurgeon February 1996, 105). "I came to the conclusion, I wouldn't say early on, but probably in the course of *Church & State* [that] if this is really going to be effective, if this is really going to be life as I tend to see life, the last third is going to have to be [an] aftermath" (Spurgeon, December 1996, 70).

10. Sim so much as admits this to Spurgeon when, describing "Dave" telling Cerebus near the end of *Minds* that everything went wrong in his life as a result of Cerebus' actions in issues 4 and 5. "If everything had worked out perfectly and Cerebus had fulfilled the destiny that was intended for him, everything would have gone off in a completely different direction.... Consequently, everything that he's gone through ... are repercussions or ripple effects from this failure to fulfill his own destiny. I'm not unmindful of the possibility that I'm in the same situation" (Spurgeon December 1996, 71).

11. Sim writes in a subsequent letter that he "spent the entire storyline looking for the Truth, the capstone that would draw everything together" (Sim 2005, 174).

12. *Church & State* and *Mothers & Daughters* are "both centered on the Big Bang," Sim tells Spurgeon. While *Mothers & Daughters* was not an intentional counterpoint to the "ultra-feminist" interpretation of the light and void as supplied by the Judge, Sim wrote it because he felt *Church & State*'s vision to be "incomplete" (Spurgeon December 1996, 73). Sim describes the anti-feminist reading of issue 186 as "the eye in the pyramid, the summit of the mountain ... or the deepest part of the pit depending on which picture suits your own view" (ibid., 75).

13. Sim tells Spurgeon "there are three parts to the equation" of *Cerebus*, namely Cerebus, Dave Sim and the reader. What Sim was attempting to do was to bring "those three individuals as close together as I possibly could" (Spurgeon December 1996, 75). He also remarks in a 2004 letter to Paul Isaacs that "Dave" is an overt homage to Chuck Dixon's 1953 cartoon *Duck Amuck*, in which Daffy Duck is tormented by his animator (see Sim, *Collected Letters 2005* [352]).

14. Notably, Sim admits in a March 2004 Q&A session: "I didn't use the fact [that Cerebus was a hermaphrodite] very much because it wasn't really of interest to me, except as a literary device, to have a character on the borderline between male and female in a huge story composed of a male cycle and a female cycle" (http://tinyurl.com/64pp6qo).

15. Sim initially intended for Cirin to be the second aardvark and "Dave" the third. Cirin instead became the third after Sim decided that, because he himself was not an aardvark, it would not work (Brownstein Winter 1997a, 12). In his introduction to the *Minds* phonebook, Sim remarks that he had since *Church & State* "a specific intention for this fourth book.... For the longest time, the final third of this very book was the furthest outpost in the *Cerebus* journey that I had marked clearly on my mental *Cerebus* map" (Sim and Gerhard 1996). Given the nature of the meeting between "Dave" and Cerebus, it seems likely Sim first conceived of this arc following his scripting the meeting between Cerebus and the Judge, which the former meeting refers to/echoes.

16. Sim later dropped the "Dave" appellation for his fictional counterpart, opting instead for an impersonal pronoun, thinking that perhaps using "Dave" might make these authorial interjections too obvious. Presenting "Dave's" dialogue with Cerebus in *Minds* as thought balloons suggests what exactly? That Dave is Cerebus' consciousness? An inner voice (and hence his guardian angel/tempting devil)? That Cerebus is merely having a conversation with himself and that "Dave" is a projection of his own God complex first evidenced during his tyrannical reign as pope? The latter is unlikely: during their exchange "Dave" tells Cerebus his life is bread and Cerebus is the baker, not "Dave"—implying that this "Dave" is not Sim himself but a fictional alter ego. Perhaps, given what Sim had in store for Cerebus, "Dave" provided Sim the distance necessary to mistreat his creation.

17. Note the change in Sim's view of Jaka in his comments on her in a "Note from the President" from *Cerebus* 114:

> I admire the character (of Jaka) far more than any of the other characters in the book. Cerebus is too much of a born loser; willfully self-destructive. Astoria is too single-minded and humorless. Lord Julius is always 'on'; the Roach too out of touch with anything approximating reality, even the Elf is too mindlessly happy all the time. When I'm writing them I'm observing from a discreet distance. I'm interested, but not to the extent of wanting to have dinner with them or anything like that. Jaka on the other hand is someone I would happily spend a lot of time with. She embodies those qualities I always look for in a woman. She has a very simple way of thinking for which she is unapologetic. She's loaded with common-sense and self-confidence. She is direct and has a low threshold for bullshit. She has virtually no interest in material possessions though she has an appreciation of them. She is almost certainly on the top rung of the karmic ladder and won't be back for another life-time.

From "Aardvark Comment," *Cerebus* 268: "For the first time he (Cerebus) was able to see Jaka precisely as she was and as she is and as she always would be: a spoiled, myopic, insensitive, self-absorbed and self-important harlot princess (quite apart from her position in the hierarchy of the city-state of Palnu)." From a 2004 letter to Dan Morris, Sim remarks that he doesn't believe that he changed Jaka's character "appreciably ... she 'reads' a little bit different as we get to know her but she was a very theatrical person all the way through. She played at being Jaka a lot of the time. People like that look very different depending on what situation they're in" (Sim, *Collected Letters 2004* 307). From a March 2004 Yahoo Group Q&A session:

> I think I kept Jaka pretty consistent. In my experience women are like cats. When you don't want them you can't get rid of them and when you do want them it's like trying to pick up lint with a magnet. All that changed was that Cerebus switched from not really wanting Jaka to really, really wanting her (after issue 74–75). As soon as you switch, they switch. Jaka is a self-absorbed aristocratic airhead. She always was [http://tinyurl.com/64pp6qo].

To go from respecting a character to calling her a materialistic airhead evinces a considerable shift in authorial intention. Sim admits in an August 2005 internet chat with readers that he

> had been as guilty as anyone through the first two hundred issues of creating really false but flattering female characters, 'admirable' domineering wives, strong independent single women, female intellectuals, strong female leaders, all the false feminist hot-button icons that earned you rave reviews and award nominations from the increasingly (or, at least, ostensibly) androgynous comic-reading public. It hadn't been false storytelling to that point, to me, because the layers of reality had actually still been there. To cite one example, I had played straight with Margaret Thatcher as a matriarch and held up her end of the discussion of what exotic dancing actually was as opposed to what Jaka wanted and needed it to be. And found [Thatcher's] side of the discussion to be the more sensible of the two. The reaction from the ostensibly androgynous audience was that I had created a genuinely terrifying presence in the Thatcher character which (ultimately, for me) just reinforced the fact that the androgynous were essentially terrified of the truth and were using their own terror of the truth to convince themselves that the truth was, therefore, intrinsically evil-why else would it be terrifying? [http://tinyurl.com/4mv68tg].

18. Elrod and Roach, for example. See *Women*.

19. In composing *Reads*, Sim was inspired by the "Fearful Symmetry" chapter of Alan Moore and Dave Gibbons' *Watchmen* (issue 5, January 1987, New York: DC Comics) (see Spurgeon, "Dave Sim" 100). Sim's text pieces alternate with a (mostly) wordless battle between Cirin and Cerebus on the eve of the Ascension. Davis' essay (issue 186) comprises the middle of the book and is perhaps the first comic book to have, aside from the cover, entirely no artwork.

20. It would not be *Cerebus*' first explicitly autobiographical moment: in discussion with Kim Thompson regarding issue 36, Sim considers "The Night Before," which details Jaka's visit with Cerebus on the eve of his election, near the conclusion of *High Society*, to be "a case of self-examination." In the issue, Cerebus believes that he is saying exactly what Jaka wants to hear, impressing her with his wealth and power, when in fact that is exactly what she *does not* want to hear. "I've had that tendency to go so far into assuming ... that I'm saying all the right things and then discovering I'm not," Sim tells Thompson. "I do put that into the character. Cerebus does not learn from it. I mean, I try to learn from it" (Thompson August 1983, 66).

21. Sim says in a 26 January 2004 letter to James W. Taylor that *Going Home* "was certainly the most rigidly mapped-out of the *Cerebus* novels" (Sim 2005, 10–11).

22. One section, entitled "Chasing YHWH," surrealistically combines Konigsberg, a satirical Woody Allen character, and a series of images that weirdly re-envision him, in impeccably rendered panels, in an Art Spiegleman-style *Maus* facemask, or as a character in a Robert Crumb underground comic, and so on.

23. On this point, a 1992 interview with Dave Sim (conducted by *Swamp Thing* artist Steve Bissette) is revelatory. As Sim tells Bissette, he had the ending of *Melmoth* (issue 150, the halfway point of the series) in his mind "pretty much from the end of *Church & State*," some four years in advance. Likewise, the endings to *Church & State* and *Jaka's Story* were, in Bissette's incredulous words, "clear in [Sim's] mind for almost a decade." At the time of the interview, Sim also claimed that certain sections of the end of *Mothers & Daughters* (which ran from issues 151 to 200) "have been vivid in my mind since '79" the year Sim had his nervous breakdown (Bissette 9–10).

24. Sim would write in response to a letter in "Aardvark Comment" that "the end of *Mothers & Daughters* ... is really the end of the formal *Cerebus* storyline" (Sim, *Cerebus* 234).

PART TWO
IGNORE IT, IT'S JUST ANOTHER REALITY

"Does This Seem Right to You?" Stories Within *Cerebus*

David Groenewegen

One of the persistently intriguing parts of *Cerebus* is Dave Sim's use of stories told within the overarching story. There are numerous examples of this, in many different forms, but all are in the service of the greater narrative and Sim's larger purpose, because Sim spent 26 years trying to represent his view of the world in which he lives, while trying to make his readers think about their view of the world, and how it differs from his. (See figure 24.)

As a key part of this, a number of characters tell stories within the larger narrative, ostensibly to "explain" things. In some cases they tell stories to Cerebus, in others they tell stories about Cerebus. Some stories are told by Cerebus himself, while others bypass Cerebus altogether to deal with other characters and concepts. Finally, there are stories that Sim tells, that seem to exist outside the story entirely, yet seek to expand upon and nail down Sim's viewpoint, or, at least, a character purporting to be Sim.

The critical aspect of most of these stories, and the thing that makes them so crucial to the overall work is the frequency with which Sim deliberately either contradicts them later on, or shows that Sim did not base the stories on the actual actions of the characters involved. That he is able to do the latter so effectively is one of the real triumphs of the comics format — only in comics can you so effectively juxtapose the seeming solidity of the written word with quite clearly different actions. In a movie, you can't show the words, only the action, in a book can only describe the action, not show it.

In most comics, indeed in most stories no matter what form they take, the long expository explanation of "what has gone before" ties up the loose ends, wraps things up. Sim likes to subvert these neat little bundles, although in the early parts of the story, such as most of the *Cerebus* volume, he often uses this staple of storytelling in a conventional way. Characters may initially lie to Cerebus for their own purposes, but eventually they tell him (and us) what was really going on. Cerebus' initial encounters with K'Cor and Henrot are good examples of this.

The arrival of Lord Julius, who has constructed his political career, indeed his life, around never telling anyone what's going on, marks a shift, but only a slight one. We know that Julius is lying all the time, so when his lies are exposed it hardly comes as a surprise. Similarly, Astoria tells Cerebus no end of stories, but as she is clearly trying to manipulate him, we come to expect little in the way of ultimate truth there either.

98   Part Two. Ignore It, It's Just Another Reality

Figure 24. Cerebus and Weisshaupt's final meeting. From *Church & State I* (© 1988 Dave Sim and Gerhard).

The various "Mind Games" issues represent a more significant turning point, where the explanations that Cerebus receives are increasingly changed and recast each time. He has things told to him that "explain" what has gone before, explanations later repudiated or shown to be false. Moreover, the pattern continues with the Judge, whose biography of Suenteus Po Po himself later denies, at the same time Sim raises questions concerning the Judge's very existence. Interestingly the Judge's final pronouncement that Cerebus will die "alone, unmourned and unloved" turns out to be completely accurate. This apparent contradiction (is the Judge "right" or is he "wrong") is one of the most compelling aspects of Sim's work, because it designed to provoke the reader into thinking about whether they think the stories are "right" or "wrong." Equally, it seems that Sim prefers not to give consistent answers to anything. Perhaps he does this to avoid the tidiness of fiction as opposed to the way life is.

Eventually though, during *Minds* Sim himself appears in the story to explain all to the protagonist. Even here, the explanations given to Cerebus remain ambiguous. Cirin vehemently denounces everything that "Dave" tells her. He also illustrates that what Cerebus knows is only what Sim chooses to tell him (by hitting him in the face with a pie and then removing and restoring the memory of the event). He is pointing out that everything about memory is fallible — Sim has stated that he doesn't recall everything in Cerebus' life (Spurgeon February 1996, 80) and that everybody has an agenda, an agenda through which one needs to sift.

Sim illustrates the strength of these agendas in the stories told about Cerebus during the overall story. These tend to be shorter, but more numerous. Many are just single lines about various perceptions of Cerebus the character. However, others are more substantial because they show someone writing about Cerebus, and what it is they are writing about him, while demonstrating his doing something quite different. This happens to a certain extent in *Going Home* where F. Stop Kennedy interprets all of Cerebus' actions in ways quite opposed to what he is actually doing (see figure 25), but is more visible in *Rick's Story* in which Rick bases a Bible on Cerebus for no apparently logical reason, although some of it seems to be hero worship, and some revenge for Cerebus' love of Jaka.

At first this seems like a critique of Bibles in general — that humans, whose thoughts,

Figure 25. "Writers ... *fabricate* things!" From *Going Home* (© 2003 Dave Sim and Gerhard).

Figure 26. Building a new religion. From *Latter Days* (© 2003 Dave Sim and Gerhard).

and prejudices influence what they are writing, and which create something quite different to that which actually occurred. Sim has said that he wrote this during his secular humanist days, when he had less faith in the Bible than he did later (Sim September/October 2005). Interestingly, Rick's Bible actually creates an environment in which Cerebus can become a messiah like figure — despite the fact that much of it seems to be a particularly nasty joke at his expense. Therefore, it serves the purpose of both moving the story along, while simultaneously inviting the reader, yet again, to question what is told and read to them.

Cerebus is aware of the unlikely nature of his ascension to messiah-hood, especially as Sim, in his incarnation as Cerebus' creator, had implied that Cerebus had thrown away his chance at a glorious destiny already. So when he retells the story during *Latter Days* (an example of Cerebus telling a story, rather than being told one), he struggles to remember what he is supposed to know and what a messiah is supposed to have done. He only knows the text of the Bible that features him so prominently because others repeatedly read it to him for years. He knows the story is not "true," he knows it did not really happen, but he recognizes that it is central to his position.

Rick's Bible demonstrates what some might see as one of the weaknesses of *Cerebus*, which is the sheer length of time that Sim has spent on it, because in his public utterances Sim is convinced of the literal truth of the Bible — if nothing else he is far more religious than he was in earlier years (Sim 2004). (See figure 26.)

By taking 26 years to complete the story, we have undoubtedly ended up with a very different *Cerebus* than the one that Sim began in the late seventies. This is because Sim has changed, just as we all change. In *Cerebus,* we have a unique piece of art precisely because it maps the changing mind and views of Dave Sim. Is there another example anywhere of a single story, with a designated end, completed in such a form, over such a long period? Diaries might capture the same change, but they are neither public, nor intended as works of fiction. Some cartoonists, notably comic strip artists like Charles Schulz, may have worked on the same creation for longer, but never with any real need to fit what they did into a coherent storyline. Sim has managed to maintain his vision, without just mechanically writing and drawing exactly what he came up with in the late seventies. The work fits within a solid structure (Sim's views on Kevillism and Cirinism are in place as far back as *High Society*), but has grabbed little bits of the times through which it has flowed, and drawn them in to the story as well, to create a story that is consistent, yet flexible enough to change with Sim.

Therefore, nifty narrative device, makes for a great deal of interesting reading and speculation, helps keep you paying attention. Terrific. Filled up all those pages. Why bother?

One of the reasons to bother is that Sim spent a quarter century experimenting with exactly what you can do with the comic book form, a statement that even his more vehement detractors are generally willing to admit. The ones who won't admit it have, in my experience, read not more than two or three issues of *Cerebus* at best. Nevertheless, that does not seem to me to be the main reason for building in all these little stories. Sim seeks to make a broader philosophical statement with *Cerebus*, and these many different stories, designing these many different views of the world to make you think. He wants the reader to question the very things he is drawing and writing. As he says in the introduction to the collected edition of *Women,* he wants you to think: does this seem right to you?

For this to work Sim has sometimes had to tell stories that move around his title character (*Jaka's Story*, *Melmoth*) or even do totally without him (large sections of *Reads*). These stories are still bound by the same rules, in that Sim is willing to question the "truth" of the story (in *Going Home* Jaka claims that Oscar's Read about her is the work of a character and completely misrepresents her), or makes the reader question the truth they are being presented with (notably in *Reads*, where Sim claims that *Cerebus* would run for two hundred issues, not 300 — although this was more effective in the original magazine form, not in a world where the later volumes are available for purchase).

And once he has done that, once he has shown all he has to show, said all he wants to say, shown all the things he does or doesn't believe, he lets Cerebus tell one last story ("Chasing YHWH"), offers an alternative viewpoint by having one of his characters question bits of it almost immediately, and then gives us the Dave Sim version of the creation and death of the universe, blending science with religion, and basically says: this is how I see it. What about you? Admittedly, the Biblical commentaries in *Latter Days* weaken this argument. The device of the unreliable narrator which has worked so effectively to this point

Figure 27. The Revelation of Truth at Last. From *The Last Day* (© 2004 Dave Sim and Gerhard).

undermines Sim's attempt to present the reader with his view of the nature of Creation and its reflection on gender issues. In public he has made it clear that the description of the Creation is that held by the author to be true (Sim June 2009). However, the commentaries upon which Sim bases his Creation are the work of Cerebus the character, who, in the same book lies about his past to attract a woman, and who pointedly goes to hell at the end. The reader who has read only the comic and not any of Sim's other interviews or writings (although Sim footnotes this section, thus drawing the outside Sim into the story), can therefore draw the conclusion that the view of Creation is deeply flawed, and that Sim is commenting on it rather than espousing it. Especially in a larger work in which so many conflicting viewpoints are also argued. (See figure 27.)

In an interview in *The Comics Journal* 185, Steve Bissette spoke about the power of imagination, and how following the path of imagination can take you "beyond this day-to-day fabric of reality we all take for granted" (Thompson March 1996, 91). Dave Sim seems to have gone down this path and emerged with a view of the world that he wanted to share, one that he knew he would have to share from within an entertainment medium. Therefore, he created a structure within which he could wrestle with his own views, and invite his readers to wrestle along with him, while at the same time entertaining and telling a story. This is a delicate balance, and to me, over the course of 300 issues he succeeded far more often than he failed. I do not agree with all of Sim's views, but many, many times forced myself to think about why. I've been thinking "Why isn't that right?" for many years now.

Aardvarkian Intertexts and True Stories

Dominick Grace

The cover of the October 2004 issue of *PMLA* includes images from Art Spiegelman's *In the Shadow of No Towers*. Of this work, Marianne Hirsch says, "Enabling reality and fantasy, historical and fictional figures, human and cartoon characters to coexist and morph into each other, it demands an extraordinarily complex response beyond just combining reading and looking" (Hirsch 2004, 1213). While perhaps no comics creator has received more serious literary attention than Spiegelman, his valorization by *PMLA* speaks strongly to the increasing seriousness with which comics are considered. However, that Spiegelman is credited with eliciting the sort of complex response Hirsh speaks to in *In the Shadow of No Towers*, a relatively slight work by Spiegelman's standards, speaks to the extent that serious academic consideration of comics is still in its infancy. Numerous works anticipate the sort of genre-bending and intertextual approach celebrated by Hirsch in Spiegelman. Dave Sim and Gerhard's *Cerebus* could better be described in terms such as those applied by Hirsch to Spiegelman; Sim also tests the limits of the comics medium in many ways, but he does so most interestingly, perhaps, in his explorations of the power of art to describe and shape (or reshape) reality. Kelly Rothenberg describes Sim and Gerhard's comic as "one of the most literary ever published" (Rothenberg 2003), and indeed from its inception *Cerebus* has been intensively interested in the nature of literature as a reflection and even creator of reality by supplanting what happened with what the story says happened. As David Groenewegen notes, in *Cerebus* Sim (and just Sim, as he alone determines the narrative trajectory) repeatedly engages in a revisionism in which he presents stories but then "deliberately either contradicts them later on, or shows that the stories are not based on the actual actions of the characters involved" (Groenewegen October/November 2004, 118). Sim interrogates the idea of a single, simple truth in a medium that, given its visual nature, would not seem amenable to such subjectivity; Sim, however, uses the tropes of comics and complex, sophisticated metafictional and intertextual devices to question the possibility of true stories.

From its inception, *Cerebus* interrogated generic distinction and easily categorizable narrative forms. The comic began as a hybridized parody of marginalized and dismissed literary genres: Sim combined the Marvel Comics adaptations of Robert E. Howard's pulp fiction *Conan the Barbarian* stories (an even lower art form translation of low art that at the time had not yet acquired its current cultural appeal) with funny animal comics by replacing the figure of Conan with a talking aardvark, Cerebus. The sword and sorcery fantasy subgenre is at the less respectable end of the continuum for a genre generally regarded as escapist and formulaic; comics generally were viewed even more than was pulp fiction at the time (1976) as childish and formulaic, and funny animal comics especially were seen as specifically for children. Indeed, part of the humor of the early *Cerebus* arises simply from the juxtaposition of the funny animal with the sword and sorcery context; some early issues might read as straight Conan-style adventures if the protagonist were a barbarian rather than a talking aardvark. However, though the earliest *Cerebus* stories themselves are generally slapdash and formulaic, even they depend upon a sophisticated intertextual interplay, in which one's ability to recognize the intertexts determines one's ability even to understand them. In these issues, Sim established generic blurring as an ongoing conceit. The world of the funny animal comic collides with the world of sword and sorcery fantasy; Cerebus looks like he belongs in a completely different universe. Sim's artistic style in the early issues is largely responsible for the sense of generic clash, as Sim exploits the various absurdities putting an anthropomorphized aardvark into fantasy situations allows. In an advancing line of mercenaries depicted in the second issue, for instance, Cerebus appears as a ridiculously diminutive figure beside the other barbarians, making what would in a Conan story be a straightforward action sequence instead a comic sequence. Even Sim's consistent rendering of everything in the strip in strict black and white (at least in the early years), with the exception of Cerebus, who is always colored with a grey toner, underscores the clash created by placing a funny animal in a barbarian fantasy. The appearance of objects literally changes when re-contextualized in relation to Cerebus stresses the point. For instance, in issue 2, the shield Cerebus acquires from his new allies shifts from a black and white line drawing to a grey object, like himself, to exaggerate the contrast between him and the other soldiers. This is a minor comic device early in the comic; later the plasticity of appearance represented here assumes greater weight.

Sim's parody quickly extended beyond the relatively limited horizon provided by barbarian fantasy. One of his earliest parody characters is Elrod, the last king of Melvinbone, based on Michael Moorcock's Elric of Melniboné. Created in the 1960s but making a two-issue guest appearance in Marvel Comics' *Conan* series in issues 14 and 15 in 1972, Sim based his depiction of Elrod on how Barry Windsor-Smith rendered Elric in these comics. Elrod came to Sim via Marvel's *Conan* comic book rather than directly from Moorcock, however, he is not derived merely from comics. His voice came from Warner Brothers cartoons; Elrod has a dialect akin to Foghorn Leghorn's. The comic effect, again, is a simple one, Moorcock's serious, melancholy albino translated into a slapstick cartoon figure, but Elrod, the first of a cast of secondary characters derived from various comics and pop culture sources, suggests Sim's broadening horizons, both comedically and in his experimentations with intertextual reference. Important as Elrod is, however, Sim's first real broadening of the potential of *Cerebus* came in issue 11, with the first appearance of The Cockroach, a parodic version of Batman who quickly became a mainstay of the comic in various reincarnations as Captain Cockroach, Moon Roach, Wolveroach, and the Punisherroach, to name a few. Sim modeled the Moon Roach persona on Moon Knight, himself obviously a Batman pastiche created by Marvel Comics.

With the Cockroach, or Cootie, as Cerebus calls him, Sim really took aim at the conventions not merely of the sub-genre of barbarian fantasy but more generally of the

Opposite: Figure 28A. The Roach drops a huge granite crescent moon on economic exploiters. From *High Society* (© 1986 Dave Sim).

entire mainstream comics world of super heroes. Sim explodes most of the more absurd conventions of super hero comics in this two-page spread from *High Society*.

First, the ridiculousness of the super hero's specialized tools are exaggerated to the point of absurdity in the huge granite crescent moon the Roach drops on those he sees as economic exploiters (figure 28A). (Any super hero wandering about a bustling metropolis is inherently absurd, but Sim stresses the point by burdening him with a gigantic boulder he presumably manages to haul around with him, unnoticed.) With Moon Roach's dialogue, Sim parodies the hyper-melodramatic language of super hero comics. This dialogue is heavy with alliteration and hyperbole, in the true Marvel style: "Unorthodox economic revenge bellow the bronchi of the simply sensational Moon Roach." Even the pacing created by the word balloon divisions and the melodrama suggested by the heavy balloon borders plays up typical super hero melodrama. Visually, as well, Sim parodies the generic conventions of the super hero comic, with his use of steep angles for perspective shots, his use of silhouettes, his kinetic, complex page design, and his use of foreshortening, as in the fifth panel of the second page, not to stress the power of the hero, as you'd find in a typical super hero book, but instead to draw our attention to Moon Roach's ridiculously over-sized feet — an ongoing gag, by the way; Sim consistently parodies the fluid gracefulness usually ascribed to super heroes by designing his action sequences to stress instead awkwardness, absurdity, and/or undramatic body parts, such as feet (figure 28B). Moon Roach's running narration of his action — interrupted occasionally by suggestions made by Kevitch, another of the Roach's multiple personalities—further parodies super-heroic hyper-melodrama in its bathetic and anti-climactic tone. This device also reflects another ongoing and increasingly important element of *Cerebus*: its increasing self-reflexivity, its move from comic to meta-comic as part of its generic play.

Figure 29, also from *High Society*, extends Sim's intertextual play. This pair of pages also features Moon Roach, but the comics referencing does not end there. The Moon Roach in this instance also echoes Spiderman, in his Roach sense; Jack Kirby's Fourth World comics from DC, in his pinging, derived from a figure (Father Box) in those series; and the pulp fiction character The Shadow, who has also had various comic book incarnations, including a run in the early seventies. In short, for a reader fully to understand the intertextual jokes on these pages, he or she must be familiar with a complex set of interwoven comics (and pulp) in-jokes. For the reader unfamiliar with comics, Moon Roach may be amusing for other reasons, not least of which is how well he parodies familiar superhero clichés, but for the comics connoisseur, the jokes are more complex and more dense.

The intertextual echoes do not end there, though. While perhaps not apparent from the bit of dialogue on these pages, the two louts Moon Roach is pummeling, Dirty Drew and Fleagle McGrew, are iterations of Yosemite Sam, with a soupçon of Robert Service's Dan McGrew, for instance. More important, though, is Moon Roach's running narrative; Moon Roach narrates his actions as he performs them. He is not the first character in *Cerebus* to do so, but he is probably the first whose version of his own story often veers radically away from what we see of the events he narrates. He is his own hero, but in the larger Cerebus world, he is, as another of his iterations comes tragically to realize much later, "comedy relief" (issue 167, collected in *Women*), not to mention mentally unbalanced. As a self-conscious narrator of his own story, the Roach functions as a relatively simple iteration of Sim's larger interest in how stories intersect and how truth derives, or does not derive, from those intersections. Because the Roach is clearly mentally unbalanced, and because we usually can see clearly and immediately the gap between his self-narratives and the

Figure 28B. Sim parodies super heroes by stressing undramatic body parts, such as feet. From *High Society* (© 1986 Dave Sim).

Figure 29. Intertextual play in *Cerebus*. From *High Society* (© 1986 Dave Sim).

reality he inhabits, his stories do not so much problematize or complicate the relationship between conflicting narratives as they privilege the external, comics narrative over the Roach's internal self-definitions. This represents an early example of the comic's increasing self-reflexivity, its move from comic to meta-comic as part of its generic play.

As Sim matured as an artist and developed the idea of treating *Cerebus* not as a set of self-contained short comics stories but rather as a sustained 300 issue, 6,000-page novel, his palette broadened significantly. Though Sim never really abandoned comics as ongoing intertexts for *Cerebus*, he expanded the comic's range of intertextual references into film (first with Lord Julius, derived from Groucho Marx) and literature. Indeed, as it progressed, *Cerebus* enfolded various literary figures and texts, notably Oscar Wilde, F. Scott Fitzgerald, Ernest Hemingway and, ultimately, the Bible in its explorations of literary construction. Increasingly, Sim used the interplay between an array of literary texts as a metaphor for the creation of belief systems and therefore of reality, especially in his extensive uses of metafictional conceits. It is perhaps not surprising, therefore, that Sim moves from parodic pastiches of marginal literary media to extensive scriptural exegesis (described as the Cerebexegesis by members of the on-line Yahoo Cerebus discussion group; the term was first used by a member named Daniel in November 2002) (Post number 9722) and the creation of a pseudo–Biblical *Book of Cerebus* that completely blurs the line between artistic creation and myth-making. As Sim has said, "I think there's a case to be made that storytellers were probably the genesis point for a lot of religions" (Atwal 1996, 84). *Cerebus*' complex intertextuality posits that narrative envisioning and revisioning problematizes our understanding life as we convert it to story; or if, as Sim suggests, "All stories are true" (a mantra he repeats in various contexts),[1] then all truth is a story.

Beginning with issues in the mid-forties (comprising part of the sequence collected as *High Society*), Sim began experimenting with prose text; by the end of the comic's run, extended prose passages, often accompanied by only one or even by no illustrations, were a common feature of the book, in blatant violation of the truism that comics should offer a balance of words and pictures, with the stress on the latter. The comic's focus even shifted away from the titular character for extended periods; once, Cerebus himself virtually disappeared from the comic for nearly a year. Issues 139 to 150, collected as *Melmoth*, focus on a retelling of the death of Oscar Wilde, with Cerebus barely present at all, appearing in passing in a catatonic state of mourning over the loss of Jaka (and clutching her doll, Missy)[2] until the end of the volume, when he emerges from his catatonia to begin the conflicts with Cirin that take up much of the subsequent three volumes. Over the last half of its run, *Cerebus* became extensively and perhaps excessively meta-fictional, especially in its juxtaposition of conventional comics with extended prose passages. These include F. Scott Fitzgerald's *The Beautiful and Damned*, Mary Hemingway's African safari journals, and the Bible. In a note on the Fitzgerald parody, in fact, Sim explicitly claims to be "'pushing the envelope' of what constitutes plagiarism, tribute, satire, and parody" (Sim and Gerhard 1998, 389). In the "Fall and the River" section of *Going Home*, what Sim does is incorporate extensive passages from the Fitzgerald novel, slightly rewritten, as a fictionalized version of Cerebus at the time, as written by the Fitzgerald analogue character F. Stop Kennedy. We see what happens to Cerebus and what Kennedy sees of Cerebus' life, side by side with Kennedy's "novel" depicting the same events in prose form and, of course, from a distant temporal perspective. The events as we see them in the comics portions happen in our readerly "now," while Kennedy's novel reflects those same events as distilled through a novelist's mind and over time. Consequently, we get two different versions of the same event simultaneously, though arguably in this instance the readerly "now" version carries more authority than the novelistic translation. Nevertheless, though the reader of *Cerebus* might recognize that the novel fictionalizes the "true" story, the reader must also recognize that such fictionalizing of fact can easily blur the edges (if not the core) of the truth; *in* Cerebus' world, what carries greater weight: what did in fact happen, or the fictionalized document of those events?

The first significant extensive example of intermingled narratives unfolds in *Jaka's Story*, in which the "present-day" narrative, involving Cerebus living with his unrequited love, Jaka, and her husband, a narrative presented in conventional comics format, is juxtaposed with a prose narrative purporting to be the story of Jaka's childhood. This prose narrative is written in a pastiche of Oscar Wilde's style (indeed, it is presented within *Cerebus* as a book by Oscar, a character explicitly modeled on Wilde), with each prose passage accompanied by a single illustration. Both the prose passage and the illustration are on otherwise blank pages; see figure 30, from *Jaka's Story*.

Both within the prose narrative and between the prose narrative and the main illustration there are disjunctions and discrepancies that require us to question the extent to which the narrative captures truth in any meaningful way; even before, as she does later, Jaka repudiates Oscar's version of her earlier life as a fabrication. However, even the pictures themselves are strangely double. Sim consistently depicts Jaka's Nurse as having the head of Missy, Jaka's doll, in inset panels, consistently suggesting the overwriting or elision of the Nurse's true face with the doll's head, as shown in figure 30. The question of what this overwriting of Nurse reflects is never answered, at least within the series.[3] Does it mean that Jaka associates Nurse with her doll and therefore sees her as a mothering, comforting figure? Certainly, the doll continues to function as an icon of comfort subsequently in the series. However, the narrative, with its association of Nurse's ministrations with flaying, twisting, and other violent acts, its association of her hands with fists, and so on, hardly invites such

AVING RISEN (THE "shine" part was both conversational formality and small irony for Nurse was, in fact, thoroughly intolerant of any outward display of morning cheerfulness – or cheerfulness at any **other** time of the day, for that matter), Jaka faced her morning bath.

As a child of privilege (being one of Lord Julius' few heirs), it would be imagined such ritual would take the form of a leisurely and self-indulgent soak until, fingers shriveled and toes puckered, she would emerge, fragrant and refreshed, from the perfumed waters.

And such it might very well have been, had her guardian been any but the funereal Nurse, steeped (as she was) in the muddy brew of arcane medical convictions endemic to the northern tribes whose grim blood flowed dourly through her resentful veins.

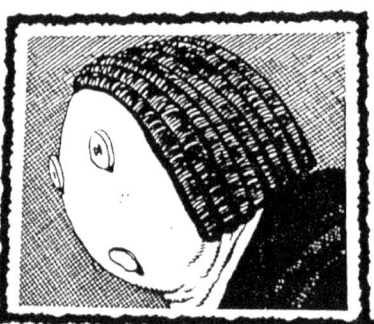

Vapours, of course, were the greatest danger. When water was heated, it released odorless, colourless and undetectable mists into the air capable of incapacitating the unwary bather.

And the vapours were not the only cause for concern.

The mere act of lying down for an extended period in water caused blood to thin and pool about one's backbone leading (inevitably, of course, like most of Nurse's consequences) to an exaggerated curvature of the spine (like the old men gathered at the gates on Market Day, their bent postures betraying youths misspent lolling carelessly beneath the corrupting surfaces of ponds and streams).

And the vapours and spinal damage were not the only dangers. There was the perfume.

O perfidious scent.

O pernicious oil.

Seeping down, down like groundwater through porous rock down, down until it was halted, arrested; accumulating and coagulating within the vulnerable tissues; there to rot until the day when, inevitably (oh, yes), the flesh would peel away in blackened and bloody strips from the very bone.

So it was that Jaka found herself each morning in her own hand-carved T'capmin marble tub knee-deep in icy well water in the sure grip of Nurse who (with firm-bristled scrub brush, a solid bar of good home-made lye soap and a lifetime of highly-developed ill-will) scraped maliciously at the few traces of grime and smudges that had managed to form since the previous morning, as if stripping twenty years worth of barnacles from a rotting hull.

All the while, nearby, the most advanced water-heating system as could be purchased with inflated Palnan crowns stood, the occasional hollow 'pong' sound its only outward sign of resentment at being made to keep its fatal vapours to itself.

an association. Does the substitution therefore suggest memory's attempt to overwrite negative experiences with positive associations? (Given the likelihood of Jaka's childhood sexual assault as a child, as discussed further blow, this idea is attractive.) Yet, the illustrations themselves seem at odds with the violent implications of Oscar's language; they suggest stillness, serenity, even elegance, not repressive violence, and Jaka herself, elsewhere in the story, asserts that nothing bad ever happened to her as a child. Coupled with her repudiation of Oscar's narration, therefore, we may be inclined to read the illustrations as of a piece with Oscar's fictionalizing of Jaka's past, and the overwriting of Nurse with Missy as an explicit marker of the fictionalizing of the past. Such a reading, in fact, would invite us to valorize the comics narrative, set in the "present," as the truth, and the illustrated prose narrative set in the "past" as therefore at least suspect, though we may then legitimately wonder why Sim devotes so much time and space to presenting a narrative that we are to read as "false."

Sim's response to a question about one of the prose passages and illustrations is perhaps telling in this respect. In issue 118, Jaka, delirious, suffers from a troubling dream of strange insect-like creatures. Here, in part, is the narrative describing these creatures: "they lacked legs, wings, and appendages of any kind (save those viscous tendrils which hung from their misshapen heads; some twitching and curious like the trunks of elephants; others limp, prey to each capricious current and draught in the room)." The passage ends with Jaka instructed, apparently by Missy, "Don't move," and forcing herself to stay still as a scream wells in her throat (Sim and Gerhard, January 1989). The narrative is no more explicit than this, and it is later in this very issue that Jaka, apparently completely seriously, asserts that nothing bad ever happened to her (and as noted above subsequently dismisses Oscar's *Jaka's Story* as a fabrication), but the illustration hints at more (figure 31). Asked about this dream and illustration, however, Sim explicitly agrees that Jaka as a child suffered some form of sexual molestation, and the dream represents a memory of that event.[4] Assuming we are willing to accept Sim's extratextual explanation of this scene, therefore, exploded is the apparent privileging of the comics narrative over the illustrated prose narrative. The "fictionalized" version in some ways (albeit obliquely and allegorically) depicts a truer past than Jaka does in her own self-narrative. One might psychoanalyze Jaka's elision of this event as an act of memory suppression or denial, of course, but perhaps the psychologically realistic explanation is less significant than the narrative disjunction the gap between different versions of Jaka's life represents. After all, Jaka's story is hardly the only one that diverges wildly, depending on whose version of it we are reading. In this instance, Jaka has constructed a narrative of her life that does not permit for such a traumatic event, so it is elided — whether consciously (Jaka is well aware of what really happened but lies about it) or unconsciously (Jaka has suppressed the memory). Which it is might affect our understanding of Jaka as a character, but which it is itself left open to the reader to attempt to determine. In other words, there is no unified, objectively "true" version of Jaka's story.

Sim's most overt play with the basic formal elements of comics as a genre as tools for metafictional exploration, though, can be found in a sequence beginning with issue 181, at the climax of which issue, we draw back from the action to view the page we have just seen re-presented on a drawing board, and then shift to a view of the eye of the creator, the comics artist we might assume is Dave Sim, though he is not so named until a subsequent

Opposite: Figure 30. A pastiche of Oscar Wilde's prose. From *Jaka's Story* (© 1990 Dave Sim and Gerhard).

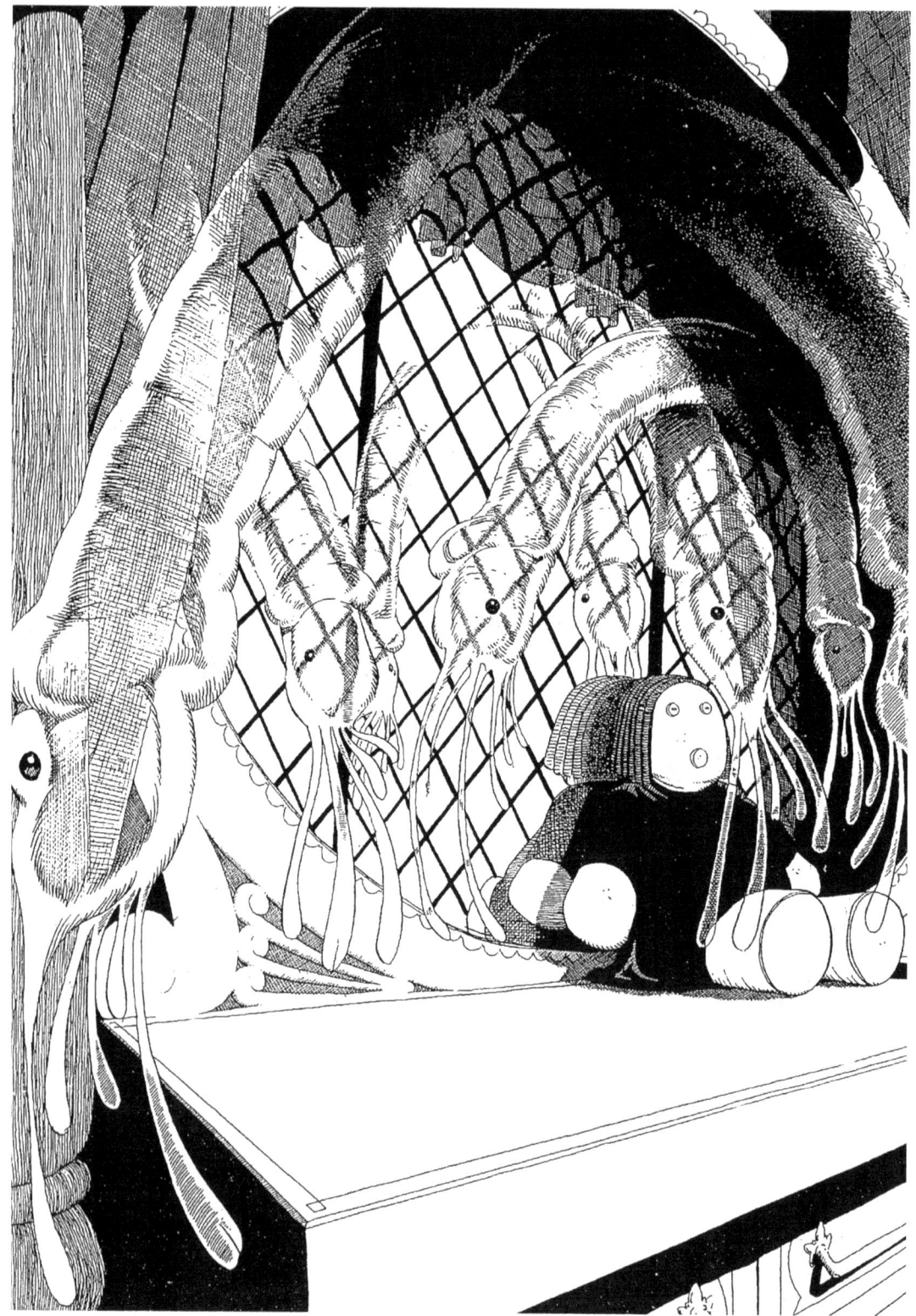

Figure 31. Imagery symbolic of sexual molestation? From *Jaka's Story* (© 1990 Dave Sim and Gerhard).

issue. The prose narrative embedding this comics sequence continues on the next page: "Viktor Davis turned away from his drawing board. Through a metaphorical haze of cigarette smoke and with perfect equanimity, he regarded his audience (as they, in turn, regarded him)" (Sim and Gerhard 1995, 144). That is, the prose passage identifies the cartoonist we have just seen, shown drawing the comics page we were looking at just before that, as Viktor Davis, not Dave Sim. Both the comics pages and the prose narrative suggest an almost Joycean detachment of the impassive artist from his work. However, even here, there is an implicit gap between the comics figure, the character Viktor Davis, and comics creator Dave Sim (whose middle name is Victor, by the way). Viktor Davis then engages in a long prose narrative that ran several issues when the book was serialized, interspersed with the ongoing comics narrative. "Viktor Davis" is clearly Dave Sim under another name — he is the writer/artist of *Cerebus*, works with Gerhard, and so on, but he is a narrativized, fictionalized version of Dave.

In *Minds*, the subsequent volume, the voice of his creator addresses Cerebus, but now this creator is not Victor Davis but "Dave," Sim's analogue within the comic. "Dave" engages in an extended dialogue with Cerebus about Cerebus' life and world, before abandoning Cerebus to his fate. "Dave" last took an active role in issue 200, though he does appear later as a bar patron to talk with Cerebus, late in *Rick's Story* (though even here, the extent to which "Dave" is actually Sim is blurred; the comic book character says he's come from Hamilton, not Kitchener, for instance). Echoed in the final books of *Cerebus*, *Latter Days* and *The Last Day*, Cerebus' interactions with "Dave" are somewhat ambiguous interactions with God. Over these issues, the reader is inclined to forget that this Dave has been presented within the prose narrative as the creation of Viktor Davis, not as a persona of Dave Sim; indeed, one could argue that "Dave" is a fictionalized version of Viktor, not the other way around, since *Reads* establishes Viktor Davis as the author of the comic we are reading, and then "Dave" appears later in that comic. Dave Sim created Viktor Davis, whom he images as the creator of the *Cerebus* comic, in which Sim introduces "Dave" as Cerebus' creator: story within story within story.

If one looks carefully at Dave's appearance at the end of *Minds*, though, one will note that the page "Dave" is drawing within *Cerebus* is not identical to the page we actually see; the page within the page includes Sim's assistant, Gerhard, looking quizzically at "Dave," a scene that does not appear on any page actually in the comic. That is, the comic within the comic is not quite the same as the comic we are reading, a subtle but important fact that ought again to invite us to distinguish between "Dave" the character in the comic and the actual author/artist. The pages seen here in fact pose fundamental questions about the creative process and about how much we can rely on what the comic seems to be telling us at any one point. Also undercut is the "Dave" that we have probably assumed is intended as a more or less accurate representative of Sim himself. In fact, as the carrot eating and "What a maroon" line suggest, "Dave" himself is, like the McGrew brothers earlier, an iteration of a Warner Brothers cartoon character, in this case the Bugs Bunny who tormented Daffy Duck (figure 32). Dave the creator goes from a detached, cool observer of his creation to a trickster.

The conclusion of *Cerebus* depends extensively on plays with narrative and interpretation, but Sim has shifted his frame of reference significantly. His earliest intertextual interfaces involved "low" culture such as comic books and pulp fiction. Over the series, Sim subsequently took on "high" culture writers such as Wilde, Fitzgerald, and Hemingway, weaving similar intertextual interpenetrations with their works. In *Rick's Story*, though, Sim anticipates the direction of his boldest intertextual play. That narrative arc presents an

almost unrecognizably translated Rick from the figure of *Jaka's Story* (indeed, one of the recurrent ways *Cerebus* problematizes the notion of truth is in the plasticity with which it treats character). During *Rick's Story*, Rick composes *The Booke of Ricke*, pseudo-scripture that, like Sim's other intertextual narratives, deals trickily with reality. As in the previous Wilde pastiche and subsequent Fitzgerald rewrite, for instance, we see clearly the contrast between the "reality" Rick experiences and his translation of it in his book. However, there is a qualitative difference between the pseudo-biography of Oscar's *Jaka's Story*, F. Stop Kennedy's *roman a clef* novel of Cerebus and Jaka and a text that purports to reveal divine truth. Though we as readers are as aware as we are in the other cases of the gaps between Rick's book and reality as it occurred, in Cerebus' world, *The Booke of Ricke* does in fact come to assume scriptural weight. Indeed, it is instrumental in Cerebus' eventual assumption of a messianic function in the final volumes of the series (once you have been pope, presumably, the only higher position you can occupy is messiah). By the end of *Latter Days* and *The Last Day*, Cerebus has parlayed the messianic function conferred on him by Rick's book into the creation of a pseudo-utopian state. Time passes. Cerebus whiles away his time engaging in detailed scriptural exegesis, narrated to us in excruciating detail over six issues of *Latter Days* under the subheading "Chasing Yoohwhoo," as Cerebus pronounces YHWH. Sim's intertextual play shifts here. Cerebus becomes the reader, and he reads scripture as conflicting narratives in dialogue with each other, God's story repeatedly co-opted, subsumed, and misread by YHWH. Rather than a coherent narrative, the Bible itself becomes the field for "contending realities," as Sim has defined the different perspectives of characters on events in the *Rick's Story* Q and A sessions; "reality" is the perspective that prevails, and Cerebus' reading of the Bible is of the contention between God and YHWH to determine reality through their versions of the master narrative.

On one level, Cerebus' exegesis function as parody of narrative interpretation, and indeed Sim has stated that originally his intent was to have Cerebus provide wacky readings of the Bible. He states in the notes to *Latter Days* that his intent was to "do a parody of the actual *content* of the Bible" and to that end, he would have a Jew show Cerebus the Torah, which Cerebus, caught up in the reading of "Rick's delusions" in *The Booke of Ricke* that allowed his transformation into the messianic Great Cerebus, would then offer his reading:

> The humor would come from the fact that Cerebus was just Cerebus. There was no 'Great' to him. So, he would read the Torah like a novel and basically spend an issue or several issues dictating this, hopefully, hilarious version of what the book was about — which would fit all the actual chapters and verses like a glove, but would be, you know, (hopefully) hilarious with all of the rabbis and priests blanching and staggering off at the end clutching the Torah [Sim and Gerhard 2003, 491].

However, and deeply ironically, perhaps, given the interview quotation I cited earlier — "I think there's a case to be made that storytellers were probably the genesis point for a lot of religions," Sim once said — while researching the Bible for this section, Sim underwent a conversion and decided to use his own, real exegesis as Cerebus'. He has forthrightly admitted that most readers will probably find his genuine views as nutty as anything he could have made up for Cerebus, so he achieves the same effect, he claims:

> If I was going to make fun of the Bible, I really needed to make fun of what was commonly accepted by most people familiar with it. If I made fun of what I thought I was reading, no

Opposite: Figure 32. Creator as trickster: Sim as Bugs Bunny. From *Minds* (© 1996 Dave Sim and Gerhard).

one was going to "get it" except me. I wandered around inside that problem for a while until I thought; Wait a minute, what if I have Cerebus just say what it is that I think that I'm reading here? It's so different from what everyone else *thinks* the book says that it'll *seem* like a parody [Sim and Gerhard 2003, 497].

Sim's religious views, aside, he's probably right. The conclusion of *Cerebus* contrasts Cerebus' receipt of an apparently divine text, the book of Cerebus, directly from God in a dream, with his utter inability not only to pass this text along to his son but also Cerebus' utter inability to get his son even to believe Cerebus' own explanation of his own past. That is, Sim obliterates the "truth" of the entire run of *Cerebus* within the world of the comic upon Cerebus' death by the new narrative of Cerebus being propounded by his son Shep-Shep, and his mother, New Joanne, whose name itself reflects her failure to understand Cerebus' story. As noted earlier, the love of Cerebus' life was Jaka, but tradition in the world within the comic book has associated Cerebus instead with a minor character named Joanne, because Sim foregrounds Joanne while eliding Jaka in *The Booke of Ricke*. At the end of *Latter Days*, we discover a young woman who is convinced Cerebus sees in her a resemblance to Joanne, which Cerebus denies; and when we see her, we know his denial is correct, for she is in fact the image of Jaka, reading Cerebus' exegesis. Therefore, the foundation of her identity as New Joanne, founder of an anti–Cerebite movement and the figure who will end Cerebus' utopia, depends on a complete misreading of the story into which she has inserted herself. The irony at the end of *Cerebus*, as Cerebus' spirit is sucked into the light — also, of course, the blank void of white paper, the absence of story — is that whatever follows (which must by definition be unknowable and unnarrated, because the comic has ended) will not only erase all the narratives we have read over 300 issues but will actively replace them with new narratives — such as F. Stop Kennedy's novelized version of Cerebus and Jaka's river voyage, perhaps.[5]

The conclusion of *Cerebus*, in effect, is that the only truth is the story that survives: but this truth is of course at odds with any notion of Truth. Perhaps the most profound irony in Cerebus is that the culminating use of intertextual metanarrative to demonstrate the contingency and unreliability of interpretation of truth consists of Sim's genuine beliefs, represented *within* the work as Cerebus' nutty misreading of the Bible and indeed used by Sim for that purpose because he knows his readers will not be able to tell parody from truth.

Notes

1. Sim first explicitly articulates the "All stories are true" conceit in *Reads* when discussing Alan Moore's theories of narrative, which lead Viktor Davis (Sim's analogue) to conclude that the idea "amounted to an alternative view of human history where fact, genuine fact, virtually did not exist. All that existed were stories, lies, myths and legends" (Sim and Gerhard 1995, 164).

2. I will have a bit more to say about Missy below. This doll becomes a major recurring symbol in the series, a role that merits more attention than can be accommodated within the parameters of this paper.

3. In 2005 and 2006, Sim engaged in a monthly question and answer session with members of the Yahoo Cerebus group. Readers sent five questions about each volume in the series to Sim, and his responses subsequently posted to the group and then stored in its files section (see http://tinyurl.com/4nx6hr7) and are well worth reading for anyone interested in Sim's explications of many of the unresolved questions in the series. One of the *Jaka's Story* questions was about this strategy. Sim explains it as serving several purposes but as, at the deepest level, reflective of what he sees as the disturbing socialization of girls to misperceive reality (e.g., by perceiving dolls as real) and who construct their relationship with the world as between themselves and Other. Here's a portion of Sim's explanation:

And that was how I pictured Jaka. Her mother dies before she's old enough to be really aware of what a mother is, so it's less easy for her to think of Missy as a baby replica-being to Jaka what Jaka is to her mother (which touches tangentially on another interesting direction: this is me. I, the little girl, am the baby and this hunk of plastic represents me. So I am both me and the Other. I am a little girl and I am a hunk of plastic. Seriously creepy, in my view), so Jaka pictures Nurse as an enlarged Missy. Missy is Other. Nurse is Other. Jaka is Jaka. So she begins to understand her relationships in those frames of reference. There is Jaka and there is Other. Some Others she has control over and some Others have control over her.

I do not think this reading is incompatible with mine, but it does have a significantly different valence.

4. See question twelve and its response in "A Cerebus Mailing List 'Talk' with Dave Sim": In response to the question, "Did Lord Julius molest young Jaka," Sim said, "Someone molested young Jaka (you guessed what the creatures in her fever dreams actually were). She's blocked out who, but Lord Julius would obviously be a suspect" (Sim March 2004).

5. Sim himself leaves what might seem the most pressing eschatological question unanswered.

While one might infer from Cerebus' decision to go towards the images of Jaka, Bear, and Ham, and from the conversion of Jaka's hands to something like talons just before Cerebus enters the light (Sim and Gerhard 2004, 237), that Cerebus has chosen wrongly and gets to spend eternity among the damned, Sim refuses to endorse that reading as required. In the final annotation in *The Last Day*, Sim's response to the question "Is Cerebus in Hell" is to say, "All I am suggesting is that making a hasty decision to Go Into the Light might not be the wisest course of action," and, "One thing is for sure, I'm not going to find out 'til I get there and neither will you" (ibid., 261).

"Why Certainly Dear Boy...": Incorporating Oscar Wilde into the Aardvark's World

Gregory John Fink

Introduction

The duality of the personal sphere and of the public sphere in the life of Oscar Wilde has been in some ways a stock theme for many writers going back to the earliest days of Wilde's fame. Contemporary writers began basing characters on Wilde as early as 1877. Most of the authors who based characters on Wilde were content to use an exaggerated caricature of one of his traits as a comic effect in their writings. Some people used Wilde's public persona as a way to comment on the esthetic movement or any of the other vogues of their era associated with Wilde and his followers. The trend to use the public aspect of Wilde as a fictional character has also had the effect of drawing people to the worlds of Wilde scholarship.

One person so affected was Dave Sim. He avidly devoured as much as could be gathered on the subject of Wilde's art and of his life in the last half of the 19th century. Sim built on his studies of Wilde and turned them first into an exploration of the nature of public image and then into a corresponding look at the factual person behind the facade. He did this by using Wilde as a character in the pages of his comic series *Cerebus*.

Wilde makes his first appearance in the second part of the *Jaka's Story* arc. Sim portrays Wilde as a man of leisure and a lover of art above all things in keeping with the more well-known aspects of Wilde's personality. A further exploration of who Oscar Wilde truly was behind the public face provides the main theme of Sim's follow up story arc, *Melmoth*. In both cases, Sim has accurately portrayed someone who took great pains to hide his factual self from prying eyes.

The idea that Wilde could have any aspect of his personality not fully known to the wider world is likely impossible. Oscar Wilde, the great icon of late 19th century art and literature, champion of the esthetic movement, proponent of stylish living and the undisputed best conversationalist of his day was somewhat of a popular subject in the writings of the early 20th century. The idea that there could be much in Wilde's past that is not already well known to any scholar willing to take the effort to read the hundreds of volumes written about the man and his works seems implausible at best. Yet Wilde was someone so wrapped up in a persona that he had created for himself that it is possible that even Wilde had forgotten whom the actual Oscar was. Sim deftly captured and portrayed both the public and the private personalities of Oscar Wilde, and did so in a sympathetic manner that allowed his readers to gain insight into the true nature of the famous author. In *Jaka's Story*, Sim presents his readers an articulate and witty exploration of the true personality of this most fascinating literary figure. In the process, Sim shows his readers the place of identity in both Cerebus' and our world.

Wilde was not the first person from our world to cross over to the world of *Cerebus*. What is distinct about Wilde is that he was the first to go beyond a cameo appearance or being a supporting character to become a starring character in his own right. Sim, in using Wilde's well-known public persona as a driving force in his story, taps into a larger and far older literary tradition. Oscar Wilde carefully designed his public persona almost from the beginning, a fact very well known by many of his contemporaries. Angela Kingston points out that Oscar Wilde's well known public face was far too fascinating a one to be ignored and that they "could not resist the temptation" (Kingston 2007, 3) of using him in their works.[1]

Who Was Oscar Wilde?

Wilde's public face is perhaps one of the most instantly recognized ones from not just the late 19th century but perhaps of the last century as well. Wilde's persona, that of the infamous talker, wit, literary genius and all around bon vivant, was as constructed as any of those that he gave to his characters. Wilde was the toast of London, Paris and New York. Many hundreds recalled meeting him and what it was that he had to say. Those who knew him took it upon themselves to tell the story of his life and many biographies turned up in the forty years following his death. There are differences in them but the overall themes of Wilde's life are the same. However, even those who were closest to him would admit that they did not know everything there was to know about him. One thing that many of them would agree on was that Oscar was, in almost all things, the ultimate disciple of the high world of art.

Wilde[2] was born in Dublin in 1854 to a prominent surgeon and a woman of literary aspirations. A good student who excelled at Greek and at poetry, Wilde entered the esthetic movement after meeting Walter Pater. Pater was a champion of the movement that held the idea of appreciating art for its own sake as one of its primary motivators. Wilde took the ideas of Pater to heart and set out to spread the esthetic movement wherever he could find a willing audience. After a lecture tour of the United States and Canada Wilde began to make a name for himself as a speaker and a wit. His writings became more and more talked of but where he really excelled was as a playwright.

Sim's focus on Wilde is not the usual one of Wilde being a celebrated dramatist. While drama would seem something that would tie Wilde into the world of Iest, Sim builds on the image of Oscar Wilde the writer instead. The device of Oscar as a writer of fiction, despite Wilde only ever having produced one actual novel, works very well in consideration of some of the wider themes that Sim chose to explore over the course of writing and drawing *Cerebus*. One of those themes was the creation and spread of identity.

Jaka's Story — Oscar, the Well-Known Author of "Reads," Presents Himself

Comics have an advantage over other art forms in that the addition of word balloons and narration can make the artist's vision plainer to the casual viewer. However, what do you do when the text on the page threatens to overwhelm the artwork itself? Can a text be a substitute for the visuals themselves? In *Cerebus*, there are occasions where what must seem at first glance to be an overabundance of text is eclipsed by the fantastic line work. This can be applied in many ways to the incredibly wordy telling of the life story of Jaka Tavers in *Jaka's Story*. It is not a fair criticism in this case as it would be difficult to contain the entire story Sim wanted to tell in the book's more than 500 pages. The story Sim had to tell, if drawn out in the traditional way, would have filled the rest of his proposed 300-issue run and then some.

In *Jaka's Story,* Sim presents the reader with the retelling of what to most readers of the book must have seemed like a very trivial part of the story of *Cerebus*. Sim sets out to give his readers a greater understanding of Jaka's back-story, a character that had, until then been an important yet relatively minor character. Jaka debuted as a tavern dancer that a drugged Cerebus falls deeply in love with. She comes and goes with little fanfare. However, there is something in what she comes to represent to Cerebus. She becomes his ideal, innocent of the machinations of the more vulgar world she inhabits, and for him an expression of true love. By the *Church & State* story arcs, Jaka has left tavern dancing and has married. She refuses Cerebus' invitation to leave everything behind to go with him into the wilds. In *Jaka's Story*, Cerebus and Jaka have crossed paths again. Cerebus still clearly loves her.

Oscar's introduction to the world of the aardvark is at first invisible to the reader. Sim splits the more traditional comic pages of his story with long sections of text excerpted from a biography of the life of Jaka Tavers. We learn from the then-anonymous author that Jaka was the niece of one of the most powerful men in the aardvark's world. Sim soon reveals the identity of our author for the story of Jaka Tavers to be a well-known author of popular reads. Sim names him simply Oscar.

Sim shows Oscar to be an overweight but immaculately dressed individual. He is highly articulate with the haughty manner of a well-born gentleman. We do not know the origin of Sim's Oscar but it is possible that he too shared a similar start in life as Wilde did. The veneer of civilization placed on the disciple of art is a deep one. The depiction of Wilde in this manner is in keeping with the well-known public persona that he took great pains to create and promote. Sim conveys the importance of a life lived for the sake of appreciating art through Oscar's applying the lens of the artist to everything around him. For example, the exchange that Wilde has with Pud Withers over the way in which Withers is keeping Jaka and Rick as essentially paid guests. Despite Withers sinking as low as to call Oscar a sodomite there is no violence in the exchange between the author and the innkeeper. Oscar corrects the mispronunciation of the word and reminds Withers that gentlemen do not resort to such slurs. He is clearly angry but far too deeply cloaked in his identity as a man of refinement to sink to that level. The assumed personality is more important to Oscar than getting his revenge so he puts aside his obvious anger in order to maintain the civilized face he has put on.

Identity as something you can create as opposed to being something you are born with is not a new idea yet Wilde took the creation to an extreme. As he did in so many other ways Wilde built the face of a man well versed in so many obscure points on the past works of art. The discussion of the origin of the guffin with Pud Withers is an example of the mastery of obscure artistic knowledge. Sim includes it to show just how well Oscar has himself mastered the creation of a public face in the same way that he has changed the face of the stone head by painting it. As simply as a little paint changes the stone head into a potent anti–Cirinist symbol a man of humble means can become the leading proponent of art in Europe. Sim plays with this public persona and uses it to drive the action in the second half of the *Jaka's Story* arc. He discards the public persona of Wilde as soon as it has served his purposes.

Melmoth — the Real Man Behind the Fake Name

The story arc that follows directly on from the *Jaka's Story* graphic novel (apart from a brief interlude not collected by Sim in these volumes) is *Melmoth*. On the surface it is difficult to comprehend why *Melmoth* is included as part of the overall arc of *Cerebus*. The main character of the series is literally a bystander (by-sitter perhaps as he sits for almost all of it on the patio of Dino's Café) to the events of the plot and does not interact with the Wilde character. Cerebus had not met Oscar in the pages of *Jaka's Story* either but Oscar was driving the characters', including Cerebus, plots forward by his encouragement of Jaka's activities in Pud Withers taproom so that he can more authentically end his book. Much as in Wilde's real life Oscar was the author of his own fall from grace in his obsession to make the perfect telling of Jaka's life. Wilde's efforts to protect his reputation in the face of the accusations of the Marquis of Queensbury were as fruitless as the ambitions of Oscar in *Jaka's Story* to capture the intimate portrait of the lost daughter of Palnu. It is fitting that a man who so carefully constructed his public image just as carefully destroyed that persona.

In *Melmoth*, Sim goes one step further in his exploration of just who Oscar Wilde truly was by exploring the last days of the literary giant's life. Much like the giant in the Wilde short story Oscar is not in a happy place in life when *Melmoth* opens. His two years at hard labor are behind him but Oscar is now a much older looking and beaten figure than he was in the pages of *Jaka's Story*. Oscar Wilde had left prison looking naturally older and more tired but as many commentators noted he was soon back to his old look after a rest in Europe. Pictures of Wilde in 1896 in Naples show him to look much like he had in 1894 but this return to health was only a temporary one. To show this would only take away from the impact of Oscar's rapid physical decline. Sim knew this well and it is a clever cheat to skip that part of the story and instead focus on the end of the summer of 1900 when the decline was evident to all that met Oscar. This choice to show Oscar Wilde as broken and aged beyond his years is in keeping with how Wilde was as soon as a few years after his release from prison. The description of Wilde at this time:

> My heart almost stood still as this once celebrated personage crossed Mme. Mickauleff's threshold. I could not believe that this was the man about whom the whole world had been talking. He was bent with a weight not of years. He had an old man's obesity. His cheeks were flabby and sagging, his eyes were dull. His manner of speech was like a blow to me, for his words came very slowly, and his sentences were timorous. He seemed grateful for the least consideration [Wilde 1979, 442].

Sim draws Oscar Wilde throughout *Melmoth* in this way. Consider the scene where Robbie and Oscar are walking back to Oscar's room (figure 33). The figure of Oscar is still fat but

Figure 33. Gerhard's inks emphasize the darkness and bring a sense of futility that seems to surround Wilde. From *Melmoth* (© 1991 Dave Sim and Gerhard).

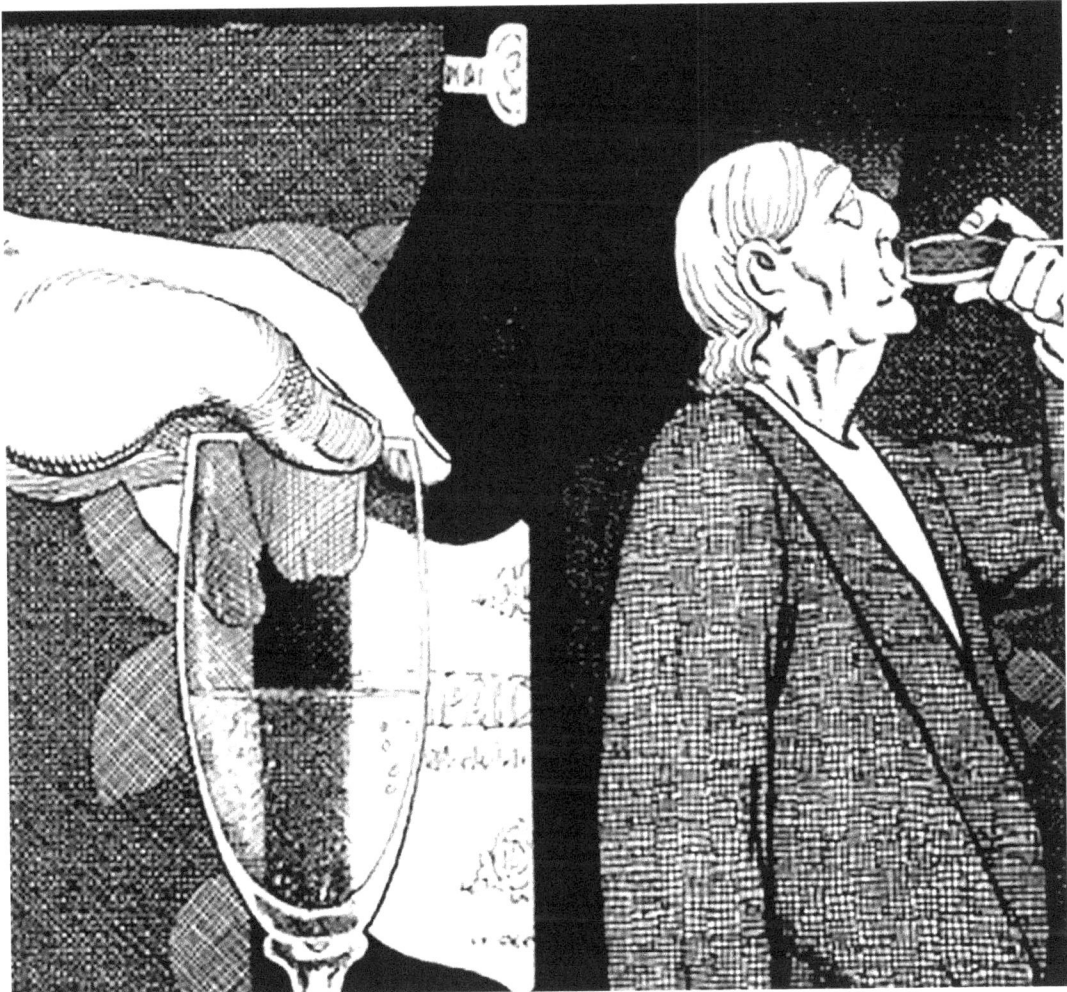

Figure 34. Wilde's continued dependence on alcohol is a factor in his decline as Sim often depicts Oscar with a glass in his hand. From *Melmoth* (© 1991 Dave Sim and Gerhard).

now he hulks and you can almost see the shuffle of his feet as he and the younger man walk down the boulevard. Stooped and bent, he looks pained by age. Gerhard's inks, bringing out the deep shadows to the face of the now broken man, emphasize the darkness and bring a sense of futility that seems to surround Wilde in the pages of *Melmoth*. It is easy to see where this description is from in the biographical writings done by men like Sherard, whom Sim references in his afterword, as well as the contemporary remembrance in the above quotation. Oscar Wilde was no longer the man that he had been but had begun to become the man that perhaps he always had been underneath it all.

It is this physical change which most seems to fascinate Sim as he dwells on the ways in which Wilde was no longer the man he had been just a few short years earlier. The years of heavy smoking and excessive drinking had played their part in prematurely aging Wilde long before the impact of his becoming a pariah following his fall from grace. Yet it is Wilde's continued dependence on alcohol that Sim sees as a factor in this decline as he often depicts Oscar with a glass in his hand (figure 34).

While overeating and overindulgence played their part, it is the impact of the exile that is the greater factor in the decline and early death of Oscar Wilde. The device of Oscar's physical decline allows Sim to show the true nature of the man Wilde breaking through the false persona of the public figure. Perhaps it is only as one's health fails and strips away much of the illusion of our lives that we truly present who we actually are to the larger world.

When looking at the way that Sim depicts Wilde over the course of *Melmoth* the putting aside of the mask of the public persona becomes one of the story's central themes. Gone for Oscar are the bon mots and light and effortless conversation. Instead, there is a lingering frailty of body and of mind. Sim shows us that as one approaches the end all illusion is shed in much the same way that falling leaves show the true shape of the tree they hid from view.

Wilde had always been larger than life but he hid the physical reality of himself much in the same way that he hid his true personality. Buried under the fine clothes and striking choices of color and style was a large man made for a very soft life. The two years at hard labor were physically punishing but the greater impact was the unmasking of Wilde's deepest secrets before an uncaring and callous world. Sim is very adept at capturing the air of futility and the loss of hope that Oscar would ever return to the heights he had once known.

Wilde took the name Melmoth as a pseudonym in a desperate attempt to hide his true self from the world. Sebastian Melmoth was the main character of a book of the same name written by a great uncle of Wilde's.[3] The title for this piece is apt as at this point of his life Oscar is as Melmoth was. Melmoth was a man cursed to live beyond his years and his only hope of escape was to try to fool someone into taking up his curse. The way that Sim shows how tired Oscar has become of life echoes what did Charles Maturin for his Melmoth in the course of his plot. Death as a release from the burden that Oscar placed on himself is not only an end to his life but it is the ultimate renewal of his reputation. By dying as he did, the maligned genius cut off before he could complete his works, Wilde managed in a strange way to guarantee his future renown. Sim was not the only one drawn to the tragic figure of Oscar Wilde but he is one of the few that explored both sides of the man's life and still managed to present a sympathetic portrayal.

Conclusions

Who can say what it is that makes someone a fully real person? Is it a faithful and accurate description of the individual backed up with the most accurate and accepted sources? Perhaps the word of key eyewitnesses is not enough to establish identity. In that situation, would photographic evidence be more useful for someone trying to convey the actuality of an individual long since passed away? If the individual in question was someone of the ordinary sort, that might be enough to ensure an accurate portrayal. However if the person in question were a very well known celebrity then this would not be enough. Celebrity brings a masking quality to the true persona of many who do become famous and this can further obscure their real selves from our knowledge. Dave Sim masterfully managed to bring out both aspects of the personality of Oscar Wilde in his work. The portrayal is a fair representation of both the public and the private sides of the Irish literary legend.

An aura of profound insight into the human condition surrounds great art. This aspect of visual arts draws in the viewer and makes the work a feast for both the eye and the soul. The esthetic movement that swept the art world of the late 19th century held this premise to be one of the key ways in which people should approach art and by doing this attempt to better their surroundings and themselves. However, the esthetes had concerns about the everyday uneducated person studying art. Their fear was that without having a substantial understanding of the iconography of the image much of the meaning of the piece is lost. By not understanding the artist's vision, the viewer cannot hope to appreciate the talent of the artist or the glory of the piece before them. Perception of the meaning of a piece, to the esthetes, was often more important than the substance of the actual work itself. In this way, the substance of the man Oscar is more noticeable in the moment of death than in the height of his influence as a dandy. A true identity always trumps a created one.

Notes

1. Kingston's book is a fascinating examination of the use of a public figure as a literary character. The influence of the book on this essay is to see the continuation by Sim of the tradition of using Wilde as a character.

2. This paragraph is a very brief amalgamation of the various biographies of Wilde. For further information, the interested student should consult some of the biographies included in the bibliography.

3. The full title of the book in question: *Melmoth the Wanderer*, written by Charles Maturin. The book, written in 1820, features a man who has made a pact with the Devil to live an extra 150 years but who has tired of the deceptions and wants to find someone to pass the curse onto. Maturin was the uncle of Wilde's mother Jane. She usually went by the name "Speranza" so the need to hide one's self behind a façade is well established in Wilde's family. As is the ability to write as it truly is a remarkable novel in and of itself.

PART THREE
BECOMING SYNONYMOUS
WITH SOMETHING INDESCRIBABLE

Seeing Sound
C. W. Marshall

The visual representation of noise within the dramatic world of comics is a defining element of the genre, allowing readers to pace narrative progress on their own terms. Sim scripts sounds, giving them a shape through letters and symbols, and that requires readers to perform a sensory transformation, processing with the eye what they associate normally with the ear. The process is not quite the same as reading a novel, though: in that case, words represent all the senses; the conventions of language use symbols to depict all the aspects of the fictional world. With comics, the process is different. The combination of image and text means that not everything abstracts into symbols of writing — what comics calls lettering. Lettering exists at a point of tension, operating both at the level of the visual and at the verbal (Kannenberg Jr. 2001, 163–92, at 165).[1] Sim processes some of the dramatic world, as he does with the real world: visual representation, framed by each panel in a sequential narrative, depicts images that the brain processes as it does visuals in the real world (with some modification, granted: two dimensions, not three; stylized representation; a different color palette, if one uses color at all; etc.). The cognitive processes are to some extent congruent. Sound in comics is different — one must see it — and as a result, the brain is both reading the panel (a process that occupies time, mirroring the passing of time as someone speaks) as well as viewing it (processing the image and other symbolism presented). Further, images relate one to another, in a sequence read and connected together in the mind as well, and related to the real world, which provides an implicit point of comparison for any fictional narrative. Of course, the process of reading comics is more neurologically complex than this, but even with this, it is possible to see considerable richness in the visual depiction of sound.

Sound in comics is not the only thing lettering represents. The tension exists when one uses words for a variety of effects within a visual field that represents one of the greatest opportunities for comics creativity. That the decoding is almost automatic — these are not things that we need to think about as we read the latest issue of our favorite superhero comic speaks to the enormous communicative power that the juxtaposition of words and image can convey. The reader's brain parses each panel, builds connections, and creates an imaginative world where anything can happen. Dave Sim's creative representation of sound in *Cerebus* embodies some of the boldest experiments ever attempted in using the visual to represent the acoustic. Throughout its run, *Cerebus* continually experimented with the visual representation of sound, creating stunning effects through his unique lettering style that are possible only within comics. Will Eisner's work anticipates some of the effects, but in terms of committed engagement with the effects possible with lettering, *Cerebus* stands alone. In this chapter, I wish to consider this distinct feature of Dave Sim's narrative technique: how Sim, as a creative artist, represents sound in *Cerebus*.

However, let us start in the Bronze Age. In Marvel Comics' *Amazing Spiderman* 121 (June 1973), Gwen Stacy falls to her death during a battle between Spiderman and the Green Goblin, commonly identified as the first death of an innocent in North American mainstream hero comics.[2] During the battle, Spiderman tries to save her, but, as the Goblin tells him on the next page, "A fall from that height would kill anyone—before they struck the ground!" (27.6). Two months later at her funeral (in issue 123), the caption can still say she was "Killed by the Green Goblin [during a battle between the Goblin and Spiderman]." However, neither of these claims is true, as a sound effect makes clear. The presence of a small "snap" in the crucial panel (ibid., 19; figure 35) shows that Gwen's neck breaks, due to the decelerating force when caught by Spiderman's web. The crucial snap remains unheard by the characters (small letters are used, and there are no other people in the panel) but it is visible to the reader (who must therefore incorporate it into the developing understanding of the larger story), and lies at odds with the narrative presented by later claims that blame the Goblin.[3] The sound effect, the lettering of which barely broaches the panel borders, problematizes the absolution the story appears to give the hero. Far from being an incidental decoration, this sound effect raises issues of ethics and responsibility, as well as narrative authority. Comics defines itself as a visual medium that integrates sequences images and words. The use of words within the sequenced panels of comics can operate in three registers: attributed text; environmental text; and narrating text. Attached directly to a character or object within the panel, or just outside of it, often through the device of thought balloons or speech balloons, is attributed text. When text is not attributed, it may exist within the dramatic frame as part of the environment within the panel, as with sound effects, or it may exist outside of the environment of the panel providing some form of narration. Such framing narration can be impersonal or can be written in the voice of one of the characters, representing thoughts, after-the-fact recollection of events, or (more tangibly) the contents of a diary or journal (as such, personal narrating text is a kind of extension of the thought balloon.) Two of these categories—attributed words spoken by characters and sound effects, are diegetic (if I may borrow a useful term from the study of music in cinema): they are presented as originating within and existing in the visual world, and have the potential to be heard by characters in the panel; framing narration, on the other hand, is non-diegetic, as are thought balloons, which have a liminal quality to them: the reader sees words on the page, but the characters within the dramatic world hear nothing.

The presence of diegetic sound within the panel also creates the experience of time: as Eisner emphasizes, time (usually) passes between panels, of course, but the presence of speech marks a duration, from which he selects only a single moment in the graphic representation (Eisner 1985, 25–30).[4] Further, "the balloon is perhaps the only element of the paginal apparatus on which the gaze definitely stops.... It is a point of anchorage, an obligatory passage" (Groensteen 2007, 79). The speech balloon demarcates a specific passage of time, and its relationship to the panel and its neighbors is crucial for establishing the reader's experience of time passing. The use of blank space within a balloon can indicate silences, and convey the importance of the few words that a character does speak. In *Cerebus* (Sim and Gerhard 1988, 926; figure 36), the large amount of blank space in Astoria's balloons gives import to the few words she says: "Now Hurry" (pause) "We haven't much time." Sim reinforces the effect by the continuity of space in panels 4 and 5. Similarly, a single text-filled panel can visually represent an ongoing, monotonous lecture that admits no interruption. Later in *Church & State*, the amount of text given to the Judge takes time to read—it extends the duration of the panel by the absence of figures in the third panel, which instead pulls back and shows the moon. The small linked balloons in panel 1 allow for the possibility of interruption; the longer ones in panel 2 do not (Sim and Gerhard 1988, 1197; figure 37).

These examples would seem to challenge Groensteen's claims that "the balloon exerts no true influence on the writing of the text, for the simple reason that it is precisely calibrated with reference to the number of words that compose the enunciation," or that "there is an implicit limit ... to the quantity of text for which a balloon can be made the receptacle" (Groensteen 2007, 84–85). This may be true for some comics lettering: the most common comics lettering uses block capitals, sans serif, which reproduce easily and yield "a graceful legibility" (Kannenberg 2001, 168 and see 173). In

Figure 35. The death of Gwen Stacey. From *Amazing Spiderman* 121 (© 1973 Marvel Comics).

a much-cited passage, Eisner calls the speech balloon a "desperation device" which "attempts to capture and make visible an ethereal element: sound" (Eisner 1985, 26). Eisner's language senses a limitation to the medium, but Sim shows the speech balloon can be an opportunity for the artist to affect the pace with which the reader encounters the narrative: the speech balloon enables the representation of sound, and time. Scott McCloud identifies a number of functions, but his analysis resists any systemic appreciation (McCloud 1993, 134). The balloon is both a container for information (an outline with a known symbolic function) and a carrier of information (the contained text) (Groensteen 2007, 68), and here the choice of the visual aspects of the contained text can help to create emotional effects in the audience.

A specific style of lettering can establish an environmental effect for a given comic, but variation can achieve local effects as well. In both cases, "letters function as an extension

Figure 36. The use of blank space within a balloon can indicate silences, and convey the importance of the few words that a character does speak. From *Church & State I* (© 1988 Dave Sim and Gerhard).

Figure 37. The small linked balloons in panel 1 allow for the possibility of interruption; the longer ones in panel 2 do not. From *Church & State I* (© 1988 Dave Sim and Gerhard).

132   Part Three. Becoming Synonymous with Something Indescribable

of the imagery" (Bongco 2000, 72). Five panels in *Rick's Story* (152.1–5; figure 38) exhibit over a dozen means of representing text, with thought bubbles and speech balloons happily alternating to represent the natural back and forth of ordinary conversation. Carrier rightly stresses a functionalist approach: "Balloons are an extraordinarily useful resource for the visual artist" (Carrier 2000 38, and 36–39 generally).

The genre of comics by its nature necessarily subverts all sensory experience to the visual, and it possesses a much richer range of means for representing tone, timbre, modulation, resonance, articulation, color, regional accents, and many other qualities of sound than do other purely visual media, such as the novel. For example, use of color, line, and the specifics of the lettering used, the presence or absence of a physical balloon, all help to identify and characterize the speakers in Grant Morrison's *Arkham Asylum: a serious house on serious Earth* (1989). Morrison literalizes specific characters with tonal color. Most creators, however, inadequately explore this range, and sound diegetics remain an underused tool in the creation of emotional engagement. While many creators, particularly of independent comics, can evolve visually distinct and evocative balloon styles or means of representing text, internal variation remains minimal.[5] There are of course exceptions, and in the late 1980s, the use of color to identify the speech of certain individuals witnessed a period of aggressive experimentation (Groensteen 2007, 74). The symbolic aspects of the

Figure 38. Five panels exhibit over a dozen means of representing text, with thought bubbles and speech balloons happily alternating to represent the natural back and forth of ordinary conversation. From *Rick's Story* (© 1998 Dave Sim and Gerhard).

visual representation of sound, its dependency upon culturally-specific icons, mean that even in extended formalist experiments, such as Ricardo Delgado's ongoing *Age of Reptiles* series, in which there are no words, no narration, and no sound effects, iconographic markers nevertheless still are used to indicate that sound is occurring — even three short lines emitting from a dinosaur's mouth show the pressures exerted by the comics medium as the rigors of Delgado's experiment are subtly undermined.

My interest in the theorization of the speech balloon and lettering then is to identify some of the variables that are available, and to isolate their use in *Cerebus*. Sim's work is often discussed only in terms of his own personal views (on women and gender issues, on religion, and on the rights of self-publishers; see elsewhere in this volume), some of which (but only some) spill into the comic itself. Noticed less is the technical virtuosity with which Sim has represented aspects of diegetic and non-diegetic sound throughout the run of *Cerebus*.

Cerebus is a story of an aardvark that dies in the final issue. This event is predicted in issue 111 (published in 1988) — Cerebus will die "alone, unmourned, and unloved" — and it constitutes one of the principle means by which Sim perpetuates and manipulates reader involvement for the last sixteen years of the series. Cerebus' motivations remain relatively one-dimensional throughout (in rough chronological order, they constitute yearnings for gold, sex, True Love, comic books, and God) as around him individuals much smarter than him manipulate and exploit him for power. While telling this story, Sim pursues a series of other literary agendas that run alongside the primary story: parodies of mainstream hero comics and homages to self-published comics; claims for the literary status of the comics medium (to be set alongside modern authors such as Oscar Wilde, F. Scott Fitzgerald, and Ernest Hemingway); explorations of the limits of free speech, authors' rights, and parody; and formalist experiments of the comics medium.[6] Sim's experimentation in layout, panel use, narrative patterns, and intertextuality all warrant deeper consideration.[7]

The creative use of the appearance of the written word in *Cerebus* does not operate in isolation: throughout the run, Sim challenges the integration of word and image as presented in the sequential narrative of comics. Depicting sound in the comics medium is an ontological difficulty, but it is one that Sim continues to meet with creativity and innovation. There have of course been discussions of sound in the medium and the effects of lettering before,[8] but using *Cerebus* as an extended test case enables us to document the range of techniques Sim has employed in his representation of speech and sound effects: my interest then is in Sim's technical accomplishment in *Cerebus* with lettering. This accomplishment can be set alongside other formal experiments conducted over the run of *Cerebus*, involving the juxtaposition of image and text (as in *Reads*, issues 175–186) or the emulation of the literary styles of Fitzgerald (in *Going Home*, issues 232–250) and Hemingway (in *Form and Void*, issues 251–265). It is within this context that one best understands an examination of Sim's representation of sound.

As an example of the variations in lettering possible, we can consider a moment near the end of *Church & State I*: Archbishop Powers is attempting to unify the Eastern and Western churches, and Cerebus is one of two people who stand in his way. His characterization is confident throughout, with a distinctive square balloon shape authorizing his pronouncements: dark lines, size of text, and underlining all convey Archbishop Powers' authority and volume, in contrast to those around him (Sim 1987b, 274). There also exists a structural echo of this point with a moment with Cirin in the second half of the series (Sim and Gerhard 1993, 157.1).[9] At a key moment (Sim 1987b, 362.4–6), however, President Weisshaupt, who is planning to create a political buffer between himself and the religious schism, suffers a heart attack, during a standoff with Cerebus (who has invoked divine wrath on those who do not give him their gold). Now the iconic nature of the imagery in this climactic scene is using a vocabulary established elsewhere in the volume.[10] Both of these conventions are invoked at the critical moment, when Weisshaupt's shouts, evoking the square balloon of Archbishop Powers, give way to silence and collapse, as his ambitions dissolve into the tiny puff in the final black balloon (Sim 1987b, 362.4–6; figure 39). Weisshaupt's authority is removed, but the reader understands his voice is slowly fading (visual metaphors are already part of our language) while pain of frustration and broken dreams comes through in the dark lines.

This is all communicated intuitively—as Carrier notes, "We are amazingly flexible at making image/word connections" (Carrier 2000, 32)—but the degree of nuance accomplished here is indeed surprising: "With comics, what is now hard to reconstruct is how the seemingly complex conventions associated with word balloons [are], without any explanation, mastered rather quickly by everyone who reads them" (ibid., 45). Successful lettering provides additional information to the readers that is not available from the words alone. The effect is additive, and *ad hoc* solutions can produce moments of

Figure 39. At the critical moment, when Weisshaupt shouts, evoking the square balloon of Bishop Powers, he gives way to silence and collapses as his ambitions dissolve into the tiny puff in the final black balloon. From *Church & State I* (© 1988 Dave Sim and Gerhard).

extraordinary emotional depth. A survey of three categories of sound representation will enable some conclusions.

Accents and Voice

Perhaps the most distinctive feature of the cast of character Sim assembles in *Cerebus* is his use of historical figures for his secondary characters: known faces from politics and cinema comedy are "cast" within the fictional world. Such anachronism (incorporating Margaret Thatcher, Groucho Marx, Oscar Wilde, George Harrison, Woody Allen, etc.) helps to create emotional attachment to recurring individuals over time, and helps the reader keep track of the extensive supporting cast, but its success is dependent upon both a contextual visual similarity as well as an ability to mimic the voices through a purely visual medium. Moreover, here we see the first distinctive feature of Sim's accomplishment, described by Scott McCloud as "dramatic variations of size and shape to portray vocal inflection on a word-to-word-basis." Artists often use this to represent a broad cultural linguistic stereotype: such as the representation of German (filtered, apparently, through Sgt. Schultz of *Hogan's Heroes*; e.g., *Cerebus* 358:3–5), and French (where a bartender offers "Lest cole"; Sim and Gerhard 1993, 220). It can simultaneously evoke Warner Brothers' cartoon characters that bear no physical similarity to the character depicted. The bartender's French accent ("I kent do eet") is at odds with Yosemite Sam ("Ah didn't hear yuh, varmint!"; ibid.). Sim has no hesitation adding layers to layers, as visual parody of one thing coexists with a textually represented acoustic parody of another. At one point, Elrod of Melvinbone, a parody of Michael Moorcock's albino fantasy hero Elric of Melniboné, appears wearing a cockroach costume because he has joined the Legion of Six-Foot Telepathic Cockroaches (a generic superhero group, apparently), and he speaks with the vocal inflections of Foghorn Leghorn: "Ah have ... I say ... Ah have arrived," who then offers "'Jaw'-'Ree'-'Vey' for the bilingually inclined" (Sim and Gerhard 1993, 186.1–2). Sim is not obliged to maintain consistently the representations of French: direct phonetic representation replaces the accented English seen with the bartender. Sim presents Swahili, in contrast, later in the series as untranslated, as it remains incomprehensible to the other characters in the scene (see Sim and Gerhard 2001, 472.1–2).[11] In this example, a speech bubble accompanies the foreign by a foreign form of speech bubble, as fat from a piece of meat drips into a campfire (figure 40).

The effect is even more dramatic with Sim's casting of actual individuals with distinctive speech patterns. Through speech patterns and word choice, the Marx Brothers, the Three Stooges, and Rodney Dangerfield, are some of the more straightforward characterizations evoked in *Cerebus*. More distinctive, though, is Prince Mick (a character drawn like Mick Jagger), identified in part only because of the audience's previous familiarity with his distinctive speech patterns: "Sow. Wha'a yew up tow t'die?" (Sim and Gerhard 1997, 165.6 ["So, what are you up to today?"]). The reader inherits and appropriates Sims's sense of language and sound: the act of reading the panel teaches the reader the accent or voice in question, and at times the effect is only possible (for me at least) when the words are actually spoken aloud. Even when his appearance is changed, his speech characteristics are sufficient to identify the character: "'s naugh' *posse* bo'" (Sim and Gerhard 1991, 76.7 ["It's not possible"]). The same is true of Mrs. Thatcher, an agent of a right-wing totalitarian government, whose speech becomes more and more exaggerated as the series progresses. Variations of size and

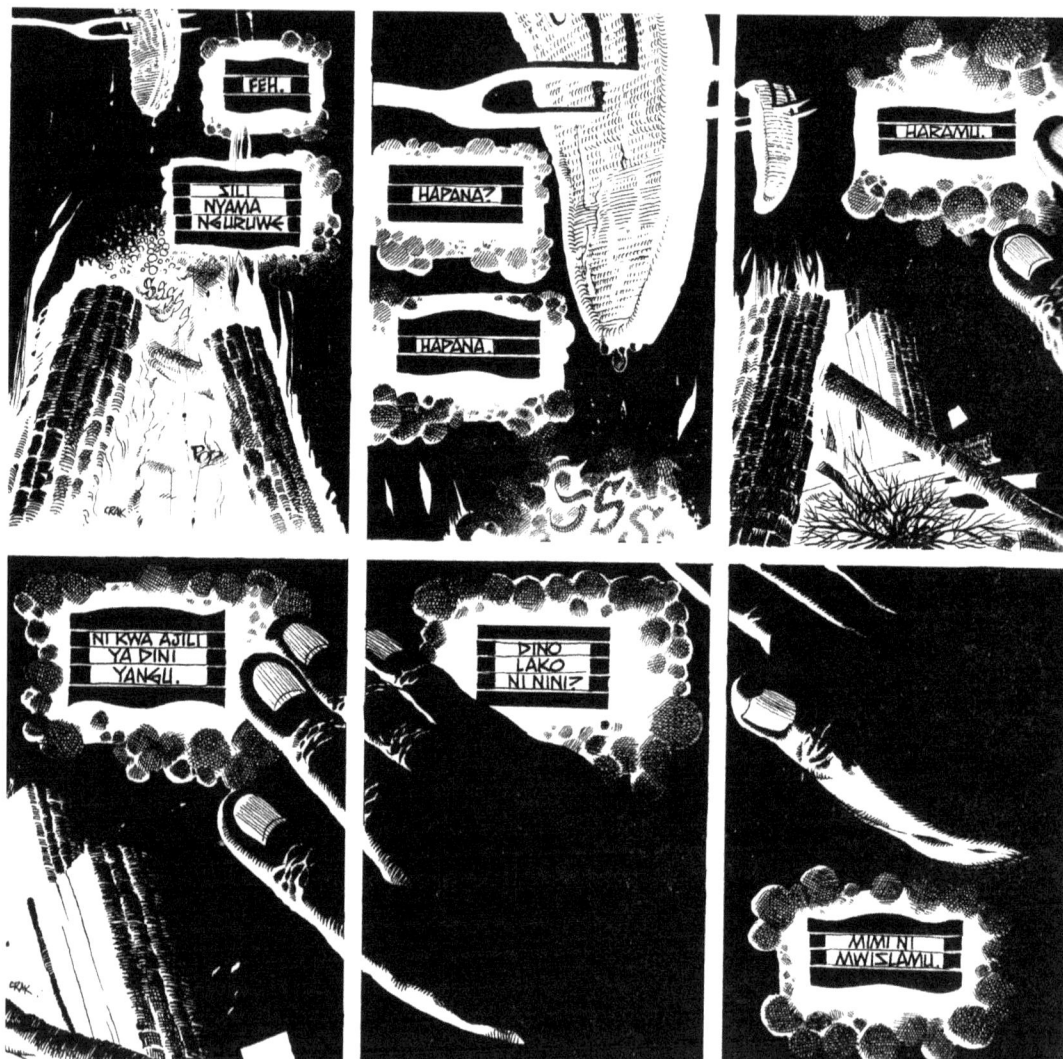

Figure 40. A speech bubble accompanies the foreign by a foreign form of speech bubble, as fat from a piece of meat drips into a campfire. From *Form and Void* (© 2001 Dave Sim and Gerhard).

shape, a curve of a baseline to indicate the rising and falling of the human voice, convey the tone and inflection of the former British Prime Minister's voice (see Sim and Gerhard 1990, 412.4–6, Sim and Gerhard 1997, 19.5, and Sim and Gerhard 1998, 57.8 for the development of the caricature).

There are also discrepancies, which serve to show that more is occurring than the speech balloons themselves would suggest. The character Oscar is one of two figures based on Oscar Wilde, and, when humbled by the presence of nobility, his florid speech is represented with exaggerated and stylized balloon and lettering, as he addresses the "Yaw Magnific'nse, Grend Lawd of the Mewst Newble City-State of Palnu" (Carrier 2000, 31)[12] (Sim and Gerhard 1990, 246:1–2; see figure 41). Oscar's scroll and exaggerated size differences in lettering convey symbolically his haughty speech.

Figure 41. Oscar's scroll and exaggerated size differences in lettering convey symbolically his haughty speech. From *Jaka's Story* (© 1990 Dave Sim and Gerhard).

Sim's innovations in representing the tension of written language and sound can manifest themselves in different ways, too. However, Sim conventionally represents his speech. It is only when Jaka parrots his words ("I understahnd Richaad has.... Chaws ... this evening," *Jaka's Story* 159:4), affecting speech mannerisms that were not in evidence when Oscar himself was speaking (Sim and Gerhard 1990, 155.1), that we see that Oscar's vocal patterns are represented only selectively (figure 42).

The precision with which Sim realizes the vocal effects leads to other aspects of characterization. The representation of the waitress in *Melmoth*, whose every statement ends with a question, forms an immediately recognizable type: "Dino said you're a really important *customer*? And I should take good care of you?" (Sim and Gerhard 1991, 114.4–5). Sim's repertoire of representing diegetic sound is replete with experiments that aggressively push the limits of representing the acoustic. As Cerebus breaks himself free of manacles holding him to a wall, Sim writes, "Cerebus did have some dialogue on this page.... It's just that none of it was printable — Dave" (Sim 1987a, 92.5). This non-diegetic use of text, replacing the voice of the editor that regularly appeared in Marvel comics of the late 1970s and early 1980s, replaces some of the sound in the panel, though the presence of two sound effects ("Snap" and "Crak") and the images of the tumbling aardvark do demonstrate that time is passing within the single panel, and that other sounds are occurring. Another experimental technique shows the layering of ever smaller balloons to represent an echo in a long corridor (Sim 1986, 493.1), emphasizing the character's isolation. The heart-shapes embedded in the

Figure 42. Oscar's vocal patterns are represented only selectively. Left, from *Jaka's Story* 155.1; right, from *Jaka's Story* 159.4 (© 1990 Dave Sim and Gerhard).

balloons of the love struck Punisherroach (Sim and Gerhard 1993, 237.6) denote nothing specific about the sound; the tenor of resonant ardor nevertheless emerges. In a sense, this is true of every speech balloon: it is all iconography and symbolic acceptance of convention. Sim can also use lettering to make a judgment about an author. While perhaps the use of an unadorned typewriter output for the words of Ham Ernestway, an Ernest Hemingway parody, connotes a constant clench-jawed mumbling (e.g., Sim and Gerhard 2001, 409.6), it also is a way of visually identifying Sims's negative views of the Hemingway — that he was a typist, but not a writer.[13] Even the positioning of the words within a balloon creates deliberate effects: when in *Going Home*, a conspirator's whisper emerges from the bushes, it is intended only for Jaka's ears, and the positioning of the text, in a balloon that presses against the head in the moonlight demonstrates that the secret whisper is intrusive (Sim and Gerhard 2000, 102.4). Later in the same panel, when Jaka is shushed, the size and central placement indicates that this sound is much more audible than anything else in the scene, and the superposition of the conspirator's balloon marks that he is repeatedly cutting her off.

Aspects of all of these elements are at work when Cerebus is trying to sleep in a room next to two people having sex: the speech balloons indicate different levels of physical activity of the couple, and the merging at the moment of climax is operating at several levels simultaneously, whereupon both again separate into the languid leisure of post-coital bliss (Sim and Gerhard 1990, 130; figure 43).

Sound Effects

The tension in the symbolic representation of sound recurs with the other diegetic mode, which is sound effects, which "in the case of sound effects, they graphically become what they describe," writes McCloud, "and give readers a rare chance to listen — with their eyes" (McCloud 1996, 146). The type of lettering, its size, placement, and the curve of the line — all these things contribute to presenting the chronological sequence within a given panel. The superposition of "flap," "bump," "thump," and

Figure 43. Speech balloons indicate different levels of physical activity. From *Jaka's Story* (© 1990 Dave Sim and Gerhard).

"bonk" in a single panel demonstrates the confusion of an addled bird as it flies away (Sim and Gerhard 1991, 448.2). The viewer recreates the bird's flustered movement with her eyes, reading left to right, as the bird regains its control and flies away at precisely the moment Sim introduces firearms for the first time into the world of Cerebus. Sim's confidence in representing diegetic sound is demonstrated in his *ad hoc* inventions (such as the *wuffa wuffa* for a dragging snowshoe, as opposed to the regular *whuf whuf* for the more sure-footed traveler, in Sim 1986, 375.1), or his creating of text to represent sound based on lexical meaning, rather than on onomatopoetic effects: in *Church & State*, bad-mannered dinner guests are given non-iconic sound effects "gulp," "chew," "gobble," and "munch," but also "wolfa wolfa," as the diners wolf their food down with Cerebus glowering at them (Sim 1987b, 661.3). For all-encompassing sound, the frame itself can assume the shape of the sound-effect: this is still diegetic sound, where the representation of sound becomes co-extensive with the space that it fills through the panel shape (e.g., Sim and Gerhard 1995,195.4–6, and, in a single-panel two-page spread, ibid., 192–93). This, to me, is more effective than expanding the scale of the diegetic sound, as when a desperate instruction to "open ... this ... fucking ... door" (Sim and Gerhard 2004, 141.1–3, 142.1) is made too extreme by the increasing distance and mushroom-cloud balloons. Three successive panels pull back the point of view for the reader, and this connotes the increase in volume, or at least the importance of the words to the character speaking.

From the first volume to the last, Sim has worked to create a credible environment: and one finds one development in his technique over 28 years in the representation of non-visual elements within the visual medium. In an early issue, relentless rain among the Pigts represented only in the image, as dense vertical lines crowd the panels (e.g., Sim 1987a, 98–105). When the rain falls on *The Last Day*, its constant *thunt thunt thunt* fills the window from which the sound emanates (68; it persists in every panel on pages 69 and 70). The sound effect's constant presence assumes tangibility, and we now see the *thunt thunt thunt* reflected on the floor during a moment's flash of lightning 71.1–8; see figure 44). The fragmentation provided by the panel borders reinforces the passage of time and the lack of movement from the unpictured Cerebus.

This substantiability can affect all diegetic sound. The lingering effects of the frosty monosyllable "What." from Jaka linger — Cerebus knows he has taken the wrong tone with her — but their residual impact, icicles on his face, assume qualities from the arctic environment in which they find themselves.[14] The reader notes the absence of a question mark (the period is important), and that the physical existence of balloons can affect characters, showing the lingering effects of speech (Sim and Gerhard 2001, 600). McCloud emphasizes the variation possible in sound effects — they are "one-shot inventions" that do not "require the same kind of methodical consistency that good balloon lettering needs" (McCloud 1996, 146). Sim shows the momentary sound of a thumb being broken with fragmented skeletal lettering (Sim and Gerhard 1990, 469.8). As with the snap of Gwen Stacey's neck, its size indicates importance, rather than actual volume. In contrast, the lingering scream just continues to grow, stretching out beyond the panel itself, as Mrs. Thatcher quietly walks away down the shadowed alley.

The world Sim creates operates by his own rules, however, and sometimes a sound effect is not just a sound effect. Some events in *Cerebus* echo through the series, creating resonances that are not detectable to the characters as they experience them. Characters hear sounds, though Sim leaves it to the reader to make sense of them. One finds a similar technique in Anton Chekhov's *The Cherry Orchard*, when at the end of act II there is the sound of a harp-string breaking, followed by a silence. Chekhov's enigmatic stage direction invites interpretation because there is no clear exegesis provided by the play itself: the sound exists in this liminal state as being both diegetic and non-diegetic simultaneously. In the same way, Sim inserts seemingly unmotivated sound effects into his series, which repeatedly occasion the observation by one of the characters that "something fell." The sounds remain diegetic — heard by characters within the narrative created — but the shape or pattern to their occurrence as the ripples extend through the series are more important for what the characters cannot perceive, but only the reader (or perhaps the re-reader) can, non-diegetically.[15]

Thoughts and Prayers

The representation of thoughts provides a comparison of Sim's presentation of diegetic sound. As before, the presence of any text in a panel necessarily evokes the passing of time. What makes the representation of thought, and particularly extended brooding, in *Cerebus* so distinctive is the stacking of balloons across panel borders, employing different combinations of line thicknesses, text styles, etc. to represent the conflicted and contradictory thoughts of a single character. The variation in panel shape, the use of brackets and different

Figure 44. The sound effect's constant presence assumes tangibility, and we now see the *thunt thunt thunt* reflected on the floor during a moment's flash of lightning. From *The Last Day* (© 2004 Dave Sim and Gerhard).

142   Part Three. Becoming Synonymous with Something Indescribable

Figure 45. Creating the impression of disconnected and leaping thoughts. From *Guys* (© 1997 Dave Sim and Gerhard).

letter sizes, and the self-correction as swearing gets partially erased or covered with the words "(no swearing)" and the multiple assents when making a good point ("Aye. Aye. Aye," each in a different but connected bubble) — all of these things (seen in the many voices in Cerebus' head in Sim and Gerhard 1997, 297; see figure 45) create the impression of disconnected and leaping thoughts in a way much more natural than the articulate and

Figure 46. Sobbing balloon shapes indicate a mournful desperation. From *Minds* (©1996 Dave Sim and and Gerhard).

properly-punctuated monologues often depicted. Unlike speech, which is linear because it takes a form governed by sequence and time, human thought (well, my own thoughts, and apparently Sims's) is less grounded in direct sequence. Sixty-two balloons concentrated in the close-up panels, form a perimeter around the nearly 40 percent of the page without any text at all (which is actually a memory): the prolonged isolation that Cerebus here feels is palpable, leaving him with nothing but his thoughts.[16]

Cerebus' self-loathing manifests itself when he chastises himself for swearing in his thoughts, and we see him adopting similar self-corrections in his unspoken prayers. A prayer in *Minds* shows him pleading, with sobbing balloon shapes indicating a mournful desperation (Sim and Gerhard 1996, 123.1–2; see figure 46). There is an antipathy here, too: Sim crosses out words rather than underlining them for emphasis and this implies a tension: these are the prayers of the agnostic repentant, both seeking help and unwilling to call undue attention to himself. Streaks of motion/light rays coincide with the crossing out of words for emphasis. Later on the same page, the reader is presented with a blank panel (ibid, 123.5), with Cerebus looking at the reader directly before adopting another tack — self-flagellation with text, with the skull and large bold letters in the word "bad" not quite evoking the sincerity he hopes to impress upon his deity. Sim uses the same technique in a later issue (Sim and Gerhard 1997, 253.3) for an angry wife talking to her husband, played by Marty Feldman. This reveals retroactively the hint of anger Cerebus feels at his *ad hoc* prayer not yet answered.[17] In using skulls-in-the-O's to represent anger, it becomes clear that Cerebus' prayer simply does not measure up in sincerity. When Cerebus finally does offer a sincere prayer, filled with regret and desperate pleading, the shaky black balloons and white letters are both moving and pathetic (Sim and Gerhard 2004, 62.2 and 63.2).

For Sim, even thought balloons have substance, and one finds this substantiality even when they do not contain words. Consider the reaction of secret observers when Jaka gives a kiss to F. Stop Kennedy (Sim and Gerhard 2000, 284.2, with the effects lingering into panels 3 and 4). The substance of each balloon separates itself, with the exclamation point shooting out like the eyes of a character in a Tex Avery cartoon. As Groensteen discusses, the balloon typically warps space around it — allowing the viewer to imagine what is behind the balloon, but letting her know that it covers nothing of substance.[18] Sim plays with that assumption.

"Play" is a useful verb in this context, for it is evident that Sim enjoys the freedom he exhibits in his representation of sound. Every reader of *Cerebus* will have personal favorites (for additional examples, consider the lettering in the images of this volume's other chapters), and this brief overview has in some ways only hinted at the artistic experiments in the series. Lettering and balloons adopt empathetic resonances with their content.[19] Once read, the examples stay with the reader, and seem to invite reading the comic aloud: "Yawan' sum scodge from Cerbusses buggid?" the drunk Cerebus asks (Sim and Gerhard 1994, 157.3; see figure 47), and Sim's readers practice aloud and repeatedly discover new fluencies with the representation of certain types of speech. Sim wrestles with the paradox of seeing sound on every page, and the results of these playful experiments constitute a crucial component of the ongoing interest of his characters.[20]

There are historical reasons why lettering remains critically unexamined. Hand lettering is labor-intensive, and places significant demands on the comics creators. Artists often subcontract lettering to those who are able to produce consistent and legible work,

Opposite: Figure 47. New fluencies with the representation of certain types of speech. From *Women* (© 1994 Dave Sim and Gerhard).

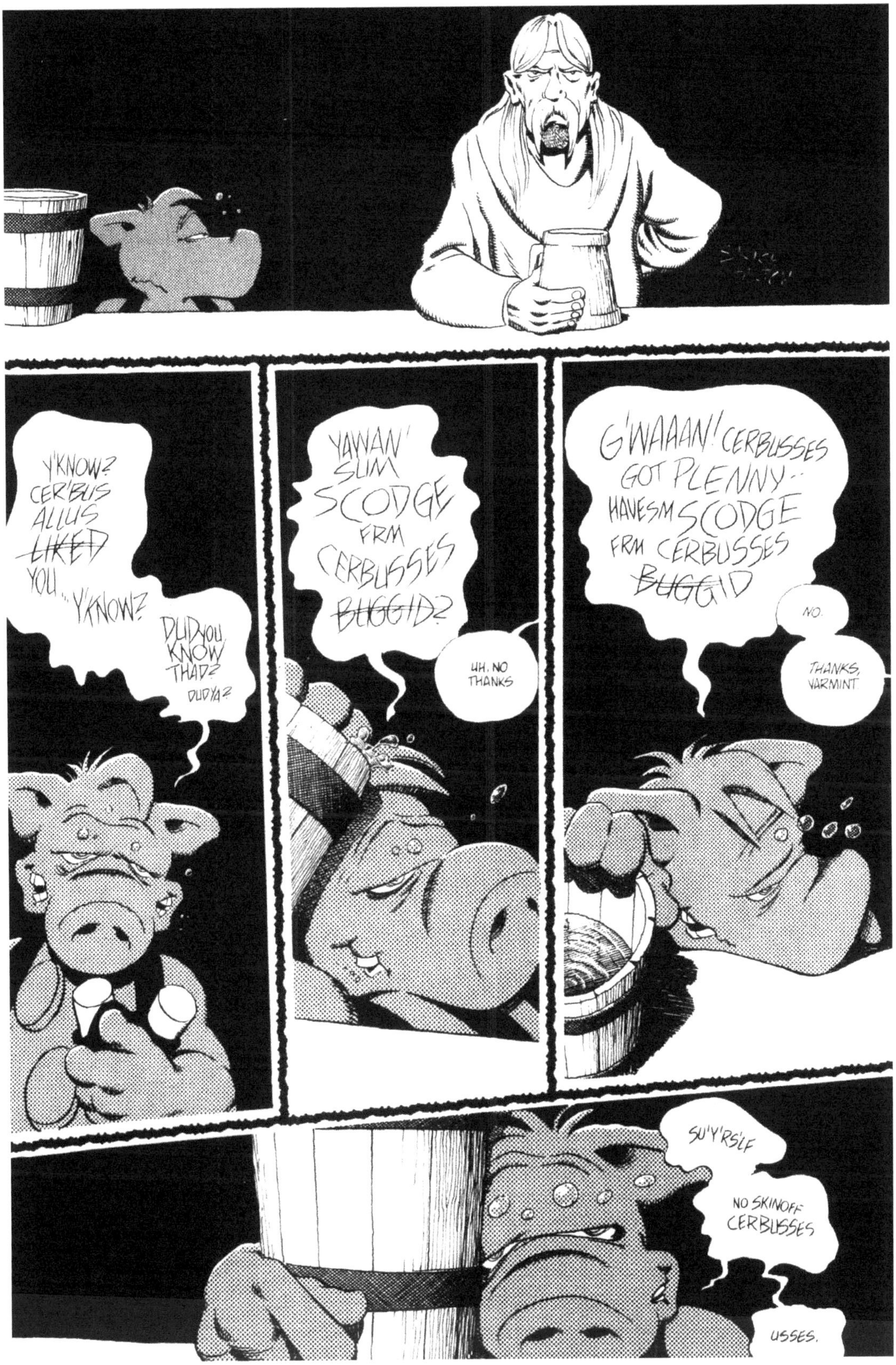

and so some creators do not consider lettering to be an opportunity for artistic expression. Though a few individuals have established considerable reputations for themselves as letterers,[21] not every writer or artist wants to engage with this additional means of producing meaning. When readers treat text as if it was unmarked, favoring content over form, there is a misleading sense that this enhances the work's literary qualities (or at least its ability to withstand critical scrutiny as literature) (Kannenberg 2001, 168).

The labor-intensive work associated with hand lettering is a critical part of the technical success of *Cerebus*. It is therefore of note that with his *glamourpuss* (2008–), Sim's current series examining (among other things) the historical and stylistic development of illustration in comics, he is using computer lettering for most of his text.

While Sim does still provide "specialty lettering," the sound effects accomplished by Sim in *Cerebus* have become less practicable given advances in computer technology and the economics of modern comics production.[22] I would therefore conclude with a paean, of sorts, for the value of hand lettering within comics. The many technical and narrative experiments and innovations Sim developed over the course of creating *Cerebus* are distinctive and repay careful attention. As more and more comics creators go to computer-generated typefaces, the opportunities for such moment-by-moment experimentation and discovery diminish. It may soon be that *Cerebus* stands alone in its aggressive and imaginative choices that will help its readers to see sound.

Notes

1. Kannenberg distinguishes narrative qualities, metanarrative qualities, and extra narrative qualities. Most of the examples considered in this chapter demonstrate metanarrative features: "the way the appearance of text can enhance the narrative in areas such as timing, characterization, or theme, as opposed to plot or structure" (Kannenberg 2001, 166). Nevertheless, this is to be selective, and all levels are operating.

2. See Blumberg, accessed 4 February 2011. For a discussion of the physics of the fall, see James Kakalios 2005, 46–52.

3. This interpretation is confirmed in the letters column to *Amazing Spiderman* 125, where editor Roy Thomas writes, "it saddens us to have to say that the whiplash effect she underwent when Spidey's webbing stopped her so suddenly was, in fact, what killed her. He couldn't have swung down in time; the action he did take resulted in her death; if he had done nothing, she still would certainly have perished. There was no way out."

4. The appearance of capturing only a single moment is, to some extent, illusory. The motion lines seen in figure 1, the presence of two sound effects that must be separated by at least a fraction of a second, etc., are all at work. In no way am I trying to reduce the imaginative possibilities of comics creators in their organization of panels.

5. See for example Bill Sienkiewicz' *Stray Toasters* (1988), Neil Gaiman's *Black Orchid* (1988), and Dr. Manhattan's blue balloons in Alan Moore's *Watchmen* (1986).

6. Some of these experiments converged in issue 186, which is part of the collection *Reads* (issues 175–86). Here Sim separates the relationship between text and image to the furthest degree in the series, though Sim reprises this in *Latter Days* with its exegesis of the Torah.

7. To take one example, twenty comics pages in *Cerebus* 20 can be arranged like a puzzle to form a "hidden Cerebus": an image that is inaccessible to the reader by nature of the comic's binding, and only alluded to visually by readers who see a part of the whole. The hidden image reinforces the fracturing psyche of the character, as Sim introduces what will be a recurring plot element, "Mind Games." See Miller and Thorne 2006, 2–8; the assembled puzzle is on p. 3.

8. See, for example Benayoun 1968; Bongco 2000, 70–74; Carrier 2000, 27–45; Eisner 1985, 10–12, 25–30; Groensteen 1997, 67–85; Kannenberg 2001; Khordoc 2001, 156–73; McCloud 1993, 134–35, 152–61; McCloud 2006, 128–47.

9. McCloud 2006, 144, uses the recapitulation as one of his examples of Sim's lettering technique. McCloud isolates the importance of vocal inflection in *Cerebus*: "Some cartoonists use dramatic variations of size and shape to portray vocal inflection on a word-to-word basis."

10. These examples are provided only to show the reader's expected familiarity with the convention being represented, not to suggest that there is an intended connection between these disparate panels. The heavy double line of the border and the interior shading help to determine the tone of bitter grumbling (which reinforces the content of the balloon; Sim 1987b, 277.3, "I hate using outdoor toilets...."). In a subsequent panel, the lettering slowly fades as Jaka chokes back tears ... her sentence is never finished but dissolves to an intention, only a thought (ibid., 479.3).

11. Typography to represent other languages in Japanese comics; see Carrier 2000, 33.

12. This use of ornate lettering draws on Walt Kelly's representation of the flimflam artist of his character P. T. Bridgeport.

13. Rothenberg, "Cerebus," identifies other parallels between Sim in *Reads* and Hemingway: "Sim just climbed on a soapbox and started preaching about female inadequacy — a charge that has been leveled against such literary greats as Ernest Hemingway."

14. Benayoun 1968, 68, discusses the physicality of balloons ("klunk"); see also Carrier 2000, 33.

15. See Miller and Thorne July 2004b, 16–25 and 43, and Sim 2004, 36–40, at 36–38.

16. On the balance of text and image on a page, see McCloud 1993, 152–61, esp. 153–55, and McCloud 1996, 128–41.

17. Note the final panel on this page, Sim and Gerhard 1997, 253.6, shows the words spoken and the speech balloon as co-extensive — there is no room for maneuver after such a directive.

18. Groensteen 1997, 71: "The balloon does not designate a natural cavity in the space that is depicted; it inscribes a zone of opacity within the 'transparent plane' that we identify as the panel."

19. For examples, consider the representation of weeping in Sim 1986, 315.2–3; compare the onomatopoetic "sniff" that is part of a soggy speech balloon in Sim 1987b, 789.6.

20. Sim has refused to allow translation of *Cerebus* into other languages, and part of the reason for this, I suggest, is his recognition of the importance of his technical accomplishment in the representation of diegetic sound.

21. Pride of place over the past two decades surely goes to Todd Klein, whose work came to prominence with Neil Gaiman's *The Sandman*. See Kannenberg 2001, 178–83. Chiarello and Klein 2004, 82–107 presents Klein's insights into lettering in detail and, for computer lettering, 108–41.

22. Kannenberg 2001, 183–91, discusses the implications of the use of computer lettering.

Negative Space and Guttural Noise: Gerhard's Psychological *Reads*

Sabin Calvert

"Gerhard is an illustrator, exclusively" [Sim and Gerhard, May 2001].

There is undeniable power in names. The name Gerhard, for example, punches quickly with a strange syllable then without warning steers the focus away in the second. The name is of Germanic, medieval origin. Translated, it means "hard spear" or possibly "brave spear." It is not a last name, decidedly male and not based in any sacred monotheistic writing. However, when placed next to a more common name such as Dave Sim, it seems mythic in its succinctness, unattached, aloof and unique. Its singularity and simplicity is misleading. It is one of the most complex names in comics. Just as Sim's own work has been eclipsed by his contentious worldview, it is perhaps best to regard Gerhard's contribution to *Cerebus* as an extension of Sim's auteur status, at worst, as his job title often indicates, a background artist.

In this chapter, I want to explore how Gerhard's work actually works. How it functions not behind the characters, not even "around" the characters but inside the characters and ultimately their author. His work underscores a sexual anxiety that digs at the very core of *Cerebus*.

Portrait of the Background Artist as a Young Man

In the early 1980s, Gerhard, a young artist working at a local art supply store in Kitchener, Ontario, began making deliveries to one Mr. Dave Sim. Sim's comic book *Cerebus* was gaining traction in a world overpopulated by brightly colored superheroes. Gerhard had some freelance pen and ink work under his belt and after some pleasantries, Gerhard asked if he would like to help him out with some ads. Sim agreed; Gerhard brought by some landscape and architectural drawings he had been working on. Impressed, Sim asked Gerhard to collaborate on a short story for Marvel's adult science fiction and fantasy quarterly *Epic Illustrated*. Their collaboration went so well that Sim asked Gerhard to begin doing backgrounds for the monthly comic. Gerhard agreed and entered into one of the longest partnerships in comics history.

September 1984 was the month Sim printed Gerhard's "backgrounds" for the second time. The title is apt as it foreshadows later events: "The Thrill of Agony and the Victory of Defeat." From 1984 to 2004 Gerhard worked on every single issue of *Cerebus* without waver, without break, dedicating the following twenty years of his life to the relentless schedule of *Cerebus*' 300 issue run. Sim would lead a new black and white pack of artists into the den of long established tradition, break new ground for independent comics creators and creator rights and gain a distribution foothold unheard of for self-published comics before or since.

Then comes the "but." Sim's divorce saddled with his LSD-induced mental breakdown, the rampant misogyny[1] and religious soul-searching ended up alienating all but its core fan base, even amongst whom the most ardent were wearing thin toward the end. Sim's working relationships eroded. Scuffles with Diamond distributors, *The Comics Journal*, groups such as Friends of Lulu, parting ways with numerous creators, as well as challenging Jeff Smith to a physical confrontation, all added up to a big divide between the independent comics world and its *de facto* Hannibal; after many brilliant strategies having to exile himself from the world he defended for so long.

At its height, *Cerebus* proudly printed distribution numbers in its masthead upwards of 37,000 a month. During the *Latter Days* story arc, sales dipped below an abysmal 6,000. Its ending, over 6,000 pages of story via a single narrator, in what should have been one of the most celebrated moments of comics history, ended like Eliot's universe, with a whimper, not a bang. Look no further than *The Comics Journal*, an early champion of Sim. Issue 263, published that very month, featured a handful of articles on the subject (mostly tepid appreciation) but put a poorly rendered, uncolored Ed Brubaker portrait on the cover. In smaller print below, the words "CEREBUS EXAMINED" appear (Groth, ed., October/November, 2004). Clearly, they were not in a celebratory mood. Yet through the tumult, Gerhard did more than weather the storm. In fact, he thrived. He thrived without pause throughout one of the most contentious and acidic comics careers.

What was the secret ingredient this partnership had that would outlast the days of Stan Lee and Jack Kirby? The closest we can find is *Love and Rockets*, yet Jaime and Gilbert Hernandez (brothers, worth mentioning) published their stories separately, and after some brief starts and stops began publishing their own books. The answer, much like *Cerebus* itself, is not simple or short. Like the adage that putting three professionals in a room produces five different answers, there are more answers than answerers here. Sim's work overshadows Gerhard's work, and Sim's work is itself overshadowed by his personality and very outspoken views. Yet Gerhard's art underscores the very nature of comics, pushing the limits of the medium to some of its greatest heights of expression. Moreover, Gerhard's art, Sim's art and political views are all metaphors for each other.

Self-Deprecation as Reflection

Gerhard: "I draw tables and chairs behind an aardvark." Yes, and Berni Wrightson smears some black stuff on a page. This quote is the most readily available on any web page or biography on Gerhard. Its extreme self-deprecation might point to the easy answer as to why Gerhard stayed with the book for so long. Nevertheless, even poor self-esteem is not worth twenty years of one's life.

This quote is a joke yet contains a shade of truth. Sim never claimed he drew an aardvark in front of tables and chairs, yet in the looking at the finished product, who can discern which came first? After all, one makes a true background for the characters, not the other way around. The work process involved Sim completely drawing his end, then Gerhard adding the rest (except for the *Guys* run). So not only was their partnership idiosyncratic but their artistic organization was as well. A comics artist who draws from a writer's script is not an illustrator, he or she is an artist. The reason being that a comics artist is writing in another language replete with its own set of traditions, rules and grammar. They are more akin to a translator.

The primary reason for Gerhard's artistic longevity was his ability to inhabit not the role of "comics artist" but of "illustrator." What does this mean? Is not all comics art necessarily illustration? Yes, but there is a fundamental difference, having to do with the role of the word in relation to the art.

Illustration is art *based* on a text. Even colloquially illustrating a point is expanding on unclear words or concepts. Comics can be and often are illustrations of a script but the script is not visible in the final product. Sim embeds the words we read into the grammar of the image. Where illustration shies away from the passage of time, relying on the words to push time forward, comics panels create the passage of time and space, using the image in the primacy of itself. The panel is fundamental to comics because it juxtaposes two "events" rather than simply offering the image as further explanation to the grammatical movement.[2] Simply put, comics begin with the image and illustration begins with the text.

Sim fully explored these tropes in *Cerebus* yet experimented with them phenomenally, which belies the power of the art and Gerhard's official role as background artist. In fact, his role and subsequent avoidance of much of the promotional world of comics allowed him

Figure 48. What you see is not what you get. From *Melmoth* (© 1991 Dave Sim and Gerhard).

avoidance of the shrapnel from battles raging in the foreground of *Cerebus*. Readers viewed Gerhard's work as simply illustrating a text, not formulating a text with images. However, the text he was illustrating was itself based on images. This unique role made a Trojan horse of the backgrounds, allowing a commentary and framework of ideas to slip by virtually unnoticed.

Setting as Fetish

Gerhard's adaption of his illustrative art to the world of comics developed along with Sim's ideology so uniformly as to be nearly imperceptible. Sim's work emphasizes Gerhard's contribution despite its often covering more real estate on the page, sometimes the entirety of the page. Readers and critics commonly view Gerhard's backgrounds as extensions of Sim's work, which it was, ideologically, in the beginning. Yet in other ways it was wholly his own. One must undertake a decoding to get at what he is saying. The psychological commentary is deep, incredible and so deftly executed as to go by unnoticed, which attests to his skill as an artist.

Gerhard made interiors exterior. He used illustration as a way to tap into the subconscious underpinnings of the author. Yet since Sim wrote no script, the illustration had to be image-based, illustrating the points of the characters in a subtle and wholly effective fashion. In the most simple of terms, the setting augments activity in fiction. These commonplace psychological surroundings, such as a thunderstorm and a dark house playing host to a murder or a sunny field delivering a pair of lovers provide visual shorthand for conveying mood. It places the reader in a state of mind. There are also subtle impressions transmitted through the geometry, vantage point and scope of a composition. Certain tall shapes suggest strength and power; small rounded shapes suggest subservience. Symmetry suggests strength; tilting horizons twist our thinking. The framing of the panel maximizes the effectiveness of visual information.

Setting and the way artists render setting is integral to the greatest of comics. The overgrown lushness of the Louisiana swamp of John Totleben and Stephen Bissette's *Swamp Thing* is worlds away from Walt Kelly's folksy backwaters milieu. Gotham City's grittiness holds a separate psychological undertone to Superman's Metropolis despite both being a metaphorical crime-ridden New York City. Compare these with Julie Doucet's claustrophobic and obsessive "actual" New York. Even Larry Marder's sparse logical and diagrammatical *Beanworld* envelops the reader in a psychological space that is unique and reliant on the characters as much as the characters' reliance on their space. We experience these worlds through these characters, and their views become fetishized by readers as an antidote to seeing the world around us. The reader identifies with the character in order to explore their world and through it a simile of reality.

The immediate surface impression transitioning into the dark heart of the psychological is the flow of labor in creating *Cerebus* and is the flow of reading *Cerebus*. There is a murky division between the two, and the line between character and setting is often blurred.

Drawing the Line

Where does Sim's world end and Gerhard's begin? It is not always clear despite being defined absolutely. The space where representation begins and resemblance ends seems easy to detect on the surface but is trickier than it appears.

The line that physically separates Gerhard and Sim's work is usually identifiable. The space surrounding the characters is stylistically, tonally and energetically different. It has greater attention to detail that is anathema to the characters yet wholly integrated into the composition. Lines that do not physically exist in the world define this difference of space. It is a mental construct — a representation of focus. Lines are a symbol of the chasm between things our eyes can focus on. The line is an ultimatum in comics because both sides are complicitly rendered, everything is in focus in each panel and each panel is in focus simultaneously. Lines are the metaphor of definition. They illustrate concepts.

Below the surface, Sim has delineated and decided these spaces but is not executor of their entirety. The line between their art is as much psychological as it is spatial. As Maurice Merleau-Ponty points out, "there are no lines visible in themselves, that neither the contour of the apple nor the border between field and meadow is in this place or that, that they are always on the near or the far side of the point we look at" (Merleau-Ponty 1972, 79). Pushing this further into the language of comics, not only is the line the definition of objects in the world, describing and defining but separating disparate modes of thinking in the juxtapositions between image and word as well as the juxtaposition of panels. Continues Merleau-Ponty: "this renders the line of object definition an uncanny power, as Paul Klee said, it 'renders visible'; it is the blueprint of a genesis of things" (ibid., 78). These things (in comics) go even further than they do in fine art, since they render the spoken word visible (as well as the unspoken thoughts in thought bubbles). What you see is not what you get (figure 48).

These divided worlds coalesce seamlessly. In order to decode Gerhard's work, Sim's own grammar of the image must be decoded since it informs the root of Gerhard's art and ultimately ends up competing with it. Sim's work also developed Gerhard's so monumentally that completely distilling them is counterproductive. They were partners, not hired hands. The codex to understanding the way Gerhard uses illustration and the way it fulfills Sim's anxiety of negative space intertwines with Sim's anxieties with women.

Let us see this in action. Figure 49 appears opposite one of the first pages of written text beginning the *Reads* story arc. On the surface, the image seems innocuous enough. Beautifully executed and pleasant,

Figure 49. One of Gerhard's illustrations coupled with the long text of "Reads." From *Reads* (© 1997 Dave Sim and Gerhard).

this image probably did not stick in the mind of too many readers at the time. The injection of long blocks of prose into a comic book was shocking enough, and what this prose contained would overtake any formalist searching into its experimentation. Yet Gerhard's symbolism underscores what Sim is saying in much the same veiled way, only using imagery rather than text. The peacock and its plumage are not only male, but also a special kind of male. The male peacock has a dazzling display that to objective human eyes, simply cannot compete with the peahen. It is the embodiment of male superiority in the most palatable of packages. Yet why not simply render a peacock? Why make this a stained-glass window? For one, stained glass has a substantially long history, specifically within the Christian church and its architecture, gaining traction in the middle ages not just for its ornate textures and stunning effectiveness in illustrating the stories of the good book, but for its symbolic qualities, as well. The stained glass window in Christian architecture represents the Immaculate Conception, the power of God (in light) passing through and creating life in the colored glass which represents the Virgin.

Another subtle clue as to Gerhard's collusion with Sim's ideas of masculinity is the Grecian vase on the sill. It is a heroic, masculine figure that provides a quiet contrast to the decidedly feminine bouquet of flowers. So here we have two representations of ornate masculinity, material evidence of the greatness of "man" which Sim would dedicate his remaining fictional life to emphasizing. Yet it is interesting how delicate and breakable these two objects are. Much like the fiction itself, there is a preciousness that contrasts deeply with the swords and caricatures, which in turn turned many readers off.

It is a stunning panel, loaded with interpretation, yet nothing, including the intent, is a matter of chance. We cannot help but notice the ominous shape lurking outside. Nor should we forget Gerhard's dedication at the onset of *Reads*: "to possessors of XX chromosomes everywhere" (Sim and Gerhard, 1995). Clearly, Sim's schismatic views were not a solitary endeavor. The key difference is that Gerhard's art deals with Sim's anxiety around gender in the space of symbols and psychological space, operating much like German expressionist sets, creating psychological moods that underscore the character's interiors in the scene. It is Sim's characters that are hyper-genderized in their physicality but it is Gerhard's art that remains a genderless reflection of the fiction that remains their trapping.

Figure 50. Alfred prepares to leave Wilde on his deathbed. From *Melmoth* (© 1991 Dave Sim and Gerhard).

Don't Call It a Background

> It seems to me fundamental to our society that- literally- an act of war is required to shuffle the feminist-homosexualist axis back into the distant *background* of our society where it belongs [Sim and Gerhard, January 2002; Emphasis mine].

It is no mistake that Sim uses the word "background" here. Not the "edge," "fringe," "gutters" nor "margin." The word choice is self-evident. The background is Sim's idea of where to relegate that-which-gives-him-anxiety. The background is where "they" will be powerless. The background is where threats lose their teeth. It is a psychological space. After all, can you point me in the direction of the societal background? It is evidence of a mind in conflict with itself. In addition, this mindset assumed the background of society and the background of a comic were completely non-threatening to Sim.

Now we must ask the question; what is a background?

In looking at a composition there is discernment between the figure(s) and the space they inhabit. In general artistic terms, it is the space or context around the figure that gives subjectivity to the subject. In Sim's terms, the context is the justification for his outrage. He remains a figure drawn in a plane with a myriad of things threatening to come into focus. He must define his background and it must *not be* empty for that would render the foreground enervate.

In using *Cerebus* as an example, Scott McCloud points out how a generically rendered character in a more realistically rendered background allows the reader to identify with the character and "mask themselves in a character and safely enter" (McCloud 1993, 43) their world. Later he puts more succinctly, "One set of lines to see. Another set of lines to be" (ibid.).

This is Sim and Gerhard at their core. Yet Sim retains "authorship" over the entire composition. Gerhard's windmills are Sim's giants. Sim's use of the written word further strains this push and pull.

Composition as Language

Just as artists in the Renaissance painted specific Biblical scenes for the church and wealthy patrons, the truly remarkable would make these scenes their own. For this reason, we remember Caravaggio's gritty images of Roman city life cast as saints and martyrs, Adam's limp hand forever awaiting divine life on the Sistine vaults, Goya's portraits of wealthy patrons' bratty children benevolently lording over their miniature empires while so many other masters with similar technical skill languish in the footnotes of history.

These footnotes are illustrators. The masters are the true artists despite the term "artist." They elevated art to a level in which their voice became one with the subject, so that we see beyond the basic representations of everyday life. Looking back at the importance of setting in comics, this place of subconscious plastered on the wall, we can begin to unpeel Gerhard's masterful (and silent) commentary on *Cerebus*.

Take this panel from *Melmoth* for example, figure 50. Oscar Wilde's light has spit its final spark and the flame is shrinking by the minute. His dear friend Alfred is about to leave, here we see him with hat in hand, the harsh morning light rendering his face into a nearly generic symbol of a face, our "lines to be." It is at the brink of melancholy, yet resolved not to show any hint of hopelessness or perhaps even hope.

Yet what richness is unfolding in Gerhard's end of the bargain? We see a profiled portrait washed in dawn, trapped in a sleepy, simple brass frame. Below this, fresh roses radiate, nearly so much as to obscure the ornate wallpaper, which has anointed itself with its own shimmer of Apollonian raiment. In seeing the picture fading, with Wilde's own *Picture of Dorian Gray* shining out from the glare with its duplicity of aesthetics, we can hear the pitiful echo of Basil begging Henry not "to take away the one person that makes my life absolutely lovely to me." The bright roses to our left hold in stark contrast with the black paneling on the right, shellacked as if embalmed, the shadow side swallowed by a black expanse of a formless suit. The roses see the plasticity of their own portraiture, their own personal Dorians in the glossy, flat wallpaper adorning Wilde's living tomb. From this seemingly simple panel we know two things: We know the flowers are dying. Moreover, we know even in his wildest, hedonistic excesses Wilde never bargained away his soul.

Behind this simple drawing of a figure, nearly ineffectual and bland and arguably awkwardly posed, can we see the true nature of what is at stake in the world. There is metaphor in this image. There is poetry completely written in images without a single word.

This Is Only a Test

One hires the illustrator and the artist for a specific representation yet one puts their own point of view in the work while the other treats it solely as a source of income with the added bonus of honing technical skill. Gerhard took on the job of an illustrator and imbued it with mastery, and in agreeing upon the label of illustrator (or "background artist," which I hope at this point you see as essentially synonymous) allowed his work to function in this illustrious capacity until the final issue.

However, this is not always a genial skill; look, for example at this two-page spread in one of the last issues of *Cerebus* (figure 51). The blank space of the page is as palpable as the dreamy, deteriorating world forming a giant Rorschach blot onto the two-page spread. There is metaphor here, as much as the *Melmoth* panel, but the sentiment is anything but genial. Here, we are faced with Cerebus dying, yet there is a challenge to the reader, direct but subtle. There is also a challenge to Sim himself here. No matter how symmetrical in appearance, it is a product of imagination fumbling around in the abstract.

The Rorschach test is a test of sanity, of seeing what is not there but in the mind. Its symmetrical, abstract nature echoes the abstract and symmetrical structure of *Cerebus*. Even this is a cloudy dream, obscuring panels and billowing hatching. In addition, remember the admonition before beginning the test; unlike the world of Dave Sim, here there are no wrong answers. There are in fact no answers, simply the ghosts of the mind guiding our eyes over the page. If you have read *Cerebus* this far, you are on your own.

Prosopagnosia is a disorder where the ability to recognize faces is hindered or disavowed. American painter Chuck Close is one of the most prominent people with this disorder. His work focuses on giant facial hyper-realism, and later a photographic rendering through cells. Gerhard may or may not suffer from prosopagnosia, but his work fits this disorder to the letter. His admonition of difficulty in rendering faces coupled with his work's complete lack of human form or face in *Cerebus* as well as much of his sketches and work post–*Cerebus* conspicuously avoids the face. Whether Gerhard suffers from prosopagnosia is of

156 Part Three. Becoming Synonymous with Something Indescribable

Figure 51A and 51B (*opposite*). The blank space of the page is as palpable as the dreamy, deteriorating world forming a giant Rorschach blot onto the two-page spread. From *The Last Day* (© 2004 Dave Sim and Gerhard).

Negative Space and Guttural Noise (Calvert) 157

little consequence, the need to find expression in areas outside the human face gives us a key to seeing how the "backgrounds" function in the work.

It is clear that the face, in all its nuance, emotion and expression holds no power of communication in Gerhard's work. With the displacement of such a vital vessel of communication coupled with the absence of words, Gerhard's work must encode Sim's ideas without using text and without using the face or body language. This is not only anathema to the way humans interact; it ensures a sort of misanthropy in its innocent guise. Make no mistake; Sim needed Gerhard to develop his expression (by freeing up his labor) just as much as Gerhard needed Sim for his (giving immaculately rendered faces up for an alternate, inhuman rendering). A world of misanthropy only functions so long as the anthropic lives.

The Open Ending

If Sim was to die before completing *Cerebus*, the instructions were explicit: Gerhard could finish the backgrounds or simply leave the images as they were and publish the remaining pages completely blank. Sim wrote nothing down for precisely this reason, so that no other person could continue his work (more to the point, profit off his passing, as *Cerebus* would enter into the public domain upon the event of its creators' deaths). This is a crucial testament to Sim's belief in the power of the word.

How strange this is! Why publish a book with X number of blank pages included to emphasize the lack of what was to be? What do these blank pages signify? Even if God had planned for Dave to shuffle off with his magnum opus incomplete, the inclusion of blank pages almost feels like a religious affront. "See these empty pages? Well, now they're wasted. Thanks a lot."

Seeing the idea of the blank page through the lens of Sim's twofold anxiety (anxiety around women and anxiety around a blank page), the reasoning becomes transparent. Without the antithesis of ink, the negative space no longer negates, it becomes a void (a word very loaded in the worldview of *Cerebus*). In the event of the failure of his grand design, he wanted to make it explicit that the void had won the battle and the war was decidedly not over.

In reading from panel to panel, we fill in a spatial and temporal discord. Gutters — the space between panels represents this psychological connection. This is the essence of comics.[3] Yet in the first half of *Cerebus* the gutters are not white (as is traditional) or black (used to varying effect to darken and slow the tone of the work). The panels filled with a line, crackling and energetic. This line is the anxiety even of the temporal. Even here the space must be non-static, something with "form." This near scribble overtakes the jump between panels and is in fact a bit jarring upon first reading. This space, dividing time, leaves too much openness to the reader, even in the idea of a panel progression. The artist must fill in the anxiety of space, representing time. As time went on, this scribbly line was lost. The battle with time proved futile and space embraced. Not with image, but with its opposition.

Rather than analyze numerous panels to show how Gerhard's art works, it is more fruitful to look at the spaces of which Sim kept him out. The spaces Sim forbid him to enter tell us what Sim was afraid of in Gerhard's art and point to how it affected *Cerebus* as a whole.

Cerebus begins with words in their traditional place in the mode of comics. As the series progressed, text gained its foothold, becoming more radical and experimental in matching the efforts of the work as an entity unto itself. No comic before *Cerebus* had used text in such a radical way. The refusal of other artists to follow in the footsteps of *Cerebus* is predominantly due to its content and as a byproduct, the effectiveness of this experimentation.

Words gained gravity as the work gained mass. As Sim played with their potential, his message became incendiary, balancing out their effectiveness with their message. *Cerebus* is the ultimate straw man precisely because of its tremendous effectiveness and its capacity for hollowness. Its soldiers rode atop the Trojan horse without bothering to crawl inside, yet it ceaselessly banged on the city gate.

Reads

When Sim enters into his roman á clef on the comics world, Gerhard is conspicuously absent from representation in its pages. He appears elsewhere in the world of comics, as in Rick Veitch's *Rare Bit Fiends*, yet receives no mention in the very comic that bears his name. Why leave him out? Why not include Gerhard somewhere in the milieu of a dozen thinly veiled people from the world of publishing wade through the rabble? Sim himself gets three distinct manifestations, why not the vice president of Aardvark-Vanaheim Incorporated? Contractual obligations?

Gerhard's absence here artistically is extremely telling. It is not an oversight. Sim's fanaticism and belief in the power of the written word is here exposed. Even mentioning Gerhard in fictional guise would assuage his anxiety, psychologically filling the space he so needs and so desperately needs to get rid of. Sim leaves Gerhard out because it is his world, his power to wield in the written word. It not only courses through the images in Cerebus in its assumed authorship but also runs a psychological current in the written word that dates all the way back to King David. This is Sim's holy space. Bringing Gerhard's name into it would shatter the illusion.

The lettered and drawn word bisects Gerhard's art; the drawn word covers objects and signs. Sometimes onomatopoeia projects the image or frames it. Sometimes it swallows it whole. The lettered word occasionally dipped its toes into Gerhard's realm, yet most of the time it stayed in the confines of thought and speech bubbles. The lettered word belies an author (or at the very least a letterer in collaborative comics) and in the arena of independent and creator-owned comics it gives the feel of a direct link to the author's hand.

Sim's lettering is astounding and universally praised, and for good reason. The lettered word performs a different function that the typed word. It has a personality beyond the written. Hybrid art is able to emphasize and give character in ways the typed word fails to do. The lettered word can also embody gender; the letterer can render it masculine or feminine.

However, the text that is most interesting and telling to Gerhard's role in *Cerebus* and indeed the key to *Cerebus* itself is the written.[4] The written word gives the illusion of universality. When typeset, authorship has the mood of objectivity and anonymity and is sometimes taken at a sort of stern face value. All that we have subjectively is the tone and style of what the text says. It commands respect in that it carries the assumption of being edited, which the lettered word does not (more so at the time of *Cerebus*' printing than today) as well as an intermediary in technology (as well as the possibility of a third party in a typist).

The words that you are now reading have a certain objectivity that the lettered word and the drawn word simply cannot reach. The letters repeated here and in everything else you read, every book, every sign, pamphlet, website, ad and letter, simply rearranged. There is a legacy in their language, unencumbered by the emotion and personality that lettering and the drawn word have inherited. A panel of a comic repeated somewhere else is simply what it is. Sim's use of the written word and typed text is nothing short of revelatory. What is most revealing about it is Sim uses it almost exclusively outside of Gerhard's reach. He explored typing in many issues, sometimes providing narrative, lore or dialogue pertaining to the scene at hand, sometimes in lieu of the thought bubble as a species of psychic talking to the reader. Later, it would guide an imagistic apostasy from comics into the world of fiction and ultimately religious text coupled with dogmatic social commentary.

Though mostly forgotten now, though it lasted throughout *Cerebus'* life and was more pervasive than the text within the actual comics' pages, the letters column grew from its own small niche, appearing sporadically to expanding into a bloated microcosm that came to weigh in at half, sometimes more than half of each issue. It displayed up and coming artists, responded to fan mail, criticism, relationship advice, the state of the world and many readers used it as a platform for their own sexual anxiety, mirroring it with Sim's own rock star status within the burgeoning world of independent comics.

This was a world free of Gerhard's hand. Few letters were addressed to him (the occasional "Dave and Ger" showed up but the recipient and responder was unambiguously singular). For a comic with two names gracing its cover, only one responded to letters. Dave Sim reveled in the written word. No dark corners, fisheye distortions, exquisitely rendered rubble or stately interiors giving silent direction unto the message. This was the domain of the word.

Sim realized this power of the word early on and used the back of the issues to address his audience directly. This culminated in issue 256 with the beginning of the notorious "Tangent." These have not been reprinted subsequently (and neither have, I might add, any of the letter columns) but Sim proclaimed them public domain and free to disseminate.

Sim's anxiety had come full circle, no longer encumbered by the baggage of the image and Gerhard's constant commentary. Yet Gerhard, still a steady workhorse, was already using his images against Sim's as astutely and masterfully as they had once serviced them. Not least of which with his introduction of photography.

Pretty Pictures

Sitting on comic book shelves across North America in July 1998 was something strange. Amidst the issues of *Sandman*, *JLA*, *Green Lantern*, *New Mutants* and other cosmic, flying be-spandexed heroes was a nature photograph: a hazy, somber sky on the brink of a storm looming over a shadowy patch of grass. A Picasso would be less out of place.

Photography had peppered the back of *Cerebus* (pictures of Sim and Ger in various places, vacationing, beaching and hanging out with women), and even appeared collaged on the cover of some issues (notably the send-ups of Dave McKean's decidedly gothic Joseph Cornell-esque *Sandman* covers), yet there was nearly always an object or a character at the center of the composition. This was something new, something weird, even for the weird world of comics. This photograph represents both a window out and a warning sign. It shows a place that is simple and free of the garish digital color palette that was taking root. The covers of the first issue of the *Going Home* story arc and its subsequent arc have nothing to do with comics and little to do with the storyline inside. They are stunning yet completely out of place. No animals, no people, just a vast expanse of nature.

Scott McCloud has said, "By de-emphasizing the appearance of the physical world in favor of the idea of form, the cartoon places itself in the world of concepts" (McCloud 1993, 41). If we follow McCloud's reasoning that the more realistic a rendering, the more attention is drawn to it as an object, is the photograph the ultimate checkmate to the game of identification and objectification? No, in fact it is quite the opposite here.

This is not a representation of reality but a capturing of actual reality, not just its depiction. More importantly, it is on the cover of a comic book, the whizz-bang selling point of the story inside. This is a warning sign. Go spend some time outside, stay away from people and enjoy the country. Here, I am pointing to the way out. It is not through a panel. The photographs Gerhard took for the following covers mirror Sim's use of the written word. They functions in a very similar way in trying to "break away" from the codes and trappings of comics and get to a "truer" art. Yet I can't help but feel that Gerhard had the idea that it would function in exactly the same way as the long literary passages inside; completely alienating the reader. The photographs would be Gerhard's turning point away from collusion into one of working against both himself and Sim's world. Whether conscious or not, this was the turning point. Everything else was done as expertly, yet the joy was not faded into the background, it was drained completely from the page.

In the end, the light, the blankness so fraught with meaning and steeped in symbolism, overtakes everything. After 3,000 pages, decades of relentless work, the severed relationships, and the public fighting and dwindling readership, negative space swallows *Cerebus*. Somehow, the anxiety refuses to leave.

Coda

Nearly three years after *Cerebus* concluded Gerhard sold his share of the company to Sim, thereby ending their professional relationship. In a wrap-up interview with Sim and Gerhard on National Public Radio in 2006, he remained quite cordial: "I don't miss the monthly schedule at all" (Gerhard, October 27, 2006). He has had nothing to do with comics since.

Another work like *Cerebus* will probably not manifest for a long time. Moreover, another collaborative effort like Gerhard and Sim's will be unlikely. For an artist to use his or her work in service of what is largely a psychological examination of another artist, let alone dedicate twenty years to the task, requires an especially dedicated genius. Not to mention a subject as deeply troubled as Sim. It would need someone as equally obsessed with obsession as Gerhard was, with just as much to say and the skill to say it without saying a word.

Notes

1. Many defenders of Sim (himself included) decry the label of "misogynist," saying that he is attacking feminism but not women per se. Yet in his own words, "All women are feminists and all feminist evidence is anecdotal" (Sim 1987a, 265). Since he uses the term "feminists" interchangeably with "women," his attack is thinly veiled; the grandest irony being that all of Sim's evidence is anecdotal, if not purposely fiction.

2. Single panel comics prove this rule with their exception. Their effectiveness depends on the lack of juxtaposition and thus is usually only effective as a gag or captured moment. Much like the film still functions in the face of the cinema.

3. Many of these ideas, and the general framework I am using to talk about comics I owe to Scott McCloud's theories on comics. His integral work *Understanding Comics* is highly recommended, as well as *Making Comics*, which expands on some of these ideas.

4. I use the word "written" interchangeably with "typed" partially for its historical reference to text prior to set type but primarily for its undertones of religiosity. The lettered word is contained in the artwork and predominantly written by hand, or at least technologically made to look handwritten. The written rests outside the space of the art as a visible script.

PART FOUR
MIND GAMES

Testing the Limits of Genre/Gender
Dominick Grace

Dave Sim's *Cerebus* is among the most innovative comics in history, challenging the medium's traditional conventions and limits. Even in its earliest days, when *Cerebus* offered a fairly straightforward parody of such sword and sorcery fantasies as *Conan the Barbarian*, it blurred generic distinctions in its combination of funny animal and barbarian fantasy conventions: Cerebus, the funny animal aardvark, is a talking animal in an otherwise human world, without either explanation of or comment on this odd (to say the least) state of affairs— at least initially, though eventually the question of what people in the world of the comic actually see when they look at him becomes a matter of some import. As the comic developed, though, and Sim's conception deepened, *Cerebus* came to challenge the accepted conventions of the comics genre, both structurally and thematically. His parodic treatment of virtually every comics genre, his consistent violation of the conventional wisdom that serial publications must offer reasonably short and self-contained narrative units that allow a reader entry at virtually any point, and his experimentation with the formal limits of what can be called comics (culminating though hardly ending in issue 186, which featured a few pages of conventional comics and then an extensive prose essay), all point to his experiments with comics as a genre.

Cerebus' blurring of formal boundaries is reflected on the comic's ideological level in Sim's experiments with gender, the edges of which he blurs in ways analogous to what he does with genre. As Sim's comic breaks down generic distinctions, his story, in its increasing focus on gender politics, works increasingly to interrogate sexual categories. The most overt manifestation of this interrogation is Cerebus' status not only as aardvark but also as hermaphrodite, a fact not revealed until issue 179, and one with widespread implications for more than just the readers' view of *Cerebus*. Cerebus the character and *Cerebus* the comic book have become the center of an exploration of the meaning of male and female as distinct and separable categories. In *Cerebus*, gender becomes not only amorphous but also an actively problematic concept. This essay attempts to address some of the implications of Sim's testing of the limits of gender, though given the scope and the complexity of the series, any conclusions reached here are provisional.

When he first appeared, Cerebus was an obvious parody of Barry Smith's *Conan the Barbarian* (figure 52). Like Conan, Cerebus was a mercenary and thief who consistently found himself tied up in the affairs of wizards and/or (more significantly, ultimately) wenches; like Conan's, Cerebus' earliest adventures were largely self-contained, single-issue ones, in which Cerebus confronted a single threat, succeeded, and proceeded to the next

Figure 52. Cerebus the Barbarian in battle. From *Cerebus* (© 1987 Dave Sim).

issue and the next threat. The adventures were very episodic and played with well-established sword-and-sorcery conventions, and new readers could pick up any early issue and grasp the basic premise quickly and easily. Sim even modeled various early characters on figures from Smith's *Conan*; indeed, one of the important recurring secondary characters, Elrod the albino, is modeled not on Michael Moorcock's Elric, but on the version of Elric depicted by Smith in issues 14 and 15 of *Conan*.

However, Sim somewhat quickly abandoned the barbarian fantasy world, undoubtedly recognizing its inherent limitations. He accelerated history radically, taking Cerebus' world from a virtual stone age to an early industrial age in fewer than 100 issues, ultimately bringing the world of the comic to a period analogous in some ways to the early 20th century. He also began to use Cerebus in a number of different roles, making him first a Prime Minister, then a pope, and finally (after a few detours) a messianic figure, extending the satirical targets of the comic well beyond the usual parameters to which comic books confine themselves. Sim's satire of social structures extends beyond the analyzing of major religious and political institutions to a more fundamental commenting on gender as the most basic and pervasive of human classification systems, even more impossible to escape than either politics or religion. The book's challenges to generic and gender limits expanded consistently as Cerebus' story unfolded. Indeed, Sim consistently pulled the rug out from under his readers. Perhaps the most significant example of this (as noted above) is the revelation in issue 179 that Cerebus is not male, as he has apparently been since the beginning, but a hermaphrodite.

With this revelation, Sim foregrounds what became the comic's primary focus, to the consternation of many readers. Sim, who earned the praise of feminist-oriented comics creators/critics such as Trina Robbins at one time, came to be regarded by many as a misogynist, especially in the pages of *The Comics Journal*, the premier magazine of comics news and criticism which is, ironically, published by Gary Groth's Fantagraphics, which also publishes an extensive line of pornographic comics in addition to the ongoing collection of the complete works of R. Crumb, perhaps the most widely-reviled cartoonist in feminist circles. The comic, and some of Sim's statements outside the parameters of the story (e.g., in the letters pages and notes of the comic, in interviews, etc.), are indeed likely to disturb and offend, but I think the most fruitful way to approach Sim's treatment of gender issues is to investigate what the work overall accomplishes through its subversions of conventional expectation.[1]

In some respects the anti-feminist themes that dominated *Cerebus* might seem surprising, even shocking, in light of the comic's apparent perspective in earlier issues, which led some to see Sim's agenda as feminist rather than anti-feminist, but, as I've already suggested, small parts of *Cerebus* are not designed to be considered in isolation from the larger work. Furthermore, a closer examination of *Cerebus* shows that, from its early issues, the comic has used gender as the basis both of humor and of more serious considerations of the social order. Sexual symbolism has played a frequent role in the comic, for instance. Sim has described the giant snake sequence in issue 15 explicitly as his giant penis story, for example. Here, Cerebus rides the snake at the leader of the Eye of the Pyramid cult; as Sim has said, "Sort of changes the meaning of the 'AAAAH' word balloon, doesn't it?" (Sim 1982a). It is easy to find multiple other examples. Perhaps the most significant of these, and one with far more serious implications, is the design of the creatures the child Jaka dreams of in *Jaka's Story*, which are explicitly insectoid but implicitly phallic, hinting at sexual abuse. Even the revelation of Cerebus' status as hermaphrodite plays on his masculine attributes; during the revelation scene, he is carrying a phallic symbol, his sword.

Though no mention is made of Cerebus' hermaphroditism until issue 179, his sexuality has been an issue of some complexity since early in the strip (figure 53). Though his behavior and his self-conception are resolutely male, even his physical design is sexually ambiguous. Significantly, he has no visible physical genitalia; as Astoria explains in *Reads*, the revelation of the required genitalia appears as desired, or willed. In other words, whether Cerebus manifests biologically as male or female is contingent on circumstance. His sexuality is latent, absent arousal; his gendered orientation makes this manifestation consistently male, though the fact of his hermaphroditism causes him ongoing stress (a subject to which I will

Figure 53. Whether Cerebus manifests biologically as male or female is contingent on circumstance. From *Reads* (© 1995 Dave Sim and Gerhard).

return shortly). His actual appearance melds traits suggestive of both male and female sexuality. On the one hand, his long snout and long tail are fairly obviously phallic, but on the other, he consists almost entirely of curved and rounded lines, and his ears, his only other prominent physical feature, are vaginal rather than phallic. Cerebus' tail has been used explicitly to make phallic jokes, as in issue 58 (collected in *Church & State I*), when he is stuffed into a too-tight pair of pants and his tail escapes out his fly, thereby appearing to be an errant (not to mention enormous) penis, to the mortification of the prim and proper woman to whom he is being introduced.

A more subtle phallic tail gesture occurs in issue 6. Cerebus directs his phallic snout toward Jaka, the tavern dancer ultimately revealed as a princess and who becomes the central female character and Cerebus' lover, while his phallic tail, functioning as a weapon, drives back into the stomach of E'lass, who has drugged Cerebus to make him attracted to Jaka in order to manipulate him (figure 54). Though this sequence appeared in print years before Cerebus was revealed as a hermaphrodite, it hints both at Cerebus' dual sexual nature (one "phallus" directed at a female, another directed into the belly of a male), and at the close interconnection between sex and aggression that Sim explores at some length throughout the comic's run. Indeed, a transgendered Cerebus has appeared at various points, at the time apparently for simple comic effect, but in the larger context of the book to establish some basis for what I take as an abiding interest in the comic in the fluidity of sexual identity. In issue 23, for instance (collected in *Cerebus*), Cerebus is disguised as a little girl

Figure 54. E'lass drugs Cerebus to make him attracted to Jaka in order to manipulate him. From *Cerebus* (© 1987 Dave Sim).

to save him from snoopy soldiers ("Madame" Dufort, by the way, who puts him in the disguise, is also a man in drag). In issue 57 (collected in *Church & State I*), Cerebus awakes after a drunken night to find himself married to Red Sophia and wearing her chain mail bikini top. Sophia herself is of course an ongoing piece of the book's commentary on gender politics, as on the one hand a bikini-mail-clad sex bomb and on the other a proficient warrior, combining conventional male and female traits.

Even secondary characters such as the Cockroach participate in this sort of fluidity. When the Cockroach first appeared, Sim had some fun with the old jokes about Batman and Robin's relationship (which has often led to speculations of pederasty). In issue 12, the Cockroach imagines living with his young protégé in "luxurious surroundings [with] the finest silk robes—a butler, and flowers—oh yes! Lots and lots of flowers!" and Cerebus, who generally refers to himself in the third person, thinks, "Cerebus is starting to wonder about this bug" (Sim 1981). The Roach's identity confusion manifests itself not only in his constant transformation into different parody superheroes but also in has radical sexual confusion, which manifests itself in a disturbing combination of desire for and loathing of both heterosexual and homosexual relationships. In a short story published in *AARGH!*, a benefit book to raise money to combat anti-homosexual legislation in Britain, Sim has the Roach's homophobic anti-perversion patrol backfire when the Roach becomes sexually aroused upon hearing a description of homosexual sex. During *Women* and *Reads*, the Roach manifests in female drag as Kay Sarah Sarah, based on the figure of Destiny in Neil Gaiman's *Sandman* series for DC. Conversely, in his identity as Punisherroach (a parody of Marvel's Punisher character), the Roach's sexual confusion manifests itself as lust channeled into violence against women, his automatic cross-bow weapon the substitute phallus with which he penetrates them. Sim closely modeled the Punisher costume he adopts on that of Marvel's Punisher, except for the tongue that protrudes from the skull design mouth, hanging down suggestively towards his genitalia.

As is suggested here, the tension between sex and violence, and between male and female, is a central concern in the comic, and has been since early in its run. The first hint of the apocalyptic storyline that governs much of the run from issue 50 to 200 comes in issue 24, when Madame Dufort, revealed as Charles X. Claremont, reveals his Apocalypse Beast: Woman Thing, a sex-reversed parody of Marvel's Man-Thing. The Apocalypse Beast is female here, but in the next issue, we discover that there have been other Apocalypse Beasts, and we meet one, Lord Roth Sump's male Sump-Thing, almost immediately. The relationship between the two Apocalypse Beasts pretty much sums up, in a humorous way, male-female relationships in *Cerebus*. They begin by fighting but very quickly end up having sex instead. Sim enacts the sex/violence equation in more serious terms a great many issues later, in one of the most-discussed sequences, in issue 94, when Pope Cerebus rapes the prisoner Astoria. Here, on the primary level of the narrative, Astoria is victim and Cerebus attacker, but elements such as the superimposition of Cerebus' head over Astoria's vagina (figure 55) suggest the sexual indeterminacy we've already discussed to some extent, and a few issues later, the comic invokes the notion of cyclical history to suggest that what happens now has happened before with the roles reversed; while condemning Astoria, Cerebus finds his consciousness in a female body, judging a male aardvark. He has, in a way, changed roles with Astoria. He, in effect, has not always been he. Male and female, on one level opposed, are, on another level, different sides of the same thing.

The creation myth that serves as the climax of *Church & State*, the extended run that consumed issues 52 to 113, presents even the origins of the universe in terms of violent sex. The male god, described as a void, rapes the female god, the light. In this sequence, we see the phallic male principle emerge *from* the female form it has entered, engaging simultaneously in an act of violent aggression and of self-creation. Many issues later, in issue 186, Sim reverses the premise, imaging the female as void and the male as light; once again, though, equating opposites. Sim repeats this pattern of reversal in his final version of the creation myth in *The Last Day*. In his final take on the creation myth, in the double issue, 289 and 290 (collected as the beginning of *The Last Day*, the final volume in the series); Sim again reverses the premises, making the light once again female. This version of the creation myth follows the Bible in making the creation of the female clearly subsequent to the creation of the male (as per Adam and Eve) and in maintaining the long-standing belief, rooted in Christianity and in Western culture generally, that the female is clearly lesser than the male. Sim's view here of course runs counter to contemporary Western belief in the equality of the sexes, but it is worth noting that an ideological, political, or societal belief does not necessarily correspond to truth. The question of the extent to which the two sexes (recognizing, of course, that the notion that there are only two sexes, rather than a sexual continuum, is itself to some extent at least arguably a construction)[2] are indeed inherently different by nature and by biology, rather than merely by social conditioning, and the question of the extent to which biologically male or biologically female humans may be "better" at some things than members of the other sex remain fraught. For every Larry Summers pilloried for suggesting that innate sexual differences need investigation and acknowledgment, there are less publicly recognized figures making similar arguments, rooted in biological study. While such conclusions as Simon Baron-Cohen's "The female brain is predominantly hard-wired for empathy. The male brain is predominantly hard-wired for understanding and building systems" (Baron-Cohen 2003, 1) are uncharacteristically blunt in such studies (though note the qualifying word "predominantly"), with provisos about findings of sex difference statistically arguing that such findings "are largely irrelevant when making decisions about individuals" (Halpern 1986, 162) common, and of course with challenges to the conclusions of such studies frequent and powerful,[3] the notion that meaningful difference between men and women can be ruled out is highly suspect.

What is more interesting to consider is that sex differences (whether they are real or whether we only think they exist) are perceptual differences. It is also essential to note that Sim's treatment, while privileging the notion of sex difference as real, and of a hierarchical relationship in which the male is higher than the female, also leaves room for overlap. That is, for Sim, biological sex may be a major factor, but the traits associated with biological sex (that is, gender: the traits that can be considered as essentially "male" or essentially "female") are not *bound* by biological sex. Even his creation myth qualifies its sexing of creation with a blurring of such distinctions. Sim imagines creation as a sort of descent from God. God brings forth God's Spirit: "In the beginning God brought forth from within Himself His Spirit" (Sim and Gerhard 2004, 2). God is clearly male in this construction, as the pronoun choice indicates, but God's creative power is also clearly more akin to mothering than fathering: he does not make something external to himself but brings forth from *within* himself a new creation. Similarly, God's Spirit is clearly male and desires to be equal to God in all things (the failure of the Spirit, unsurprisingly perhaps, is to desire to be as God) and therefore to bring forth from himself a creature equal to himself. Unlike God, however, the Spirit cannot do so independently; God must act to bring forth from within the Spirit

Figure 55. The superimposition of Cerebus' head over Astoria's vagina suggests sexual indeterminacy. From *Church & State II* (© 1988 Dave Sim and Gerhard).

the Word, around which matter gathers to be then the source of Light. Again, the male Spirit is also akin to the female here, at least in relation to God, whose agency is necessary to bring forth the Word, around which matter then coalesces, from which matter then emerges the Light, at God's command. Sim presents the Light as explicitly female, and inferior in relation to the Spirit as the Spirit is in relation to God.

The Light, therefore, is two removes from God (Sim's cosmology seems to owe as much to Plato as to Scripture) but, like the Spirit, also wishes equality and to bring forth from itself its equal. The key difference established between the Spirit and the Light at this point is the Spirit's horror at further division (in which the Spirit echoes God) and the Light's delight in it. The Spirit desires to merge, the Light to multiply, so many of the further spirits brought forth from the Spirit then merge, becoming heavier and sinking, while those from the Light simply multiply. These contrasting impulses come to represent the contrasting male and female principles, but again, the association reverses. When animals come forth upon the earth, those which merely multiply without merging (that is, those that do not pair-bond or herd) are the male spirits, whereas the male Spirit was the one that established merging rather than just multiplying, while those that multiply and merge (that is, those that *do* pair-bond or herd) are female spirits, whereas the female Light was the spirit that multiplied only. Biologically, of course, both sorts of creatures must be both male *and* female in order to reproduce at all, since biological creatures, unlike spirits, do not as a rule procreate parthogenetically, so in creatures of the flesh, the concept of a male versus a female spirit is inherently in conflict with the biology of the creature: creatures with male spirits may have male or female bodies; creatures with female spirits may have male or female bodies.

Represented biologically, this complexity in men and women has special urgency, since they are, in Sim as in scripture, made in the image of God. However, being made in the image of God complicates the question not simply because there are two sexes but because of how Sim explicitly images their creation. God made man (as in the biologically male human, not humans in general) in God's image, except that in his midst he has "an image of God's spirit" (Sim and Gerhard 2004, 24): his genitalia. That is, the male genitalia, the most overt marking of male biological sex, are the image not of God but of God's Spirit, the secondary creature that is masculine in one respect but feminine relative to God. Woman is made from man's breast but has two breasts, which Sim's pseudo-scriptural text describes as "a marveil and a desire unto the spirit in the midst of the man which [...] doeth desire to be joined unto them" (ibid., 27).[4] Sim's note is especially interesting: "I think, as 'living metaphors' go, it only stands to reason that God created woman (basically) as an enlarged counterpart to the man's penis. That is, a woman's size relative to a penis is analogous to the size of 'the light' relative to God's spirit (the disparity in size originating in the mandate to create equally — God's spirit having come forth from within God and, thereby, containing more inherent greatness in a smaller 'space' than the primordial 'light' which was, for want of a better term, 'non-deistic' in origin)." While establishing a difference and a hierarchy in which the female is inferior to the male, this creation also establishes an analogy between the male and female principle and renders the most overtly male trait of the man, paradoxically, also the most female. Or, to put it another way, what draws a man to a woman is his essentially female core.

This brings us back, in a roundabout way, to Cerebus' hermaphroditism. This hermaphrodism represents the complexity of gender in *Cerebus*. Though biology makes most creatures one sex or the other, and though one's nature most frequently orients one's gender sense as either masculine or feminine (i.e. males tend to be gendered masculine and females feminine), Cerebus is not that simple. Indeed, Sim repeatedly challenges simple binary sexual difference, however much he also insists on its importance. Yoohwhoo, or YHWH, is in one sense the female antithesis of God. She is also, however, he/she/it, the tripartite combination of possibilities that might be seen as corresponding to divine, human and devilish possibilities. Sim explores this idea extensively in the "Cerebexegesis," the lengthy scriptural exegesis in which Cerebus engages in *Latter Days*. Frequently, biologically male characters (Joseph, for instance) function on one level of the narrative as literal men but on another as representatives of or analogues for Yoohwhoo—that is, as representations of the "female." As in Cerebus' Genesis story in his *Book of Cerebus*, the gender association of the creature varies depending on the narrative level or the direction of the relationship.

Sim anticipates this idea visually in *Rick's Story* in Rick's propensity for perceiving the same thing simultaneously in multiple terms. This applies to women, whom he can perceive as devil, woman, or angel, reflected also visually in this depiction of Cerebus. Sim visibly renders Cerebus' potential to be different things (figure 56).

Rick is himself defined by Cerebus as a girly-boy, because he reacts girlishly in some situations. For instance, when he is slightly hurt, he whines in pain and egregiously exaggerates his injury, which is not a manly way to behave, at least in Cerebus' eyes. Cerebus also sees Rick as a big baby, which is of course in some ways an analogous view. This image of Cerebus giving an infantilized Rick a bottle literalizes this notion (figure 57). It also of course places Cerebus in yet another female-analogous position, "mothering" Rick. Cerebus attempts to make Rick more masculine, while Rick reads everything Cerebus says as having religious significance, producing the *Booke of Ricke*, which serves as the scripture that allows for Cerebus' eventual assumption of complete power in *Latter Days*. In a way, therefore, Cerebus' "mothering" of Rick in fact allows Rick to become a man and achieve the great end of writing a prophetic text. The link between girly-boy Rick and hermaphrodite Cerebus returns as a minor but important element in *The Last Day*. One of the various religious schismatic groups (Le Sanctuary Upper Felda des Ricke et Joanne, Lesbiennes) has latched on to Cerebus' appellation for Rick and used it as the basis of their own theology:

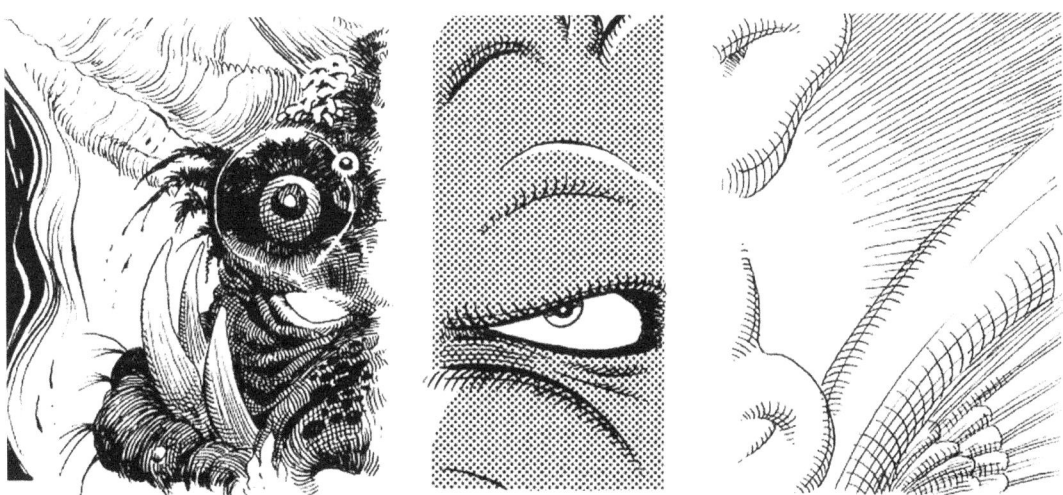

Figure 56. Sim visibly renders Cerebus' potential to be different things. From *Rick's Story* (© 1998 Dave Sim and Gerhard).

Figure 57. Cerebus sees Rick as a big baby. From *Rick's Story* (© 1998 Dave Sim and Gerhard).

The adherents of the LSUFdReJL—citing the following passage from NEW JOANNE'S original interview notes [ref. The Sanctuary vs. The Seat of Truth: The Book of Cerebus Foundational Dogma, NEW JOANNE, Cast-Iron Fallopian Tube Press, Panrovy, 1311 page 287 (originally published in an edited form in Friends of Yoohwhoo Trés Glam Second Issue, Summersmith, 104 Cast-Iron Fallopian Tube Press): "It was just like Girlyboy (Cerebus thought) to keep all the self-contained verses to himself Pardon? Oh. [Laughs] Girlyboy. That was the nickname Cerebus had for Rick back in the original Sanctuary. Cerebus never called him that to his face, of course."—believe that Rick, like Cerebus, was a fully developed hermaphrodite and-owing to his greater size and weight-played the "butch" role to Cerebus' "femme" role in their relationship [Sim and Gerhard 2004, 99].[5]

Part of the point here, of course, is that this reading is manifestly wrong, as anyone who read *Rick's Story* will know, and in that regard, this passage is entirely of a piece with the recurrent problematizing of reading/interpreting in *Cerebus* generally. It is also a reading that reverses both the literal implications of Cerebus' words as quoted here (by what logic would the Girly-boy be the butch role?) but also the implied gender relationship between Cerebus and Rick at the time—not an implicit lovers' relationship, to be sure, yet nevertheless one with the gender implications of mother/child. The hermaphroditism serves to clarify the extent to which the gender assignment is largely arbitrary. On the level of biology, perhaps, it is inherent, but otherwise gender becomes a function of one's role and relative status.

Cerebus, as we have noted repeatedly, behaves and conceives of himself as male, but he is biologically both male and female. As a result of discovering his hermaphroditism, Cerebus has suffered recurrent angst about his sexual identity, assuming that his biology must, or might, mean that he is, as he puts it (albeit under elisions suggesting his desire not to confront the possibility), a "faggot." Sex with a male would not violate his heterosexuality biologically, since he has female sex organs, but it would violate his sense of sexual identity as male. What he fails to recognize, and what *Cerebus* is, I think, ultimately working towards articulating, is that such sexual evaluations are largely socially constructed, having little to do with actual biology or with a grasp of the complexity of the world as it is. Astoria notes, in the sequence from issue 94 discussed earlier, that Cerebus' sexual desire is an acquired taste; indeed, in early issues of *Cerebus*, Cerebus is singularly uninterested in sex, except when under the influence of drugs, as mentioned earlier. Once he acquires it, though, it comes to define him even beyond the flesh. After Cerebus' death, the tripartite image he sees in the light (former war comrade and friend Bear; literary idol Ham Ernestway; and Jaka) interests him primarily for the figure of Jaka—the "she" part of the equation and Cerebus' sexual ideal (New Joanne, as she comes to call herself, drew Cerebus' attention because she closely resembled Jaka, not Joanne). Unsurprisingly, the dead manifest in the afterworld as idealized versions of their physical selves; the dead Cerebus is Cerebus in his prime, not the old, decrepit, and maimed Cerebus who died. This idea is so conventional as to be unremarkable, but Sim stresses his point by explicitly sexing the spirit. When Cerebus' spirit focuses on Jaka, he assumes his "Rabbi" identity (a Captain Marvel—the real Captain Marvel, not the Marvel one—parody). Part of the Rabbi's disguise to pass as gentile was a false foreskin removed when he assumed his Jewish identity. As Cerebus moves toward the light, we see him popping off the fake foreskin (figure 58), not only a particularly fleshly thing for a spirit to do but one with obviously sexual implications in the context. Cerebus is preparing himself for sex with Jaka, literalizing the maleness of his self-identity. Arguably, it is this insistence on his maleness that determines his eternal fate. Sim has refused to answer definitively the question of whether Cerebus ends up in hell, but certainly the end of *The Last Day* suggests that being dragged into the light by the talon-like fingers that Jaka's hands have in the final image of her in the comic is unlikely to be heavenly.

As Suenteus Po argues in *Reads*, it is the either/or insistence on a distinction between male and female that is problematic: "It makes as much sense for you to contemplate the

Figure 58. As Cerebus moves toward the light, we see him popping off the fake foreskin. From *The Last Day* (© 2004 Dave Sim and Gerhard).

relative merits of complimentary natures ... to determine which, of the two, is pre-eminent as it would for a fly on my windowsill to question whether it was better for me to move my bishop or my queen in a game of chess" (Sim and Gerhard 1995, 60). The conception of self and other when manifested in sexual terms leads, in *Cerebus*, to a world in chaos; male against female or female against male is to miss the point, *Cerebus* argues. Biological sexual difference is a fact; gender is a constructed difference. Cerebus' biology is both male and female, but his gender is male; his sexual identity is constructed, not innate. Through its exploration of gender, through its blurring of gender distinctions, and through its basic reversals enacted over the vast scope of its run, *Cerebus*, I would argue, treats gender conventions as it treats genre conventions, inverting, transgressing against, and ultimately exploding them.

Notes

1. The storm of controversy over Sim's putative misogyny had perhaps its most overt manifestation in such incidents as *The Comics Journal*'s labeling of Sim as a misogynist on the cover of issue 174 and printing an illustration inside the issue of Sim as a Naziesque warden of a concentration camp for women. Sim's perception is that he's so widely viewed as a misogynist that in 2007 he started sending correspondents a form letter saying, "If you want a response to your letter or submission all you have to do is to return this form letter stating for the record (and I reserve the right to post your name on the internet under the heading): 'I don't believe Dave Sim is a misogynist.' Or enter your name on the wiki page devoted to it at the Yahoo Cerebus discussion group" (letter to Stanley Leiber, available at http://tinyurl.com/4947p8r). The wiki page referred to ended up being a petition hosted at http://www.ipetitions.com/ petition/davesim. To date (February 2011) there are 277 signatures. For the record: I have not signed the petition. Also for the record: I do not believe Dave Sim is a misogynist (neither as he nor as the dictionary define the term), but I do not think signing a petition to that effect serves any purpose.

2. Sim himself refers in "Chasing Scott," the annotations to *Going Home*, to six principal "genders" (though his quotation marks around the term invite some skepticism about how seriously he takes the concept: "masculine heterosexualist," "female heterosexualist, female bisexual, lesbian, gay male, and gay bisexualist," as well as numerous other minor categories: "transsexuals, the transsexually inclined, tomboy heterosexualists, transvestites, or perhaps the only pinpoint minority really relevant to the discussion [of Cerebus]: genuine hermaphrodites" (Sim and Gerhard 1998).

3. It is beyond the scope of this paper (and my expertise) to even pretend to explore this controversial topic at any length; Halpern noted over fifteen years ago that "thousands, maybe even tens of thousands, of journal articles and books have been written that address this topic" (Halpern 1986, 13). I wish merely to suggest that in adopting the positions that a) there are real differences between the sexes and b) these differences may speak to the relative strengths or weaknesses of each sex, Sim may be at odds with sociological orthodoxy, but he is not necessarily wrong. Certainly, there are scientists who agree with him.

4. It is interesting that Sim connects male genitalia with the *breasts*, rather than the genitalia, of women. The draw of the female, perhaps, is not simply to the gratification of sexual desire but to the more complex web of associations between lover and mother; breasts are not simply sexual organs but also nurturing and comforting ones. The draw is still biological, of course, but the desire for the breast incorporates to some degree at least psychology as well as the fundamental procreative urge.

5. I am uncomfortably aware that Sim here is skewering precisely the sort of self-servicing interpretive gesture I am engaged in myself in this paper, and that Sim is profoundly suspicious of the merits of the works of us "scholar squirrels," as he refers to academics in "Chasing Scott" (Sim and Gerhard 1998), a term borrowed from Gore Vidal. Indeed, I doubt he would view my reading as valid. However, I am inclined to trust the art, not the artist, and I believe that *Cerebus* and Sim's personal beliefs are not necessarily identical.

Anti–Feminist Aardvark?
Gender, Subjectivity and Authorship
Isaac J. Mayeux

Cerebus is a comic about guys. The men in Dave Sim's work include ineffectual wannabe superheroes, smug would-be messiahs, washed-up rock stars, and scheming bureaucrats. Despite this varied cast of male characters, fans and critics often focus on Sim's portrayal of his female characters, all of whom call attention to patriarchal aggression in some capacity. Feminist critics have long attacked the ideology of masculine dominance. Despite this critique, models of aggressive, dominant masculinity remain at the center of academic and popular discourse. *Cerebus* uses its female characters— most especially Cirin and Astoria, who represent second-wave and third-wave feminism respectively — to analyze feminism and to posit an answer as to why the discourse on masculinity has progressed so slowly. Sim employs the characters of Astoria and Cirin to critique the Feminist movement for preoccupying itself with the narrative of patriarchal aggression as an excuse to gain power. Nonetheless, *Cerebus* also uses the character of Jaka to offer its own critique of patriarchy.

There is little scholarship that acknowledges Sim's work, much less scholarly work that examines gender representation in *Cerebus*. The series is consistently mentioned in the many works that argue to establish the legitimacy of the comics genre (see Dardess 1995, 214; Hatfield 2005, 29; McCloud 1994, 87; Sabin 1993, 231), though none of these works analyze the text in a serious, sustained way. Other works, such as Kelly Rothenberg's "Cerebus: An Aardvark on the Edge," focus on *Cerebus* solely, but they review the general history of Sim's work, rather than analyze a particular feature of it.

Because literary scholars have yet to recognize *Cerebus* as a text worthy of discussion, the internet contains the liveliest conversations about the aardvark. Even a casual interaction with the many message boards, fan sites, and blogs that discuss *Cerebus* reveals that the greatest controversy surrounding the work is its representation of women. Sim's detractors have labeled him a misogynist. One former fan went as far as to say that "Until Sim can confess that he is the working definition of a misogynist, I will never buy another comic written or illustrated by Dave Sim or acknowledge Dave Sim in any way ever again" (Champion 2008). While many fans can still appreciate Sim's comics regardless of his personal views, others conflate *Cerebus* and Sim, treating them as one entity.

Unfortunately, the impulse to see *Cerebus* and Sim as one could very well end a productive scholarly conversation on *Cerebus* before it starts. People still debate whether Sim is a misogynist, and that debate would likely eclipse all other discourse on *Cerebus* if readers collapse Sim and his work into one entity. Furthermore, literary criticism is a field closely aligned with feminism. If the discourse on this graphic novel never rises above the question of misogyny, literary critics will likely ignore *Cerebus* altogether because they have heard that it expresses a hatred for women. Such an outcome would be a loss for both the broader field of literary studies and the relatively new study of the graphic novel. While the former would benefit from the way that Sim confronts and de-familiarizes various aspects of contemporary discourse (gender, religion, politics, and so on), the latter would gain from Sim's formal ingenuity. At points, Sim forces the reader to turn the book sideways or upside down in order to keep reading. He often intercuts his narratives with pages of uninterrupted prose. As critics of the graphic novel continue to unravel the ways that comics make meaning, *Cerebus* represents the testing and transgressing of the conventional boundaries that comics readers expect. Critics must not ostracize a work with so much to offer.

Ultimately, critics must evaluate *Cerebus* apart from anything Dave Sim says in an interview about the intellectual capacity of women. The fact that Sim has asserted that there is a "substantial body of evidence — increasing every day — that indicates women are intellectually inferior to men," has no bearing on the meaning present in his work (Sim 2008b). Umberto Eco has pointed out that once an author creates a work for the general public, the work exists independently of the author. For Eco, the text holds meaning — not so much the reader or the author. The artist "has the right to react as a model reader" (Eco 1992, 194). For instance, Eco may try to refute what he regards as an over interpretation of *Foucault's Pendulum*, but he does so with the same facts at his disposal as any other reader. Eco must interpret his own novel, rather than simply say, "I did not mean that!" *Cerebus* is a text with significance independent of its author. Sim's (Sim 2008b) interactions with his fans affirm this idea. When presented with a reader's theory, he typically responds to it based on the textual evidence that supports or refutes the theory. Comments like "Well, that would be interesting, wouldn't it?" and "Well, obviously that would be my view," reflect that *Cerebus* contains a good deal of ambiguity, and that it is not the author's job to present the reader with the final, unquestionable reading of a work. Sim seems to agree with Eco that while the author creates the work, the reader interprets it. The author's intentions do not make one interpretation better than another is. Rather, the text supplies meaning and allows for multiple interpretations. The text does not speak in a univocal language.

Regardless of Sim's views on women, *Cerebus* is a self-contained world that operates according to its own logic and the conventions of the graphic novel. An outstanding convention of the graphic novel generally — and of *Cerebus* in particular — is the notion of "cartooning. In *Understanding Comics*, Scott McCloud compares cartooning to the realistic portrait, asserting that "by stripping down an image to its essential 'meaning,' an artist can amplify that meaning in a way that realistic art can't" (McCloud 1993, 30–31). McCloud notes that film critics will often use the term "cartoon" when discussing live action films to denote when a character or story takes on intensified symbolic meaning. Cartooning becomes a tool with which the author can bring certain details or ideas into focus, just as a frame can exclude or intensify certain details in a photograph. Sim cartoons the characters Cirin, Astoria, and Jaka to great effect. The reader can easily identify them with second wave feminism, third wave feminism, and traditional patriarchy, respectively.

In his famous essay, originally printed in issue 186, Sim referred to women as "emo-

Opposite: Figure 59. Uneven lines around her body suggest quivering. From *High Society* (© 1986 Dave Sim).

tion-based beings," yet the character of Astoria completely subverts such a notion (Sim and Gerhard 1995). For Astoria, emotions are tools for power. In *High Society*, the second volume of the series, she often manipulates the Roach's feelings of anger, sadness, or love to accomplish her goals. More importantly, she uses the stereotype of the irrational woman to trick Cerebus. After the Moon Roach kills a banker at Astoria's behest, Cerebus follows him back to Astoria's house. When Cerebus explains his intentions to turn the Roach in, Astoria attempts to dissuade him by crying. When that fails to deter the aardvark, she tearfully suggests that he take the Moon Roach costume. In order to cover up her part in the Roach's murders, she emphasizes her irrationality, saying, "I should never have kept it—somewhere in the back of my mind, I always hoped he could give up the Moon Roach voluntarily." In a final effort, she stresses her own emotional frailty (Sim draws uneven lines around her body to suggest quivering, see figure 59) and tells Cerebus, "Then you shan't feel too badly when I kill myself." When Astoria later appears in the aardvark's hotel suite, it becomes clear that she was using the narrative of the emotionally frail woman to her advantage. In the first of these two scenes, her constant movement marks Astoria's irrationality. In the second scene, Astoria remains stationary, and the artist juxtaposes lack of movement and immutably closed eyes with the frenzied action of Cerebus' fight with the Roach (figure 60). Furthermore, she quickly establishes control over the other two, telling Cerebus to agree to a three percent "increase on Palnan goods," and telling the Roach to go away. Both obey. This scene cements Astoria's status as a stoic and rational character.

Astoria's rationality defies the stereotype of the overly-emotional woman, but the most important facet of her character is that she is a stand-in for third-wave feminism. Third wave feminism describes the various types of feminism that both sprouted out of and began to question second wave feminism. Many of this new generation winced under the controlling tendencies of their intellectual forerunners, especially in relation to sex (see Queen and Comella 2008, 274–275; Tong 2009, 3–5). As Cirin's rebellious daughter, Astoria represents the next stage in the movement—Kevillism. Astoria's Kevillist movement opposes Cirinism in its dislike of rigid hierarchies. Significantly, while Cirin wants to regulate publications concerning sex, Astoria views sex as one of her greatest weapons. By the fifth panel of Astoria's introduction, she has seduced the Roach so that she can use him as her personal assassin ("Hey—what d'yuh think yer doin'? Hey! Hey*ymph*!" says the Roach, off to the side of the panel). Thirty pages later, she tries the same trick with Cerebus. She grabs the aardvark and rolls around with him on the floor. Cerebus threatens to hurt her if she does not stop, to which she replies, "Ooooh! That sounds like fun!" (Sim 1986, 147). In an obvious nod to real life feminism, both Cirin and Astoria have written manifestoes for their respective movements, and in Astoria's she writes, "The penis is an organ without scruple, without humanity, without common sense. Those women who understand this fact and make use of it have at their command all the resources of the modern world" (Sim and Gerhard 1994, 8). While many Second-wave feminists saw sex as a tool of Patriarchy, Astoria, like sex-positive third-wave feminists, sees sex as a tool for the liberation of women.

Astoria's character arc forms *Cerebus'* first major criticism of the feminist movement. Whether she is manipulating the Iestan legislature, Iestan financial institutions, or Cerebus, every action Astoria takes is for more power, but power for the sake of freedom for herself and other women. She supports Republicanism in Iest because she believes that "in time,

Opposite: Figure 60. Sim juxtaposes lack of movement and immutably closed eyes with the frenzied action of Cerebus' fight with the Roach. From *High Society* (© 1986 Dave Sim).

that it can lead to women getting the vote" (Sim 1986, 502). By the eighth volume of the story, however, Astoria begins to see "the hypocrisy of her own position." She wanted to teach her followers, the Kevillists, to be strong, independent women. Her movement was to have no leaders, and they would share decision-making. Yet, she acted as a despot guiding her followers "towards blind and unquestioning obedience" (Sim and Gerhard 1994, 205). Astoria uses the narrative of equality to mask her real motive of gaining power for its own sake. Consequently, *Cerebus* critiques third-wave feminists not for lacking intelligence or even for their agenda of equality, but for manipulating others with the ideology of freedom — in effect, using the idea of freedom to gain power over others, thereby repeating a narrative of domination.

In spite of this critique, Sim allows Astoria to redeem herself, transcending her status as a rational would-be autocrat. Astoria's character arc reaches its conclusion when Suenteus Po deftly argues that political and religious power imprisons the individual, even the one wielding the power. He addresses Astoria, Cirin, and Cerebus, telling Astoria that she was free the moment she left her entourage, and could have remained free had she escaped into the anonymity of the crowds. He exposes their hypocrisy. For all his efforts, Astoria is the only one who listens. Sim grants Astoria a moment of enlightenment. While Po speaks, the panels focused on him. Several panels zoom in on Po's face — Po physically fills the space of the comic, producing the effect of an enlarged presence and authority (Sim and Gerhard 1995, 84). Confronted with her own hypocrisy, Astoria gives a speech in which she and her words fill pages. As she confesses to various misdeeds, Sim splits the page into three panels, each one containing Astoria's profile. Cerebus and Cirin stand in the middle, and Astoria dwarfs them, signifying that she has reached a heightened state of mind (figure 61). In this heightened state, she recognizes that her actions have all been for the sake of more power: "It's a charade" (ibid., 100). She recognizes that more power will only imprison her. Astoria leaves the church, giving up all efforts to dominate others. Despite the fact that Astoria is the least masculine of the characters involved in this scene, Sim establishes her as a wise character willing to change in pursuit of freedom. Astoria represents a critique of third-wave feminism, yet her choice to remove herself from the struggle for power implies that feminists are not wrong to desire equality for women. Rather, *Cerebus* insists that feminists are wrong to use that narrative as a means to domination.

Cirin represents the appropriation of the militant aggression that feminists would typically attribute to patriarchy. bell hooks, for instance, defines patriarchy as a political-social system that insists that males are inherently dominating, superior to everything and everyone deemed weak, especially females, and endowed with the right to dominate and rule over the weak and to maintain that dominance through various forms of psychological terrorism and violence (hooks 2004, 18). Cirin takes this definition and replaces "patriarchy" with "matriarchy." Rather than oppose patriarchal masculinity with a new template of femininity, Cirin adopts those destructive masculine behaviors. Sim codes Cirin as a masculine character by drawing her as a physically imposing figure — larger than most of the characters with whom she shares the frame (figure 62) — but he also chooses to draw her as a cloaked figure. The image invokes Islamic nations that require women be covered at all times. Perhaps more importantly, her cloak suggests her status as an assassin, covert violence being the crux of her power. The cloak and its link to fascism imply that *Cerebus* does not critique

Opposite: Figure 61. Sim splits the page into three panels, each one containing Astoria's profile. From *Reads* (© 1995 Dave Sim and Gerhard).

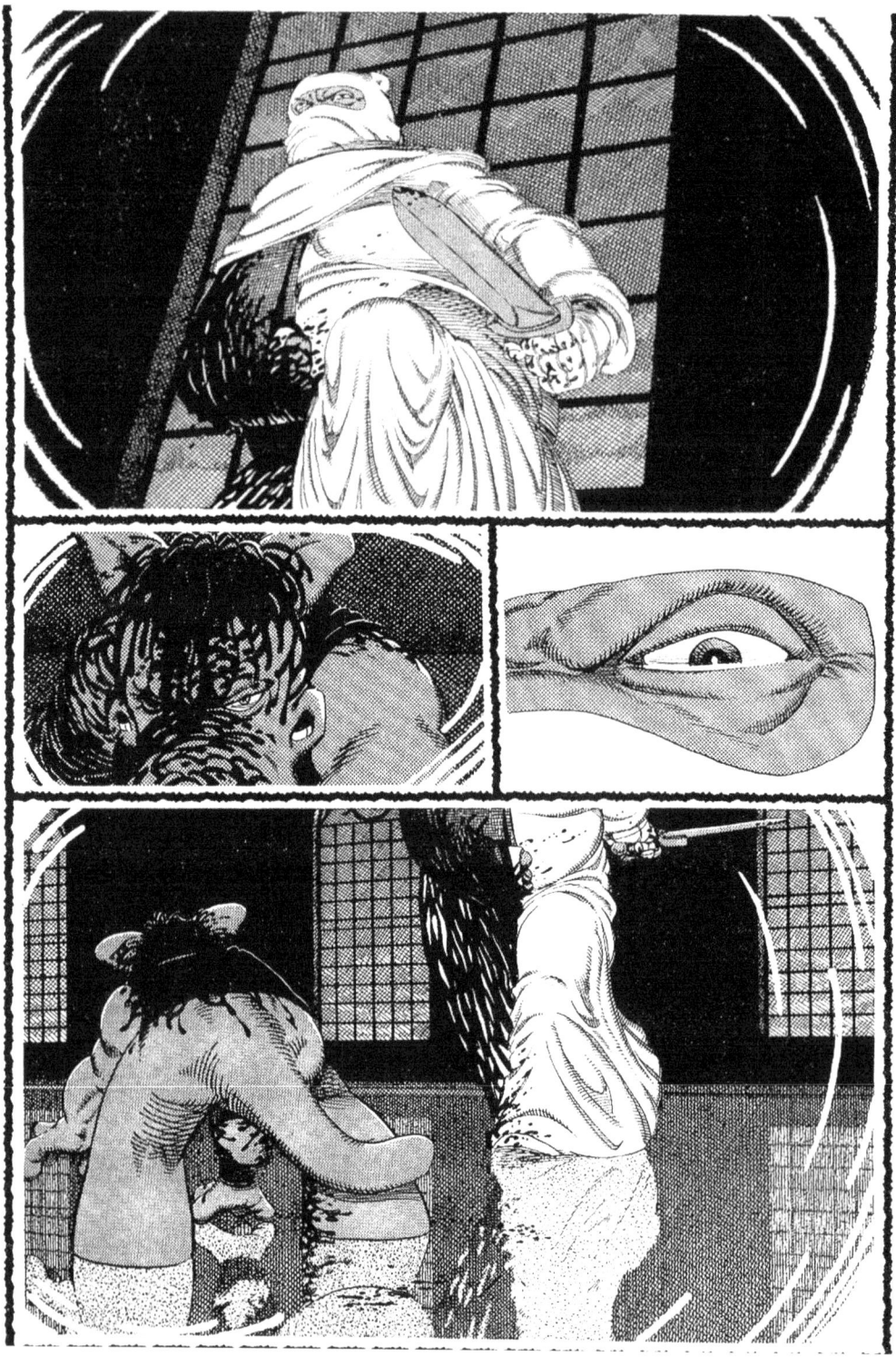

Figure 62. Cirin as a masculine character with a physically imposing figure. From *Reads* (© 1995 Dave Sim and Gerhard).

the movement for women's equality, or even the idea that women are superior to men, but rather exposes the impulse to use the ideology of women's rights to dominate others and inhibit their freedom.

Sim's critique gains greater force when one realizes that Cirin stands in for not only second wave feminism, but also second wave feminism as embodied by Catharine MacKinnon. Oddly enough, MacKinnon sees quilts as an exemplar of women's artistic contributions to society (MacKinnon 1987, 39). Judith Evans goes as far as to say that a "woman-culture" for MacKinnon "is about making quilts" (Evans 1995, 88). Like MacKinnon, Cirin conceives of her movement in terms of quilt-making. As Cirinism spreads, quilting circles become the center of economic and political life—a place to trade information, distribute resources, and, of course, create works of art (Sim and Gerhard 1996, passim).

More importantly, Cirin resembles MacKinnon in her obsession with censorship. What is perhaps MacKinnon's most outstanding feature as a writer is her unrelenting opposition to pornography. As a lawyer, MacKinnon argues that pornography violates the Constitutional right to equality (MacKinnon 200, 80). More concretely, she has stated that pornography "is a technologically sophisticated traffic in women" (MacKinnon 1991, 195). In short, MacKinnon argues that pornography should be illegal. In a similar vein, Cirin's regime outlaws all activity that objectifies women. For instance, the Cirinists arrest Jaka because she is a dancer in a tavern. In fact, they originally intend to execute her for her crimes, but Jaka claims diplomatic immunity as the niece of Lord Julius. In the same instance, the Cirinists arrest Oscar because he is a "book writer" (Sim and Gerhard 1990). He has "No artistic license" (ibid.). Read in this light, *Cerebus* critiques MacKinnon, and second wave feminism as a whole, for attempting to regulate what types of speech are legally permissible.

Sim extends this critique when he explains the origin of Cirinism in *Minds*. When Sim enters his own world as the character "Dave," he explains to Cerebus that Cirin hijacked both her name and her movement from the real Cirin. The original Cirin was a scholar who created a movement based on simple living, equality, and economic independence for women. Cirin the aardvark, whose name was originally Serna, led the communal safety branch of the revolution. As the revolution grows, the communal safety officers contribute less to the work force and take more of the resources. Eventually, Cirin the aardvark decides to avoid the consequences of her actions and take complete control of the revolution in one stroke. Through either psychic manipulation or old-fashioned interrogation, she convinces her followers that she is Cirin, and that the real Cirin is actually Serna, head of communal safety. She declares "Serna" a traitor to the revolution, and then orders her minions to shave Serna's head and sew her lips shut to prevent her from revealing the truth. This incident resembles the myth of Philomela, whose brother-in-law, Tereus, raped her and cut out her tongue to silence her. Tereus' actions indicate a desire to suppress the feminine voice and control a woman's ability to talk with whomever she pleases. Similarly, Cirin's actions expose her penchant for censorship, her movement built upon the silencing of a woman. Sim the artist makes the parallel explicit in his attention to "Serna's" blood-drenched and later atrophied mouth (figure 63). Cirin's decision to silence "Serna" is a misogynistic act of mythic proportions. She has co-opted patriarchal tactics.

This myth is especially relevant to this episode of *Cerebus* because of the response by Procne, Philomela's sister and Tereus' wife. Philomela weaves a tapestry detailing what happened and sends it to Procne, who decides to punish her husband by killing their son, the

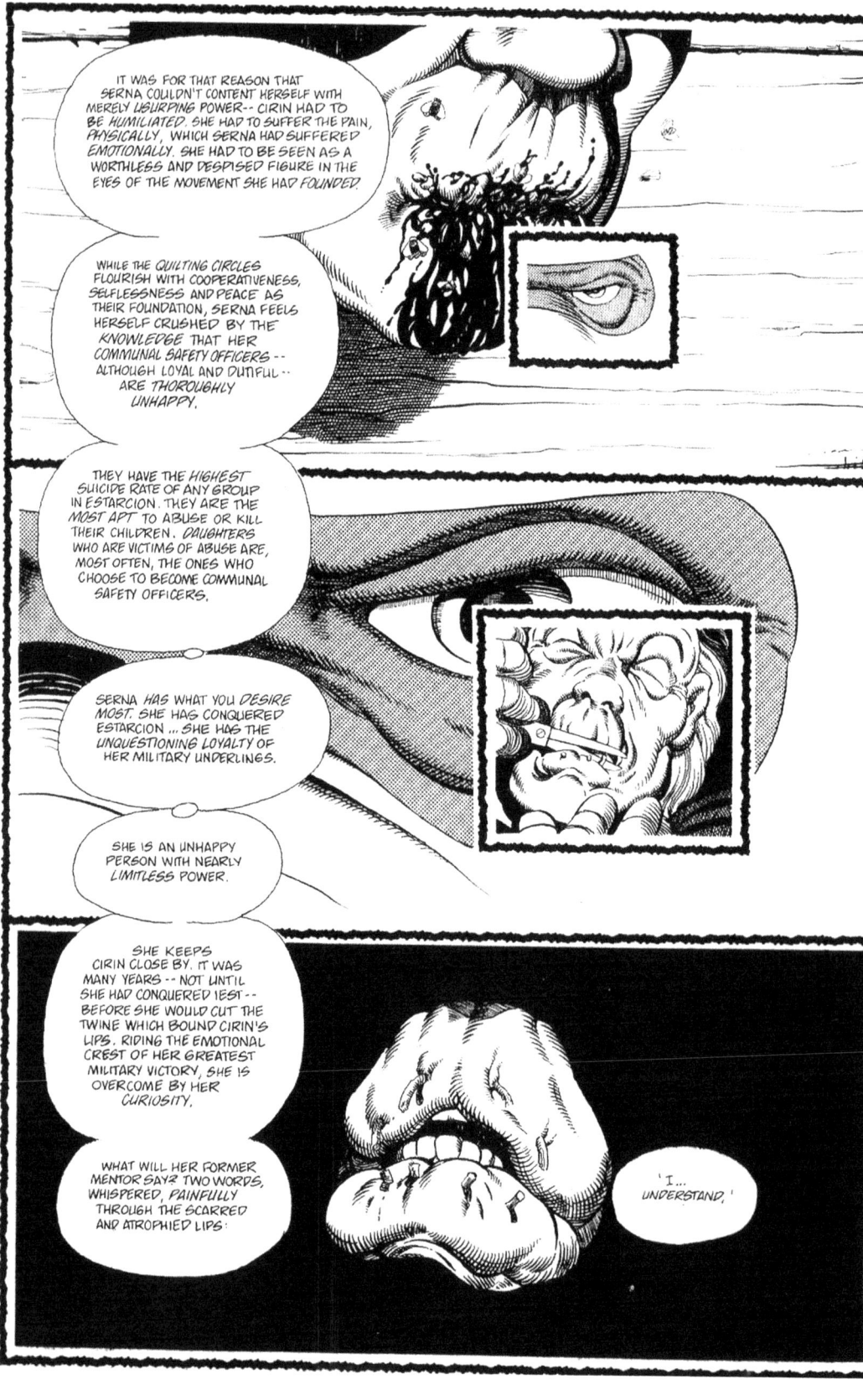

product of their marriage, and serving him to Tereus as a meal. This choice parallels Cirin's actions because, as Jessica Lugo observes, "[Procne] has adopted his [Tereus'] barbarous nature, and decides by a primal, vengeful code of honor that Tereus' punishment should fit his crime" (Lugo 2007, 403). Like Procne, Cirin retaliates against male domination, but does so by adopting the same logic as that oppressive ideology. Cirin's matriarchy depends upon patriarchal domination, upon the silencing of women.

Cirin's interactions with her underlings cement the idea that she embodies the feminine appropriation of patriarchal domination. In a moment of clarity in *Women*, Cirin confesses to General Greer that she encourages her "own sycophants" to flatter her. She admits that when she reviewed transcripts of conversations, "All that would cause offense to me was excluded, stripped away and hidden from me. Like a man. Very like a man" (Sim and Gerhard 1994, 150). Again, Cirin silences all dissent, but she recognizes her hypocrisy, at least for a moment. Because the comment, "Like a man," comes from Cirin, this moment should hardly be taken as Sim's admission that men inherently silence dissent. Rather, Cirin realizes that she exemplifies the destructive stereotype of masculinity that she herself created. Not surprisingly, Cirin later executes General Greer for agreeing that she was "like a man," on grounds of treason against the goddess, thus silencing another female voice to eliminate the threat to her power (ibid., 165).

By repeating scenarios in which Cirin judges what types of speech are acceptable and punishes women who violate her arbitrary boundaries, Sim turns MacKinnon's own critique of patriarchy back on her:

> "When you are powerless, you don't just speak differently. A lot, you don't speak. Your speech is not just differently articulated, it is silenced. Eliminated, gone. You aren't just deprived of a language with which to articulate your distinctiveness, although you are; you are deprived of a life out of which articulation might come" [MacKinnon 1987, 39].

Cerebus implies that by trying to silence certain types of speech, MacKinnon uses the same tactics of domination that she decries.

While Astoria and Cirin represent powerful women using egalitarian ideology to gain more power, Sim cartoons Jaka as a victim of masculine domination, patriarchal ideology. Jaka has no identity outside of the men in her life — whether it be Lord Julius, Pud, Rick, or Cerebus. Jaka's identity as a dancer affords her some level of independence, but she ultimately sacrifices that identity by marrying Rick, and that marriage fails to live up to its promise. Jaka must support Rick, who spends his time with Oscar instead of looking for work. The marriage culminates with Rick striking Jaka and declaring his hatred for her after discovering that she aborted her first pregnancy. That Jaka's marriage is concluded by an episode of male violence affirms her status as a victim. Thus, *Cerebus* characterizes patriarchy, via its representation of marriage, as a system that perpetrates violence against women.

If Sim's indictment of traditional marriage softens because Jaka's marriage to Rick in *Jaka's Story* is less than traditional, Sim concretely emphasizes how marriage destroys Jaka in *Minds*. During his conversation in space with the aardvark, "Dave" runs through multiple hypothetical scenarios in which Cerebus and Jaka are married, all of them resulting in Cerebus abusing Jaka. In the first scenario, Jaka is submissive but unhappy. "Dave" explains that she plans to leave and that he "can make her love you — but I can't make her love

Opposite: Figure 63. Cirin's actions expose her penchant for censorship, her movement built upon the silencing of a woman. From *Minds* (© 1996 Dave Sim and Gerhard).

Figure 64. Sim captures the brutality of the situation by placing Cerebus' fist at the center of the frame. From *Minds* (© 1996 Dave Sim and Gerhard).

Figure 65. Jaka hangs herself. From *Minds* (© 1996 Dave Sim and Gerhard).

stronger than her need to be happy ... or her instinct for self-preservation" (Sim and Gerhard 1996, 209). This first marital scenario presents traditional, male-led marriage as a dreary and dangerous proposition for the woman. According to "Dave," Jaka will leave to protect herself. Cerebus then demands that "Dave" create a story in which Jaka will be happy no matter what, which results in Cerebus hitting Jaka in the eye and then the nose. Sim captures the brutality of the situation by placing Cerebus' fist at the center of the frame (figure 64). Realizing that Jaka will look ugly if he hits her, he tells "Dave," "Okay! You make her happy to stay with Cerebus no matter what. *And* you make it so Cerebus never hits her *ever*, or threatens to hit her." What follows is a twenty-four-page story in which Cerebus cheats on Jaka, and she hangs herself (figure 65). The repetition of abuse in marriage, no matter how "Dave" modifies the rules, implies that marriage is an inherently unsafe state of being for the woman. Far from arguing in favor of male dominance and superiority, *Cerebus* destabilizes patriarchal domination.

Another instance in which Jaka is subject to masculine domination exists only in the mind of Pud. Throughout *Jaka's Story*, Pud fantasizes about Jaka. With each imagined interaction, he comes closer and closer to raping her. When he finally violates Jaka's personal space with the intention of raping her, she vomits on him. This prevents Pud from carrying out his fantasy. Moreover, Pud's repeated fantasy unmasks the danger of a femininity that identifies women as sex objects. His exchange with Jaka is economic in nature: she dances in his tavern, and he pays her in groceries. In his mind, Jaka should offer her body as a commodity in exchange for goods from his store. Pud is the product of an ideology that treats women not as people but as sex objects. By cultivating the fraught relationship between Jaka and Pud, *Cerebus* comments on the notion that men should control women.

One of the worst abuses Jaka suffers comes when Lord Julius, her uncle, molests her. This is a point that gains much of its force from its subtlety. The reader only knows of Jaka's sexual abuse from feverish dreams she has involving phallic insects, apparently full of semen. The author's preoccupation with sexual violence highlights the tyranny of a system in which women are subservient to men. Sim has refrained from naming a culprit, but he has admitted, "Lord Julius would obviously be a suspect" (Sim 2008a). He is the only suspect, considering that any other suspect would be someone unimportant to the narrative. Nonetheless, the story itself suggests Julius as Jaka's abuser. In his cosmic exchange with Cerebus, "Dave" relates how Jaka has commissioned a painting of herself and Lord Julius, calling it, "Her first tentative step on the road to a brighter future where she will escape the prison in which she finds herself. She will rediscover the world ... and, in so doing ... rediscover herself" (Sim and Gerhard 1996, 144). Jaka herself chose the content of the painting and hopes to use it to express how she feels to Lord Julius, yet the painting contains truths of which Jaka is not consciously aware. In M. Zulli's painting, Jaka sits with her arms wrapped around her legs, protecting her breasts and vagina (figure 66). On the other side of the frame, Lord Julius stands in front of a podium, fingering a cigar in his left hand—the phallic object—while his right hand sits in his pocket—a vaginal symbol. The artist's choice to occupy Lord Julius's hands with both a phallic and vaginal object evokes the molestation of a young girl, unable to engage in sexual intercourse. This painting reconstructs Lord Julius's violation of his niece, while simultaneously providing an explanation for his avoidance of her. Jaka's choice of M. Zulli as her artist supports this reading of the painting. Zulli's audition painting portrayed Jaka masturbating while wearing the Palnu flag. At least unconsciously, Jaka understood that what she wanted to express to her uncle was sexual in nature. The idea that an uncle would molest his niece is damning. The critique

Figure 66. The painting contains truths of which Jaka is not consciously aware. From *Minds* (© 1996 Dave Sim and Gerhard).

is stronger in this case, however, because Lord Julius was the man in whom Jaka had found her identity as the Princess of Palnu. It was that context that allowed, perhaps even encouraged, Lord Julius to violate his niece; that *Cerebus* portrays Jaka as a casualty of masculine oppression fits well with bell hooks' description of patriarchy as a system that preys upon "everyone deemed weak, especially females." Sim's work may not be a rallying cry for sisterhood, but it is certainly much more *feminist-friendly* than many have given it credit. The character of Jaka exposes the oppression of patriarchy.

If *Cerebus* indicts feminism for using the narrative of masculine aggression for its own gain, yet also agrees with the critique to some extent, readers must ask, "What does this graphic novel have to say about alternative models of masculinity?" What drives Sim's work is not an obsession with or revulsion for women, but a fixation on masculinity. His work illuminates the question of what it means to be a man,to be a person expected to fulfill certain expectations of masculinity. A part of Scott McCloud's idea of cartooning involves "masking." A more abstractly rendered character allows the reader to inhabit safely a more realistic environment (such as the one Gerhard draws). The more abstract the character, the more relatable that character becomes. The eponymous protagonist of *Cerebus* is easily the most abstract character in the series. Other characters often have direct referents in the real world, such as Margaret Thatcher, but Cerebus' distinct lack of physical detail allows Sim to use his character as a depository for masculine anxieties. As Cerebus progresses from mercenary to prime minister to pope and so on, the changes in his character tell us more about what it means, or can mean, to be a man.

The Aardvark and the Beautiful Women: Male Sexuality and Gender Politics
Mario N. Castro

Cerebus is arguably one of the most inaccessible comic books in history. It is also one of the few graphic novels which it is seemingly impossible to separate from its creator. Sim is, in a way, a creator who likes to provoke through his artistic statements. As a result, the public knows more about the creator than his creation, a perception that has worsened after decades of accusations of misogyny.

It is essential for critics and historians to change their approach to the work of Dave Sim. We have to stop using Sim's official declarations and commentaries about his own work and begin conceiving of *Cerebus* as what it really is: the most ambitious graphic novel ever published, an epic achievement containing nearly unlimited potential for critical analysis.

Cerebus works as an evolving narrative that moves from the most specific ideas to the most general abstraction. It begins as a parody of fantasy pulp fiction, then metamorphizes into a complex deconstruction of economy, religion and finally, gender. This essay will work in a similar manner, by dividing the body of the analysis into two main parts: the first part will focus on the concept of gender through a Bourdieuan approach, which considers gender as an arbitrary construction. This section will also deal with the gender characteristics of Cerebus, the main protagonist, and the unusual aspects of his relationships with Red Sophia and Astoria in *High Society* and *Church & State*. The second part of this essay centers on gender politics and female representation in the fictional world of Estarcion. This section explores the concept of gender superiority and subalternity (those outside the hegemonic power structure) as presented in the longest storyline of the series, *Mothers & Daughters*. Due to *Cerebus'* length, it is not possible to summarize all the events and characters that appear throughout the series. This critical analysis is intended as a mere introduction. The rest is up to the reader.

A Virgin, Hermaphrodite Barbarian: Male Dominance and Gender Construction

One of the most controversial aspects of feminism lies in the fact that its theoretical background works, in most cases, within a semiotic system determined by a male perspective. This is particularly notable when dealing with concepts such as "gender" and "women."

According to Judith Butler, "The subject of women is no longer understood in stable or abiding terms" (Butler 1990, 1). As performative agents, women exist inside a symbolic universe perfectly conceived to justify the superiority of men in all aspects of society. This process arises as a product of Freudian theory, the writings of Greek philosophers and the semiological interpretations of culture and language, which have maintained a definitive intellectual vocabulary that effectively invalidates the existence of "women" as female construction. Instead, the entire female culture has essentially evolved and developed around male misconceptions of what a "woman" should be.

Pierre Bourdieu, in his essay entitled "Masculine Domination," asserts that the biggest mistake of feminist scholars has been to focus their analysis on the domestic space, instead of state and social institutions, where the symbolic means of control are much more prevalent. Bourdieu believes that gender domination works primarily on a linguistic level. If one inserts a determined semiotic construct in the habitus, then is possible that certain terms or words alter the hierarchical aspects—like the consideration of the superiority/inferiority of women—of the social matrix. In some aspects, this particular thesis is similar to the notorious statement of Julia Kristeva in *The Power of Horror*: "Strictly speaking, 'women' cannot be said to exist" (Kristeva 1982, 19). From Bourdieu's perspective, the most surprising aspect of male domination is its effective use of communication as a system of arbitrary meanings that have created a set of gender archetypes:

> It is clear that in these areas one must above all restore the paradoxical character of *doxa* while at the same time dismantling the processes responsible for this transformation of history into nature, of cultural arbitrariness into the *natural*. And to do so, one has to adopt the point of view on our own world and our own vision of the world which is that of the anthropologist, capable of showing that the principle of division (*nomos*) which founds the difference between male and female as we (mis)recognize it is simultaneously arbitrary, contingent, and also socio-logically necessary [Bourdieu 200, 2].

What Bourdieu infers is that language uses a wide variety of concepts that immediately evokes in the listener certain predefined aspects of "masculinity" and "femininity." Simple antonyms such as erect/flaccid, up/down, hard/soft, refer directly to stereotypical (or more specifically, *idiosyncratic*) aspects of gender oppositions: the hardness of the penis against the softness of the vagina, the upper/active position of men in intercourse with the passive/lower role of women. Behind the *signifier* lies an extensive net of semiotic implications that try to unify the performativity of the body with established paradigms about sex.

Cerebus is a valuable object of study—even alongside its contradictory nature and sudden shifts in tone—because of its literary ambitions and the way that it constantly challenges the usual archetypes about gender and sexuality, the best example being its main character. In several ways, the evolution of Cerebus' sexuality directly parallels the development and tone of the plot. In the first issues, he is characterized as an ambitious and cunning mercenary, but also as bad-tempered, violent and misanthropic. Though his behavior and attitude is stereotypically "male"—fond of alcohol, dim witted and unrefined—he doesn't seem to have a sexual interest in women and most of the time he considers them either as strange and annoying creatures, or both. Sim presents this ambivalent attitude in the narrative through Cerebus' complex relationships with the main female characters of the story.

The first direct mention of Cerebus' sexuality happens in the first part of the *Church & State* story arc (issue 57): Weisshaupt, one of the main political antagonists in this storyline, blackmails Cerebus and forces him into accepting a fake marriage with Red Sophia, a character originally portrayed as a one-note parody of Roy Thomas and Barry

Windsor-Smith's *Red Sonja*, a female warrior who only sleeps with men who defeat her in combat. As Cerebus is unable to escape the political machinations of Weisshaupt, he agrees to retake his position as Prime Minister of Iest and wait for a chance to betray him. This chance for betrayal occurs when Cerebus manages to obtain the title of Pope of the Southern Church.

In this section of the story, Sim uses the bizarre relationship between Cerebus and Red Sophia to mock the usual clichés of a "forced" or "uncomfortable" marriage. Sim reduces Sophia, in particular, from a powerful and sensual warrior into a "trophy wife," a woman who only serves a political function. In Cerebus' case, his attitude towards his new status as a married man turns from mere tolerance to passive-aggressiveness. This situation worsens with the appearance of Mrs. Henrot-Gutch, his insensitive and emasculating mother-in-law. Though Cerebus never physically hurts or attacks Red Sophia in any way, it is obvious that the marriage rapidly runs its course.

Most of the marital fights revolve around Cerebus' obsession with sex and are parodic in tone. A particularly notorious moment occurs when Red Sophia reveals, by screaming from a window, the peculiar sexual fetishes of her husband: "Hey! Everybody! Most Holy likes me to tie him up and tickle his feet with my tongue!" (Sim and Gerhard April 1985).

The first marriage of Cerebus marks the point where the character transitions from an almost asexual, passive character, into the sexual archetype of a virile, active, dominant man, an aspect that only acquires a much more grotesque connotation in his relationship with Astoria. With Red Sophia's marriage, Sim challenges, in an ironical tone, the most common aspects of religious-based marriages: a mercenary (the typical model of masculinity in the sword and sorcery genre) only becomes sexually "active" when he becomes pope.

High Society marks the first appearance of Astoria (issue 31). Characterized as the ex-wife of Lord Julius (the powerful ruler of Palnu), Astoria is an astute and cold woman with extensive experience in political stratagems. She easily manages to manipulate Cerebus and later, becomes the director of his election campaign for the job of Prime Minister. During this time, they sleep together as a couple in his suite at the Regency Hotel, but Sim implies that there's no type of sexual contact between them.

Astoria is involved in two of the most prominent events in *Church & State*. The first one is the assassination of the Pope of the Western Church by her own hands. The second, and much more important to the hypothesis of this essay, is her apparent "rape" by Cerebus the Pope. This incident takes place in issue 94, in the middle of Astoria's interrogation regarding the killing of the Lion of Serrea. After a brutal exchange between Astoria and Cerebus, she tries to "buy" her freedom by "helping" Cerebus with one of his so-called "acquired tastes." While referring to this, she removes her underwear and places it on Cerebus' head. Then, she reveals that his unusual approach to sex is a result of idiosyncratic rules (which also may indicate that Cerebus was a virgin up until his marriage with Red Sophia): "Oh, I forgot. You can't, can you? As a *good orthodox tarimite*, unless you're *married*, isn't that right?" (Sim and Gerhard January 1987) (italics mine). In an instant, he gags and blindfolds her and using his power as pope, divorces Red Sophia and "marries" Astoria. Then he proceeds to rape her. This controversial sequence was followed by a heated debate between readers and critics of the series that extended for several months. The struggle centered on the particular nature of Cerebus' action and if it actually qualifies as statutory rape or some kind of consensual sex.

Instead of focusing on the most subjective or polemic aspects of this incident, I will focus my analysis on the visually aesthetic devices that Sim uses in this complex scene. The entire sequence lasts five pages and starts on page sixteen, just when Cerebus blindfolds Astoria, and finishes at the end of the issue, resulting in a grand total of 24 frames. Sim places the point-of-view of the "camera" on Astoria's eyes, providing a visual intention that completely opposes the techniques used in pornography.

The object of any erotic material, but particularly the ones directed at heterosexual male viewers, is to provide a feeling of *sexual stimuli*. Always placed in front of the women/actress, this point of view is a technique that creates a connection with the receptor that must imagine himself in place of the male actor penetrating the woman. The camera *simulates* a dominant position in which the woman is an "object" that's sexually possessed. It establishes a visual illusion by catering to the desires of the male watcher. Observes Linda Williams, "This logic was not just a matter of centering the narrative images; the spectator, too, had to be metaphorically centered within the illusory world created out of an assemblage of shots" (Williams 1989, 65). The pornographic material provides a voyeuristic representation that imitates a real-life sexual scenario. Sim designed the rape of Astoria, on the other hand, to be visually unpleasant, placing the reader in a "passive" position: the one of the victim. We do not see what is happening because of Astoria's blindfold, so the entire sequence develops in the dark. As *receptors*, we construct the scene in our minds only through sounds and dialogue ("I've never been ... so humiliated ... in my life"). The sequence and the issue end when Cerebus falls asleep.

The following issue, number 95, begins with a dream sequence. We see Cerebus dressed as a mercenary, running in what appears to be some sort of sewer. On page three, a gigantic black chain falls on Cerebus' head. He tries to lift it, but it becomes heavier and heavier until it crushes him. On page six, we see Cerebus asleep on Astoria's lap. The point-of-view of the "camera" reverts to the "active" position by placing the female in the center of the image. Sim present us with a typical example of female coercion by a powerful male, yet he visually presents it through atypical aesthetic devices. The sequence challenges the semiotic construction of arbitrary concepts such as active/passive and dominance/subordination. Sim visually deconstructs gender, providing an ambiguous tone to the rape. Sim enhances this ambiguity in a dream sequence that graphically represents the "guilt" of Cerebus in the form of a heavy chain.

The central question of issues 94 and 95 is simple: Does Cerebus' act constitute a rape? What is clear from the scene is that Astoria intended to manipulate Cerebus, a possibility that correlates with the usual counterargument used in trials or in public perception regarding the ethical "blame" of the female victim (the controversial assessment of "she was asking for it"). Astoria confesses in *Mothers & Daughters* that she intended to "provoke" Cerebus so she could get pregnant—the reason, a hidden political agenda (Sim and Gerhard February 1994). She also reveals that Cerebus is a *hermaphrodite*; his body includes "both male and female genitalia." Then, she explains that the erection "seals his uterus when engaging in intercourse" (ibid.). Sim thus poses the question of the performativity of the body and its relation with gender as a construct.

At his best, Sim's opinions regarding gender politics and feminism are insightful and revolutionary. At his worst, they're contradictory and extreme. Even alongside his militant anti-feminism, the character of Cerebus seems fitting proof that Sim believes in the concept of "gender." At least, there must be a definitive difference between biology and the psychological aspects of the individual. Sim uses the concept frequently in both *Reads* and "Tangent" (by far the most controversial of his writings), yet this may arise from the fact that he does not believe in gender equality. The narrative and characters in *Cerebus* clearly entail that women and men are *different*; they can't be equal, and that semiological differentiation is also sociologically necessary and thus, one of them must be superior to the other. However, it also seems that there is the possibility of the presence of "blind spots," little "holes" that seemingly avoid the feminine/masculine paradigm. In Bourdieuan terms, these would be exceptions in the arbitrary construction of gender inside the social matrix, open spaces where the characteristics of each sex overlap each other.

The complex behavior and attitude of Cerebus provides a fascinating new perspective to the ongoing debate of gender and sex. By the last 100 issues of the series, Sim characterizes Cerebus as a hyper-sexualized male. Throughout *Minds* and *Guys,* Cerebus is perverted, volatile and mildly insane. Curiously enough, he seems to "slip" constantly into the female territory. Like a "woman," he's narcissistic and impulsive, flaws that are mocked by Bear (a long time friend from his mercenary days), referring to Cerebus as "chick shit" (Sim and Gerhard, September 1996). Bourdieu asserts, "The worst humiliation for a man is to be turned into a woman" (Bourdieu 2000, 22). Virility is a code validated by other males. Cerebus' physical deformation and conflicted personality symbolically represent a male who cannot be completely "masculine," despite his sexual prowess and political power. Ultimately, he doesn't really understand the logic behind the aspects of virility and instead, his male behavior emerges as self-preservation instinct.

The Mother and the Daughter: Gender Politics and Female Representation

The complex religious aspects of the world of Estarcion serve different narrative purposes. In most cases, they are plot devices that have symbolic functions, such as the implication of religious institutions to political economies or the theological conception of the male/female duality. In the latter, the Western represents the male perspective and Eastern Churches, both ruled by the belief of a masculine god named Tarim. Just like the Roman Catholic Church, men exclusively constitute its doctrine and internal hierarchy. In the opposite spectrum lies the Church of the True Goddess Terim; the most modern version of this "feminist" church is the Cirinist movement, a highly militarized matriarchy, and Kevillism (founded by Astoria). The conflict between these two factions is the center of the longest story arc in *Cerebus*, entitled *Mothers & Daughters*.

Cirin, a scholar of matriarchal societies in Upper Felda, and her assistant Serna, founded Cirinism as a form of communal society focused on agriculture and an ascetic life. Cirin summarized all its theoretical and philosophical aspects in a treatise entitled "The Five Cornerstones." Cirin proposed the idea of a "matriarchy" as a desperate solution to the brutal consequences of the one-century occupation of the Sepran Army. The war resulted in the massacre of every man and child between the ages of five and forty, leaving a starving community formed exclusively by women, old men and children (Sim and Gerhard May 1995). The Cirinists introduced large white robes as an obligatory dress code, establishing a physical equality between all the women of the community and thus, eliminating all superficial aspects of fashion and beauty. Cirinists direct all the energy and workforce to harvesting food and raising the children. This activity is named "quilting" and the community of women is then known as the "Motherhood" (ibid.). They divide food rations equally and tools and utensils belong to all members of the community. Men, on the other hand, have no influence or power in the motherhood and only serve a reproductive function:

> As quilting spreads to the adjacent farm communities, commerce declines in Harwell: the few shops close, the farmer's marketplace is sparsely attended, which leads to the accelerated growth of quilting which leads to a further decline in commerce. And so on. The old men of the village council meet infrequently and then not at all — They soon join the remaining farmers in community taverns supplied with ale and hard liquor by the motherhood. The men drink and the women work [ibid.].

The concept of gendered spaces semiotically determines the female or male nature of certain public or domestic places. The structure of patriarchal societies of the 19th century demonstrates that "initial status differences between women and men create certain types of gendered spaces ... that institutionalized spatial segregation then reinforces prevailing male advantages" (Spain 1992, 33). Cirinism inverts this mechanism by tolerating the existence of single male space: the tavern. By limiting the male movement into one area, Cirinists can control and exclude men from any socio-economic activity, effectively rendering them *invisible*. The tavern becomes a space of symbolic domination. To achieve this, Serna (who's in charge of communal safety) slowly trains a select number of mothers (the more physically powerful, the better) to serve as a group of mercenaries, killing all men who oppose the matriarchy or that partake in domestic violence.

In many ways, the Cirinist movement inverts the status of women in Ancient Greece. The matriarchy opposes the notion of women as "vessels" of the male seed, and instead the mothers are the *creators* of life, the center of the human existence, while men are mere "givers" of seed, perverted creatures who disrupt the female space. In Spivakian terms, men are the subalterns in the Cirinist movement. They are completely excluded from historical and economical discourse. The system forces them to stay in a single space because they lack a determined social function. If a man becomes a widow or never marries, he can choose to die in the tavern where he would have access to unlimited supplies of food and shelter. In semiotic terms, they "cannot speak."

Despite this, the presence of men in Cirinism challenges the usual definition of subalternity. Spivak states that "the Word 'subaltern' is losing its definitive power because it has become a kind of buzzword for any group that wants something that it does not have" (Spivak 1996, 190). Despite the effectiveness of Cirinism, it remains a hierarchical system based on the extreme aspects of gender superiority. From a more critical perspective, Cirin's obsession with motherhood replicates the oppressiveness of a patriarchy, justifying the presence of gender expectations. It establishes an enclosed system where exclusively mothers determine the power and means of control. By contrast, daughters do not have any type of influence inside the community and only become active and valuable members when they give birth to a child. This form of oppression ultimately leads to the formation of Kevillism.

Women chronicles the intellectual struggle between Cirin and Astoria, the founder of Kevillism, Cirinism's competing ideology, the ideology of "daughters." This fight is represented through brief excerpts of their writings (*Kevillist Origins* and *The New Matriarchy*, respectively), which Sim has placed on facing pages, as if to give physical form to both the immediacy of their argument, and its intensely immediate competition for dominance. Even though both agree on certain ideas (women as a superior gender, the Alcohol Sanction imposed on the motherhood, the danger of men), their main disagreement arises from the basic hierarchy of Cirinism and the role of women in a communal society:

> The matriarchists misinterpret, intentionally I think, the true nature of a woman. They persist in the notion that a woman must adhere to a single male, forming a family unit that they then endeavor to dominate as a superior force. This is nonsensical. The best working model for a woman's life is the beehive; a solitary queen, serviced and catered to by a diverse group of males who exist exclusively to advance her cause.... The woman who owns the allegiance of the wealthiest, the strongest and the most brilliant of consorts; to her pass the reigns of absolute power. Inevitably she will rise, like heavy cream through thin milk, to the very summit of human existence. Astoria—*Kevillist Origins* [Sim and Gerhard November 1992].

This debate arises from an intergenerational conflict and it's a clear reference to the sexual revolution of the 1960s and women's liberation movement of the 1970s. The traditional women, raised to become wives and mothers, clash with the aspirations of sexual freedom and power of their daughters. The struggle of contemporary values against conservative values is determined by the traditional "wife" and family unit against the new vision of women capable of standing as equals to the other sex. This separation of the social expectations of "womanhood" and the sexual and economical liberation of "women" is directly addressed in *Cerebus* through the development of Countess Michelle Detin and Jaka Tavers.

Michelle had a very brief role in *Church & State,* only appearing in six issues (*Cerebus* 53 — 56 and 83 — 84) as a mysterious and rich countess who asks Cerebus for advice regarding her taxes. He decides to stay for a couple of days, while he finishes his political memoir titled "On Governing." During that time, she and Cerebus engage in several intriguing conversations about politics and gender. When asked if she considers herself a Kevillist or a Cirinist, she answers, "I'm not really sure myself" (Sim August 1983). She mentions his desire of having children and her small chances of actually getting married, alongside the disadvantages of a Cirinist government. They are interrupted in the middle of their conversation by the Wolveroach, a parody of Wolverine, and Vichy, an anarcho-romantic suitor of the Countess. Through issues 54 to 56, it becomes quite clear that men are attracted to Michelle as a substitute of the maternal figure, a profile that she seems to adopt in a condescending manner. This strange attraction that Michelle poses on men is almost immediately extended to Cerebus and later, pointed out in a humorous tone in issue 56 by Charles X. Claremont (an omnipresent being who possesses the body of the Wolveroach): "Cheer up, you're three feet tall, you look about five years old, you have the demeanor of an orphaned puppy and a need for a mother-substitute upon which I could float his holiness' trading fleet.... You'll find someone else in no time" (Sim November 1983). In her second appearance in issues 83 and 84, she is reduced to this motherly role by taking care of the Secret Sacred Wars Roach and the McGrew brothers as if they were little children, "This is nothing—you should see them when it's time for them to get their jammies on" (Sim and Gerhard March 1986). Sim designed the Countess as the perfect archetype of the "unwilling mother," a woman who turns from a sensual and independent female to a mere figure that fills the inner oedipal desires of men.

Sim originally introduced Jaka Tavers in issue 6. The episode follows a couple of thieves, who drug Cerebus in a failed attempt at extracting from his head the location of a secret treasure. The plan backfires and Cerebus falls madly in love with Jaka only to forget everything by the end of the issue. However, the memory of Jaka remains in his subconscious and during the rest of the series; she becomes his main love interest. This naive love later turns into blind obsession, an infatuation with the "idea" of Jaka. As the series narrative develops, she makes brief appearances in *High Society* (issue 36), where she returns Cerebus' sword, and later in *Church & State* (issue 74) as a married and pregnant woman. These events culminate in *Jaka's Story*, a pseudo-biography of Jaka written in a poetic

Oscar-Wilde-like prose by a character only referred to, fittingly, as "Oscar." This volume contains two storylines: one set in the past, depicted as long pages of text and minimal art depicting Jaka's childhood; and a second one set in the present, after the military conquest of the Cirinists. This plot twist forces Cerebus to hide in a tavern, owned by a man named Pud, where Jaka and her husband Rick are currently living.

The narration centered on Jaka's past symbolically chronicles her transition from childhood to womanhood. Her precocious physical development, her introduction to a complex aristocratic world she secretly hates and her inner desire of being recognized by her "uncle," Lord Julius, leads to a sentiment of despair which results in a hasty escape from Palnu on her thirteenth birthday. The implications of Jaka's actions through most of the series have mixed feelings: she wishes a "normal" life, an existence far away from the luxurious lifestyle of the bourgeois. Sim depicts Jaka as self-centered, selfish and a little childish, but also as a caring and intelligent woman. Gradually, it becomes quite clear that she doesn't seem to care for the attention of males, even if this contradicts her obsession with dancing, a talent that puts her in danger several times. She becomes, unwillingly, a "solitary queen" (the "beehive" as mentioned by Astoria in *Kevillist Origins*): a female filled with the attentions and the desires of men (in this case by the perverse triangle of Cerebus, Rick and Pud), an independent, sexually liberated woman with no desires of raising family. In much more simple terms, Jaka is a modern woman dedicated to her career. This leads to a tragic conclusion: a group of Cirinist soldiers kill Pud and a customer while Jaka, Oscar and Rick are imprisoned (Cerebus is not present at the time of the arrest). We discover that Cirinist law prohibits dancing or employing a dancer as it "objectifies" women (Sim and Gerhard June 1990). After a rushed trial, the couple is freed by the recommendation of Mrs. Thatcher and the diplomatic tricks of Lord Julius, who apparently knew the location of Jaka since the very beginning. However, before releasing them, Mrs. Thatcher reveals to Rick that Jaka had an abortion using an exotic plant: "Your wife went to number thirteen, Littlecollege in her sixth month, Mr. Nash.... Ask your wife. Ask her what the baby's gender was. What it would have been" (Sim and Gerhard July 1990). Sim unambiguously implies that Jaka aborted the fetus because of fear, as the burden of raising a child may jeopardize the marriage and ruin her career as a dancer. Whether this action was triggered to save the marriage (as Rick was unemployed at that moment) or for selfish reasons, or both, is left unanswered.

Michelle is the perfect equivalent of Jaka. Michelle is a peasant who becomes an aristocrat, Jaka an aristocrat who becomes a peasant. Men for unknown reasons at some point in their lives manipulate both. They never explicitly state if they are Kevillists or Cirinists, but Sim reduces them in the story to exact mother and daughter archetypes: Michelle turns into a mother-substitute and Jaka becomes a sort of femme-fatale who ruins the lives of various men. The fascinating aspect of this opposition is that the characters never met, Michelle only briefly appears in the series while Jaka is one of the main secondary characters. Importantly, they are characters developed before the *Mothers & Daughters* arc, which establishes them as prior symbolic devices that provide a clear context to the events that are about to come.

Conclusions

In an interview for *The Comics Journal* 184, Sim states that *Cerebus* 1 to 200 represents "the completion of the story. The yin and yang. The ultra-female reading. The ultra-male reading ... You make up your mind which one's the pit and which one's the top of the mountain" (Spurgeon December 1996, 73). At a first glance, there is a clear correlation between the evolution of the narrative style and the specific "novels" that compose the plot of *Cerebus*. *Women* and *Jaka's Story* relates to *Guys* and *Rick's Story*. The theological and sociological explorations of *Church & State* directly influence the cosmological analysis in *Form & Void* and *Latter Days*. This also explains the sudden shift in tone of the series. The narrative and humor in the first 200 issues is subtle and "refined," even when dealing with hard topics like sexuality and violence. The art is simple and cartoony. Thus, a reader can consider this the *ultra-female reading* of the story. However, when the plot reaches the *Guys* (issue 201) arc, the humor and style become chaotic, extreme and mean-spirited. The art reaches an almost photorealistic quality and entire issues are devoted to sexist jokes or scenarios created to degrade women, hence the idea of an *ultra-male reading*. The differences are, in fact, so astonishing that a reader could view them as two different works.

Kelly Rothenberg, in his essay titled "Cerebus: An Aardvark on the Edge," states that Sim's "master plan at the end of the *Cerebus* series is to present the male and female viewpoints together as an overall picture of Cerebus' world" (Rothenberg 1993). Sim's views about gender politics and religion drastically change over time, which leads to the conflicted nature of the work which changes from an apparently objective analysis of both genders into a theological examination that justifies the viewpoint of men's superiority over women. Nevertheless, beyond the implications of Sim's misogyny or his religious conversion or the public controversies regarding the publication of the series, there is a much more important question to ask here. Namely, is it possible to view *Cerebus the Aardvark* as a legitimate work of literature? Does it really present us with a challenging view about the relationships of men and women?

A pivotal moment in *Minds* relates to the surprising exposure of Cirin's deepest secret: she is in fact Serna, the assistant of Cirin, who stole her identity. This revelation directly relates to the events of issue 163. After losing in a chess match with Suenteus Po, Cerebus appears directly above the house of the real Cirin and immediately falls through the roof, landing on a couch. She then proceeds to give him a long monologue dealing with the nature of men and women:

> All women read minds, with very few exceptions. It's a little more complicated than that. "Woman's intuition" is a nice way of putting it. "Women are more sensitive" is another way of putting it. A not-so-nice way of putting it is that women rape men's minds the way men rape women's bodies. It is not an exact analogy, of course, because rape is invasion and invasion is the man's way; absorption and consumption are the woman's way; that's the way they are built. Consider the two genders, one that invades and violates and the other that absorbs and consumes. The nice way of putting it is that they're complementary. The not-so-nice way of putting it is that they deserve each other; serve each other right [Sim and Gerhard November 1992].

Perhaps Sim truly believes in men's superiority or the inherent evils of women or that there's a female god impersonating the real God. Even if that's the case, Sim can't negate the existence of women. Just like the real Cirin states, men and women are inseparable concepts. They are a *duality*. One can only exist by opposing the other. This is essence of the epic storyline of *Cerebus*: a terrifying tale that chronicles the consequences of dogmatism, of believing that a gender is superior to the other. The "nice way of putting it" is that they *need* each other. And "the not-so-nice way of putting it"? They are equally as bad.

PART FIVE
YE BOOKE OF SIM

YHWH's Story, or, How to Laugh While Reading "Chasing YHWH" and Still Have Enough Stamina for *The Last Day*

Edward M. Komara

The "Chasing YHWH" section of the *Latter Days* volume is one of the densest portions of *Cerebus the Aardvark* by Dave Sim with Gerhard. The reason for it is Cerebus' line-by-line exegesis ("Cerebexegesis" as Sim shared with a correspondent [Sim 2005, 64–66]) of the Book of *Genesis*, brought to Cerebus as part of a Torah scroll by a visitor named Konigsberg.[1] Sim packs many pages with only this exegetical text in small type. While the series was still appearing in single issues, one reader wrote that "Chasing YHWH" was less entertaining than, say, the eighth issue of *Pink Panther* or a 1973 issue of *TV Guide* (Sim 2005, 40–41). Another suggested that most clergy would find the commentary "heretical" (to which Sim added "and probably blasphemous" [ibid., 201]). Many respondents on the Yahoo Cerebus group confessed hating the storyline (ibid., 64–66). Even after the *Latter Days* volume appeared in November 2003, appreciation for "Chasing YHWH" remained unchanged. One reader wrote in 2004 to Sim that he liked the overall *Cerebus the Aardvark* storyline until he came to the "really bad interpretations of the Bible" (ibid., 424).

Not all readers were quite so vocal and hostile. I, for one, admit to skipping over the text pieces when I first read the original issues. So apparently did the writers of the issue-summaries for the Cerebus Wiki (*Cerebus Wiki*); while they provide details of the external events happening to Konigsberg in issues 280 to 287, most of their summaries of the drama within the commentary are limited to "Cerebus continues his reading of the Torah." Sim has remained steadfast in the importance of Cerebus' *Genesis* exegesis, affirming it as the "capstone [to the storyline that] needed to be addressed on its own terms once it was found" (Sim 2005, 4–6). Rather than rejection or ignorance, the commentary deserves affirmation as functional within *Cerebus*, understanding as structurally important in relation to the series finale. Furthermore, it is important that the reader realize that much of the commentary's humor results from the disparity between Cerebus' fictional times and our historical times. As Cerebus proceeds further in his explication, the narrower that disparity will become. As a result, in the later parts of the "Chasing YHWH" sequence, we will find with less frequency words and pictures that seem funny, but nonetheless we will continue to realize the "universal condition of existence" that Sim ascribes to the Torah (Sim 2005, 173).

The Story So Far....

After stints as a barbarian, Prime Minister, and Pope, Cerebus becomes a fugitive when another aardvark, Cirin, conquers the lands where he lives and establishes a matriarchal dictatorship. Early in his wanderings, Cerebus comes upon an old love, Jaka, who introduces him to her husband Rick, and he stays with them for some time. When Cirin's soldiers arrest Jaka, Rick, and a writer friend Oscar, Cerebus initially believes them to be dead, but he recovers from his shock when he learns that Jaka is still alive. His sole face-to-face confrontation of Cirin ends inconclusively and bloodily for both aardvarks and Cirin remains in power. Sometime later, Cerebus and Rick meet again and reacquaint themselves in the bar where Cerebus is working. Rick and Jaka had long been divorced, and his experiences in Cirinist captivity left him mentally scarred, perhaps mildly insane. Rick writes the sacred *Booke of Ricke* in which he sets down various sayings of Cerebus and the physical measurements of the bar. Shortly after Rick's final departure, Jaka by chance enters the bar, and Cerebus falls in love again with her. Their trip to Cerebus' childhood hometown ends disastrously when upon arrival Cerebus learns both of his parents had died recently; ashamed for having been absent when his father died, he dismisses Jaka and resumes his fugitive wanderings. From imminent Cirinist execution, three "Wise Fellows" who follow the teachings contained in the *Booke of Ricke* save him. With their help and a locally raised male army, Cerebus frees from Cirinist control the immediate region, in which he establishes his own state. It is there that a man named Konigsberg brings a scroll copy of the Torah, in accordance with a wish from the dying Rick; Cerebus sets about reading and interpreting it (figure 67).

I first read the "Chasing YHWH" issues as a monthly subscriber to *Cerebus*. Each of the original issues provided twenty pages of story, no more and no less, along with Sim's introductory "Note from the President" and various back features and essays. With such a strict and regular page count, *Cerebus*-time to publishing-time was elastic, always slower or quicker; a dramatic scene that took place within one day of *Cerebus'* story-timeframe might take three issues to be published fully, hence about a little over two months in the monthly subscriber's time to receive and read; in the case of the "Chasing YHWH" storyline, eight months of published issues covered ten years of Cerebus' life, during which he read and explicated the events of approximately 2370 years as related by the *Book of Genesis*. Reading the issues while each appeared obviously made for a more time-stretching experience than reading them collected as part of the *Latter Days* reprint volume.

When gathered in the *Latter Days* volume, the complete sequence has the appearance of a transition, leading from the opening credits of a 1970s Woody Allen film and the first pages of Konigsberg's diary, through many years to a much later time when Konigsberg is old (if not already dead), the transcript of Cerebus' commentaries completed, and a reader is "flipping through" the Exodus section of those commentaries in Cerebus' presence (that reader may or may not be Cerebus' future wife New Joanne, who is seen only at the very end of *Latter Days*). However, while reading each issue for the first time, I could see only twenty pages, and so I felt uncertain as to where Sim was heading with "Chasing YHWH," and as to whether the commentaries were worth slogging through.

Principles

When I decided to read the "Cerebexegesis" for a second time, this time in the *Latter Days* volume, I set for myself a few principles in order to understand it better within the

Figure 67. Cerebus and Konigsberg examining the Torah scroll. From *Latter Days* (© 2003 Dave Sim and Gerhard).

context of the overall series. One principle is to understand the commentary in the context of the larger *Cerebus* story. The historical tradition behind *Genesis* and the rest of the Torah place the origins of these texts around 1200 B.C. to 1000 B.C.. The story of *Cerebus* takes place in an era of time that may be unrelated to any of the eras in our written history. Its fictional events take place before, after, during, or even beyond the time of the Biblical writers.[2] Sim published the "Chasing YHWH" issues in 2002 and 2003. Because of these wide intervals in time, we should consider Cerebus' comments on *Genesis* according to only his fictional character within his fictional setting as conceived by Sim. A second principle is that the discrepancies in how the fictional Cerebus (would have) read *Genesis* in his timeframe, how the historical Hebrews wrote that book approximately 3100 years ago, and how we read it today should be taken not as breaks in Sim's conceptual continuity, but as disparities in which we may find humor. The third principle is to keep separate what Cerebus as character mused during his reading of the Torah from what Sim realized from his own study of the Torah and has discussed in public.[3] To be sure, Sim has sustained in himself and for himself the same basic thoughts conveyed in the "Cerebexegesis," a few of which are unusual (if not unorthodox) to the interpretations prevailing in our time (figure 68). Nonetheless, before responding to Sim on a matter of Torah or Bible interpretation in a context other than in the *Cerebus* story, we have to consider what Sim has said in the context of our present times and settings. The fourth principle I lay down is based on the *Cerebus* series as a whole as moral, and not just in the "Chasing YHWH" sequence. The temptation is to select individual moral moments in the *Cerebus* story and apply them to our times as literal and ethical directives. Succumbing to that temptation has resulted in many of the misunderstandings existing today about both *Cerebus* and its author. Rather, if I do discuss such moral passages in this study, I will try to do so not as an ethical system, but as a more flexible, but no less moral, form of the parable. Finally, for this study, I use as my sources the published issues and their collection as the reprint volume *Latter Days*, various editions of the Bible, and Sim's letters and other published comments.

Interpreting Genesis *1:4*

Cerebus' interpretation of the first three *Genesis* verses is similar to orthodox interpretations. However, where Cerebus begins to depart from us is at *Genesis* 1:4, which his text reads as "God divided himself betweene the light and betweene the dark." This verse is the linchpin of Cerebus' commentary. In all that small type on the printed page, its interpretation is easy to miss. Nonetheless, our appreciation begins here. The conventional understanding of this passage by our Western culture is that God had distinguished light from darkness, rendering day distinct from night. Cerebus offers an alternate reading— which God divided *himself* in two parts, giving his prevailing self-portion to the darkness, and his newly derived portion to the light — an interpretation not thought of in our Christian culture. This interpretation should be jarring to every *Cerebus* reader familiar with *Genesis*, forcing at least a second reading (if not the chuckle that it deserves).

What is the textual basis of *Genesis* 1:4? After all, the translations of the Bible commonly available give it as:

(*New International Version*, 1984): God saw that the light was good, and he separated the light from the darkness.
(*Jerusalem Bible*, 1966): God saw that light was good, and God divided light from darkness.
(Douay-Rheims): And God saw the light that it was good; and he divided the light from the darkness.

Sim used a photographic facsimile of the 1611 King James Bible, mostly for its Jacobean style of English translation (Sim and Gerhard 2003, 491).[4] In the body of the printed text, *Genesis* 1:4 reads: "And God saw the light, that it was good: and God divided the light from the darkenesse." By the word "divided" is an indication for a margin note to the left, which reads "Heb[rew] betweene the light and between the darknesse." If one refers to the Hebrew text[5] and reads *Genesis* 1:4 literally to the Hebrew characters, it would read:

is *God's house*. [laughs] Which—to Yoohwhoo—it *is*, now. And he *anoints the rock!* [laughs and laughs] *The rock is going to be his church!* "*And he called the name of that place Beth-el*". Literally, the House of God—to which Yoohwhoo is compelled to add, "*but the name of that citie was called Luz, at the first.*" At the first, sure [laughs] but not now, Yoohwhoo. Now, it's the House of God. "*And Iacob vowed a vow, saying, If God will be with me, and will keepe me in this way that I goe, and will giue me bread to eate, and raiment to put on, so that I come againe to my fathers house in peace: then shall the Yoohwhoo be my God.*" You can almost hear Yoohwhoo letting out a big sigh of relief at that *last* line. A little too soon as it turns out: "*And this stone which I haue set for a pillar, shall be Gods house: and of all that thou shalt giue me, I will surely giue the tenth vnto thee.*" So, *nine*-tenths of whatever Jacob gets, Jacob keeps and *one*-tenth of whatever Jacob gets [laughs] Jacob will give to his rock. [looks around the Sanctuary] Hard to believe that the idea for all this [laughs] came from a rock. Jacob is a very, very funny guy. He just doesn't *know* that he's a very, very funny guy. Okay. Chapter twenty-nine. "*Then Iacob lift up his feet, and came into the land of the children of the East. And he looked, and behold, a well in the field, and loe, there three flocks of sheepe lying by it: for out of that wel they watered the flocks: and a great stone was vpon the welles mouth.*" [laughs and laughs and laughs a *lot* through this part of the story] God is going along with it! Why not? If he can pretend for *Hagar* that His house is inside of a *well*, what kind of a big problem would it be for God to put His new house on top of His *old* house? No problem at all. "*And thither were all the flockes gathered, and they rolled the stone from the wels mouth, & watered the sheepe, and put the stone againe vpon the wels mouth in his place.*" [laughs] God knows his place! Inside the stone on top of the well's mouth. "*And Iacob said vnto them, My brethren whence be ye? and they saide, Of Haran are we. And he said vnto them, Know ye Laban the sonne of Nahor?*" [laughs]. Laban isn't the son of Nahor. Laban is the son of *Bethuel*. Bethuel is the son of Nahor. [laughs] Jacob can't remember who is whose father and who is whose grandfather any better than Yoohwhoo can! "*And they sayde, We knowe. And he said vnto them, Is there peace to him? and they said, He is well: and behold, Rachel his daughter commeth with the sheepe.*" [laughs] See, this is the part where Jacob, like Abraham's servant did, is supposed to say something in his heart like "Let it come to pass that the damsel to whom I shall say, let down thy pitcher and give the cattle drink, etc. etc." And he was probably thinking that he'd have to kill a few hours until the cattlemen showed up. Instead, here she comes with *the sheep* and he gets so nervous when he finds out that *this is her!* that it comes out: "*And hee said, Loe, yet the day is great, neither is it time that the cattell should be gathered together: water yee the sheepe, and goe and feed.*" [laughs] All the guys by the well must've thought he had lost his mind! "*And they said, We cannot, vntill all the flockes bee gathered together, and till they rolle the stone from the welles mouth: then wee water the sheepe. And while hee yet spake with them, Rachel came with her fathers sheepe: for she kept them. And it came to passe, when Iacob saw Rachel the daughter of Laban his mothers brother; that Iacob went neere, and rolled the stone from the wels mouth, and watered the flocke of Laban his mothers brother.*" [laughs] What a comedian! He's got it *backwards*. He's supposed to think in his heart of something Laban's daughter can do to identify herself to *him* and instead [laughs] he takes *one* look at her and *he* rolls the stone off of the well's mouth and *he* waters all the sheep for *her*. [laughs] "*And Iacob kissed Rachel, and lifted vp his voice, and wept.*" [laughs] This boy really knows how to play "hard-to-get". "*And Iacob told Rachel, that hee was her fathers brother, and that hee was Rebekahs sonne: and she ranne and told her father.*" [laughs]. Well, he was *half* right. [laughs]. He's Rebekah's son, but he sure isn't Rachel's father's brother. He's Rachel's father's *nephew*. Can you imagine when Rachel came running in? [laughs] Your brother is here! The son of Rebekah! "Oh, crap," he must've thought with this excited young girl bouncing all around him. [laughs] "Not *this* again." "*And it came to passe, when Laban heard the hearing of Iacob his sisters sonne, that he runne to meet him, and imbraced him, and kissed him, & brought him to his house: and hee tolde Laban all these things. And Laban said to him, Surely thou art my bone and my flesh: and he abode with him a moneth of daies.*" [laughs] "My bone and my flesh," that's what Adam called *Hawwa*: "bone of my bone and flesh of my flesh" [laughs] So Laban [dangling his hand from a limp wrist] has figured Jacob out in the first five seconds. [laughs] Oh, Laban is going to take this one re-e-al slow after what happened with Rebekah. Oh, this is going to be fun. Stick around, kid. Which Jacob does. Which gives Laban a month to figure out what he's going to do with him. So, a month later, Laban just…pops…him with: "*And Laban said vnto Iacob, Because thou art my brother, shouldest thou therefore serue me for nought? Tell me, what shall thy wages be?*" Well, the answer to *that* is: who said *I* was going to serve *you?* The elder is supposed to serve the *younger*. If *anybody* serves *anybody, you* should be serving *me*, Uncle Laban. But that's "man stuff" and Yoohwhoo and Jacob don't [laughs] don't know from "man stuff". *Jacob's* only reaction is, Wages? Hmm. [laughs] What do I want for my wages to serve my brother Laban? Oh, this kid is "easy pickings" all right. "*And Laban had two daughters: the name of the elder was Leah, and the name of the yonger Rachel. Leah was tender eyed: but Rachel was beautiful and well fauoured. And Iacob loued Rachel, and said, I will serue thee seuen years for Rachel thy yonger daughter. And Laban said, It is better that I giue her to thee, then that I should giue her to another man: abide with me.*" Jacob completely misses the insult: It's better that I give her to you than to someone like me. You know, to another *man*. Whatever Jacob is [laughs] a man wouldn't serve another man for *seven years* just for a *wife*. What?

Figure 68. Sample page of Cerebexegesis text. From *Latter Days* (© 2003 Dave Sim and Gerhard).

(Hebrew/English) uira aleim atheaur ki-tub uibdl aleim bin eaur ubin echshk / and-he-is-seeing Elohim the light that good and-he-is separating Elohim between the-light and-between the darkness.

Therefore, the King James translators had added that marginal note to try to reclaim a literal reading of that Hebrew verse. To be sure, the Septuagint Bible translated from Hebrew to Greek sometime in the second and first centuries B.C. followed closely the Hebrew source (kai diechoerisen ho theos ana meson tou phoetos kai ana meson tou skotous). But in the late 4th century A.D. in his Latin Vulgate translation, St. Jerome did not keep that structure (et vidit Deus lucem quod esset bona et divisit lucem ac tenebras = and God saw light which was good and he divided light from darkness).[6] When subsequent editions of the King James Bible text appeared, that marginal note was dropped, and so present-day readers have become more used to the St. Jerome style of rendering of that verse than the Hebrew original. Sim knows only English, admitting in his published correspondence that he is "unilingual" and has "a meager aptitude for languages."[7] Still, in making full use of the 1611 English translation of *Genesis* 1:4 and its literal marginal note, Sim infuses fully the written English style of the Jacobean era, and he restores the verbal arrangement of the Hebrew original text, while leaving himself enough flexibility as author of *Cerebus* to allow an alternate reading, whether in earnest or in parody.

Dividing the Commentaries into Manageable Portions

On the basis that God divided himself into his older darkness self (named God) and his newly-derived light self (yet to be named), Cerebus dictates eight commentaries on *Genesis* chapters one through thirty-eight, each commentary separated by one year or more in the aardvark's life:

Table 1: Timeframe of Cerebus' Exegesis of the Book of *Genesis* within the *Cerebus* Chronology

Latter Days page number	Cerebus calendar year	Commentary number	Coverage
288	Year 68	Konigsberg brings Torah to Cerebus	
290–300	Year 70	Commentary 1	*Genesis* 1:1 to 2:4
305–316	Year 71	Commentary 2	*Genesis* 2:4 to 4:24 (with *Genesis* 5, the list of Adam's descendants, implicit on 316–317 [Cerebus: "And that's the end of Chapter Five!"])
316–317	Year 71	Commentary 3	*Genesis* 6 to 9
330–340	Year 73	Commentary 4	*Genesis* 10 to 17
343–355	Year 75	Commentary 5	*Genesis* 18 to 22
364–377	Year 79	Commentary 6	*Genesis* 23 to 28:31
384–404	Year 80	Commentary 7	*Genesis* 29:32 to 33
411–421	Year 81	Commentary 8	*Genesis* 34 to 38
423–431	After year 81 (indefinite)	Subsequent commentary: an unnamed reader [perhaps Cerebus' future	All presented excerpts treat *Exodus* 4:1–11, 14:13–14, 15:6–8, 18:27,

wife New Joanne] is skimming through the remainder of Cerebus' Torah commentaries	19:24, 20:3–11, 21:21, 24:9–11, 24:12–14, and chapters 25 to 31 in brief

During these eleven years of Cerebexegesis, a new layer of *Genesis* narrative-interpretation gradually emerges. To realize this new layer, we need to concentrate on the two halves of God (the light part will be renamed YHWH) as the main characters in *Genesis*. That means the humans like Adam, Eve, Noah, and Abraham are secondary pawns. This is very different from how Jews and Christians have conventionally read *Genesis*, with the single undivided God (including the YHWH, not recognized as a separate entity) and the human figures as the interactive main characters.

Naming YHWH

Before reviewing Cerebus' version of *Genesis* from this alternate perspective, we should see how Cerebus names and thus introduces the light part of God as a figure from *Genesis*. Near the end of the first commentary, Cerebus asks Konigsberg about chapter 2.4 (and I will cite from the facsimile 1611 King James Bible): "These are the generations of the heavens, and of the earth, when they were created; in the day that the LORD God made the earth and the heavens...." From the ensuing conversation, we will have to presume that the scroll text that Cerebus and Konigsberg are examining has "YHWH" in place of "LORD."

> CEREBUS: Here's a question Cerebus had right off the bat about chapter two. [Points at verse four] How in the heck do you *pronounce* this?
> KONIGSBERG: Pronounce what?
> CEREBUS: *This*. This right HERE.
> KONIGSBERG: OH! The Tetragrammaton. You ... uh ... you *DON'T* actually.
> CEREBUS: "DON'T" WHAT.
> KONIGSBERG: Pronounce it. It's the Ineffable Name of God.
> CEREBUS: "The in-WHAT-able name of God"?
> KONIGSBERG: "Ineffable." Ineffable means "too overpowering to be expressed in WORDS — too lofty or sacred to be uttered aloud." Legend says that during TEMPLE WORSHIP when the High Priest would SPEAK The Name everyone would bang cymbals really LOUDLY so you couldn't hear the pronunciation. In the WRITTEN Torah the VOWELS are missing so that all you get are the unpronounceable consonants: "YHWH" ... ... which the GOYIM (don't ask me why) ... ... translate as "LORD" ... ... all in CAPITALS.
> CEREBUS: So *THAT'S* it. The *VOWELS* are missing, eh? [No "a"] or "e" or "i" or "o" or "u."[8]
> KONIGSBERG: The thing is no one knows WHICH vowels are missing, HOW *MANY* vowels are missing, or WHICH PART of The Name they're missing FROM.
> CEREBUS: In THAT case ... LET's call her: ... "YOOHWHOO" [Sim and Gerhard 2003, 298–300].

The shock of seeing a rendering of something regarded as sacred into something so girlishly feminine has to produce a reaction in the reader, whether laughter or a flinch. And lest there is any doubt on the pronunciation of "Yoohwhoo"—you hoo, or you woo—Sim explains in his notes to *Latter Days* (ibid., 501) that the command "O Yoohwhoo! Believe!" (ibid., 304) is his homophonetic joke on the Koran salutation "O, You who believe."

From the moment that Cerebus reformulated the Tetragrammaton from the ineffable YHWH to the effable Yoohwhoo(figure 69), he henceforth refers to the light-portion of

Figure 69. Cerebus giving the effable name "Yoowhoo." From *Latter Days* (© 2003 Dave Sim and Gerhard).

God as female in gender, using "she" and "her" as pronouns. Up until then, Cerebus didn't even know what to make of that separated portion from God. For example, here he is explicating *Genesis* 1:5:

> Cerebus: The evening—Night, God, the elder being—comes first. The morning—Day, the light, the younger being—came after God. The part of God that separated from God or the part of God's spirit that separated from God's spirit and that is.... NOW ... inside ... the light ... [Thinks] [Sighs] ... has no idea how it got in there. Or ... just in general ... what the heck is going on [Sim and Gerhard 2003, 291].

Once he confers the name Yoohwhoo on the light portion of God, he has a more secure grasp (granted, it is his own grasp) of that entity, so from that point in the commentary he is less concerned with what Yoohwhoo is than what Yoohwhoo does.

Commentary Digests

With God and Yoohwhoo now established as two separate and distinct beings, how they interact with each other is Cerebus' main concern, and the impact of what they do on the humans is of less concern. Here are digests of his explication of *Genesis* one through thirty-eight, by commentary portion:

Commentary 1: God alone begins creating the heavens and the earth. Upon creating darkness and light, he divides his spirit in two, one to darkness known as "God," the other to light to be named later as YHWH or Yoohwhoo. During the remaining days of creation, God tries to help Yoohwhoo "feel" better by "explaining" the world to her. When God sets about creating man and woman, Yoohwhoo agrees but only on condition that humans do not have dominion over the Earth (which Yoowhoo identifies with) or the cattle.

Commentary 2: Yoowhoo tells an alternate version of the creation, in which everything comes into being in one day, not one week, with the plants and the herbs taking precedence. God creates Adam and, from Adam's rib, Eve. Yoohwhoo tells them to eat from the forbidden Tree of Knowledge of Good and Evil, and she gets Eve to blame it on the snake. During the expulsion of Adam only—Eve remains in the Garden—God explains to Yoohwhoo that Yoowhoo's desire to be one flesh with God and hence *be God* is what has gotten her in trouble. Yoowhoo places a guard at the Garden's entrance to keep Adam and other future men out, not to keep Eve and other women in. As a result of conjugal visits to Adam, Eve conceives Cain and Abel. Cain kills Abel, and upon fleeing he founds the city of Enoch in order to evade Yoowhoo's curse and thus get other men to farm for him. With Adam and Eve's third son, Seth, men begin worshipping Yoohwhoo.

Commentary 3: Where Yoohwhoo saw fruitfulness in the generations of man, God saw wickedness. So in an attempt to be one flesh with God, Yoohwhoo offers to destroy the earth. God accepts the offer but asks that Noah and two of each kind of animal be spared out of compassion. The flood covers not the whole earth, but only the small area familiar to Yoohwhoo (who thus becomes fooled into thinking the whole earth was destroyed). During the post-flood covenant with Noah, God and Yoohwhoo disagree regarding man's dominion over cattle. God uses Noah's drunken episode as an occasion to mock Yoohwhoo for having had Adam and Eve eat from the Tree of Knowledge of Good and Evil.

Commentary 4: Yoohwhoo disapproves of the construction of the Tower of Babel, and to stop that work, she orders God to give different languages to the men. Among God's later generations, Yoohwhoo takes a special interest in Abram, thinking he may help her understand "what is going on" with God. Yoohwhoo encourages Abram's cattle sacrifice to her, in order to prove her point to God that men including Abram could be evil enough for God to kill.

Instead of killing Abram, God surprises Yoohwhoo by having Abram and his brother separated from each other. Lot is captured by four kings, but is rescued by Abram. God arranges for Melchizedek to bless Abram as possessor of heaven and earth, which infuriates Yoohwhoo as she thinks herself as possessor of earth. But then Abram declares Yoohwhoo as the Most High God and the possessor of heaven and earth; in return, Yoohwhoo promises Abram descendants. Hagar's birth of Ishmael leads Yoohwhoo to resume thinking that she is a God — upon which, God himself renames Abram to Abraham and directs to ritual circumcision, thus superseding Yoohwhoo's covenant with Abraham, and showing Yoohwhoo just who *is* God.

Commentary 5: Yoohwhoo sends angels in the form of three men to tell Abraham and Sarah that a natural son will be born to them. Abraham's discussion with the three angels/men regarding the cities of Sodom and Gomorrah demonstrates that "the way of the Yoohwhoo"— having everything done in the way Yoohwhoo wants it done — might not be exactly the way that Yoohwhoo wants it done. As a threat to remind Yoohwhoo of his power, God destroys Sodom and Gomorrah; furthermore, he permits Lot and his daughters to have new children towards saving their race. Meanwhile, Yoohwhoo takes credit for Sarah's birth of Isaac, and so she has Sarah order Abraham to cast out Hagar and Ishmael — which Abraham does on God's advice. Yoohwhoo then has Abraham bring up an old dispute with Abimelech regarding a water well, during the course of which Abimelech and Pichol affirm Yoohwhoo, upon which Yoohwhoo thinks she is "matching point for point" with God. Yoohwhoo thinks that she is Abraham and God is Isaac, or alternatively that she is Isaac and God is Abraham — in short, whether she is the son of God, or God is the son of Yoohwhoo. In response, God directs Abraham to sacrifice Isaac, in order to show Yoowhoo that God is God, and that Yoohwhoo should be as faithful to God as are Abraham and Isaac. When Yoohwhoo stays Abraham's hand from carrying out the sacrifice, she loses that dispute with God.

Commentary 6: Sarah dies, and is buried by Abraham among God's people in Hebron. Yoohwhoo follows the meeting of Rebekah and Isaac as if it is a love story. Later she regards the couple's twins as God (Esau; elder, having emerged from the womb first) and Yoowhoo (Jacob; younger); but in truth Esau is Yoohwhoo and Jacob is God, so Esau's selling his birthright to Jacob is a reversal on Yoohwhoo, who would be henceforth to serve God. Desperate, Yoohwhoo sends Esau to Gerar to renew Abraham's covenant, and Esau is made blessed of the Yoohwhoo. The incident of Jacob fooling Isaac into giving him Esau's blessing is God's way of fooling Yoohwhoo into thinking that she is still having her way. But Isaac's telling Esau "you shall break thy yoke" is God's way of saying to Yoohwhoo that the elder (whether God or Esau) is not going to serve the younger forever (whether Yoohwhoo or Jacob). Jacob dreams of the ladder to heaven, which signifies that God's angels are moving to Earth, and Yoohwhoo's angels are moving to heaven, showing that Yoohwhoo is in command. But upon waking, Jacob dedicates his pillow on which he had the dream as God's house, and Yoohwhoo can be that God if she protects Jacob back to his father's house. God and Yoohwhoo do not interfere with Jacob's dealing with Laban regarding the latter's daughters.

Commentary 7: Each of the births of Jacob's children gives God occasions to say to Yoohwhoo that: (1) Yoohwhoo cannot and will not become one flesh with God; (2) God will see and hear and judge Yoohwhoo, but he will not be any more joined to her than Jacob is joined to Leah; and (3) when Yoohwhoo shows good judgment, God will take away his reproach from her. One of Yoohwhoo's "good judgments" is having Jacob steal Laban's cattle, upon which Laban's daughter Rachel steals her father's pagan idols. Rachel's theft is a manifestation of a joke from God: that Rebekah, Laban, Leah, and Rachel are all pagans instead of Yoohwhoo's people. Also, God tells Laban not to go "from good to bad" when accosting Jacob about the cattle, thus disappointing Yoohwhoo's expectation for retaliatory violence. Furthermore, Laban (as God) accuses Jacob (as Yoohwhoo) of holding his daughters captive — hence reminding Yoohwhoo that God created woman. God intends the covenant made by Laban and Jacob to parody the covenant made by Abimelech and Abraham.

Anointing one of the covenant rocks means designating a son or heir (Jacob's son Joseph being a logical choice)—an act that acknowledges God as the One God, and thus Yoohwhoo loses hold on the prevailing covenant. Jacob wrestles with Yoohwhoo's angel, who demands to be blessed and the blessing to go to Yoohwhoo and not to Joseph (and in this way, Yoohwhoo can regain control of the covenants).

Commentary 8: God says that Shechem's defilement of Dinah is as wrong as Yoohwhoo blocking Adam from the garden and Eve. God wants Jacob to build an actual altar at Bethel, not some flimsy "joke" altar that he built for Yoohwhoo. God echoes Yoohwhoo's covenant to Jacob. Yoohwhoo tells God to make Jacob's wife Rachel pregnant again—an action that Cerebus calls bad judgment—since Jacob violated Laban's curse by having children with his wives' maids, the consequences will involve the next child born, Joseph. Yoohwhoo identifies with Joseph. Joseph being sold into slavery is God's way of reinforcing to Yoohwhoo that captivity is wrong, namely the garden. God identifies with Judah. Yoohwhoo kills Judah's son Er, and Onan for transmitting "the seed of God' representative" without her (Yoohwhoo's) participation. With Yoohwhoo's help, Er's widow Tamar deceives Judah into sex by dressing as a harlot. By evading death by execution, Tamar scores a win on Yoohwhoo's behalf.

In summary, the light part of God named YHWH (or Yoohwhoo as named by Cerebus) embedded herself into the earth and began acting in an emotional, female-like, self-fictional (if not self-delusional) manner in response to the darkness male-like God. At first she tried cleaving or being of one flesh with God, and then trying to be God. When Yoohwhoo failed to succeed at either, she then began a different strategy that is, directing God to carry out various actions, while at the same time trying to take control of the covenants with men. As Cerebus remarks, "Although Yoohwhoo is calling the shots, it is God's 'hands' that are making all her crazy ideas real" (Sim and Gerhard 2003, 421).[9]

Sim and the Historians

In prevailing Jewish and Christian interpretations of the Torah, God and YHWH are the same. A historical explanation for this combination is that the five books of the Torah as we now possess and read them may be ancient conflations of four manuscripts (or manuscript sources). Two of the designations for the derived sources, J and E, have been used since a 1780 publication by Johann Gottfried Eichhorn; one set of stories referring to YHWH was called J, because the German J and V in "Jehovah" were and are pronounced like the Y and W in "YHWH" and in the English "Yahweh," and the other set of stories referring to El or Elohim, the Hebrew name for God, was called E. Before long, other scholars discerned a source, they called P (short for Priests) within the E set of stories. Finally, the style of the Book of Deuteronomy was thought to be different from J, E, and P, and so that book (aside from its last few verses) was called a fourth source unto itself (Friedman 1997, 52).[10] The conflation of these sources into the Torah as analyzed by Biblical historians is supposed to have occurred in stages: J and E most likely combined sometime after the Assyrian conquest of Israel in 722 B.C., with P interwoven into those texts and Deuteronomy added around the mid–400s B.C. (ibid., 225).[11]

While planning and writing the "Chasing YHWH" commentaries, Sim was fully aware of the traditional interpretation of the Torah.[12] As he wrote for the *Latter Days* collection, "If I was going to make fun of the Bible, I really needed to make fun of what was commonly accepted by most Biblical scholars and by most people familiar with it" (p.497). Making such fun meant not being beholden to the research model of four conflated sources to the

Torah. It also meant not adhering to the rabbinical Jewish or Christian interpretations as well. The *Cerebus* timeline takes place apart from the time of Moses (the purported traditional author of the Torah) freed Sim from these academic and religious denominational restrictions. However, taking and reading the Torah away from its traditional time and its traditional land may be asking too much of his audience. Such retrojection of the Torah may be seen as a risk, or instead as Sim saw it, a "new writerly idea — that the Torah was a universal condition of existence" (Sim 2008a, 173). Accepting that universal condition of existence for the Torah enables in the reader an objective perspective, to which discrepancies in our present-day historical and denominational approaches in reading the Torah and the rest of the Bible may be noticed, delighted, laughed with, or laughed at. Sim's own acceptance of that same condition earned him the opportunity to admit later on, both in the frames of the *Cerebus* storyline and of his (and our) present times, that "God played along with all this [the efforts to understand the Mosaic Law Code and the Talmud, which seem YHWH-ist to Sim] because YHWH was our choice" (Sim 2005, 565). As readers, we need not agree uncritically with Sim's admission. However, by suspending our disbelief in our own timeframe, and at the same time by reading with increasing seriousness to Cerebus' Torah reading, the fictional and present timeframes might draw together and eventually to coincide. Their common element is the Torah, its universal presence abiding in Cerebus' world and in ours.

YHWH as Female Among Us, Here and Now?

Why does Sim's presentation of a masculine/feminine duality in God at the beginning of time seem alien or strange to us? Should it seem that strange to us? I ask this seriously because of a blogspot that a colleague showed me, the blog *The Blue God of Judaism*. This website features material written and posted by Rabbi Robert dos Santos Teixeira that explores "the similarities between YHWH / Judaism and Shiva / Shivaism." One particular piece, "The Blue God of Judaism," posted 22 July 2010, grabbed my attention, not so much for its argument that the color of the Jewish God is blue, but more the assertion in the third paragraph:

> This article aims to contribute to and further recent discussion of YHWH's masculine form, i.e., the Lord's body. Hopefully, in so doing, long-overlooked similarities between YHWH and Shiva will receive due attention, and the feminine form of YHWH (footnote 4) will re-emerge more fully, thereby triggering a re-appreciation for the life-creating and life-sustaining oneness of the divine masculine and the divine feminine, perhaps the most ancient tenet of Judaism [*The Blue God of Judaism*].

Intrigued, I looked immediately to that footnote:

> See Judith M. Hadley, *The Cult of Asherah in Ancient Israel and Judah: Evidence for a Hebrew Goddess* (Cambridge: University Press, 2000) and Mark Sameth, "Who Is He? He Is She: The Secret Four-Letter Name of God," *CCAR Journal: A Reform Jewish Quarterly* (Summer 2008): 22–28. Sameth points out that the Tetragrammaton (Yud Hay Vov Hay) when written in reverse (Hay Vov Hay Yud) forms the Hebrew words hu and hi, he and she in English. He goes on to write: "And that is why our Jewish mystics, before donning their tallitot or tefellin in prayer, recite a kavanah, a mystical intention, to unite Yud Hay and Vov Hay l'shem yichud, for the sake of God's unification. And that's why the mystical book Sefer Bahir teaches that the meaning of the large bet, which opens the Torah, is the union of the two

principles of the masculine and feminine, united in the primordial act of Creation" (page 25). Five, maybe six years ago, a homeless Jewish man by the name of Mordecai, who frequented Jackson Square, in New Orleans, told me of reversing the four-letter name to form the Hebrew equivalent of He-She. In my view, He-She and the countless images of Shiva and Shakti in sexual embrace point to the same reality, the masculine and feminine creative, divine forces are (ecstatically) united, thus making the continuation of life possible [ibid.].

The viability of Teixeira's thesis aside, his statement and the accompanying footnote quoted just now seem to argue for both the divine feminine and the divine masculine as present during the time of creation. Nevertheless, despite that intriguing similarity, I recognize that Teixeira and Sim differ regarding where and how the divine masculine joins the divine feminine. Teixeira sees the masculine and feminine as joined together in YHWH, while Sim sees them joined in God initially, and then separated by God, who manages to retain the divine progenerative masculine impulse, thereby creating the rest of the world by himself, while YHWH is solely the void feminine. Furthermore, while Teixeira views YHWH with God as creative, Sim views her as argumentative with God, demanding, and destructive. Nonetheless, Sim is not alone in presenting the creating divinity embodying male and female.

Setting Up the Last Day

Does the depiction of God and Yoohwhoo as related by Cerebus through Torah exegesis have an abiding and credible truth within the story's setting? That is, is Cerebus laughably wrong and alone in his interpretation of the Torah, or would another person within the confines of the same story interpret *Genesis* 1:4 in the same way as Cerebus and proceed to describe the feminine at odds with the masculine? If we have just now examined a blog post by someone other than Dave Sim on the divine male/female oneness at and during creation, we cannot entirely discount the possibility of someone else among the *Cerebus* characters giving an interpretation of the Torah similar to what Cerebus offers. If we grant ourselves that possibility, then we should ask from where is Cerebus drawing for his exegesis? Is he drawing from a divine revelation, or from his experiences, observations, and surroundings? Throughout *Cerebus*, many things are revealed to the title character, although whether what is revealed is true or false is a recurring question, and whether the revealer is divine or mortal is posed with each revelation. Considering the circumstances in the story leading to the Torah being delivered to Cerebus, brought about by other characters that age and die, I would venture to say that Cerebus is not working from a divine revelation, but his Cerebexegesis does prepare him to recognize a divine revelation when it is eventually shown to him — that true revelation would be the account of the creation of the world presented in the *Cerebus* double-issue 289 and 290 (Sim and Gerhard 2004, 1–40).[13]

Therefore, for his commentaries it appears that Cerebus is drawing from his context, experiences and observations, with which we are familiar to the extent of the story told to us up until then. With God and Yoohwhoo being the divine masculine and feminine at creation, and with their interactions with mortal men, it is possible to regard them as the archetypes of what gods and higher beings would seem to man. Once one has realized that God and Yoohwhoo are two different beings, each of a different gender, one should think about re-reading the whole *Cerebus* storyline. Sim suffuses several parts of the series with religious discussions of the male god Tarim and the opposing female god Terim, such as that between Pope Cerebus and his prisoner Astoria in *Church & State II*. There are two ways of reading this and other episodes on religion. One is by using the Torah commentary as the highest and longest-abiding perspective point, from which one can view the particular gods Tarim and Terim. The other is by reviewing Cerebus' discussions (arguments, really: some of them are shouts) about Tarim and Terim as influential (on a small and particular scale, to be sure) on his later interpretation of the Torah. Either and both ways of reading—to and from the Torah—are in accordance with Sim's description of the function of the Torah commentaries as "the capstone" to the whole series (Sim 2008a, 5). The more striking capstones in architecture are pointed, like the top of the Washington Monument in Washington DC, or the tops of the Egyptian pyramids. These instances reduce the capstone's sides from three dimensions to one dimension. Likewise, the Cerebexegesis pulls together the disparate comic timeframes into one common and serious setting for character, reader, and Torah. If this *Cerebus* series capstone ends at a point, it ends at the revelation prologue beginning *The Last Day*.

Jaka's Story and Latter Days as Counterparts

The visual format of the "Chasing YHWH" sequence was prose text in small type at the sides and/or bottom of a static panel (figure 70). It had been used in previous installments of *Cerebus*, namely *Jaka's Story*, *Reads*, and *Rick's Story*. Because the format in *Reads* parodies the "reads" serial publications described in the narrative, I am going to disregard that instance in this discussion. *Rick's Story* is pertinent, but for reasons which I explain below, I will set that aside momentarily from this comparison.

Jaka's Story is a counterpart to *Latter Days* in three ways. One: *Jaka's Story* focuses on the title character, a tavern dancer, and not on Cerebus. Two: Jaka's husband Rick instigates another character's (Oscar) writing a reads-story about Jaka by providing the source stories. Three: the willful and often delusional views she has of the males around her. As Sim explains, "the title [*Jaka's Story*] refers to the fact that Jaka is holding a series of untenable situations in stasis just by virtue of being Jaka. The marriage [with Rick] isn't much of a marriage but she's holding it together single-handedly with her perception of it. She is working to make Rick into her perception of who Rick should be—a process and a perception of which he is completely unaware and bears no resemblance to who he is. Her job is not actually a job; it is a complete transparent pretence, a total fiction that she is maintaining by ignoring who she knows Pud to be and what she knows his interests are and play-acting the fiction. Moreover, she does the same thing with Cerebus. Holds him in a complete stasis in her orbit by casting him in a role that fits the fiction she's woven about her marriage and her job" (Sim 2005, 559).

Parallels to these three ways can be drawn for Yoohwhoo. The first parallel is that while the graphic novel is titled *Latter Days*, that title comes from the Torah (see Sim 2005, 167), a great deal of its content being Yoohwhoo in nature; to that extent, it may be said that this graphic novel eventually comes to focus on the character behind the source of the title, Yoohwhoo. A second is that Jaka's husband Rick instigated another character's (Cerebus)

Opposite: Figure 70. The sheer bulk of the "Cerebexegesis" text in the "Chasing YHWH" section of *Latter Days* overwhelms and bogs down many readers. From *Latter Days* (© 2003 Sim and Gerhard).

river *"become into"* four heads? And what the heck does "become into" *mean*? No idea, but guess what? The heads have *names*! *"The name of the first Pison: that it which compasseth the whole land of Hauilah, where is gold."* It was at this point that Cerebus got the definite impression that a certain element of…scope…was missing from Yoohwhoo's version of events. *"And the gold of that land good: There Bdellium and the Onix stone."* You know what Cerebus means? Like the next verse is going to tell you a great place to buy dish-towels and placemats. *"And the name of the second riuer Gihon: the same it that compasseth the whole land of Cush."* The second *river*. See, Cerebus thought we were talking about the *heads* that the river *"became into"*. Never been married, eh? See, you learn to just nod and smile at this kind of stuff. The more you don't understand? The more you nod and smile. *"And the name of the third riuer Hiddekel: that which goeth toward the East of Assyria: and the fourth riuer is Euphrates."* At this point, the bell rings and we all get to *leave* geography class and go *back* to Ancient History class. *"And the Yoohwhoo God tooke the man, and put him into the garden of Eden, to dresse it, and to keepe it."* See, if you've never been married, at *this* point you would ask yourself, *self?* Why does Yoohwhoo God repeat verse 8 practically word-for-word here in verse 15? If you *have* been married—like *Cerebus* has—you just nod and smile and think, "Okay, *now* she's remembered where she was in the story *before* she got distracted by the part about the rivers." *"And the Yoohwhoo God commanded the man, saying, Of euery tree of the garden, eating thou shalt eate. But of the tree of the knowledge of good and euill, thou shalt not eate of it: for in the day that thou eatest thereof, dying thou shalt die."* Okay, so basically Yoohwhoo God created the heavens and the earth in one day, all the plants and herbs *before* they were in the ground, formed a man out of the *dust* of the ground, planted a garden with a tree of *life* and a tree of *knowledge of good and evil*, *put* the man *in* the garden, and told him *not* to eat the fruit of the second tree or he would die. Well. [thinks] *That* certainly answers all of Cerebus' questions about how everything came to be. *"And the Yoohwhoo God said, It not good that the man should be alone: I will make him a helpe meet as before him."* As *before* him? There was a "help-meet" *before* the man? And what the heck is a "help meet," anyway? It's okay, Cerebus reminds himself, it's okay—just keep nodding and smiling. Which is getting difficult at this point because there are—*obviously*—you know, *major parts of the story MISSING here*. But…as Cerebus came to learn when he was *married*: if you just keep nodding and smiling, most of the time—gradually, but eventually— you *will* be *given* the missing pieces as you…*you* know…go along. Whereas IF, instead, you *yell* really loud, "YOOHWHOO GOD, WHAT IN THE *HECK* ARE YOU *TALKING ABOUT?*" All you're going to accomplish is to hurt her feelings and get her so upset she can't *remember* what she was talking about and she'll get all huffy and she won't talk to you for a few days. So: *"And out of the ground the Yoohwhoo God formed euery beast of the field, and euery foule of the aire and brought vnto the man, to see what he would call them: and whatsoeuer the man called euery creature, that the name thereof. And the man called names to all cattell, and to the foule of the aire, and to euery beast of the fielde: but for the man there was not found a helpe meete for him."* Aha! thought Cerebus (all of his nodding and smiling having finally paid off): It's a *compromise!* Remember when God tried to make the deal with the earth? To give the man and the-female-of-the-man dominion over everything *except* the whales? And the earth left out the earth and the

dictating a commentary about Yoohwhoo by requesting Konigsberg's ancestor to provide a text to the aardvark. A third way is the willful and often delusional views Yoohwhoo has of the males—deity and mortals alike—with whom she interacts. To use Sim's description of Jaka above as a base, "Yoohwhoo is holding a series of untenable situations in stasis just by virtue of being Yoohwhoo. The relationship with God isn't much of a relationship but she's holding it together single-handedly with her perception of it. She is working to make God into her perception of who God should be—a process and a perception of which He is completely unaware and bears no resemblance to who He is. Her job isn't actually a job; it's a complete transparent pretence, a total fiction that she's maintaining by ignoring who she knows individual men to be and what she knows their interests are and play-acting the fiction."

Not all three senses of *Rick's Story* are similar to those in the two books focusing on Jaka and Yoohwhoo. To be sure, one similarity is that the graphic novel focuses on the title character, Rick. A second is that he instigates his own writing about himself and Cerebus. However, the third sense for Rick does not correspond to those for Jaka and Yoohwhoo. To be sure, he does have his delusions, but they are about particular people, such as Cerebus and Joanne, a woman with whom he interacts in the novel's plot, but one cannot be certain he has such delusions about all aardvarks and women. Despite the similarity of *Rick's Story* as title to *Jaka's Story*, they are not thematic counterparts.

Moreover, *Rick's Story* is not a structural counterpart to *Jaka's Story*, but *Latter Days* is. In a Yahoo online question and answer session, Sim wrote of the 300 issues of *Cerebus the Aardvark* consisting of two equal parts, issues 1–150, and 151–300, the first half being a "male cycle," the second half being a "female cycle." *Jaka's Story* ran for 25 issues, followed by a twelve-issue "short story" *Melmoth*, which depicted the death of Oscar Wilde.[14] Those two books were the last two portions of the series' first part. *Latter Days* ran for 23 issues (issues 266 to 288) followed only by the final twelve issue numbers comprising *The Last Day*, containing the double-issue revelation prologue, and the last ten single issues depicting the last events and death of Cerebus. These two books were the last two portions of the series' second part. Taking note of this structural symmetry would enhance the thematic symmetry of *Latter Days* to *Jaka's Story*.

Conclusion: Pace Yourself

The sheer bulk of the "Cerebexegesis" text in the "Chasing YHWH" section of *Latter Days* overwhelms and bogs down many readers. However, if they were to read it faster, and in the same manner that they have read *Jaka's Story (figure 71)*, they would give themselves an opportunity to understand the structural role of *Latter Days*, and thus recognize the function of and an appropriate reading pace for *The Last Day*. I advise patience while reading the commentaries, because they confirm much of the behavior by various characters in the earlier *Cerebus* stories, and they pave the way for the revelation that follows. The more we follow Cerebus' interpretation of the Torah, the more we too are prepared for the revelation he later receives. Yet I think it is permissible to pause sometimes while reading the commentaries to wonder if, as a 1980 movie title put it, "The Gods Must Be Crazy."

NOTES

1. "Konigsberg" is the birth surname of comedian/director Woody Allen, and Sim bases his character Konigsberg on Allen.

2. Alexx Kay (*The Cerebus Timeline*) suggests approximately 4000 B.C.E., based on remarks made near the close of *Church & State II* by the Judge, later shown in the series to be unreliable. However, in two published letters, Sim has suggested that Cerebus' world may be a separate world parallel to our own. "Cerebus' world and our world are either the same world at different time periods (such that history just repeats itself in slightly modified patterns) or Cerebus' world is just typical of a solar system like our own. With these conditions, you produce the same elements just in a different mix (Muslims, Egyptians, Mary Hemingway, and the Sphinx). I would speculate that what seems intricate, unique and convoluted to us is perhaps as basic as God can get it. The earth and everyone living on it and everyone who ever lived on it are like the most basic kind of Lego pieces, the hydrogen atom among life forms, in order to give us the greatest chance of understanding how exponentially and vastly greater our souls are" (Sim 2005, 428). From the other letter: "When Rick has his religious experience, particularly the evergreen tree that was burning but not being consumed, well, that's an obvious Moshe reference, likewise the introduction of the Torah into the book. It was a new writerly idea — that the Torah was a universal condition of existence, leaving it an open question as to whether the *Cerebus* storyline takes place on earth in the distant past, earth in the distant future, or a planet light years away from earth. All planets are the earth with a YHWH inside of them, an Abraham, an Isaac, a Jacob, etc. etc. The story always unfolds the same way. The permutations and twists and turns all take place after the Age of Prophets, but the Age of Prophets is carved in stone" (Sim 2005, 173).

3. Sim has included his realizations from reading the Bible in his correspondence *Collected Letters 2004* and *Collected Letters 2*, in the back notes to the reprint volumes *Latter Days* and *The Last Day*, and in his public speaking such as the talk he gave at the 1 October 2006 St. Bonaventure University event "Ye Bookes of Cerebus."

4. A digitized facsimile of that same imprint is available for examination free

Figure 71. A world about to be transformed. From *Jaka's Story* (© 1990 Dave Sim and Gerhard).

online on the website of the Schoenberg Center for Electronic Text and Image. http://tinyurl.com/3ekkbno.

5. I used the interlinear Hebrew/English version on the Scripture4all Foundation website. http://tinyurl.com/3xmmozw.

6. It is very likely that John Wyclif's Middle English translation of the Bible followed Jerome's Latin Vulgate, as Wyclif renders that verse as "And God seiy the liyt, that it was good, and he departide the liyt from derknessis."

7. Sim, letter to Billy Beach, 29 May 2004, and Sim, letter to Emilio Englade, 6 February 2004, both in Sim 2005, pages 565 and 55 respectively.

8. Where that panel appears in the original issue 280 [unnumbered page 20] and on page 300 of *Latter Days*, Cerebus' mention of the vowel "a" is missing, apparently left out by mistake by Sim while lettering the page. See Figure 3.

9. Sim's letters to Billy Beach in the *Collected Letters 2004* and *Collected Letters 2* provide many detailed thoughts about the relationship of God and Yoohwhoo, especially 30 April 2004 (Sim 2005, 446–450).

10. Sim in the notes to *Latter Days* [496] refers to Dimont 1962; second edition 2004.

11. Friedman suggests that the biblical Ezra was the redactor who shaped the Torah in our received form.

12. Sim learned of this through a *Cerebus* reader, Claude Flowers, as acknowledged by Sim in his notes in *Latter Days* (Sim and Gerhard 2003, 495–497).

13. In a 2004 letter to Steve Bolhafner, Sim explains that the "Chasing YHWH" commentary "explained how I see *Genesis*," but that the prologue revelation to *The Last Day* is "how I see the first chapter of *Genesis*" (Sim 2005, 64–66). There is an awesome and terrifying truth within that prologue, such that even if a reader decides to reject the revelation as unscientific and nonhistorical, he — or she — has to acknowledge and accept its parabolic power. Sim's public remarks since 2004 suggest that the revelation's divine quality is too strong to be contained in a printed comic book (I hardly dare to say that quality is "ineffable").

14. As Sim discussed in 1992 in a Usenet question-and-answer session, the dying Oscar Wilde in *Melmoth* is a different person than the Oscar arrested in *Jaka's Story* and briefly seen imprisoned in *Flight*.

Appendix:
An Introduction to
the *Cerebus* "Phonebooks"
Lenny Cooper

Cerebus

One of the more interesting aspects of a novel that takes 26 years to write is the ability to see its author develop as an artist. This volume includes a satire/tribute/homage to Robert E. Howard's *Conan* series (or, more accurately, to the Roy Thomas and Barry Windsor-Smith early 1970s Marvel Comics adaptation). There are some very funny passages, and the sequential art and rendering, while far simpler than the later phonebooks, are clearer and at times easier to follow. At mid-point of this volume, allegedly influenced by a powerful drug experience, Sim's story becomes increasingly complicated as Sim lays down many of the plot points that developed in coming decades. He introduces key characters, including Lord Julius, Sim's brilliant homage to Groucho Marx, The Cockroach, Sim's all-purpose superhero parody template, and Jaka, Cerebus' love interest. As well, the religious and political landscape of Estarcion, the world in which Cerebus roams, becomes better defined.

High Society

When asked which their favorite of the phonebooks is, many *Cerebus* readers name *High Society*. Truthfully, this is perhaps a correct estimation, in terms of sheer comedic/satiric effect. Sim may have grown as an artist in terms of writing and drawing proficiency, yet he was never funnier than in this early volume. Add to the mix Sim's take on politics, including Cerebus' campaign for Prime Minister. *High Society* is replete with memorable characters, hilarious moments, and sharp satire—not just of politics—but also of basic human interaction. In one chapter, Jaka returns, giving Cerebus' character greater emotional depth and resonance. While the art clearly is not up to Sim's later standards, it still represents a major step forward from the simpler composition of the pages in the previous volume. One can see Sim trying new techniques, in his control over time and space on the page. Overall, *High Society* bursts with creativity and energy.

Church & State

In *Church & State* Sim ups his game to a higher level and it is exhilarating to see the transformation in both writing and art. The most obvious change is the addition of Gerhard as background artist, making the world of Cerebus more complete and solid, as if everything snapped into focus. This is true, too, for the writing, as Sim constructs a detailed exploration of the relationship between religion and politics, focused through the prism of power. In a story that literally stretches into the heavens, Sim examines political and religious machinations. The Roach returns to lampoon superheroes. Mick Jagger and Keith Richards arrive in fine parody form. Sim introduces the theme of creation as the byproduct of contrasting opposing forces. The exhilarating finale leaves the reader breathless, as Cerebus ponders the meaning of a prophecy that will haunt him for the rest of his life.

Jaka's Story

Where *Church & State* maintains a macro view of Cerebus' world, *Jaka's Story* is a much smaller, though no less profound, story. Sim superbly fleshes out Jaka, introduces her husband Rick and Oscar, a delightful analogue of Oscar Wilde. While the story has smaller scope than its predecessor does, its insights are razor sharp. Sim brilliantly dissects his characters, while simultaneously telling Jaka's back-story in "The Daughters of Palnu," a novel within a novel, introducing the theme of stories being told on different levels of reality. At the end, Sim draws these various threads together, weaving this personal story back into the tapestry of the larger world in which it is set, to devastating results.

Melmoth

With *Melmoth*, Sim again changes direction. As with *Jaka's Story*, *Melmoth* is a microcosm (at eleven issues the shortest of *Cerebus*' story arcs), detailing the final days of Sebastien Melmoth, another Oscar Wilde analogue. Sim and Gerhard's meticulous attention to detail evidences their continued development as comics artists and Sim departs more and more from traditional comic book page design. Cerebus becomes a minor supporting role yet at the end of the day Sim and Gerhard provide the reader with a small powerful story about the death of a brilliant man in a totalitarian society.

Mothers & Daughters 1: Flight

Sim returns to the macrocosm with *Flight*, as this phonebook focuses on Cirin and the fascist state which she rules, as well as providing further insight into the mysterious Suenteus Po, with whom Cerebus communicates in the series' numerous "Mind Game" segments. Rounding out the fun, we have the return of the Roach in yet another superhero parody.

Mothers & Daughters 2: Women

Sim sharpens the focus of his exploration of Mothers & Daughters and their roles in society, starting with a delicious lampooning of Oprah Winfrey. We are also introduced to Swoon, Sim's hilarious send up of Neil Gaiman's *Sandman*, through the (many) eyes of the Roach. Sim continues to enrich the series' mythology, giving us further insight into the minds and dreams of Cirin, Jaka, Astoria and Cerebus.

Mothers & Daughters 3: Reads

In this, the series' most controversial phonebook, Sim deepens his examination of women in society, and he does so in a way that, for some, forever brands him a misogynist. Notwithstanding one's views on the issues presented, in *Reads* Sim goes fascinatingly postmodern, presenting the character of Victor Reid, a clear Dave Sim analogue that retains a level of fictional detachment, espousing views that may or may not be those of Sim himself. A thought provoking volume that stretches the boundaries of what can be accomplished in the comics medium.

Mothers & Daughters 4: Minds

Sim further blurs the boundaries of fiction and reality, with the introduction of "Dave," Cerebus' creator. Sim provides key details of the history of Cerebus' world and the roots of Cirinism, wrapping up the plot points introduced in *Cerebus*, effectively ending the major narrative arc in place since the first phonebook.

Guys

Sim returns to the microcosm, as the society shaking events of the previous volumes give way to the insular community of a bar, to where the Cirinist regime has confined its men. Sim delves deep into the male persona, and does so with sharp precision and satire. The result is what some readers deem the funniest *Cerebus* phonebook since *High Society*.

Rick's Story

Rick's Story is a pivotal, if problematic, phonebook, if not for its story, a parody of the Bible and further exploration of gender politics, then for the effect it would have on its creator. As such, by the end of the novel, it is clear that there are, in Cerebus' world, higher powers at work. This volume, as well as the previous one, marks a revolution in Sim and Gerhard's art, with breathtaking page designs that perfectly capture each character's specific view of reality, tempered either by alcohol or by religious fervor.

Going Home 1: Going Home

Jaka returns at the end of *Rick's Story* and *Going Home* largely concerns her relationship with Cerebus and is among the sharpest most astutely written parts of the entire *Cerebus* novel. Sim also introduces F. Stop Kennedy, Sim's take on F. Scott Fitzgerald, returning to the theme of multiple levels of reality, amplified in F. Stop's drunken musings.

Going Home 2: Form & Void

Form & Void continues Cerebus and Jaka's trek through Estarcion and relationship hell. In this volume, Sim introduces Ham Ernestway, Sim's stand-in for Ernest Hemingway, and his wife Mary. This phonebook features breathtaking naturalist artwork as Sim and Gerhard offer stunning views of a region of Estarcion that bears striking similarity to the Serengeti. In the final segment, which takes Cerebus back to his roots, Sim pulls the story into a powerful climax, setting the scene for the final story arc.

Latter Days Book I: Latter Days

In the final story arc, Sim returns to the macrocosm. Decades pass and Cerebus ages. While this volume initially appears to focus on humor, with the hilarious introduction of the Three Wise Fellows, it quickly veers into biblical exegesis, as an older Cerebus performs a painstaking analysis of the early chapters of *Genesis*. Still, the volume still finds time to poke fun at its usual targets—religion, politics, and comic books, with the introduction of Spore, a parody of Todd McFarlane's popular Spawn character—in addition to a delightful parody of Woody Allen.

Latter Days Book II: The Last Day

With *The Last Day*, Sim returns to the microcosm. Jumping ahead several decades from the previous volume, we see Cerebus' final day, alone in his room, as he ponders his life and reviews some of the choices that lead him to his final moments. Throughout it all, as ever, is some terrific art, highlighted by Gerhard's meticulous set design. There is still time left for some final drama, and the ultimate culmination of the story, tying together the final pieces. At the end of the day, Cerebus is presented with what Sim suggests are the inevitable consequences of his choices.

Bibliography

Atwal, Sandy. 1996. "An Interview with *Cerebus* Creator, Writer and Illustrator, Dave Sim." *Filler!* 4: 62–87.
Baron-Cohen, Simon. 2003. *The Essential Difference: Male and Female Brains and the Truth About Autism.* New York: Basic.
Beaty, Bart. September 1998. "*Pickle, Poot,* and the Cerebus Effect." *The Comics Journal* 207: 1–2.
Bell, Blake. 2002. *I Have to Live with This Guy!* Raleigh, NC: TwoMorrows.
Bell, John. 1986. *Canuck Comics.* Montreal, Quebec: Matrix .
Benayoun, Robert. 1968. *Vroom tchac zouvie, le ballon dans la bande dessinée.* Paris: André Balland.
Bissette, Stephen R. 1992. "Sim on Cerebus." *Comics Interview* 107: 8–39.
"Blood and Thunder." March 1993. *The Comics Journal* 157: 20–21.
_____. April 1995. *The Comics Journal* 176: 5–10.
_____. August 2001. *The Comics Journal* 236: 3–9.
_____. June 2003. "Dear Dave: A Blood and Thunder Special." *The Comics Journal* 253: 12–18.
The Blue God of Judaism. http://tinyurl.com/45x2v3x.
Blumberg, Arnold T. "'The Night Gwen Stacy Died': The End of Innocence and the Birth of the Bronze Age." *Reconstruction* 3.4. http://tinyurl.com/62mh6r4.
Bongco, Mila. 2000. *Reading Comics: Language, Culture, and the Concept of the Superhero in Comic Books.* New York: Garland.
Bourdieu, Pierre. 2002. *Masculine Domination.* Stanford: Stanford University Press.
Brownstein, Charles. Winter 1997. "Dave Sim: 20 Years of Cerebus," *Feature Magazine*: 4–30.
_____. Winter 1997b. "Gerhard: 20 Years of Cerebus." *Feature Magazine*: 31–37.
Butler, Judith. 1990. *Gender Trouble: Feminism and the Subversion of Identity.* London: Routledge.
Carrier, David. 2000. *The Aesthetics of Comics.* University Park: Penn State University Press.
Cerebus Wiki. http://www.cereb.us/wiki/.
Champion, Edward. "Dave Sim: The Stalin of Comics." http://www.edrants.com/dave-sim-the-stalin-of-comics.
Chiarello, Mark, and Todd Klein. 2004. *The DC Comics Guide to Coloring and Lettering Comics.* New York: Watson-Guptill.
Coleman, Jenny. 2009. "An Introduction to Feminisms in a Postfeminist Age." *Women's Studies Journal* 23.
Cosh, Colby. October/November 2004. "Our Northern Neighbors, the Cirinists." *The Comics Journal* 263: 125–128.
Coville, Jamie. July 2005. "Dave Sim Interview." *Coville's Clubhouse.* http://tinyurl.com/4c8cw75.
Dardess, George. 1995. "Bringing Comic Books to Class." *College English* 57.
Darnall, Stephen. November 1993. "Spotlight On: Dave Sim." *Hero Illustrated* 5: 64–66.
DeCandido, Keith R.A. February 1990. "Talking Heads." *The Comics Journal* 134: 38–41.
Decker, Dwight R. March 1982. "From Elfland to Smallville." *The Comics Journal* 71: 55–56.
_____. July 1984. "News Feature." *The Comics Journal* 91: 11–12.
Dimont, Max I. 2004. *Jews, God and History,* 2d ed. New York: Simon & Schuster.
Douglas, Alfred Bruce, Lord. 1950. *Oscar Wilde: A Summing-Up.* London: Richards.
Eco, Umberto. 1992. *Interpretation and Overinterpretation.* Cambridge: Cambridge University Press.
Eichhorn, Johann Gottfried. 1780–1783. *Einleitung in das Alte Testament.* 5 volumes. Leipzig, Germany.
Eisner, Will. 1985. *Comics and Sequential Art,* expanded edition. Tamarac, FL: Poorhouse.
Fawcett, Hilary. 2006. "Fashioning the Second Wave: Issues across Generations." *Studies in the Literary Imagination* 39.

Fiore, R. March 1982. "Comics in 1981: The Age of the Alternatives." *The Comics Journal* 71: 35.
———. September 1987. "Funnybook Roulette." *The Comics Journal* 117: 37.
———. October 1990. "I Survived Jaka's Story." *The Comics Journal* 138: 37–38.
———. October/November 2004. "Quixote Triumphant." *The Comics Journal* 263: 104–111.
Friedman, Richard Elliott. 1997. *Who Wrote the Bible?* San Francisco: Harper San Francisco.
Gerhard. October 27, 2006. "Interview with Laura Jones." National Public Radio KUER 90.1. Salt Lake City.
Grant, Paul M. May 1993. "Dave Sim Redux." *Wizard* 21: 56–59.
Groenewegen, David. October/November 2004. "Does This Seem Right to You? Stories Within *Cerebus*." *The Comics Journal* 263: 118–20.
Groensteen, Thierry. 2007. *The System of Comics*. Tr. Bart Beaty and Nick Nguyen. Jackson: University of Mississippi Press.
Groth, Gary. April 1988. "In Defense of Bud Plant." *The Comics Journal* 121: 3.
———. April 1988. "Diamond Backs Down." *The Comics Journal* 121: 7.
———. June 1988. "Sim-Diamond Clash Again." *The Comics Journal* 122: 20.
———. July 1988. "Dave Sim Speaks on Publishing." *The Comics Journal* 123: 5–8.
———. August 1988. "Bud Plant Sells Out to Diamond." *The Comics Journal* 124: 16–17.
———. August 1988. "Funnybook Roulette." *The Comics Journal* 124: 25–27.
———. February 1991. "Dear Dave: A Reply to Dave Sim." *The Comics Journal* 140: 3–4.
———. August 1992. "Comics: The New Culture of Illiteracy, or: Why the World Is Turning to Shit Part 563." *The Comics Journal* 152: 3–6.
———. January 1993. "The Two Daves, or the Babbitization of Dave Sim." *The Comics Journal* 155: 3–7.
———. February 2000. "The Time of the Toad: The Comics Profession 1980–2000." *The Comics Journal* 220: 3–5.
Halpern, Diane F. 1986. *Sex Differences in Cognitive Abilities*. Hillsdale, NJ: Lawrence Erlbaum Associates.
Harris, Frank. 1938. *Oscar Wilde*. London: Constable.
Hatfield, Charles. 2005. *Alternative Comics: An Emerging Literature*. Jackson: University Press of Mississippi.
Hirsch, Marianne. 2004. "Editor's Column: Collateral Damage." *PMLA* 119: 1209–1215.
Holland, Vyvyanm. 1954. *Son of Oscar Wilde*. Boston: Dutton.
hooks, bell. 2004. *The Will to Change: Men, Masculinity, and Love*. New York: Atria Books.
Kakalios, James. 2005. *The Physics of Superheroes*. New York: Gotham.
Kannenberg, Gene, Jr. 2001. "Graphic Text, Graphic Context: Interpreting Custom Fonts and Hands in Contemporary Comics," in Paul Gutjahr and Megan Benton, eds., *Illuminating Letters: Typography and Literary Interpretation*. Amherst: University of Massachusetts Press: 163–192.
Kay, Alexx. *The Cerebus Timeline* version 5.0. http://tinyurl.com/3rp8ckk.
Khordoc, Catherine. 2001. "The Comic Book's Soundtrack: Visual Sound Effects in *Asterix*," in R. Varnum and C. T. Gibbons, eds., *The Language of Comics: Word and Image*. Jackson: University of Mississippi Press: 156–173.
Krieder, Tim. 2011. "Irredeemable: Dave Sim's *Cerebus*." *The Comics Journal* 301: 337–375.
Kingston, Angela. 2007. *Oscar Wilde as a Character in Victorian Fiction*. London: Palgrave Macmillan.
Kreiner, Rich. October/November 2004. "Can *Cerebus* Survive Dave Sim?" *The Comics Journal* 263: 101–102.
Kristeva, Julia. 1982. *The Power of Horror*. New York: Columbia University Press.
Lugo, Jessica. 2007. "Blood, Barbarism, and Belly Laughs: Shakespeare's Titus and Ovid's Philomela." *English Studies: A Journal of English Language and Literature* 88: 401–417.
Lydon, Neil. 1992. *No More Sex War: The Failures of Feminism*. London: Sinclair-Stevenson.
MacDonald, Heidi. July 1985. "Dave Sim." *The Comics Journal* 100: 144–148, and 185.
———. February 1987. "Generally Speaking." *The Comics Journal* 114: 95.
———. February 1993. "That's Just Dave: The Former Viktor Davis." *The Comics Journal* 174: 117–18.
MacKinnon, Catherine. 1987. *Feminism Unmodified: Discourses on Life and Law*. Cambridge: Harvard University Press.
———. 1991. *Toward a Feminist State*. Cambridge: Harvard University Press.
———. 2006. "Equality and Speech," in Jessica Spector, ed., *Prostitution and Pornography: Philosophical Debate About the Sex Industry*. Stanford: Stanford University Press: 80–105.
McCloud, Scott. 1993. *Understanding Comics: The Invisible Art*. Northampton, NA: Kitchen Sink.
———. 2006. *Making Comics: Storytelling Secrets of Comics, Manga and Graphic Novels*. New York: Harper.

McDonnell, David. March 1983. "Dave and Deni Sim: Part One." *Comics Scene* 8, 2: 6–9.
McKeown, Patrick. June 1991. "Dear Dave." *The Comics Journal* 144: 30.
Merleau-Ponty, Maurice. 1972. "Eye and Mind" in *Aesthetics*, edited by Harold Osborne. London: Oxford University Press: 58–63.
Mikhail, E. H. 1979. *Oscar Wilde: Interviews and Recollections*, vols. 1 and 2. London: Macmillan.
Miller, Craig, and John Thorne. July 2004a. "Dave Sim Interview." *Following Cerebus* 1: 2–15.
_____. July 2004b. "Following the Trail of Something That Fell." *Following Cerebus* 1: 16–25 and 43.
_____. 2006. "No More Games: Mind Games and Beyond in *Cerebus*." *Following Cerebus* 8: 2–8.
Palmer, Tom, Jr. June 1996. "The Wizard Q&A: Dave Sim." *Wizard* 78: 80–81.
Pearson, A. November 1993. *Fear and Loathing* 21: 20–22.
Phillips, Gene. October 1981. "Aardvark High." *The Comics Journal* 67: 51–52.
Queen, Carol, and Lynn Comella. 2008. "The Necessary Revolution: Sex-Positive Feminism in the Post-Barnard Era." *The Communication Review* 11: 274–291.
Reynolds, Adrian. 1993. "Dave Sim and Gerhard Interview." http://tinyurl.com/6dsdeax.
Rothenberg, Kelly. 2003. "Cerebus: An Aardvark on the Edge (A Brief History of Dave Sim and His Independent Comic Book)." *Americana: The Journal of American Popular Culture 1900 to Present* 2, no. 1: n. pg.
Rubinstein, Anne. February 1993. "The Saddest Fate." *The Comics Journal* 174: 120.
Sabin, Roger. 1993. *Adult Comics: An Introduction*. New York: Routledge.
Sherard, Robert. 1916. *The Real Oscar Wilde*. London: T. Wener Laurie.
Shooter, Jim. August 29, 2011. *Jim Shooter* blog post. http://tinyurl.com/3f8qqu7.
Shulgan, Christopher. November 2003. "Comic Book Anti-Hero!" *Saturday Night*: 50.
Sim, Dave. December-January 1977-1978 to July 1984. *Cerebus* issues 1 through 64. Kitchener, Ontario: Aardvark-Vanaheim.
_____. 1982a. *Swords of Cerebus Volume 2*. Kitchener, Ontario: Aardvark-Vanaheim.
_____. 1982b. *Swords of Cerebus Volume 3*. Kitchener, Ontario: Aardvark-Vanaheim.
_____. 1982c. *Swords of Cerebus Volume 4*. Kitchener, Ontario: Aardvark-Vanaheim.
_____. 1986. *High Society*. Kitchener, Ontario: Aardvark-Vanaheim
_____. 1987a. *Cerebus*. Kitchener, Ontario: Aardvark-Vanaheim.
_____. 1987b. *Church & State I*. Kitchener, Ontario: Aardvark-Vanaheim.
_____. June 16, 1989. Introduction to *Cerebus Bi-Weekly* 15. Kitchener, Ontario: Aardvark-Vanaheim.
_____. August 25, 1989. Introduction to *Cerebus Bi-Weekly* 20. Kitchener, Ontario: Aardvark-Vanaheim.
_____. March 1990. *High Society* 4. Kitchener, Ontario: Aardvark-Vanaheim.
_____. July 2001. "Sim: Dave Sim Responds to a Call for Submissions." *The Comics Journal* 235: 68–69.
_____. August 2001. "Letter." *The Comics Journal* 236: 3–4.
_____. February 2004. "Dear Allen." *The Comics Journal* 258: 11–21.
_____. March 2004. "A Cerebus Mailing List 'Talk' with Dave Sim." http://tinyurl.com/64pp6qo.
_____. 2004. "About Last Issue," *Following Cerebus* 2: 36–40.
_____. 2004. "Monthly Q&A" http://groups.yahoo.com/group/cerebus/files.
_____. September-October 2005. "Dave Answers 6 Questions: September / October 2005." http://tinyurl.com/3z5ytto.
_____. 2005. *Collected Letters 2004*. Kitchener, Ontario: Aardvark-Vanaheim.
_____. 2008a. *Collected Letters 2*. Aardvark-Vanaheim.
_____. 2008b. "Faxes Between Chester Brown and Dave Sim." http://groups.yahoo.com/group/cerebus/files.
_____. April 2009–present. *Cerebus Archive*. Kitchener, Ontario: Aardvark-Vanaheim.
_____. 2009. "On Writing Cerebus," in Pat Harrigan and Noah Wardrip-Fruin eds., *Third Person: Authoring and Exploring Vast Narratives*. Cambridge: MIT Press: 41–46.
_____. 2011. "Now I'll Ask You One." *Strawman Comics.com*, http: www.strawman.com.
_____. "Dave Sim Live." http://tinyurl.com/4nx6hr7.
_____. "The Dave Sim Usenet Interview." http://tinyurl.com/3p4abn7.
_____. The Dave Sim Usenet Interview. http://tinyurl.com/6h6drxf.
_____, and Gerhard. August 1984 to March 2004. *Cerebus* issues 65 through 300. Kitchener, Ontario: Aardvark-Vanaheim.
_____, and _____. 1988. *Church & State II*. Kitchener, Ontario: Aardvark-Vanaheim.
_____, and _____. 1990. *Jaka's Story*. Kitchener, Ontario: Aardvark-Vanaheim.
_____, and _____. 1992. *Melmoth*. Kitchener, Ontario: Aardvark-Vanaheim.
_____, and _____. 1993. *Cerebus Zero*. Kitchener, Ontario: Aardvark-Vanaheim.

_____, and _____. 1993. *Flight*. Kitchener, Ontario: Aardvark-Vanaheim.
_____, and _____. 1994. *Women*. Kitchener, Ontario: Aardvark-Vanaheim.
_____, and _____. 1995. *Reads*. Kitchener, Ontario: Aardvark-Vanaheim.
_____, and _____. 1996. *Minds*. Kitchener, Ontario: Aardvark-Vanaheim.
_____, and _____. 1997. *Guys*. Kitchener, Ontario: Aardvark-Vanaheim.
_____, and _____. 1997. *Rick's Story*. Kitchener: Ontario: Aardvark-Vanaheim.
_____, and _____. 1999. *Going Home*. Kitchener, Ontario: Aardvark-Vanaheim.
_____, and _____. 2001. *Form & Void*. Kitchener, Ontario: Aardvark-Vanaheim.
_____, and _____. 2003. *Latter Days*. Kitchener, Ontario: Aardvark-Vanaheim.
_____, and _____. 2004. *The Last Day*. Kitchener, Ontario: Aardvark-Vanaheim.
Spain, Daphne. 1992. *Gendered Spaces*. Chapel Hill: University of North Carolina Press.
Spivak, Gayatri Chakravorty, Donna Landry, and Gerald M. MacLean. 1996. *The Spivak Reader: Selected Works of Gayatri Chakravorty Spivak*. London: Routledge.
Spurgeon, Tom. February 1996. "Dave Sim." *The Comics Journal* 184: 68–106.
_____. December 1996. "Dave Sim Part II." *The Comics Journal* 192: 69–89.
Stephen, Reneé. October/November 2004. "Masculinity's Last Hope, or Creepily Paranoid Misogynist? An Open Letter to Dave Sim." *The Comics Journal* 263: 129–132.
Thompson, Kim. December 1979. "Good Aardvark Art." *The Comics Journal* 52: 25–26.
_____. July 1983. "Dave and Deni Sim Part One." *The Comics Journal* 82: 66–78.
_____. August 1983. "Dave and Deni Sim Part Two." *The Comics Journal* 83: 59–125.
_____. March 1996. "Back to the Drawing Board: Steve Bissette Interview." *The Comics Journal* 185: 42–99.
_____, and J. Hagey. February 1993. "The Story That Wasn't: 'Reads' and the Comics Industry." *The Comics Journal* 174: 112–17.
_____, and Steve Ringgenberg. October 1982. "Aardvark-Vanaheim Prepares Three Projects." *The Comics Journal* 76: 25.
Tong, Rosemarie. 2009. *Feminist Thought: A More Comprehensive Introduction*. Boulder, CO: Westview.
Viola, Ken, director. 1987. *Masters of Comic Book Art*. Burbank, CA: Rhino/WEA Home Video. (VHS).
Wilde, Oscar. 2007. *Oscar Wilde: A Life in Letters*. New York: Carroll and Graf.
Williams, Linda. 1989. *Hard Core: Power, Pleasure, and the "Frenzy of the Visible."* San Diego: University of California Press.
Wolk, Douglas. 2007. "Dave Sim: Aardvark Politick." *Reading Comics: How Graphic Novels Work and What They Mean*. Cambridge, MA: Da Capo: 289–303.

About the Contributors

Sabin **Calvert** is a comics artist and writer living in Brooklyn. His work has appeared in *World War 3 Illustrated*, and *Awesome 2: Awesomer*. His book *Gorgeous Clothed Flies* was a 2010 Printed Matter Awards for Artist recipient and excerpts appeared in *Neo-Integrity* by Keith Mayerson and the Comics Edition show at the Museum of Comics and Cartoon Art. He publishes his own web comic, *Symptom of the Universe*.

Mario N. **Castro** graduated from the Autonomous University of Nuevo León with a bachelor's degree in Mexican literature. He is a translator and journalist.

Lenny **Cooper** is a lifelong comic book reader and advocate for the treatment of the comic book medium as a vehicle for serious (as well as silly) artistic expression. He is a decades-long fan of *Cerebus*, as well as a moderator for the Cerebus Yahoo Group. He is an attorney in New York.

Sebastian **Domsch** teaches at Munich University. Besides working as a reviewer for several newspapers, in Germany, he has written two books, edited one volume on 21st-century American fiction and co-edited two other volumes. He is also co-editor of an ongoing dictionary of contemporary authors, introducing graphic novelists.

Gregory John **Fink**, a master's candidate in history at the University of Alberta, has had a lifelong interest in the study of comics and cartoons. His studies led to collaboration with Bill Blackbeard that saw the publication of a collection of *Krazy Kat* daily cartoons in 2001.

Dominick **Grace** is an associate professor of English at Brescia University College. He has published or presented conference papers on literature from almost every century, from the 14th to the 21st, but is especially interested in Chaucer and Shakespeare, popular culture texts, science fiction, comic books, and popular music.

David **Groenewegen** is a librarian who lives and works in Melbourne, Australia. He has been a contributing writer to *The Comics Journal*.

Eric **Hoffman** is an independent scholar in Connecticut. He is a widely published writer, with work appearing in journals as diverse as *American Communist History*, *Isis*, *Jacket*, *Poetry Flash*, *Rain Taxi*, *Smartish Pace* and *Talisman*. He is the author of several books of poetry, including *Everything Is Actual* and *The American Eye*.

Edward M. **Komara** is the Crane Librarian at the Julia E. Crane Music Library at the State University of New York at Potsdam. He is the author of *The Road to Robert Johnson* and *The Dial Recordings of Charlie Parker*, editor of *The Encyclopedia of the Blues* and of *Chasin' That Devil Music* by Gayle Wardlow and a reviewer of books and CDs for *Notes: The Journal of the Music Library Association* and the *ARSC (Association of Recorded Sound Collections) Journal*.

C. W. **Marshall** is an associate professor of classics at the University of British Columbia. He is the author of *The Stagecraft and Performance of Roman Comedy* and many articles on ancient theatre. He is co-editor of *Classics and Comics* and co-editor of volumes on *Battlestar Galactica* and *The Wire*.

Isaac J. **Mayeux** is a professor in the University of Dayton English Department. His master's thesis was on Dave Sim: "The Anxious Aardvark Sees the Light: Divine Masculinity in Dave Sim's Cerebus." He lives in Dayton, Ohio.

Index

Numbers in **bold italics** indicate pages with illustrations.

"Aardvark Comment" 62, 64, 69, 78, 80, 84, 90, 94–96, 160
Adams, Neal 8, 14, 23, 27, 78
Allen, Woody 53, 73, 96, 135, 200, 214, 219; *see also* Konigsberg
Alternative Comics (Hatfield) 5, 6, 59
Astoria 25, 36, 38, 42, 44, 77, 86, 89, 95, 97, ***130***, 165, 168, ***169***, 172, 175, 176, 178, 180, ***181***, 185, 190, 192–197, 212, 218; *see also* Kevillism

Barks, Carl 5, 13, 26, 63
Batman 2, 23, 27, 66, 70, 74, 84, 104, 167
Bear 89, 117, 173, 194
The Beavers 10, 12, ***13***
Bell, Blake 9, 15, 21, 30, 63
Bissette, Stephen R. 7, 8, 26, 33, 35, 36, 38, 41, 42, 92, 96, 102
Booke of Ricke 87, 99–101, 113, 115, 116, 171, 200
"A Boy and His Aardvark" (Brennan/Sim) 14–15, 21
Brennan, T. Casey 14–15, 21
Brownstein, Charles 64, 82, 86, 92

"Cerebexegesis" 53, 56, ***57***, 59, 100–102, 108, 115, 171, 199, 200, 202, ***203***, 205, 211, 212, ***213***, 214
Cerebus: aborted fanzine 15, 16, 18; ascensions 77, 78, 82, 85, 88–90, 96, 100; backgrounds 149–151, 153–155, 158; comics parody in 23, 24, 30, 66, 67, 70–73, 104–106, 127, 133, 135, 148, 163, 165, 167, 175, 217, 218; creation myth explored 168–171, 198, 211, 212; experimentation in 6, 23, 27, 70, 71, 104, 133, 146, 153, 159, 163; fantasy elements in 1, 6, 9, 18, 27, 28, 34, 38, 60, 67, 69, 80, 91, 104, 135, 163, 164; gender in 3, 4, 22, 38, 39, 41, 42, 45, ***47***, 49, 50, 60, 77, 86, 88, 89, 91, 102, 133, 153, 159, 161, 163, 165, 166, 167, 169–175, 185, 189, 190, 193–198, 207, 210, 211, 219; as graphic novel 6, 28, 34, 35, 59, 64, 67, 73, 81, 82, 121, 176, 189, 190, 212, 214; history in 27, 164, 165, 202; humor in 1, 65, 69, 73, 74, 76, 104, 115, 168, 196, 198, 202, 219; intertextual references 108, 109, 111, 113, 116, 118–125; narrative structure 3, 25, ***28***, 65, 67–70, 71, 73–94, 127, 163, 164, 190; panels in 141, 142, ***143***, 144, 150, 152, 158; publishing schedule 1, 6, 12, 20, 25, 26, 28; political satire in 2, 25, 44, 71, 80, 165; prose text in 108, 109, 111, 197, 212, ***213***, 214, ***215***; religious satire in 3, 51, 53, 59, 71, 115, 165; representation of sound in 127–147, 159, 160; satire in 1, 2, 3, 71, 72; as search for truth 85, 86, 87, 91, 95–97, 101–103, 106, 108, 109, 111, 115, 116, 125, 168, 172; as story of a life 84, 85; unreliable narrators 3, 39, 87–92, 97–102, 103, 106, 108, 109, 111, 115, 116, 163; word balloons in 129, 142, ***143***, 144
Cerebus (character): as barbarian 2, 7, 16, 21, 23, 71, 73, 85, 88, 103, 104, 163, ***164***, 190, 200; death of 2, 40, 98, 116, 117, 133, 155, 173; as messiah 3, 53, 56, 59, 89, 100, 116; as pope 2, 36, 74, 88, 89, 95, 115, 165, 168, 189, 192, 200, 212; as prime minister 25, 40, 81, 82, 88, 137, 165, 189, 192, 200, 217; rape of Astoria 2, 33, 36, 38, 168, 183, 192, 193; relationship with Jaka 2–4, 38, 39, 41, 51, 53, 88, 89, 120, 185, ***186***, ***187***, 188, 196, 197; sexual identity 88, 95, 163, 165, 166, 170–172, 174, 190–194
Cerebus ("phonebook") 164, 217
Cerebus Archive 13, 62, 69
"Cerebus Effect" 65, 57, 85, 151
Cerebus TV 13, 18, 62
"Chasing Scott" 60, 174
"Chasing YHWH" 4, 59, 96, 101, 115, 199, 200, 201, 202, 209, ***212***, 212, 214, 216
Church & State 2, 3, 28, 31, 38, 40–42, 44, 45, 49, 60, 80–82, 85, 86, 88, 91, 94–96, ***98***, 120, 129, ***130***, ***131***, 133, ***134***, 140, 166–168, ***169***, 190–192, 196, 198, 212, 215, 217, 218
Cirin 42, 44, 51, 53, 85, 87–89, 90, 95, 96, 99, 109, 133, 175, 176, 178, 180, ***182***, 183, 185, ***186***, 194, 195, 198, 200, 218
Cirinism 2, 3, 39, 41, 42, ***43***, 44, 51, 53, 60, 62, 80, 85, 90, 101, 121, 178, 183, 194–197, 200, 218, 219
Claremont, Charles X. 30, 168, 196

227

228　Index

Collected Letters 2 62, 216
Collected Letters 2004 62, 95, 215, 216
comic books: conventions 5, 6, 9, 15, 23, 25, 30, 31, 38, 63, 64; creator's rights 19, 30, 33, 36; distribution methods 1, 6, 20, 34, 35, 62, 65–68, 149; fanzines 6–11, 15, 16, 18, 22; shops 5, 6, 7, 9, 15, 35; studio system 5, 11, 12, 19, 20, 27, 36, 65–66, 71, 106; super-hero as dominant genre 1, 5, 6, 12, 25, 27, 66, 148; underground comix 5–7, 9, 10, 15, 34, 66, 67, 96
Comics Code Authority 5, 6, 7, 66
The Comics Journal 2, 14, 20, 26, 30, 33, 34, 36, 38, 39, 45, 49, 78, 84; criticism of *Cerebus* and Sim 2, 27, 33, 36, 38, 41, 45, 46, 49, 59, 149, 165, 174; *see also* Fiore, R.; Groth, Gary; Hagey, J.; Spurgeon, Tom; Thompson; Kim
Conan the Barbarian 1, 7, 9, 10, 11, 16, 18, 22, 23, 26, 28, 67, 68, 71, 85, 103, 104, 163, 164, 217; *see also* Howard, Robert E.; Thomas, Roy; Windsor-Smith, Barry
A Contract with God (Eisner) 34, 66, 81
Crumb, Robert 49, 96, 165

Dark Fantasy 15, 16, 18
"Dave" 51, *52*, 87, 89, 90, 95, 99, 113, 183
Davis, Viktor 22, 45, 49–51, 59, 77, 78, 86, 87, 90, 92, 113, 116
Day, Gene 10–15, 18, 19, 21–23, 27, 44, 63
DC Comics 5, 6, 8, 13, 19–21, 23, 39, 33, 35, 36, 45, 64, 67, 72, 84, 95, 106, 168, 212
Detin, Countess Michelle 196, 197
Drucker, Mort 2, 91, 92

Earnestway, Ham 78, 139, 219; *see also* Hemingway, Ernest
Eastman, Kevin 33, 35, 36
Eisner, Will 5, 7, 28, 34, 66, 81, 129, 146
Elfquest 6, 21, 28, 71, 81

Elric of Melniboné 1, 18, 71, 73, 104, 135, 164;
Elrod 72, 73, 96, 104, 135, 164
Estarcion 1, 3, 23, 26, 47, 76, 80, 190, 194, 217, 219

The Fantastic Four 30, 33, 94
feminism 41, 42, 45, 49, 50, 61, 64, 77, 85, 86, 88, 90–96, 161, 165, 175, 176, 178, 180, 182, 183–185, 189, 190, 191, 193; *see also* homosexuality; Marxism
Fiore, R. 1, 7, 36, 38, 41, 60, 62; *see also The Comics Journal*
Fitzgerald, F. Scott 60, 108, 109, 113, 115, 133, 219; *see also* Kennedy, F. Stop
Fleagle, Dirty Drew 106, 113, 196
Flight 44, 86, 216, 218
Form & Void 133, *136*, 198, 219
Friedrich, Michael 6, 11, 21, 23

Gaiman, Neil 30, 146, 147, 168, 218
George (The Judge) 2, 45, 60, 82, *83*, 85–89, 95, 98, 129, *131*, 185, 208, 215
Gerber, Steve 18, 26, 30
Gerhard 1, 2, 18, 25, 33–36, *34*, 41, 62, 63, 70, 77, 85, 94, 103, 113, 122, 123, 199, 217–219; contribution to *Cerebus* 2, 18, 31, *32*, 33, 70, 148–162
Gibbons, Dave 34, 35, 96
glamourpuss 8, 44, 62
Going Home 51, 53, 59, *60*, 61, 78, 90, 91, 93, 96, *99*, 99, 101, 109, 134, 139, 160, 174, 219
Groth, Gary 20, 33, 38, 45, 54, *55*, 59; *see also The Comics Journal*
Guys 50, 51, 89, 92–94, *142*, 150, 194, 198, 219

Hagey, J. 45, 49, 59; *see also The Comics Journal*
Hatfield, Charles 5, 6, 34, 59
Hemingway, Ernest 108, 113, 146, 219; *see also* Earnestway, Ham
Hemingway, Mary 109, 215, 219
Henrot-Gutch, Mrs. 97, 192
High Society 2, 3, 13, 25, 28, 30, 34, 35, 38, 40, 44, 63–65, 78, 80, 81, 85, 86, 91, 94, 96, 101, 104, *105*, 106, *107*, *108*, 108, 177, 178, 190, 192, 196, 217, 219
homosexuality 39, 40, 42, 60, 93, 154; *see also* feminism; Marxism
Howard, Robert E. 11, 18, 67, 68, 103, 217; *see also Conan the Barbarian* and *Red Sonja*
Howard the Duck 1, 7, 18, 21, 26, 30, 80

Iest 2, 38, 81, 119, 178, 192
Illusionism 80, 89; *see also* Po, Suenteus

Jagger, Mick 135, 218
Jaka's Story 2–5, 38–42, 51, 53, 59, 64, 78, 80, 82, 84–86, 89, 90, 94, 96, 101, 109, *110*, 111, *112*, 115, 116, 118, 119, 120, 121, *137*, 137, *138*, *139*, 165, 185, 188, 196, 198, 212, 214, *215*, 216, 218
Joanne 116, 173

Kennedy, F. Stop *61*, 78, 90, 99, 109, 115, 116, 144, 219; *see also* Fitzgerald, F. Scott
Kevillism 3, 42, 44, 86, 101, 178, 194, 195, 180, 196, 197; *see also* Astoria
Kirby, Jack 30, 33, 94, 106, 149
Konigsberg 53, *56*, 63, 96, 199, 200, *201*, 204, 205, 214, 219; *see also* Allen, Woody
Kremer, Harry 9, 13–15, 21; *see also* Now and Then Books; *Now and Then Times*

Laird, Peter 33, 35, 36
The Last Day 53, *58*, 59, 113, 115, 117, 140, *141*, *156*, 168, 171, *173*, 173, 199, 211, 212, 214–216, 219
Latter Days 4, 51, 53, 59, 60, 62, 78, 88, 91, 93, *100*, 100, 101, 113, 115, 116, 146, 149, 171, 198, 199, 200, *201*, 202, *203*, 204, 205, *206*, 209, 212, *213*, 214–216, 219
Lee, Stan 33, 94, 149
Lord Julius 27, 73, 80, 95, 97, 108, 117, *137*, 183, 185, 188, *189*, 189, 192, 197, 217; *see also* Marx, Groucho

Loubert, Denise 7, 9, 14, 15, 16, 18, 19, 21–23, 26, 30, 31, 63, 64
Loubert, Michael 15, 16, 21, *22*, 67, 94
Love and Rockets 3, 8, 149

MacKinnon, Catherine 49, 183, 185
Mailer, Norman 28, 49, 64, 86
Marvel Comics 1, 5, 6, 8, 11, 13, 18, 19, 20–22, 30, 31, 33, 35, 36, 63, 64, 67, 72, 103, 104, 106, 128, *129*, 137, 148, 168, 173, 217
Marx, Groucho 1, 27, 74, 108, 135, 136; *see also* Lord Julius
Marxism 42, 61, 64, 86, 92, 93; *see also* feminism; homosexuality
McCloud, Scott 129, 135, 139, 140, 146, 154, 161, 162, 176, 189
McDonnell, David 15, 28, 30
McFarlane, Todd 36, 53, 62, 217
McGrew, Fleagle 106, 113, 196
Melmoth 38, 40–42, 59, 60, 84–86, 90, 96, 101, 109, 118, 121–123, *122*, *123*, 124, 137, 150, 153–155, 214, 216, 218; *see also* Melmoth, Sebastien; Oscar; Wilde, Oscar
Melmoth, Sebastien 40, 41, 84, 90, 218; *see also* Melmoth; Oscar; Wilde, Oscar
Miller, Craig 62, 85, 89
"Mind Games" 70, 78, *79*, 98, 218
Minds 50, 51, *52*, 86, 90–95, 99, 113, *115*, *116*, *120*, *143*, 144, 183, 185, *186*, *187*, *189*, 194, 198, 218
misogyny 41, 42, 45, 49, 60, 91, 149, 161, 165, 174–176, 183, 190, 198, 218; *see also* Sim, Dave
Missy 109, 111, *112*, 116–117
Moon Knight 25, 30, 104
Moorcock, Michael 1, 18, 71, 73, 104, 135, 164
Moore, Alan 34–36, 87, 96, 116, 146
Morris, Dan 78, 82, 87, 95
Mothers & Daughters 3, 40, 42, 44, 51, 80, 85–88, 92, 95, 96, 190, 193, 194, 197, 218

New Joanne 116, 172, 173, 200, 205
"Note from the President" 89, 90, 94, 95, 200
Now and Then Books 9, 14, 15
Now and Then Times 9, 13, 16
Nurse 109, *110*, 111, 117

Oktoberfest (Sim) 13, 14
Oscar 39–41, 78, 87, 89, 90, 101, 109, 111, 115, 120, 121, *123*, 124, 135, 136, *137*, 137, *138*, 139, 183, 185, 197, 200, 212, 218

Palmer, Tom, Jr. 8, 20, 26, 81, 82, 94
Palnu 26, 27, 40, 80, 95, 136, 167, 178, 188, 189, 192, 197, 218
"Palnu Trilogy" 27, 40, 80
Phantacea (Sim) 18, 19, 21
Pigts 88, 140
Pini, Richard 6, 21, 28, 36, 81
Pini, Wendy 6, 21, 28, 71, 81
Po, Suenteus 44, 51, 80, 85, 87, 89, 98, 173, 180, 198, 218; *see also* Illusionism

Reads 4, 22, 44, 45, *47*, 49–51, 60, 78, 86, 88, 90, 92, 94, 96, 101, 113, 116, 133, 146, 147, *152*, 152, 153, 159, *165*, 165, 168, 173
Red Sonja 18, 23, 30, 72, 192; *see also* Howard, Robert E.; Red Sophia; Thomas Roy; Windsor-Smith, Barry
Red Sophia 27, 72, 167, 190–192; *see also* Red Sonja
Revolt: 3000 (Sim) 19–21
Rick 2, 38, 39, 41, *47*, 49, 51, 53, 64, 87–91, 99–101, 115, 116, 120, *132*, 137, 171, *172*, 172, 178, 185, 194, 197, 198, 200, 212, 214, 215, 218, 219
Rick's Story 51, 53, 78, 88–90, 92, 93, 99, 113, 115, 117, *132*, 132, 133, *171*, 171, *172*, 198, 212, 214, 219
The Roach 1, 10, 23, *24*, 25, 27, 30, *31*, 60, 64, 72, 80, 95, 96, 104, *105*, 106, *107*, *108*, 108, 135, 139, 167–169, 178, 217, 218
Rothenberg, Kelly 103, 146, 175, 198

Seuling, Phil 6, 21, 25

Shooter, Jim 19, 63, 64
Sienkiewicz, Bill 25, 35, 146
Sim, Dave: accusations of misogyny 13, 41, 45, 49, 51, 65, 91, 149, 161, 165, 174–176, 183, 190, 198, 218; anti-feminism 3, 4, 38–42, 44, 45, *47*, 49, 50, 60, 63, 77, 85, 86, 88, 90–92, 95, 152, 153, 158, 161, 165, 169, 176, 182–185; artistic development 69, 70; collaborations with Gene Day 11–14; ComicGraphics studio 14, 19; on creative freedom 20, 39, 91, 92; critique of graphic novel definition 34, 35, 81, 82; fanzine work 8–11, 15, 16, 18; freelance work 14, 17–20; influences 7, 10, 13, 14, 18, 23, 26; lettering style 2, 4, 127–147, 159, 160; LSD overdose 25, 26, 78, 104, 111, 149; opposition to merchandising 30, 33; relationship with Loubert 15, 30, 31; religious awakening 51, 60, 63, 64, 77, 91, 93, 101, 115–116, 133, 198; self-publishing 1, 2, 3, 7, 12, 16, 19, 20, 21, 23, 27, 28, 33, 35, 36, 45, 62–64
Spawn 36, 53, *54*, 62, 219
Spiderman 2, 66, 128, 106, *129*, 129
Spurgeon, Tom 9, 25, 38–40, 44, 49–51, 81, 84, 85; *see also The Comics Journal*
Superman 8, 66, 71, 84, 85, 151

"Tangent" 44, 160, 193
Tarim 78, 192, 194, 211, 212
Tavers, Jaka 2, 3, 25, 38, 39, 49, 53, 64, 75, 87–91, 95, 96, 100, 101, 109, 111, 115–117, 120, 121, 137, *138*, 139, 140, 147, 165–167, 173, 175, 176, 183, 185, *186*, *187*, 188, *189*, 189, 196–198, 200, 212, 214, *215*, 217–219
Terim 78, 88, 89, 194, 211, 212
Thatcher, Margaret 40, 96, 135, 189
Thatcher, Mrs. 40, 137, 141, 197
Thomas, Roy 18, 26, 146, 191, 217; *see also Conan the Barbarian; Red Sonja*
Thompson, Kim 8, 18–20, 26, 27, 45, 49, 51, 59, 63, 78, 80,

84, 96; *see also The Comics Journal*
Three Stooges 53, 62, 136
Three Wise Fellows 53, 62, 219
Torah 59, 62, 85, 91, 99, 100, 108, 115, 170, 199–216

Upper Felda 171, 194

Watchmen 34, 96, 146
Weisshaupt, Adam 25, 80, 98, 133, **134**, 191, 192

Wilde, Oscar 38, 40, 48, 60, 84, 90, 108, 109, *111*, 113, 115, 118, 119–125, **122**, 133, 135, 136, **153**, 154, 155, 197, 214, 216, 218; *see also Melmoth*; Melmoth, Sebastien; Oscar
Windsor-Smith, Barry 8, 9, 14, 16, 18, 21, 23, 26, 28, 70, 104, 163, 164, 191, 192, 217; *see also Conan the Barbarian; Red Sonja*

Withers, Pud 25, 39, 90, 98, 120, 121, 185, 188, 197, 212
Women 44, 50, 78, 86, 94, 185, 195, 198, 218
Wrightson, Berni 8, 14, 149

Yoohwhoo 78, 115, 171, 172, 205, 207–209, 211, 212, 214, 216